HOPE
IN AN AGE OF
TERROR

HOPE
IN AN AGE OF
TERROR

PAUL J. DaPONTE

ORBIS ✪ BOOKS
Maryknoll, New York 10545

Founded in 1970, Orbis Books endeavors to publish works that enlighten the mind, nourish the spirit, and challenge the conscience. The publishing arm of the Maryknoll Fathers and Brothers, Orbis seeks to explore the global dimensions of the Christian faith and mission, to invite dialogue with diverse cultures and religious traditions, and to serve the cause of reconciliation and peace. The books published reflect the views of their authors and do not represent the official position of the Maryknoll Society. To learn more about Maryknoll and Orbis Books, please visit our website at www.maryknollsociety.org.

Library of Congress Cataloging-in-Publication Data

DaPonte, Paul J.
    Hope in an age of terror / Paul J. DaPonte.
        p.   cm.
    Includes bibliographical references (p.   ) and index.
    ISBN 978–1–57075–843–0 (pbk.)
    1. Suffering – Religious aspects – Christianity. 2. September 11 Terrorist
Attacks, 2001 – Religious aspects – Christianity. 3. Terrorism – Religious aspects –
Christianity. 4. Good and evil. 5. Hope – Religious aspects – Christianity. I. Title.
BT736.15.D37 2009
231′.8 – dc22
                                                              2009009544

For Simeon and Seraphina

I pray that God will grant you wisdom to find creative ways
to practice embrace in our world shot through with violence.

— Miroslav Volf, concluding his remarks at the
United Nations annual International Prayer Breakfast
on September 11, 2001, unaware that only blocks away
the World Trade Towers had just imploded.

Contents

Acknowledgments

This book is a theology of testimony. The discussion on God it provides arises largely from the witness of those who have been, in the words of the poet, "acquainted with the night." Priority of testimony is appropriate in a church whose rock foundation has always been the faith of martyrs. Even those who serve as the book's main dialogue partners — Miroslav Volf, John Zizioulas, Paul Fiddes — are all theologians who attest compellingly to God's relationality. You can't do that from too far away. Theirs is a theology of participation.

I wish to testify to the many people who have helped me write this book. In particular, I would like to thank Susan Perry and the editorial staff at Orbis Books for the excellent suggestions they have made for the developing manuscript. I wish to thank my theology students at Boston College who, without realizing it, are already well acquainted with this book in its various stages of composition. I am grateful for the endless support of friends, especially Emmanuel Nathan and Br. Benedict Hirsch, O.S.B., who have been for me faithful dialogue partners in theology, and family, especially Anthony and Carolyn DaPonte, my parents, who have been an endless source of encouragement. And I would like to thank my wife, Adrianne Nagy DaPonte, whose faith in me and belief in this project have really made all the difference.

General Introduction

Dust seems an incongruous image to ponder at the beginning of a theological reflection on 9/11. On that day, in 2001, an endless barrage of graphic footage interrupted regularly televised programs and routinely regulated lives. It captured a horror replete with the real, with things tangible, heavy, stark — twisted steel, shattered glass, mounds of concrete rubble. On that day it was the terrible *weight* of destruction we were seeing and struggling to believe.

Nevertheless, it is the image of dust — gray, wind-born, ephemeral — that we remember most. It descended, danced in the air, piled and drifted. Dust appeared to be covering everything, but in actual fact, it was everything that had been turned into dust. That's what dust is — it is everything that once was.

As a powerful, multivalent symbol, dust is common to scriptural imagery and liturgical practice. From the beginning, the Yahwist explains how "the Lord God formed man from the dust of the ground, and breathed into his nostrils the breath of life" (Gen. 2:7). In trying to make sense of his own terrible suffering, Job ponders, "Your hand fashioned and made me; and now you turn and destroy me. Remember that you fashioned me like clay; and will you turn me to dust again?" (9:8–9). Likewise the psalmist wonders: "What profit is there in my death, if I go down to the Pit? Will the dust praise you? Will it tell of your faithfulness?" (30:9). And it is this very same image each year that inaugurates the church's Lenten journey — a smudge of ash with the instruction, "Remember, you are dust, and unto dust you shall return."

Quite fittingly, then, this theological study begins with dust. It is a somber image for a terrible tragedy. But like the primordial dust of Genesis, it is also a hopeful reminder of the very Spirit and power of God that animates, one that compels the prophet to proclaim: "O dwellers in the dust, awake and sing for joy!" (Isa. 26:19). The dust of the ground can bring forth life, even the dust of Ground Zero.

This work is an attempt to articulate a Christian response to the terrorist attacks of September 11, 2001. It is a theological reflection on evil and suffering, violence and revenge, identity and otherness, but it is, foremost, a response. It is offered as an answer to the urgent question that has so often been asked in perilous times: *What are we to do, now that they have done this to us? How should we respond to this injury, this evil?* The question means that the answer fits appropriately within the category of political theology, but it is just as important a concern to pastoral and practical theology.

A number of challenges soon become evident. An obvious one involves the decision itself to pursue a theological investigation, while all around angry, impassioned voices are calling for swift, decisive, usually retributive action — an official military response in no uncertain terms. The present theological reflection, although making use of the views of philosophers and political and social scientists, does not consider the urgent realities of state security and cannot serve as a recommendation for government policy. At the same time, of course, every political theology worth the name strives to influence the moral milieu in which public policy is made.

Another challenge in writing a response like this one is that it needs to be done in a timely enough fashion so as to retain a tenable connection to the originating event. If it comes too late, it loses the urgency of the historical link that called forth the response in the first place. On the other hand, if the response is rushed, if it attempts to be intriguing rather than insightful, it runs the risk of being no more than an impassioned "knee-jerk" — triggered words, rather than the careful, reasoned response that is needed. Culminating as it does some years after the terrorist attacks on the United States, the present work is offered as a sustained reflection on themes relevant to the tragedy, one that could only have come about with the passage of some time, so as to encourage that kind of deeply human response that flows from a changed perspective, a conversion of heart. Indeed, the dust has to settle, as it were, before one can begin to see clearly.

The three parts that follow have been given names, or, more properly, metonyms, that likewise suggest the passage of time. Part 1 is called "9/10"; part 2 is "9/11"; part 3, "9/12." Together they form an examination of the terrorist attacks through a consideration of history, crisis, and hope.

The first part — September 10 — situates the question of God and suffering within a long tradition of reflection on that most fundamental of theological concerns and seeks to specify an adequate language with which to proceed. After setting forth preliminary guidelines, it explores the traditional approaches to theodicy and gives a critical appraisal and, finally, rejection of the theoretical, theodical option. The exigencies of catastrophe make clear the need for a more active and compassionate theological response to suffering than the ones provided by traditional theodicies with their pat, all-purpose answers, one that searches for God not in specious abstractions but in the urgent questions that arise from actual, historical crises themselves. Only in this way can our theologizing be adequately engaged with the plight of suffering humanity. We are right to opt for what provisionally might be called "catastrophe" theology over traditional theodicies if the former leads us to the side of the suffering one, since only there are we able to explore our God questions most humanly and in the presence of Christ who suffered too. The challenge, then, of such an approach is the commitment to remain courageously "open-eyed" before the concrete occurrences of evil in history, firmly resolving to avoid that tendency of turning evil into a mere abstract notion. Doing so only segregates the very real experience of suffering from our theologizing and renders our theology lame. We must take heed of the history of suffering to derive a theology that makes a difference, as the impact of the Holocaust on theology makes clear.

Responsible theology after Auschwitz cannot ignore the historical fact of the dust and ashes of, among others, 6 million Jews. Responsible theology penetrates the evil *in situ* to discover the otherwise hidden machinations of evil's toll on suffering humanity. In this way political philosopher Hannah Arendt was able to perceptively characterize the "banality" of evildoers' attitudes toward their deeds. For the sake of suffering humanity, theologians are similarly charged to name what they see, when and where they see it. We can confront 9/11 and the challenge of global terrorism only after we have heeded what we have learned of the evil and suffering of "9/10."

Taking the history of suffering seriously, Miroslav Volf has looked penetratingly at the evil of recent times and has given it a name — the evil of exclusion. From his own experience in war-ravaged Croatia, Volf identifies the human propensity of excluding the other as a grave cause of suffering in our time. In chapter 4 this evil of exclusion is further probed to discern its concrete manifestations in recent history: in the quest for pure identity, in the problem of envy and scapegoating, in domination systems, and in the tendency to demonize the enemy other. The actual mechanisms of evil lead irrevocably to violence, and as the tragic history of the twentieth century makes clear, we have had our fill of violence. The history of "9/10" has been written in blood because violence always begets more violence. September 10 is the age of revenge. Its banner is aptly captured in a few lines from Auden's war poem "September 1, 1939":

I and the public know
What all schoolchildren learn
Those to whom evil is done
Do evil in return.[1]

The overall aim of part 1 is to offer a methodology for our theology of suffering. In doing so, it necessarily encounters the thorny question of how to handle the painful memory of suffering, one answer to which is offered in the final chapter of the book.

Our commitment to a theology of suffering that avoids the dangers of abstracting evil leads to part 2's reflection on terrorism via an investigation of the 9/11 attacks. A brief review of what occurred precedes an investigation of the aftermath of the attack and a consideration of historical and conjunctural causes. One oft-heard characterization of the destructive act that has ushered in the twenty-first century invokes the biblical genre of Apocalypse. By reflecting on certain symbols that loomed large in the tragedy — towers, ashes, and smoke — we see that the truest apocalyptic unveiling is shown to be an unveiling of violence itself, as theologian James Alison has recognized.

Chapter 4 examines definitions and categories of terrorism, including a study of terrorism as a by-product of and reaction against modernity. One particularly troubling aspect of much contemporary terrorist activity is the relationship between violence and certain religious motivations. The work of René Girard assists our understanding of mimetic rivalry and the mechanism of sacrifice. The topic of identity, explored in part 1 in connection with the evil of exclusion, resumes. The attempt to establish identity based on exclusion of the other is writ dangerously large in the many horrifying occurrences of suicidal bombing.

The chapter revisits a number of the dimensions of evil already explored in part 1 — exclusion, domination, violence, revenge — but now further examined with regard to the terrorist tragedy. This is the crux of a catastrophe theology that takes suffering seriously in the concrete realm. In particular, we inspect the role of organized forgetting, the death of community, the influence of totalitarian multimedia powers, and the troubling collision and collusion of fundamentalisms. A new way of discerning the perennial evil of revenge presents itself in the 9/11 world: "blowback" — the unforeseen consequences of past military and political interventions.

Some observers have claimed that we cannot understand the terrorist mind-set without first taking seriously the apparent problem of humiliation experienced in many societies that tend to breed terrorist activity. Central to this claim is that the terrorism of 9/11 cannot simply be attributed to factors such as poverty, lack of education, or fanaticism. To humiliate means to *bring low;* humiliation is the experience of shame before others that follows from having been put down and brought low, a very real sense of the loss of dignity that points to the passivity of *passio,* that is, of suffering. It is clear how 9/11 brought low many buildings peopled with many innocent lives. What has not *chop* been so readily considered is the role of humiliation as a driving motivation in terrorist activity, a matter that, in turn, begs a most provocative question: *Do we play a part in making our own terrorists?* This is not the only question to be asked. Of course, we must also consider questions that point to the terrorists themselves, for example, *How does Islamists' rejection of Western values contribute to the rise of global terrorism today?* Still, we cannot avoid asking those difficult questions that point to ourselves.

Part 2 — 9/11 — ends with a consideration of God at Ground Zero. This, too, gets to the heart of catastrophe theology: Where is God in the midst of our suffering? Since Auschwitz it has become clear that theoretical theodicy can offer no adequate response. And still the question seems never to go away. Indeed, where was God at Ground Zero? If we can ask that question, and we cannot help but ask it in the midst of every tragedy, then can we also dare to speak of the *ground zeroing* of God? That is to say, if our experience of suffering necessarily challenges our given understanding of God, what characteristics of our image of God have been (or should be) obliterated? Are there, for example, certain aspects of onto-theological monotheism that encourage the evil tendency of exclusionary practice? What kind of God-talk best pro- *Critics review!* motes a peaceful humanum? How can reflection on God as community — the insights of social Trinitarian theology — help heal a world marred by division and devastation?

The final part of the present study, "9/12," insures that the present work is best considered a contribution — a present-day articulation — of a theology of hope. Trinitarian "self-donation" or "self-giving," in sharp contrast to the horrors of the terrorist's violent self-sacrifice, is proposed as the promise of a hope-filled future wherein the call to arms of enmity is overshadowed by the call to the arms of embrace. Volf's model for reconciliation is explored in terms of the embracing arms of the prodigal's father, the outstretched arms of the Crucified for the godless, and the open arms of Trinitarian *perichoresis.* John Zizioulas's theology of God as communion provides a lens through which we

can further explore the social implications of a truly robust Trinitarian understanding of God. The central problem of identity is revisited and reconceived
in terms of the dialogical construction of selves in reciprocal self-surrender.
This is the Christian's identity, embodied by Christ's example of *kenosis,* of
self-emptying for the other. Here, in Christ, we find *humility,* in contrast to the
passive humiliation previously considered: humility means to empty *oneself.* It
comes via the Latin *humilis,* from *humus,* that is, ground — once again, dust.

An anatomy of forgiveness follows, as a response to the anatomy of revenge
investigated in the first part. It is founded on an enhanced recognition of the
solidarity of humanity in sin and suffering and fortified in the transforming
event of the Eucharist. Only with such a foundation, our study concludes, can
we pursue the dangerous, almost unimaginable, future secured by the God of
love and set out before us as the only option left open to us in Christ — that
of embracing, within the greater embrace of the God of love, all those who
hurt us, even those who terrorize. It is here that we find the Christian response
that we have been striving to articulate all along. Only this response provides
healing to the wound that lingers in the memory of suffering. For truly remembering 9/11 can adequately take place only within God's re-*membering* of a
divided human community.

PART ONE

9/10

I T CAN BE SAID that the subject of our investigation in this first part is nothing less than the long and terrible history of human suffering. Such a topic, however, is too vast a canvas to take in at once. More feasibly, "9/10" represents an effort to understand a certain self-perpetuating dynamic in human history that has instigated and intensified so much of the suffering of recent times. It offers a theological reflection on the evil and suffering of exclusion and revenge that has darkened too many of the history pages of the twentieth century now come to a close. Only by taking those dark chapters seriously can we dare to hope in the promise of the future. A theology that takes suffering seriously is the guide and goal of our investigation.

Political theology is first and foremost a theology that is sensitive to suffering. According to Johann-Baptist Metz, theology is "political" in a substantial and not superficial or incidental way through its basic impetus, a *conversio ad passionem,* and through its governing category, the *memoria passionis,* which is particularly sensitive to the sufferings of the "stranger-other."[1] The centrality of suffering in such political theology can otherwise be called a "theodicy-sensitive" one, but, most importantly, only if our theodical efforts remain in the practical realm: "Suffering...should not pose the theodicy question as a theoretical question but rather as a practical question."[2] This challenge to any serious theology of suffering amounts to a reformulation of the traditional approach to theodicy. True political theology situates the question of God within the persistent memory of suffering, taking into account "the way one's own preformulated certainties are wounded by the misfortune of others."[3] Articulating a theology of suffering that is both committed to remaining open-eyed in concrete, actual history and to hearing the persistent echoes of the memory of past suffering is the aim of part 1. It is precisely this courageous remembrance of the painful past, for Metz "the only universal category of humanity open to us,"[4] that can potentially change the future by grounding it in hope.

CHAPTER ONE

The Question of God and Suffering

That difficult memory of suffering brings to the fore a consideration of theodicy. This chapter examines the historical and cultural underpinnings of the theodical tradition and then investigates its potential usefulness for a contemporary theology of suffering. Before we turn to that task, however, some preliminary considerations on suffering and sin are in order.

SUFFERING AND SIN: PRELIMINARY CONSIDERATIONS

First, and most importantly, all talk about God and human suffering must necessarily proceed from a commitment to open-minded reflection and to the development of a long memory. Hypothetically, if a list could ever be made of the names of all of suffering humanity from time immemorial to the present, those names would most assuredly conflict with our own biased accounts of the victors and the vanquished, the perpetrators and the innocent. Human suffering, however, is the great equalizer. To an extent it characterizes every life in every place at every time. As such, when discussing, honestly and humanly, the question of God and suffering, we should find ourselves, unavoidably, all-inclusive.

Secondly, all quantitative arguments about suffering must be bracketed. Although the scale of catastrophe and the enormity of tragedy vary with each occurrence and on some level cannot escape being grasped synoptically, in the end, human suffering does not tolerate objective comparisons easily. When we get right down to it, there really is no meaning to the notion of a sum total of pain and suffering. Each individual's real suffering is always too much suffering. Again, the magnitude of large-scale suffering prompts its own kind of protest and its own set of urgent questions. But the caution remains to take care not to trivialize suffering when it appears on a seemingly small scale. Simply put, pain hurts. That is already enough information. At the same time, we cannot afford to be simplistic:

9

This is not to say that all suffering is the same, as if it does not matter whether someone experiences a concentration camp or a fall from a bicycle. Suffering is present in both cases, but the extent to which it manifests itself is infinitely different. In a skin injury we may perhaps, upon reflection, discover the "why?" of suffering, but in the darkness of Auschwitz this question is so overwhelming that we can hardly cope with it anymore.[1]

Thirdly, it must be acknowledged from the outset that when we approach the topics of suffering and the presence of evil, we are standing very much in the face of dark mystery. Accordingly, it must be seen that a theology of suffering does not derive from a winning argument. All we can ever do is to strive to offer the best theology of suffering that we can, which may come down to the most helpful or meaningful one, even when experience compels us to end our statements about suffering with more question marks than periods.

Finally, by way of preliminary observations, it must be said that although the ability to empathize is a great gift in coming to terms with the problem of human suffering, we must admit our limits. We are compelled to do whatever we can to understand the suffering of the other. But at the same time we must acknowledge that between ourselves and the one in pain there exists an often wide and sometimes unbridgeable chasm.

THE QUESTION OF EVIL
(AND THEODICY'S ATTEMPT AT AN ANSWER)

Our purpose here is not to define the nature or origin of evil or to exhaust the congested catalogue of human suffering within recent history. Rather, our present aim is to outline the basic approaches to theodicy by investigating the claims made by a particular modern theodicist, John Hick. At this point in our discussion, it matters less *how* evil has come about; it is sufficient *that* evil is here and is a present reality and constant challenge to theistic belief systems. Still, a few basic distinctions are in order.

Although a perennial mystery, the concept of evil is usually examined on a number of different levels. Traditionally, the term "natural evil" is used to describe the pain and suffering caused by disease, disaster, and other harmful forces in the world. "Moral evil," on the other hand, is that evil which results from human choices, the pain and suffering people cause one another through their deceit, malice, or cruelty. Moral evil is sometimes called personal or human evil to emphasize the role of individual freedom, but many theologians broaden the concept to include those evils that have a more systemic base. Structural evil is the product of large-scale human systems; it is the suffering unleashed by oppressive political regimes, wars, exploitative economic systems, technological advances, and other human inventions and organizations.

Another way to examine the problem of evil is to make a distinction between passive and active evil. One way to state this difference is to call the former "suffering" (the evil that people undergo) and the latter "sin" — (the evil that people do not just passively undergo but actually commit). Abraham van de Beek observes such a distinction, pointing out that suffering is *passio,* in which human beings are first of all passive:

> [Suffering] is whatever violates the wholeness of life, and wherever peace (in the absolute sense) is violated. Suffering occurred in the concentration camps. Suffering occurs where people die of hunger, or are wasted by debilitating illness, where animals are tortured. Suffering occurs where people are forced, helplessly, to watch the suffering of others; it occurs in the sense of powerlessness with which prisoners see their fellow prisoners executed; it throbs in the powerlessness with which people watch a loved one die of a deadly disease.[2]

Yet the evil that is suffering cannot be easily isolated from the evil that is sin. As van de Beek's analysis suggests, any discussion of the reality of evil inevitably reveals the interconnectedness of sin and suffering. On the question of origins: Does suffering enter the world through sin, or does sin make its home in a world of misery? Or do both sin and suffering appear as simultaneous realities in a world that is open to evil? In the realm of human relationships, it seems almost a commonplace to observe that the sin of one person is the suffering of another, and that the very word "oppressor" implies the existence of one oppressed. But beyond this, it also seems true to say that every act of sin is, in itself, a certain kind of suffering. Does not the sinner, through the very act of sin, demonize himself or herself in the eyes of society, causing feelings of inferiority and hostility, which in turn lead to further acts of victimization and self-contempt? Still further, it seems to be part of the very insidiousness of evil that people sometimes seek out their own suffering in order to escape from extreme isolation and psychic agony. Sin and suffering seem inseparably intertwined in the act of suicide. Conversely, there can also be a powerful sense that suffering somehow serves a purpose or plan, perhaps as a form of training or spiritual conditioning in which we are purged in order to grow into a more worthy humanity.[3]

Although the mystery of evil manifests itself in evidently distinguishable forms of suffering and sin, it is clear that one of these two terms cannot remain in isolation from the other. They are inextricably intertwined as dual features of the same dark reality. Once again, our purposes preclude a more in-depth investigation of the nature and origin of evil in favor of an analysis of some of the ways that believers in God have struggled to come to terms with the reality of evil as a given. We proceed, then, to examine the topic of theodicy.

Insofar as it is grounded in one of humanity's most urgent questions, what it means to suffer in the presence of God, theodicy is as old as humanity's quest for meaning itself. In terms of its formulation as a philosophical problem, it traces at least as far back as the Ancient Greeks, apparently to Epicurus (341–270 B.C.E.).[4] However, the term "theodicy" itself has a relatively recent provenance. The word is a neologism of the German philosopher Gottfried Wilhelm Leibniz (1646–1716), a combination of the Greek words *theos,* god, and *dike,* righteousness.[5] Its etymology is also its clearest definition: it is an attempt to justify God's righteousness in a world beset by suffering, even as the evidence against such a benevolent design seems uncontestable. There are two traditional starting points in such an endeavor: God's omnipotence or God's goodness. Choosing either of the starting points means having to defend the other. Thus if theodicy begins with the premise of God's omnipotence, holding that all things flow from God's hands and are in God's control, then the burden becomes a justification of God's goodness, since the position must be maintained in the face of the reality of suffering and evil. If, on the other hand, theodicy begins with God's love, care, and concern for creation, then the onus of justification lies on the side of God's power, that is, if God could have created a world without evil and could have created humanity without a propensity toward sin, then why hasn't God done so? Most theodical thinking proceeds from variations on this central dilemma. Characteristic of all of them, however, is Christian theology's emphasis on free will and responsibility. "To be a person is to be a finite center of freedom, a (relatively) self-directing agent responsible for one's own decisions."[6] According to Hick, there are two classic strains of thought in the history and development of theodicy in the Christian tradition: the Augustinian approach and the Irenaean approach.[7] After introducing them, we shall return to the question of the legitimacy of the theodicy option in a forthcoming section.

The theodicy attributed to Augustine (354–430) reflects the influence of Plato's concept of forms, specifically in that the world is perceived to be filled with particular things that are imperfect copies of their perfect forms. The presence of evil in the world is thus an indication that the world has fallen short of its intended perfection. Accordingly, evil is not a separate power but a deprivation, a lack of goodness. Augustine's understanding of original sin holds that evil came into the world at the levels of creation that possessed free will, those of the angels and humanity. By choosing evil, human beings entered a fallen state, becoming subject to the revolt of the flesh against the spirit and incurring a guilt that is transmitted by carnal generation.[8] Furthermore, humanity's turning away from God was a moral evil that infected an originally perfect world, unleashing all manner of natural evil — earthquakes, diseases, etc. — as penal consequences for such defection. Thus, for Augustine, all evil is either sin or the punishment for sin.[9] The great judgment will occur at the end of history, and those who cooperated with God's offer of salvation will enter eternal reward, while those who rejected it will enter eternal damnation.

> The Augustinian theodicy fulfills the intention lying behind it, which is to clear the creator of any responsibility for the existence of evil by loading that responsibility without remainder upon the creature. Evil stems from the culpable misuse of creaturely freedom in a tragic act of cosmic significance, the prehistory of the human race — an act that was prefigured in the heavenly realms by the incomprehensible fall of some of the angels, chief of whom is now Satan, God's enemy.[10]

A number of criticisms have been leveled against Augustine's alleged theodicy. Hick observes that the basic criticism lies in Augustine's vision of a perfectly created world containing no evil, which was made to follow a divinely preordained plan, but which has nevertheless gone awry. It is illogical to presume that human beings, even with the gift of their own free will, could make a choice for evil that never existed in a perfectly created world in the first place. Secondly, it is clearly impossible to allow Augustine's conception of the prelapsarian world in light of modern scientific theories of evolution and cosmology. The human species gradually emerged from lower forms of life with limited moral awareness, and science has proven that disease and natural disasters did indeed occur long before the appearance of the first *homo sapiens*. Likewise, it is difficult to conceive of any constructive purpose for Augustine's understanding of eternal damnation, which seems not to rectify but rather to

fortify the presence of evil in the structure of the universe. In spite of the difficulties inherent in the position, Hick claims that Augustine's so-called theodicy
has achieved an overall prominence in traditional Catholic thinking on the
topic, in no small part due to the support lent to it in the later Middle Ages
by Thomas Aquinas (1226–74).[11]

The second major approach to theodicy examined by Hick is actually antecedent to that of Augustine. Irenaeus (c. 130–c. 202), the early Greek-speaking
church father, had already offered a different response to the problem of evil,
which, unlike Augustine's, does not presuppose an initial state of human perfection.[12] According to Irenaeus, God created the human race in two extended
stages, corresponding to the reference in Genesis 1:26 to God's *image,* whereby
immature humanity is first endowed with the intelligence needed for moral
and spiritual development; and, secondly, to God's *likeness,* the stage now taking place, where humanity is transformed, through its own freedom, from
human animals into true sons and daughters of God.[13] Within a process of
humanization, human beings grow into their intended state of perfection.
Thus, Irenaeus's theological anthropology regards the human situation as characterized by a fundamental tension between selfishness and morality. Whereas
selfishness arises from the primitive and bestial instinct for survival, the call
of morality and religion leads to the realization of a perfected, God-centered
humanity, the true end (rather than beginning) of creation.

According to the Irenaean approach, then, moral evil is the "necessary condition of the creation of humanity at an epistemic distance from God, in a
state in which one has a genuine freedom in relation to one's Maker and can
freely develop, in response to God's noncoercive presence, toward one's own
fulfillment as a child of God."[14] Moreover, even the presence of natural evil,
for example, the suffering and pain derived from instances of disease and disaster, while incapable of being positively attributed to God's will, do at least
seem more at home in a world created not simply for the endless enjoyment of
pleasure but rather for the enabling of true personhood among human beings.
Still, allowing for the presence of evil and suffering as a necessary condition
for human fulfillment does not guarantee that such a goal is inevitable in life.
In fact, sometimes the sheer enormity of pain and suffering that many people
encounter seems to hinder rather than enhance the process of humanization
under discussion. Accordingly, Hick's understanding of Irenaeus's theodicy
necessarily points to the subject of life after death, to some greater future
good that must justify all the suffering endured in the human journey toward
personhood, and that would allow the continuation of that process for those

for whom the imbalance of evil and suffering on earth was far too damaging to allow wholesome integration into a greater humanity.

> In his foresight he knew human weakness and what would result from it. In his love and power he will surpass the substance of our created nature. It was appropriate that the nature first appear and only later that the mortal be surpassed and absorbed by immortality, the corruptible by incorruptibility; that by acquiring the knowledge of good and evil, human beings should be made according to the image and likeness of God.[15]

The so-called Irenaean model of theodicy does contain a certain logical consistency with regard to the reality of evil and the role of human freedom within the process of humanization, one that is more consonant with modern knowledge than that proposed by Augustine. This teleological or developmental theodicy is the one that Hick himself prefers, referring to it as a theodicy of "soul making." Yet criticisms have been voiced against this type of theodicy as well. The Irenaean view, for example, rejects the traditional Christian notion of the Fall of humanity. However, as Hick points out, it is still possible to recover a rehabilitated version of the Fall tradition if, rather than referring to the loss of an idealized state already enjoyed, it could be reinterpreted to point to a state yet to be realized. The overall vision of this interpretation of the doctrine would no longer then be the immense gap between our perfect progenitors and our fallen selves, but rather the distance between our striving selves and what, according to the divine intention, we are destined to be.[16] Likewise, despite the relative soundness of the Irenaean conception of a person-making world, which must incorporate the presence of evil and suffering as necessary conditions for its realization, there seems to arise a relative weakness with this form of justification in the historical cases of extremely horrendous acts of evil and suffering. The horrific reality of Auschwitz, for example, stands as a stark challenge to any overly facile reduction of evil and suffering to their use as tools for human realization.[17]

The Augustinian and Irenaean models represent the two major approaches to theodicy in traditional Christian thought in which an attempt is made to resolve the dilemma of evil in a world created by a benevolent God. Both models do justice to the primacy of human free will, the prerequisite of any serious discussion about God, evil, and human suffering. Each model attempts to integrate the two main, though conflicting elements in every such calculus, namely, God's omnipotence and God's goodness. In so doing, one model begins with a primordial state of perfection, from which evil appears as a privation of its intended form, while the other ends with the perfection of creation, which could be achieved only within an atmosphere of tensile struggle between the higher spiritual and baser primitive human instinct. The challenge we must now face regarding theodicy involves a question of a more existential nature, namely, do these theodicies work? Do they provide meaning for humanity in search of answers (or even clues to answers) to their most urgently and painfully posed questions? Do they cast any light into the dark valley of misery, grief, and disbelief that often engulfs human beings on that journey toward discovery and self-actualization? Is theodicy a viable and useful enterprise capable of seriously engaging contemporary men and women in their most vital, existential concerns? Perhaps these questions can be answered in a satisfactory way only when they are posed within the actual, concrete context of human suffering itself. Indeed, perhaps it is only through the real experience of evil, be it moral or metaphysical, and of suffering, however actively or passively borne, that we are capable of producing an authentically human response to suffering of any worth.

CATASTROPHE AS CATALYST

We endeavor to determine the suitability of the theodicy option for theologizing on suffering in our time. It has been presented by way of John Hick's understanding of its two main theological paradigms, the Augustinian and Irenaean models, both of which function as decidedly theoretical responses to the *why* question of suffering by employing largely philosophical abstractions of evil that ignore historical reality. This part — *9/10* — is precisely about history, specifically that of the twentieth century, in all of its catastrophic realism. That history cannot be isolated from theology.

Because the problems of God, the presence of evil, and the existence of suffering seem always to have characterized the long history of theological and philosophical inquiry, it is fair to say that such questioning is here to stay. To some extent, human existence has been and will remain fragile and fraught with peril. Notwithstanding the considerable merits of ever-advancing technologies, human beings continue to succumb to diseases old and new, perish from predicted and unpredicted natural disasters, deteriorate from every evil intent and deliberate cruelty, and, of course, still end up having to face one day the inevitable and frightening prospects of old age and demise. The exigencies of life always seem to prompt the kind of questioning that ensures the continuity of the search for meaning in the face of evil and suffering as an engaging and most urgent theological pursuit.

A question, then, can be carefully posed: Does not catastrophe itself serve as a reliable catalyst for meaningful theologizing? By catastrophe we do not simply mean a sudden disaster, such as the devastation wrought by a hurricane, but rather, getting to the root meaning of the Greek term — "a down-turning," as in the overturning of an order or system. The question of catastrophe as catalyst rests on a basic observation of ourselves and others in the midst of suffering and must be asked when we consider the evident limitations of ahistorical theodicy. In the encounter with evil and suffering, the most urgent questions about life (and, therefore, theological questions) simply happen: they promptly and freely, even naturally, surface on their own. Such questions are not the product of esoteric speculation and philosophical problem-solving. They emerge, rather, as an almost automatic response, a kind of built-in theological reflex. When we suffer, we cry, "Oh God." This is theology in its raw material.

An important caveat must be made. To say that catastrophe prompts questioning on the deepest level of ultimate concern is not the same as saying that suffering is itself a good, a human value. That doloristic tendency has prompted the very dangerous practice of seeking out suffering for its own character-building potential and leads to the inhuman (and therefore un-Christian) decision to permit rather than protest unjust structures and systems that inflict suffering and destroy rather than nurture the humanum.

> Suffering is meaningless, at least in the first instance. This means that we have to fight against suffering with all our possibilities, especially when it is a matter of innocent suffering. To use the word "meaningless" is to indicate that suffering should not exist. This affirmation is of capital importance because an overhasty attribution of meaning to suffering leads to a cease-fire in the battle against suffering. The immediate attribution of meaning and the insensitivity to concrete suffering constitute a vicious circle.[18]

It is questions that are under consideration here, not answers. We are attempting to locate the impulse behind the motivation to theodicize. Again, the observation is repeated that these kinds of questions of the most profound nature, which seem to arise almost as an automatic response to suffering and evil, suggest that theology properly begins at the level of human crisis. If that is so, and precisely because the world in which we live is a world where calamity and disaster are in no short supply, does it not also suggest that, at the dawning of this twenty-first century and third millennium, the proper situation for theologizing — at least in the form of such urgent questions — is by the wheelchair rather than in the armchair? What is the role and relevance of theology in our time? Or to pose the same question more graphically: In a world where airplanes are readily hijacked by terrorists and transformed into live human bombs targeted at crowded office towers, does not theology discover (rediscover?) one of its most urgent purposes — precisely in those desperate spaces where human beings cry out in agony and bewilderment? Can theology afford to keep the history of suffering at bay?

The recent publication of an "alternative" history of philosophy underscores the question at hand. In *Evil and Modern Thought,* Susan Neiman recasts the whole of Western philosophy as a history of attempting to come to terms with the problem of evil and suffering.[19] In particular, the author contends that the problem of evil is the guiding force of modern thought in its entirety. In examining the intellectual reactions to various catastrophes throughout modern history, Neiman identifies the devastating Lisbon earthquake of 1755 and the Nazi attempt to eradicate European Jewry in the Second World War as two central poles of inquiry by which we can locate the beginning and end of the modern. "Focusing on points of doubt and crisis allow us to examine our guiding assumptions by examining what challenges them at points where they break down: What threatens our sense of the world?"[20] When reflecting upon the toll of suffering evoked by disaster, in particular, the enormous, large-scale calamities of the twentieth century, we must realize that among the more grievous casualties to be reckoned with is the death of those prevailing parameters of understanding that had hitherto provided sense and stability in a world of contingencies. Neiman makes the point that conceptual resources themselves necessarily pass away. The case of the Lisbon earthquake illustrates the point quite clearly. "Since Lisbon, natural evils no longer have any seemly relation to moral evils, hence they no longer have meaning at all. Natural disaster is the object of attempts at prediction and control, not of interpretation."[21]

We might ask what an "alternative" history of theology would look like if, in like manner, it could be arranged according to the various theological responses elicited by victims in their experiences of evil and suffering? Or can we question whether such a history of Christian theology, compiled in terms of intellectual responses to human suffering, could ever rightly be called "alternative" in the first place? We turn our attention now to an investigation of one such human catastrophe, one that (one hopes) profoundly and irrevocably reshaped the tenor of theological inquiry.

CHAPTER TWO

Auschwitz

Evil and Suffering in the Twentieth Century
First Reflection

As we have just implied, a recasting of theology from the perspective of the suffering one is perhaps more readily available to the theologian than to the philosopher engaged in argument. Jewish and Christian theologies are bound up in history, rooted in the foundational experience of liberation from enslavement and the bondage of evil. Respect for the concreteness of experience in Jewish and Christian theology grounds us in the present task of reflecting on the role of catastrophe in the generation of meaningful theology.

Once again, our central aim is to explore what changes in our understanding of the problem of evil and suffering reveal about the changes in our understanding of ourselves, about our place in the world, and about God. To pursue this direction we must take heed of those key turning points — boundary crossings — that often follow in the wake of human catastrophe. A reckoning of the devastation of any catastrophe must always include conceptual damage — the shattering of structures that had hitherto allowed people to cope with and continue living life. As Neiman explains, after the Lisbon earthquake of 1755, it became easier and necessary to distinguish between natural and moral evil; after Lisbon, moral categories would be limited only to those human beings capable of realizing them. Evil would come to be identified with evil intent. After the horrors of the *Shoah,* however, the very idea of applying moral categories would be questioned.[1]

At this point it is helpful to recall that the titles of the three main parts of the present work — 9/10, 9/11, and 9/12 — reflect our central concern with the problem of terrorism in our time. Using them should in no way imply that terrorism is a new phenomenon that commenced in the last second half of the year 2001 in New York City and Washington, D.C. It is, rather, an attempt to concretize, in shorthand, a major source of suffering afflicting many areas of the world, one with a long history and, hopefully, not as long a future,

and therefore one begging to be investigated not only as a political, sociological, or psychological problem, but, just as urgently, as a philosophical and
theological one.

Indeed, for many people, the date "September 11" already has become syn-
onymous with terrorism, much in the way that the name "Auschwitz" has
become a byword for human depravity. Such references become metonymous,
yet in their very specificity prohibit facile comparisons with seemingly similar
catastrophes. An actual date, like an actual place, safeguards our remembering from mere abstractions about suffering. In this way, "the authority of
those who suffer" compels us to speak of Auschwitz as unique because uniqueness implies a necessary incommensurability whatever the historical context:
"nowhere in the twentieth century does the absolute prohibition against making comparisons — and by such comparisons neutralizing the catastrophe —
show itself so clearly and unavoidably as it does in that which we signify
with the word 'Auschwitz.' "[2] Thus, our investigation of Auschwitz respects
its uniqueness, or, as Metz explains, its prohibition against comparisons. And
yet such uniqueness does not rule out the possibility, even the probability,
of the establishment of precedents of evil occurring in human history that
increase the potential of their repeatability. Hannah Arendt considers the
phenomenon:

> It is in the very nature of things human that every act that has once made
> its appearance and has been recorded in the history of mankind has a
> potentiality long after its actuality has become a thing of the past. No
> punishment has ever possessed enough power of deterrence to prevent
> the commission of crimes. On the contrary, whatever the punishment,
> once a specific crime has appeared for the first time, its reappearance is
> more likely than its initial emergence could ever have been.[3]

Arendt's observation is all the more compelling in light of the terrible statistics
of suffering resulting from war in the twentieth century. Between 1500 and
1900, there were approximately 589 wars and more than 141,901,000 deaths.
Between 1900 and 1995, there were more than 250 wars with approximately
109,746,000 deaths, 62 million of which were civilians. Thus the twentieth
century alone accounts for more than 40 percent of all war deaths since 1500.[4]

The observations of Metz and Arendt point to the underlying rationale
of the present investigation. The theologian must be sensitive to both the
uniqueness of every catastrophe of human suffering and to the potential for
precedence that each catastrophe brings with its every appearance. Our aim

is thus to investigate twentieth-century suffering by focusing on one unique episode, reflecting on where we have been in order to better understand where we are now and where we may be going.

HISTORICAL BACKGROUND

Our investigation leads us to World War II and the years immediately preceding it, 1933–45, during which time the Nazi regime in Germany and in Nazi-occupied Europe attempted to destroy European Jewry in a widespread operation of genocide. While we cannot pursue an exhaustive sociopolitical analysis of the causes and effects of the Holocaust, we can at least initiate the discussion by situating it within a historical framework and by defining our terms.

The word "holocaust" itself comes from the Greek *holos* meaning "whole" and *caustos* meaning "burnt." Originally, "holocaust" referred to any sacrifice consumed by fire, but the term gradually came to mean sacrifice on a large scale and, by the seventeenth century, had come to connote a massive slaughter of persons. In Hebrew, the Holocaust is called *Shoah* — a great, destructive wind — a term that avoids the denotation of sacrifice altogether, implying instead the notion of catastrophe. The crime of "genocide," literally the "annihilation of a race," was defined by the United Nations Convention of 1948 as "acts committed to destroy in whole or in part a national, ethnic, racial or religious group as such."[5] Thus here, the Holocaust, *Shoah,* refers to the vast and calculated program of genocide intended and implemented by the Nazis as the "Final Solution" to what they called "the Jewish problem" in an effort to make the territories under their control *judenrein* — cleansed of Jews.

Although a precise accounting of total deaths can never be ascertained, simply because of the staggering numbers of victims involved, it is commonly held that nearly 6 million Jews perished in the Nazi death camps.[6] However, this systematic campaign of extermination was directed at all Jews, not on the basis of Judaism but rather on what was presumed to be a shared Jewish racial nature. "For Nazi ideology, a Jew was a Jew. All belonged to one racial nature, which Nazism regarded as inimical to the national 'purity' of the Aryan race."[7] At the time, 6 million Jews represented roughly two-thirds of the European Jewish population and one-third of the Jewish population worldwide, and that same number included 90 percent of the rabbis and religious scholars of Eastern and Western European Judaism. As such, Rosemary Radford Ruether considers the Holocaust an attempt to pull up an entire culture by the roots: it was "more than the killing of a large number of individuals. It was ethnocide, the effort to destroy a people as a cultural entity."[8]

Of course, the Holocaust cannot be viewed apart from the long and terrible history of anti-Semitism that has afflicted the Jewish people throughout the ages.[9] Frequent outbursts of persecution, ghettoization, and killing had long followed the Jews in their plight of mass migration often spurred by destructive and murderous frenzies — for example, the dreaded pogroms of Czarist Russia and the terrible waves of anti-Jewish violence that occurred well into the Russian Civil War period of 1919–21.[10] However, the Holocaust cannot be adequately understood as just another, albeit enormous-scale, pogrom. Although persecution of the Jews at the hands of the Nazis was sporadic and thuggish in the 1920s and gradually grew in intensification during heightened moments of persecution, such as the notorious *Kristallnacht* of November 9–10, 1938, never before had the Jewish people been the object of the state-sanctioned, wholesale annihilation known as the "Final Solution of the Jewish problem."

Richard Rubenstein and John Roth distinguish between "hot" and "cool" destructiveness in the practical implementation of the Nazi program of extermination. Whereas Russian pogroms can be understood as resulting from "hot" moments of mass emotion, the Final Solution on the whole, although punctuated by moments of intense and sadistic cruelty, is the product of a "cool" method of killing.[11] "The aim of most of the commanders was to diminish rather than intensify the emotional component of the killing operation, rendering it as impersonal and as cold-bloodedly systematic as possible."[12]

Rubenstein and Roth further point out that unlike earlier pogroms that were never the result of legitimate acts of government, the Final Solution, by contrast, was the product of officially sanctioned actions taken by legally authorized agents of the state. "The program of total extermination was organized and implemented by the German state at the zenith of its power with the full cooperation of every major German political, social, religious, and business institution. No assault of remotely comparable power had ever been inflicted upon the Jews in their entire history."[13]

A "cool" approach with an official sanction could render a highly efficient killing machine. Factory methods of mass production were employed as the killing was conducted on an assembly-line basis at concentration camps and extermination centers. When Heinrich Himmler, leader of the SS, observed that his killing squads — *Einsatzgruppen* — found the task of machine-gunning groups of Jewish men, women, and children too labor intensive and emotionally taxing, other methods of extermination, most notably gassing, were employed. The rates of killing are astounding. "At Auschwitz, which became the largest killing center, the magnitude of death was the equivalent of one death per minute, day and night, for a period of three years."[14]

Even the most cursory of introductions to the Holocaust, such as the one offered here, implies something of its uniqueness in history. While it remains a topic of contention, many scholars do insist that the Nazi project of extermination was indeed unprecedented at least for the reasons mentioned above, namely, because of its sanction as a legal directive of an officially recognized government and because its explicit objective was the genocide of an entire people simply because they were deemed unworthy, as a race, to live. We can begin to see, then, that it is the category of intention that contributes to the unprecedented quality of the Holocaust. Even more so, it was the specifically genocidal intent of the Nazis themselves, since the total eradication of world Jewry was integral to their identity and purposive behavior.[15] In that sense, we agree with Yehuda Bauer's claim that it was properly the evil perpetrated by the Nazi regime that was unique in history.[16] The problem, however, with setting genocidal intentionality as the sole, determining factor of uniqueness is that it is very difficult to conceive of a single intentionality when confronting the enormity of the Holocaust. The category of intentionality remains an abstraction unless we take heed of the concrete acts that flowed from it.[17] To whatever extent the uniqueness of the Holocaust can ever be objectively determined, we can at least investigate some of the ways in which this catastrophe changed our ways of thinking about God and humanity, suffering and evil in the world. For indeed, "the Holocaust was a boundary-crossing event, one of those moments in history which changes everything before and after, even if the substance and direction of the change take time to dawn on human consciousness."[18]

MUSELMÄNNER

A disturbing problem emerges whenever we approach the topic of the human person after Auschwitz. We must, as theology bids us, begin with the testimony of victims, but who can adequately speak for them? What we know of the atrocities of the camps comes from the victims who survived, but as Emil Fackenheim points out, the only complete witnesses to the terror are those who cannot speak for themselves. These are not only the 6 million dead, but also those members of a new and frightening sub-category of humanity—

muselmänner — as they became known in the camps, the skin-and-bone, walking dead of Auschwitz and the other death camps. Primo Levi, an Auschwitz survivor, describes them:

> Their life is short, but their number is endless; they the *muselmänner,* the drowned, form the backbone of the camp, an anonymous mass, continuously renewed and always identical, of non-men who march and labour in silence, the divine spark dead within them, already too empty really to suffer. One hesitates to call them living; one hesitates to call their death death.[19]

It is only the *muselmann* — the already half-dead victim — that can provide the most realistic portrait of the human person after Auschwitz and who alone could have rendered a complete witness. In Fackenheim's view, the *muselmann* stands as the most original and characteristic product of the Third Reich, "the person who is dead while alive and whose death is no longer a human death."[20]

Hannah Arendt explores the process by which "living corpses" were prepared and mass-produced in the concentration camps. The first step involves the killing of the juridical person, achieved by placing the concentration camp outside the normal penal system and by selecting inmates outside of normal juridical procedures. A completely arbitrary system is thereby established aiming at destroying the civil rights of the entire population. "The destruction of a man's rights, the killing of the juridical person in him, is a prerequisite for dominating him entirely."[21] The second step in preparing living corpses is, according to Arendt, the murder of the moral person. The second killing creates a widespread anonymity that renders death itself anonymous and that precludes the possibility of martyrdom. Death, then, becomes void of meaning.

> When a man is faced with the alternative of betraying and thus murdering his friends or of sending his wife and children, for whom he is in every way responsible, to their death; when even suicide would mean the immediate murder of his own family — how is he to decide? The alternative is no longer between good and evil, but between murder and murder.[22]

Camp conditions were designed to make the exercise of conscience pointless and the possibility of doing good unrealizable. With the death of the moral person thus achieved, the final stage in the preparation of living corpses is the death of individuality. After the deaths of the juridical and moral persons,

Arendt observes that the death of the individual is almost always successful. It is also the death of the individual that accounts for the relatively small number of serious revolts of any consequence. "For to destroy individuality is to destroy spontaneity, man's power to begin something new out of his own resources, something new which cannot be explained on the basis of reactions to environment and events."[23] In Arendt's view, the totalitarian methodology of gradual killing employed by the Nazis aimed at excising the human from the human person. The death of the juridical person caused outrage; the death of the moral person brought despair. And the death of the individual produced horror at the sight of the human person reduced to a state of beastliness.

To some extent, such a portrait of the suffering "human" is misleading inasmuch as the Nazi project of extermination required its perpetrators to regard their victims as essentially subhuman. Only in this way could the abominations and killings take place so efficiently and regularly and on such an enormous scale. One SS pamphlet makes the case quite clearly:

> From a biological view he seems completely normal. He has hands and feet and a sort of brain. He has eyes and a mouth. But, in fact, he is a completely different creature, a horror. He only looks human, with a human face, but his spirit is lower than that of an animal. A terrible chaos runs rampant in this creature, an awful urge for destruction, primitive desires, unparalleled evil, a monster, a subhuman.[24]

A program of dehumanization was effectively employed by forcing victims to look and act like animals. Void of the normal distinguishing marks of humanity, victims could all the more easily be "herded" onto "cattle cars" and "branded" with "cattle prods." Further depersonalization would be effected by stripping prisoners of the individuality of their own clothing, cramming them into straw-lined pens and depriving them of adequate sanitation. Terrence Des Pres describes this logic of destruction as a process of "excremental assault" whereby Nazi camp officials severely restricted the time and place at which prisoners could eliminate their waste. Poor diet inevitably caused dysentery which in turn compelled prisoners to "illegally" use the toilet. The "excremental assault" actually began when the Jews were first herded like animals into cattle cars and transported to camps. Forced to stand during the seemingly endless journey, it was often impossible for the victims to avoid vomiting, defecating, or urinating where they stood.[25] Likewise, notorious medical experiments, such as those conducted by the powerful I. G. Farben

Chemical Trust, found an abundant supply of "laboratory animals" from cooperating camp officials at Auschwitz: "In contemplation of experiments with
a new soporific drug, we would appreciate your procuring for us a number
of women.... We received our answer but consider the price of 200 marks
a woman excessive. We propose to pay not more than 170 marks a head. If
agreeable, we will take possession of the women. Despite their emaciated condition, they were found satisfactory.... The tests were made. All subjects died.
We shall contact you shortly on the subject of a new load."[26]

Another effective metaphor for dehumanization was the Nazi predilection
for likening Jews to dirt, bacilli, or disease. Adolf Hitler openly confessed in
conversation over dinner one evening:

> The discovery of the Jewish virus is one of the greatest revolutions that
> have taken place in the world. The battle in which we are engaged
> today is of the same sort as the battle waged, during the last century,
> by Pasteur and Koch. How many diseases have their origin in the Jewish
> virus!... We shall regain our health only by eliminating the Jew.[27]

Dehumanization thus provided the key stratagem to the Nazi genocide.
Stripping victims of their integrity, dignity, and identity through the implementation of camp policies aimed at eliminating any semblance of a prisoner's
humanity allowed for an efficient and extensive killing operation.

The evil of Auschwitz degraded the humanity not only of victims but of
victimizers as well. Observing the anthropology of perpetrators, Didier Pollefeyt acknowledges an underlying disunity or "doubling" of lives, public and
private. By compartmentalizing their professional and personal lives, camp
officials could maintain a daytime schedule of cruelty and murder followed by
an evening of civility and gentility shared with family and friends.[28] An inner
fragmentation occurs in the attempt to reconcile obedience to immoral orders
with a sense of private moral self-respect. That is to say, the external violence
committed against camp prisoners required that an inner violence take place
within the collective psyche of camp officials. Ordinary human compassion
quite literally needed to be imprisoned.[29]

And yet this phenomenon of fragmentation does not necessarily preclude
the occurrence of sadistic brutality for its own sake. Surely there were some
Nazi officials for whom camp life provided an opportunity to participate in
a boundless festival of cruelty. At the very least there seems to have been, for
many perpetrators, a basic enjoyment of and thrill in the exercise of power. By
rendering victims powerless, camp officials further reduced them to a means,

while the power holder remained the sole end. Accordingly, Pollefeyt considers the enjoyment of the exercise of power to be the central passion underlying the evil in the death camps, rather than the sadistic enjoyment of inflicting pain on others.[30]

The portrait of the human person at Auschwitz is shocking. Rather than the "Enlightened" view of the person as end in himself or herself, and far from the Bible's image and likeness of God, the human person as victim is a *muselmann*, a nonperson stripped of identity and integrity. Moreover, the human person as victimizer is an unfeeling automaton capable of perpetrating the most heinous of crimes on a daily basis, as a matter of course, and who, through an inner fragmentation of self, manages to render the human in the other utterly subhuman.

THE OTHER AS THE PROBLEM

Our task is to examine the process by which a select group of human beings is identified, persecuted, and, as was the case of European Jews in the first half of the twentieth century, systematically eliminated as the embodiment of the disturbing and threatening "other" who does not belong. It is a process characterized by a vicious circle of defining enemies and making victims, a dynamic that undergirds much of the abhorrent history of warfare in the twentieth century.

Although still motivated by the promise of Enlightenment ideals and encouraged by the rapid acceleration of technological improvements, Europe in the early part of the twentieth century was haunted by a number of fears and anxieties that coincided with a preoccupation with national identity and domestic consolidation. In *Mirror of Destruction: War, Genocide, and Modern Identity,* Omer Bartov examines the tense sociopolitical atmosphere of late nineteenth- and early twentieth-century Europe, an era of intensive nation-state building, when "ambiguous identities produced tremendous social, political, and psychological tensions, which in turn made for that complex relationship between creativity and disintegration, ingenuity and annihilation, so typical of our century."[31]

The longstanding presence of two such "ambiguous identity" groups, the Gypsies and the Jews, conflicted with the prevailing quest for a sense of national identity and solidarity. Of the two groups, the Gypsies, because of their apparent preference for maintaining their own traditional cultural distinctiveness, proved to be, strangely, less of a problem. The Jews, on the other

hand, due to their still recent legal emancipation, were in the midst of undergoing a massive "coming out of the ghetto," exhibited in a growing desire to
achieve the full potential of political and economic integration into Gentile
society, while still maintaining many distinctive features of their Jewish identity, as well as ties to other Jews across national borders. As a result, the Jewish
people came to represent the ultimate "insider as outsider."

> Thus the Jews served as both proof of and metaphor for the immense
> integrative powers of the new nation-state; simultaneously, they came
> to symbolize its exclusionary potential.... In this sense, the Jews can be
> seen as the paradigmatic example of the preoccupation with identity and
> solidarity, exclusion and victimization that numerous states or at least
> some of their agencies have manifested in the modern era.[32]

By the end of World War I, and with greater fervor after the nomination
of Adolf Hitler as chancellor in 1933, increasing numbers of Germans began
to identify the Jews as their most dangerous domestic enemy. The very elusive
quality of this enemy meant that the Jews could be perceived as the metaphor-
ical embodiment of all other opponents, domestic and foreign, of the defeated
German nation struggling for recovery. As such, the indistinguishable nature of
the emancipated, assimilated Jew could easily be conflated with other anonymous and threatening forces in society, such as the new economic forces of the
modern industrial state. And since the Jews seemed to greatly benefit from the
process, they could easily be identified as the chief instigators of the suffering
it caused.[33] In projecting the image of the "pernicious" Jew as real enemy of
the state and root cause of all of its problems, the Nazi party's efforts to "filter"
the composition of the *Volk* and strengthen its homogeneity simultaneously
effected a consolidation of its own power.

According to anthropologist Alexander Laban Hinton, modernity has long
necessitated the essentialization or reification of difference, a tendency that
has emerged as a quest for national homogeneity and racial purity. What is
unique in the case of Nazi ideology is that "difference was biologized into an
immutable physiological essence that could not be changed.... People, like
other species and the physical world itself, had a 'nature' that could be appre-
hended, classified and theorized. Otherness became an immutable fact."[34]

The process of identifying the other as "Jew" was the frightening prelude to
the justification of the exclusion and ultimate elimination of that other. Jean
Améry remembers:

It didn't begin until 1935, when I was sitting over a newspaper in a Vienna coffeehouse and was studying the Nuremberg Laws, which had just been enacted across the border in Germany. I needed only to skim them and already I could perceive that they applied to me. Society, concretized in the National Socialist German state, which the world recognized absolutely as the legitimate representative of the German people, had just made me formally and beyond any question a Jew, or rather it had given a new dimension to what I had already known earlier, but which at the time was of no great consequence to me, namely that I was a Jew.[35]

In *Becoming Evil: How Ordinary People Commit Genocide and Mass Killing,* James Waller examines the process by which the "social death" of victims is initiated — the legitimization of the "other" as enemy — through the mechanism of "us-them thinking."[36] According to Waller, a salient characteristic of the dynamics of group formation is that its members, regardless of any shared history, blood relation, or prior similarity, sense the existence of boundaries that separate them from groups and that, in turn, invariably lead to comparisons hostile to outsiders. This boundary situation is effected by the use of *social categorizations* — cognitive tools that separate, classify, and order our greater social environment. In itself it is a mechanism quite natural to the human mind, a universal process by which an incredibly complex world of information is sorted, filtered, and actively processed. It is also, however, the behavioral manifestation of the universal psychological tendencies of ethnocentrism and xenophobia.[37]

In general, the process involves assigning people to in-groups and out-groups and follows a predictable pattern consisting of, first, the *assumed similarity effect* whereby individuals within the group are perceived as more similar to "us" than out-group members; second, whereby in-group members view out-group members as all alike; third, the *accentuation effect* in which differences between our group and the out-group are exaggerated; and finally, the *in-group bias,* in which members of the in-group are preferred and favored over those the out-group. Social death intensifies as the pattern progresses to this final stage of in-group preference, which, Waller claims, derives from a basic motivational need to increase our own self-esteem. When a group becomes an extension of ourselves, our own sense of self-esteem is augmented. But for self-esteem to be enhanced, there must be an overall perception of the superiority of the in-group, an eventuality more or less guaranteed by the tendencies toward exaggeration exhibited in the us-them thinking of the earlier effects. We become, in Waller's words, "cognitive misers" preferring not to see subtleties and nuances, opting instead for sweeping categorical judgments based on diametrically opposed views of good and evil:

> If we know something about one out-group member, we are likely to feel that we know something about all of them. Similarly, since we assume that out-group members are highly similar, or essentially interchangeable, we can use our handy social group stereotype to quickly interpret an individual out-group member's behavior. They are, after all, all alike. Why waste our cognitive energy on attending to potentially distinctive information about a specific individual in the out-group?[38]

Group-favoritism, in itself, does not automatically spur antagonism toward out-groups. But it does provide a fertile breeding ground for conflict and contempt whenever vital interests are perceived to be threatened. Such dichotomous "us-them" thinking prompts a dualistic vision of good and evil. "We are innocent; they are guilty. We are the victims; they are the victimizers. It is rarely *our* enemy or *an* enemy, but *the* enemy — a usage of the definitive article that hints of something fixed and immutable, abstract and evil."[39]

BANALITY

In this section on the evil of Auschwitz, our focus remains on the salient features of the manifestations of evil rather than on its essence or origin. Accordingly, we speak of evil primarily as an adjective and use it to qualify a particular event or action or being. We do so to avoid a reification of the notion of evil — of making it substantial in a metaphysical sense — and in the awareness that evil, used as a noun, can only be such in abstraction. Often there comes a point when philosophical abstractions of evil are unavoidable and even helpful in coming to terms with this elusive and complex dimension of human existence. But any attempt to avoid the slow and sobering inspection of the terrible "facts" of evil in history can only hinder our quest for understanding, dull our capacity to see evil where it exists, and weaken our resolve to eradicate from in our midst. This very point accompanies us in our efforts to identify and interpret the evil(s) of Auschwitz — at once too massive to grasp and yet horrifyingly real in each concrete episode of atrocity.

The point also brings us to a consideration of one particularly contentious characterization of that evil, namely, its *banality*. In 1963, Hannah Arendt published *Eichmann in Jerusalem: A Report on the Banality of Evil* — her investigative account of the 1961 trial and conviction of Adolf Eichmann, notorious SS member and chief architect of the logistics of the killing enterprise at Auschwitz. She coined the phrase to express the disturbing air of normality that characterized both the commission of evil at the hands of many Nazis as well as its almost nonchalant recollection as displayed in the courtroom.

> The trouble with Eichmann was precisely that so many were like him, and that the many were neither perverted nor sadistic, that they were, and still are, terribly and terrifyingly normal. From the viewpoint of our loyal institutions and of our moral standards of judgment, this normality was much more terrifying than all the atrocities put together, for it implied — as had been said at Nuremburg over and over again by the defendants and their counsels — that this new type of criminal, who is in actual fact *hostis generis humani* [an enemy of all humanity], commits his crimes under circumstances that make it well-nigh impossible for him to know or feel that he is doing wrong.[40]

To be sure, "banality of evil" is a shocking juxtaposition of words. Arendt's intention was to draw our attention to the insidious guise that evil can take. It is a chilling observation: evil conceals itself most effectively in the quotidian. With regard to the ensuing controversy about the phrase, it is easy to see how some could misinterpret Arendt's insight as meaning that the commission of evil is itself normal. Pollefeyt, however, correctly points out that Arendt's comment is a description of the evil of the criminal rather than a characterization of evil itself, and, as such, remains a misleading articulation of an astute observation. Thus clarified, the phrase under consideration provides a grave admonition for our times: "precisely because evil is such an ordinary human ability, we can never banalize it, but should always take it seriously as a universal possibility."[41]

The very banality of the evil existing in the perpetrators of the Holocaust is seen in their compliance with the bureaucratic machine of prescriptions and rules that stifled any questioning or soul-searching. In this way, the banality found in the criminals indicates a restriction of human creativity and the commitment to the good. Banality suggests that the human person has been rendered an unthinking and unfeeling automaton. At root here is the question of whether the perpetrators of the evil of Auschwitz are better regarded as moral monsters rather than real human beings. At stake here is much that can be said about our understanding of the reality of evil and human complicity with it. For if the perpetrators of evil in the Nazi regime were moral monsters, then we have to regard the Holocaust as an anomaly, an aberration in human history, a view that makes it easy to take the dangerous path toward the belief that the Holocaust was a one-time event that, under our vigilant eye, could never happen again. We thus "keep" evil in one time and place, as we would, say, an exhibit in a war museum: evil is more manageable and easier to see if seen from a distance, far away in the Germany of the 1930s and 1940s — and conveniently away from ourselves in our own day. But entertaining that delusion brings about the very likelihood of recurrence that it aims to prevent. For moral monsters can be numbered; there were, after all, only so many of them. But human beings are everywhere, and, heeding Arendt's warning, so too is the potential for evil.[42] The enormity of the problem is clear. And it has everything to do with the way in which the problem of evil, after Auschwitz, is approached and the efficacy with which it is combated.

The fact that in our time the word "Nazi" has become a byword for evil incarnate suggests not only an awareness of the utter depravity of the policies of the Third Reich but also indicates the cultural proclivity to limit evil to one place and time, as just discussed. Of course, no one can deny that the despicable acts perpetrated against the Jews and other groups deemed "undesirable" by the Nazis were anything but evil. But the conclusion should not lead us to the dualistic kind of thinking that sets the wholly good on one side against the purely evil on the other — an option, tellingly, that bears the same sinister predilection toward demonizing the other so characteristic of the Nazi mind-set. The question, therefore, confronts us urgently: What exactly is it that compels us to demonize? In his analysis, Pollefeyt answers in a word: fear.

> People very easily choose for the monstrous interpretation of evil because this is very comforting, especially in the context of the Nazi genocide. The idea that human beings who murder every day are not fundamentally different from us, is very threatening for our own identity. It is very comforting, if we can say that such criminals are sick, extremely racist, sadistic, or possessed by the devil. In this way, we very carefully locate evil outside ourselves, thereby enabling us to condemn it in a moralistic manner in the other.... Evil then becomes the guilt of the Other, the immoral individual, the extreme antisemite, the supreme antagonist. The other is doing evil for evil's sake, whereas we know ourselves by experience, we long for goodness, integrity and authenticity.[43]

When we resist the temptation toward simplistic, dualistic thinking, we are afforded an opportunity for a more realistic probing of the problem of evil in all its complexities (not to mention familiarities). At Auschwitz, particularly, we become aware of the influence of other significant factors that made it possible for ordinary, even banal, people to become perpetrators of some of the most heinous crimes ever committed.

MODERNITY

In his important study *Modernity and the Holocaust,* Zygmunt Bauman provides a useful analysis of racism and its relation to the peculiar forces and features of modern times. In particular, Bauman makes the claim that the Holocaust was the result of a certain resonance between racism and the overarching worldview and attendant practices of modernity.[44]

We began to consider in a previous section the question of how the threat of the encroaching advances of modernity — especially the perceived rule of economic and monetary values — came to be associated with Jewish racial characteristics, which eventually made the strategy of the elimination of the Jews tantamount to a rejection of the modern order. In this way, there appears to be an essentially premodern character to Nazi racism. As a threat to the traditional *volkisch* way of life, the social upheaval associated with modernity could be attributed, conveniently and effectively, to the presence of precisely that foreign and unwelcome element of society that seemed to benefit most from it. Notwithstanding the antimodern features of the racist policies against the Jews, racism is essentially a modern phenomenon insofar as it depends on the advancement of modern science, modern technology, and modern forms of state power: "Modernity made racism possible; an era that declared achievement to be the only measure of human worth needed a theory of ascription to redeem boundary-drawing and boundary-guarding concerns under new conditions which made boundary-crossing easier than ever before."[45]

Racism can be defined only by a practice of which it is a part and which it, in turn, rationalizes. It is a practice that combines strategies of architecture (demolition) and gardening (weeding) with that of medicine (amputation) and is therefore emblematic of the modern quest for self-control and self-administration. It is a practice "in the service of the construction of an artificial social order, through cutting out elements of the present reality that neither fit the visualized perfect reality, nor can be changed so that they do."[46] Racism is a declaration that a certain group of people cannot be controlled or incorporated into the prevailing rational order. Their problems or defects cannot be ameliorated. They remain alien to the culture because the culture cannot cultivate them. As such, racism is inevitably associated with the strategy of estrangement.

Racism thrives in the modern milieu, with its stress on the unprecedented ability to improve human conditions according to the rational reorganization of human affairs, its reliance on the power of scientific, technological, and cultural manipulation, and its unbridled ambition toward the creation of the design of a perfect society. In the case of the Third Reich, that perfect design required two quintessentially modern hinges; the enthronement of nature as the new deity, which made science its main cult of worship, and its activist, engineering attitude toward nature, which allowed the power of science to reshape reality.[47]

Racism, furthermore, requires a mode of implementation that can guarantee the efficient realization of its ends, and to that extent, modern bureaucracy provided the ready means. Nazi racist aims necessitated tremendous resources, an expansive division of labor, and an extensive mobilization of forces to achieve its end of separation, isolation, and, ultimately, extermination. The concentration and regulation of power, resources, and managerial skills characteristic of modern bureaucracies was operative in the coolly rational implementation of every step of Hitler's social engineering programs.

At Auschwitz, concern for economic efficiency combined with advances in technology and improved killing methods paved the way for the industrialization of mass murder. A clear concatenation of technological innovations culminated in the vast concentration camp system developed and run by the Economic Central Office of the SS (WVHA). Extermination camps were fashioned on the assembly-line factory model designed to operate smoothly, efficiently, and cost-effectively. Jews, now referred to as *Stücke* (pieces), were to be "processed" through the following final phases: transport, selection, preparation (confiscation of belongings, stripping, shaving by inmate barbers), gassing (carbon monoxide or, at Auschwitz, Zyklon B hydrogen cyanide), extraction of gold dental work, transport of corpses to crematoria, burning, removal of ashes, disposal of ashes in adjoining marshes or for the use of fertilizer at nearby SS farms, shipment of personal items back to Germany, including shorn hair to be used as insulation and upholstery fabric, and, finally, elimination of any residual evidence. At an optimum rate, the Jews were to be "processed" within six hours from their arrival by train.[48]

The characteristically modern features of the Nazi racist enterprise — its immense bureaucratic structure, its reliance on science and technology, and its implementation of modern business and industrial production techniques — all contribute to the unprecedented nature of the Holocaust and its designation as the world's first truly modern genocide. The vast killing operation became an exemplar of the modern virtues of rational planning, optimum efficiency, and technological ingenuity. Indeed, at Auschwitz, "nothing was wasted except human beings."[49]

GLIMPSES OF GOD AT AUSCHWITZ

We have explored some of the ways in which the Holocaust has impacted the various dimensions of the *human* question: how a new nadir of humanity appeared in the death camps, namely, the walking dead *muselmänner* and the power-intoxicated perpetrators no longer moved by the sight of human suffering and, indeed, empowered to produce it. We have noted the utter banality that accompanies the commission of evil in modern times; how vast bureaucratic structures effectively stifle the screams of their tortured victims, and how advanced science and technology, divorced from human value systems, can bring about the industrialization of mass murder. Finally, though in some ways most significantly, we have seen that the evil culminating at Auschwitz first germinated in the form of a perception of the "other" as the problem — the threatening force and elusive enemy requiring extermination for the sake of the purity of a race deemed superior.

But what of *God* at Auschwitz? How did the experience of radical evil and prolonged human suffering affect the perceptions, apprehensions, and evocations of the divine? Who was God at Auschwitz? Does the God of the camps look like the God of the Bible? Where was God at Auschwitz? In distant heavens? Or in the smoke and ashes blackening those heavens?

Perhaps it is only through personal witness that we can begin to find answers to such pressing questions about God. Statistics, historical analyses, and theological interpretations all have their place in the pursuit of understanding the effects of such suffering on humanity in the midst of the camp's culture of death. But when it comes to struggling specifically with God and wrestling with God-concepts, when believing means squinting to see even the faintest glimpse of the holy in the midst of a living hell, then personal witness and experience embedded in narrative take on a new and urgent significance. Franklin

Sherman writes of the difficulty of capturing both the *intensity* and *extensity* of large-scale catastrophe.

> Once one has entered to any extent into the suffering of one single individual caught in the nameless terror of the pogroms and the persecutions, the deportations and the death camps, it is difficult to multiply this, say by sixtyfold and still retain one's grasp upon the problem. To multiply it by six hundredfold, by six thousandfold, by sixty thousandfold, by six hundred thousandfold, by six millionfold, is impossible. And so one's mind, reeling, returns to the picture of the single individual. We see him then, not only in himself, but as prototypical of the whole number of sufferers.[50]

This should not imply that religious opinions and testimonies of survivors are necessarily normative for theology. But neither are they without significance for the normative and structural features of a growing faith tradition grappling with a calamitous interruption such as the Holocaust, a struggle that, unavoidably, takes time — even a great amount of time — to dawn on human consciousness.

The present inquiry on God at Auschwitz needs to confront the greater characterization of the biblical God and of the history of God's people struggling to be faithful to that God in the face of suffering and adversity. Particularly in this regard, we must remember that the Bible bears witness to a long history of argument with and insistent questioning of the living God. Biblical faith demands such questioning precisely because claims for justice and the desire to understand God's involvement in human affairs arise from the very heart of faith. Eliezer Berkovits concurs: "It is the faith of Abraham in God that cannot tolerate injustice on the part of God. This is also the essence of Job's dilemma. The sustained fire of his plaint is not derived from his personal plight, but from the passion of his faith."[51] As such, the questioning of God's providence in the death camps occurred very much within the normative tradition of questioning found in the Bible. We thus have all the more reason to remember and value the questioning of victims, just as Elie Wiesel remembers the words of an elderly friend, recalled at the beginning of *Night:* "I pray to the God within me that He will give me the strength to ask Him the right questions."[52]

We turn now to a brief survey of a few of the glimpses of God captured in the urgent questioning taking place in the death camps. There are a number of other God impressions that have been depicted in the numerous volumes of testimonies of Holocaust survivors. Those chosen, however, do seem to reflect a degree of commonly shared experience. They also bespeak of that phenomenon introduced earlier in the section entitled "Catastrophe as Catalyst," which is here now reemphasized: "Focusing on points of doubt and crisis allow us to examine our guiding assumptions by examining what challenges them at points where they break down: what threatens our sense of the sense of the world?"[53]

The Silent God

It's the end. God is no longer with us . . . I know. One has no right to say things like that. I know. Man is too small, too humble and inconsiderable to seek to understand the mysterious ways of God. But what can I do? I'm not a sage, one of the elect, nor a saint. I'm just an ordinary creature of flesh and blood. I've got eyes, too, and I can see what they're doing here. Where is the Divine Mercy? Where is God? How can I believe, how could anyone believe in this merciful God?[54]

The silent God of Auschwitz was encountered by the people of the Covenant. The fact is an unavoidable starting point for a reflection on the God that many found to be silent or altogether absent in the death camps. It is essential as our point of departure because in attempting to come to terms with the horrors of the experience of divine alienation, both Judaism and Christianity must strive to show that the occurrence of the Holocaust is consistent with a biblical understanding of God as interpreted, rabbinically and ecclesially, over the centuries. Scripture, as articulated in the classic Jewish and Christian theological positions, depicts God as having chosen Israel as the object of divine concern. As interpreted and revered, the scriptural traditions do not imply that God will prevent any individual from suffering, even the suffering to be endured by an innocent individual, as the book of Job makes clear. What God does promise is to protect this people if they remain faithful to the Law, warning that infidelity to the Law will most assuredly result in grave and dire consequences for the people. We thus encounter the shock to both Jewish and Christian religious sensibilities in confrontation with the silent God of the death camps. Moreover, the underlying shock begs a further, disruptive question: Should the Holocaust be considered as yet another instance of divine punishment for infidelity on the part of God's people? As Rubenstein and Roth indicate, the question can be posed shockingly: "Did God use Adolf Hitler to inflict terrible suffering upon six million Jews, including more than one million children, plus more than six million others who perished in the Nazi murders of defenseless people?"[55] For Rubenstein, the God of history died at Auschwitz.[56] Religious explanations no longer seem adequate to explain this degree of suffering. Emil Fackenheim is downright adamant: "Not a single one of the six million died because they had failed to keep the divine-Jewish covenant: they all died because their great-grandparents *had* kept it.... Here is the rock on which the 'for our sins we are punished' suffers total shipwreck."[57] If we cannot grasp the gravity of the problem in this way, then what are the ramifications of the silent God, encountered by millions of God's people, for faith in the wake of catastrophe?[58] And if we do choose to see God's punishing hand, then is the resulting portrait of such an abusive God any better?[59]

The Abusing God

Is there a God who takes part in the personal destiny of man? It becomes difficult for me to believe so, for this God has now for years permitted torrents of blood and suffering, mountains of horror and despair, to be engendered against mankind by a few hundred thousand, bestialized, spiritually diseased and deluded individuals — men in any case incapable of any normal human feeling. He has allowed millions of decent people to suffer and die.[60]

Perhaps the most poignant and soul-wrenching witness to the abusing God is found in the book of Job. Job strains, in the midst of his own insurmountable suffering, to glimpse the faithful and just God of righteousness and mercy.

> Does it seem good to you to oppress,
> to despise the work of your hands
> and favor the designs of the wicked?
>
> (Job 10:3)

> Your hands fashioned and made me;
> and now you turn and destroy me.
> Remember that you fashioned me like clay;
> and will you turn me to dust again?
> Did you not pour me out like milk
> and curdle me like cheese?   (Job 10:8–10)

Job's suffering is profound. But Job is one man, and at some point, a pressing moral question is justified: Is this normative account of one man's ordeal with undeserved suffering enough of a comforting answer to sustain millions in prolonged agony who are crying out to a God of justice and love that they once thought they knew? In other words, at what point are quantitative questions, here regarding 6 million victims, only satisfied by qualitative answers, here a changed notion of God? G. Baudler offers a further way of addressing this question in an insightful study examining how Judaism, Christianity, and Islam understand God "not as an abstraction but as a power of destiny perceived in different ways and called by various names (El, Yahweh, Abba)."[61] His study on Job is especially instructive in that it explores the ramifications of meaning in the designation of Job's God as El, with its bull-like omnipotence, partially adopted from primitive Canaanite religion. But Baudler points out that the more developed biblical notion of the Hebrew God is Yahweh, "I-am-there." As a result, for Job the final word on suffering lies in God's infinite majesty and otherness and in man's posture of humble and silent submission before it, what amounts to a regressive response in light of Judaism's later history of covenantal relationship with God.

> But Judaism as a whole does not make this regression. Judaism is the Yahweh religion. Unlike Job, Jews hold fast to Yahweh as the covenant God, and they also cling to lamentation and accusation in the face of suffering. Jews do not, as Job did, hold their hands over their mouths and remain dumb before El's power (cf. Job 40:5). Rather the attitude of the suffering, just Israel is the same attitude as that of the Jews — *hold fast to lamentation.* . . . The Yahweh-believing Jew holds unfalteringly to the covenant and never tires of suing God to keep the blessed covenant promises. . . . This is the genuine Jewish-Yahweh believing attitude in light of the Holocaust and gruesome, incomprehensible suffering and injustice.[62]

Perhaps what is most normative in this moving biblical episode is not the resolution to Job's suffering but his epistemological crisis itself, his struggle with a God who challenges his expectations. And just as we find in Job, perhaps it is especially narrative theology that can do justice to the enormity of the questions posed.[63]

The Suffering God

> The men died quickly but the child did not: "Where is God? Where is He?" someone behind me asked. . . . But the third rope was still moving; being so light the child was still alive. For more than a half an hour

he stayed there, struggling between life and death, dying in slow agony under our eyes. And we had to look him full in the face.... Behind me, I heard the same man asking: "Where is God now?" And I heard a voice within me answer him: "Where is he? Here he is — He is hanging here on this gallows."[64]

The idea of a suffering God is not new. There are several passages in the Bible that make the assertion that God is with us in our sufferings (Ps. 23:4; Ps. 139). Colin Eimer points out that "in the same breath that the biblical prophets establish a connection between abandonment of the covenant and consequent suffering, they also speak of God's continuing love. The *Shekhinah,* the divine presence, has gone into exile with the people. God will be with them, will not abandon them, and will ultimately return them to their land and former glory. To match the tears we weep by the waters of Babylon, God also weeps."[65] But what of this notion of God's own suffering, of a God so close to us that our suffering becomes a part of God as God's own?[66] Dorothee Sölle argues that after the Holocaust, we have the duty to modify the traditional doctrine of an all-loving, omnipotent Deity. God after Auschwitz is all-loving, but not all-powerful. God should be perceived as on the side of victims, suffering along with them. "In view of the Holocaust I cannot talk simply of 'losing' God: chance participation compels one to other forms of speaking of God and must lead beyond the omnipotent and all-loving God."[67]

Of course, Sölle's view is at the same time a rejection of the theodicy question. There no longer remains the need to justify God's omnipotence, but even more than that, the same view asserts that after the devastation, there no longer remains the desire to defend an all-powerful, eternal, and unchanging God. "The religious question of suffering is no longer the one so often heard: How can God permit that? But a more difficult one, which first has to be studied: How does our pain become God's pain and how does God's pain appear in our pain?"[68] For Sölle, the God of the Patriarchs, omnipotent, unchanging, beyond need and vulnerability, the God of hierarchical thought, this God is not worthy of worship. When we speak of God's pain and suffering we no longer think of God in purely masculine imagery. God is then our mother who consoles us and comforts us and holds us in our pain. "God cannot comfort us if she were not bound to us in pain, if she did not have this wonderful and exceptional ability to feel the pain of another in her own body, suffering with us, existing with us."[69]

Perhaps we are right to conclude, with Sölle, that an omnipotent God who imposes suffering and looks down on Auschwitz is a sadist. If the God of power is dead, however, how is the God of weakness still God? Can God suffer and still remain divine? For Christians the discussion leads inevitably to Calvary. But can the cross offer both Jews and Christians a means of coming to terms with the death of 6 million Jews? In *The Creative Suffering of God,* Paul Fiddes warns that "we cannot and must not suppose that death only enters into the being of God in the cross of Jesus or that God only overcomes death there. Wherever trust in God is created, death ceases to be the instrument of hostile non-being."[70] Thus, for believers both Jewish and Christian, it is trust, a trust even unto death, which allows the encounter. "Death becomes the place where we trust God to preserve our relationships with him and others, rather than being the place of the curse where all relationships are broken. Death is changed in the sense that our perception of it has changed and because we ourselves are changed."[71]

A changed perception of death would indeed provide a certain spiritual sustenance in our time of suffering. But when we are speaking of a concern for attitudinal changes, are we not drawing close to the philosophical approach to dealing with suffering encountered in traditional theodicies, even if here we are trying to envision a God who suffers along with us? Death may indeed be the place where we trust God to preserve our relationships. But we are right to ask whether Auschwitz is the place where trust is likely to take root and allow such a fundamental reorientation toward God. Something of the problem is left unaddressed, something requiring our appreciation of God's presence not only in our passive suffering but in our active resistance as well.

CHAPTER THREE

Exclusion

Evil and Suffering in the Twentieth Century
Second Reflection

We have chosen to highlight one instance, Auschwitz, out of many twentieth-century catastrophes — the annals of suffering are horrendous and indisputable — to illustrate in detail both the magnitude of suffering that characterizes the catastrophes of our time, such as the many genocides the world has witnessed in the last hundred years (6 million Jews perished in just one genocidal episode) as well as the evil-inducing mechanisms that typically lurk beneath all of its horrible manifestations. We have done so, moreover, in an effort to anchor the discussion of evil and suffering, as much as possible, in the realm of the concrete, to the point of including the staggering statistics of the numbered dead, reflections on relevant historical and cultural factors, even the gruesome methods of murder made possible through modern technology and bureaucratic planning. The resulting analysis is disturbing in its graphic realism, and intentionally so, since, as we have already suggested, most theological reflection on human suffering falters in the detached, speculative realm.

This concrete approach does, moreover, yield certain categories by which the scandal of twentieth-century suffering can be further explored and understood. One such theme is the problem of *exclusion*. Exclusion stands as the main instigator of the hatred that has led to the inestimable suffering of the past century. According to Miroslav Volf, "exclusion...names an objective evil."[1]

Volf views the problem of exclusion as a fundamental disruption of God's creative activity as depicted in the first chapter of Genesis.[2] There, the account of creation follows an intricate pattern of both "separating" and "binding together": God separates the light from the darkness, the water from the land, etc., but also brings entities together — humans to each other as complements and to the rest of creation as stewards, as well as to God as bearers of the divine image. This twofold process provides a powerful conception of the way that the human person is formed: identity is not just a matter of dividing but of *connecting*.

> The human self is formed not through a simple rejection of the other — through a binary logic of opposition and negation — but through a complex process of "taking in" and "keeping out." We are who we are not because we are separate from the others who are next to us, but because we are *both* separate *and* connected, *both* distinct *and* related; the boundaries that mark our identities are both barriers and bridges.[3]

The conjunction is crucial here: we are speaking of both separating *and* binding in a process that results in patterns of human interdependence — a phenomenon Volf calls *differentiation*. Creation by separation alone would result in self-enclosed, self-identical, isolated beings, which in turn would lead to relationships of repression and domination.[4]

For our purposes, Volf's interest in God's creative "separating and binding together" is especially relevant for its ramifications for a conception of sin. Significantly, if creation is a matter of differentiation, then sin represents a violent reconfiguration of divinely ordained patterns of interdependence. Sin as exclusion thus occurs as either a transgression against the *separating* aspect of creative differentiation — a failure to recognize the other as belonging to the pattern of interdependence and rendering that other an inferior being, a mere assimilation of the self by forcing the other to be like the self or by subjugating the other to the self — or as a transgression against the *binding* aspect of differentiation, whereby the ties that bind are cut so as to allow the self to achieve a position of sovereign independence, which invariably turns the other into an enemy to be combated and driven away or a nonentity to be disregarded and thrown away. "Exclusion takes place when the violence of expulsion, assimilation, or subjugation and the indifference of abandonment replace the dynamics of taking in and keeping out as well as the mutuality of giving and receiving."[5]

The conception of sin as exclusion thus comes down to a disruption of the fundamental relationship of self to other(s). The position offers an insightful key through which we can interpret the identity-based conflict at the heart of so much of the past century's disturbing chronicle of suffering and inhumanity. We will return to an investigation of Volf's understanding of sin and forgiveness in part 3.

IDENTITY

Most deep-rooted conflicts should be understood as problems related to identity, specifically when human identity needs remain unsatisfied or become threatened:

> Deep-rooted conflict is about identity: the beliefs, values, culture, spirituality, meaning systems, relationships, history, imagination, and capacity to act that form the core of an individual or group. Identity can be defined by needs, which are variously described...as human identity needs, ontological needs (needs relating to the nature of being), or simply human needs. The unique and particular satisfiers of human needs make up the unique and particular identity of a given individual or group. Deep-rooted conflict occurs when the most significant human needs satisfiers of a group are taken away or threatened.[6]

Deep-rooted (identity) conflicts generally occur within relational systems, that is, within a context in which parties have to deal with one another frequently through factors such as geographical proximity or other political exigencies. With relational systems, there is a self (the individual or group from whose vantage point the story is told), and there is an other (to whom the individual or group relates).[7] Self-other dynamics can be understood against a background of closed and exclusive relational systems where only one relationship matters to the parties involved, or against a less restrictive background where self and other are open to other relationships. Still, self and other are both part of other relational systems that may be influenced by their own particular relationship system. Self and other may occupy a relational system as friends or as enemies, through common interests, activities, or objects of desire.

Such a study of self-other dynamics is crucial to this reflection on suffering linked to identity conflicts, especially when these do lead to outbursts of hatred and violence. Here it is particularly worthwhile to consider the thought of the most significant twentieth-century philosopher of the self-other relationship: Emmanuel Levinas.

TOTALITY VS. INFINITY

It makes sense to highlight in this reflection on suffering in the twentieth century an analysis of the self-other dynamic from a Levinasian perspective. According to Richard J. Bernstein, Levinas's entire philosophical project is best understood as an ethical response to the horror of the evil that has erupted in the past century.[8] Our study of suffering *in extremis* at Auschwitz conveys the shocking brutality of totalitarian systems that historically have sought to remove (and even eliminate) the other from the purview of the self. In sharp contrast, Levinas emphasizes the infinite responsibility for the other person in his insistence on the primacy of ethics as first philosophy.

Levinas highlights the contrast inherent in the concepts of *totality* and *infinity* in his discourse on the self-other relationship, providing a useful tool by which we can examine the violence at the heart of much deep-rooted conflict. According to Levinas, "totality" suggests that mode of living in which the core of a person's being can be known, grasped, and controlled in its entirety. "Individuals are reduced to being bearers of forces that command them unbeknown to themselves. The meaning of individuals (invisible outside this totality) is derived from the totality."[9] For Levinas, totality represents a violent assault in its attempt to confine what is beyond confinement.

In contrast, "infinity" refers to the vast world of the interiority of the other (transcendent exteriority of the self), which can never by fully known or contained, let alone manipulated or controlled. "The idea of infinity is transcendence itself, the overflowing of an adequate idea. If totality cannot be constituted it is because Infinity does not permit itself to be integrated. It is not the insufficiency of the I that prevents totalization, but the Infinity of the Other."[10] For Levinas, the fullness of humanity is encountered in the infinity of the other.

The concepts of totality and infinity allow us to understand Levinas's central concern with ethics as first philosophy and his overall indictment of Western philosophy as a whole in its preoccupation with ontology.[11] For by totalizing, Levinas means any relation to otherness that is reducible to comprehension or understanding. That is to say, the very act of comprehending, of understanding via correlation, reciprocity, symmetry, recognition, etc., which, in itself, characterizes ontological relationships with the human other, forms totalities where there is and can only be infinity.

> When I totalize, I conceive of the relation to the other from some imagined point that would be outside of it and I turn myself into a theoretical spectator on the social world of which I am really part, and in which I am an agent . . . [but] there is no view from nowhere. Every view is from somewhere and the ethical relation is a description from the point of view of an agent in the social world and not a spectator upon it.[12]

Here is the crux of the critique of the ontological relation to the other where everything is known always already within the horizon of Being. Levinas's critique of totality is, moreover, a critique of the history of philosophy — "an attempt at universal synthesis, a reduction of all experience, of all that is reasonable, to a totality wherein consciousness embraces the world, leaves nothing other outside of itself, and thus becomes absolute thought. The consciousness of self is at the same time the consciousness of the whole."[13] Totalizing presupposes a hubristic and impossible knowing whereby every alterity is reduced to the Same.[14] And yet the other overflows comprehension.

According to Levinas, it is only the *face* of the Other that cannot be captured or portrayed. The human face is beyond reduction. It cannot even be seen, as perception is always already a containment. "It is what cannot become a content, which your thought would embrace; it is uncontainable, it leads you beyond. It is in this that the signification of the face makes it escape from being, as a correlate of a knowing."[15] The face appeals to me, not to be known but to be faced.

> There is first the very uprightness of the face, its upright exposure, without defense. The skin of the face is that which stays most naked, most destitute. It is the most naked, though with a decent nudity. It is the most destitute also: there is an essential poverty in the face; the proof of this is that one tries to mask this poverty by putting on poses, by taking on a countenance. The face is exposed, menaces, as if inviting us to an act of violence. At the same time, the face is what forbids us to kill.[16]

The face refers to the part of the body, the central zone of the head, as well as that quality which transcends it, the other's corporeal self-presence manifest through the gaze or appeal we are exposed to. The face speaks, and in so doing renders all discourse possible. Its first speech is always and everywhere: *Thou shalt not kill.*[17] The face is vulnerable and weak in its nakedness. It speaks to me, as Levinas points out, with an authority, as if *from on high.* It is a commandment, and it is spoken to me. Levinas makes the important distinction between the *saying* and the *said:* even though every saying bears a content, it is the event of the saying that prevents me from doing nothing and merely contemplating that which is spoken. It compels me to respond. Responsibility is the only authentic relationship to the Other.

Here we can see, in Levinas's self-other dialectics, the priority of ethics. The face speaks to me, and I must find the resources to respond to the call. The command of the face orders me in a nonsymmetrical relationship that does not concern itself with reciprocity. I am beholden. Even more so, according to Levinas, this is how I, the self, am authentically defined — as beckoned by the other.

> Constituting itself in the very movement wherein being responsible for the other devolves on it, subjectivity goes to the point of substitution for the other. It assumes the condition — or the uncondition — of hostage. Subjectivity as such is initially hostage; it answers to the point of expiating for others. . . . The ontological condition undoes itself, or is undone, in the human condition or uncondition. To be human means to live as if one were not a being among beings. As if, through human spirituality, the categories of being inverted into an "otherwise than being."[18]

Clearly, for Levinas, ethics takes on the priority (away from ontology) through its insistence on ultimate responsibility for the other which, in turn, defines humanity. "I am I in the sole measure that I am responsible, a non-interchangeable I."[19] We could paraphrase Levinas's same point here to recast it more boldly: *I am I, being responsible*, which is to say: *I am really only I,* ʌʅoʇ *because of you.* qʋ ʇʇ ·

THE OTHER AS THE ANSWER

An exhaustive investigation of Levinas's ethics is beyond the scope of this project. As a matter of fact, Levinas's oeuvre does not resemble the typically comprehensive system of moral principles and regulations that one expects to find in a fully elaborated ethical program. Instead, Levinas offers a foundation and a vision centered on the fundamental obligation to the other. For our purposes, we want to consider the implications of Levinas's starting point — his stance against Western thought's suppression of alterity — for our reflection on twentieth-century evil and suffering rooted in identity conflict arising from the self-other dynamic.

The answer, as introduced above, lies in the significance of the face of the other. Levinas uses an extreme and radical language — the self is held hostage in his or her obligation to the other, that substitution for the other places demands on me that make me responsible even for my persecutors — to demonstrate the importance of grappling with the problem of human suffering by attending to the centrality of the self-other relationship.

Much is at stake. For not to be obsessed with the other from the other's place "on high" is to be trapped inside the confines of one's ego.[20] The self's true humanity takes root only in the appeal of the other to the self and in the self's obligatory answer in responsibility. For Levinas, ethics does not follow from an ontological foundation that provides a basis for right conduct; again, Levinas sees ontology as an attempt to grasp the world as a totality from some impossible outside that does not exist. All thinking about what it means to be a human being must therefore begin with ethics in the first place. Most importantly, this means that ethics cannot be rooted exclusively in the traditional idea that we are all the same, and that, based on the awareness of our common humanity, we will live out a responsible ethics.

> The thought — or rather the cliché — is that if I realized how much the other was like me I would automatically feel a desire to help. But...the danger in grounding ethics in the idea that we are all "fundamentally the same" is that a door is opened for a Holocaust. One only has to believe that some people are not "really" the same to destroy all the force of such a grounding.[21]

Levinas's ethics, thus, not only leaves room for the category of difference but actually insists upon it. It is the other precisely in his or her alterity that imposes the demand of ethics and that safeguards it from the totalizing designs of universalizing thought. Indeed, once the other is grasped in intelligibility, the alterity of the other is diminished. The other is the opening to infinity, marked by transcendence and exteriority insofar as it is outside the powers of the self-same.

Infinity's primacy lies in its anteriority to the totalizing project of ontology. As we have seen, this means that the strong foundation of ethics is precisely its *weak* — but all the more compelling — experience of the other; by "weak" here we mean *unarmed,* both offensively and defensively; its normative force is derived from nowhere else but from this experience of the face. "The experience of the face of the other, as *the* founding experience for metaphysical reflection and *a* founding experience for all nonviolent reflection, justifies itself at the moment of its appearance, and by the very fact of its appearance."[22] As an ethical experience the face itself induces responsibility.

USELESS SUFFERING

Levinas's insistence that the other person can never be reduced to comprehension, that inexhaustible infinity resides not on some lofty ontological plane but rather in the face of the other who calls out to me in naked vulnerability and even takes hostage of me through his demand for responsible action, that this truly ethical facing is necessarily constitutive of subjectivity and identity, indicates, in the end, a wholly human course to take in our efforts to come to terms with the problem of human suffering.

Levinas undertakes a phenomenology of suffering, pointing out that the experience of suffering is not comparable to any other experience of a datum of consciousness, such as that of sound, or color, or contact, inasmuch as the content of suffering is an "in-spite-of consciousness," making its content unassumable. It is "an unwelcome superfluity, that is inscribed in a sensorial content, penetrating, as suffering, the dimensions of meaning that seem to open themselves to it, or becomes grafted to it."[23] Suffering is at once what disturbs order and the disturbance itself; it cannot be integrated into a meaningful whole. Therefore, one rejects it. It is not just the consciousness of rejection but the rejection itself. Levinas describes suffering as a backward consciousness that operates not as a grasp but as a revulsion. As a refusal of meaning it thrusts itself forward as a sensible quality. Thus suffering involves both the content and modality. It is the way in which, within a consciousness, the unbearable is not borne, and this modality registers itself as a datum of consciousness. Thus, the structure of suffering is contradictory. "Contradiction *qua* sensation: the ache of pain — woe."[24] Suffering consciousness is consciousness of its woe.

Earlier, by way of our introductory exposé of Hick's understanding of traditional approaches to theodicy, the passivity of suffering — *passio* — is noted as a defining characteristic, occurring as powerlessness thrust upon those undergoing it.[25] Here Levinas sketches the phenomenality of that passivity, the contradictory structure of suffering described above, where taking into consciousness no longer is a taking but a submission, indeed a "submission to submission" insofar as passivity, a modality, signifies as a quiddity, independent of its conceptual opposition to activity.[26] Thus, the passivity of suffering is not simply the other side of activity, as in the case of the (comparatively active) passivity of ordinary experience in which the senses "receive," culminating in perception. This is passivity beyond the conceptual. Nor is it to be understood simply in terms of a curtailment of freedom.

> The humanity of those who suffer is overwhelmed by the evil that rends it, otherwise than by non-freedom: violently and cruelly, more irremissibly than the negation that dominates or paralyzes the act of non-freedom. What counts in the non-freedom or the submission of suffering is the concreteness of the *not* . . . the *not* of evil, a negativity extending as

far as to the realm of un-meaning. All evil related back to suffering. It is the impasse of life and of being.[27]

Thus, suffering is absurdity, and pain is its deepest expression and loudest outburst. Most importantly, for Levinas, suffering is, in its very phenomenality, useless. It is "for nothing."

But it is precisely here — in the absurdity of suffering — that Levinas's appeal to the other penetrates with the greatest meaning. For resonating within the groan of the other's pain is the original opening toward meaningful care. In the pure suffering of the other, a beyond appears in the form of the interhuman:

> In this perspective there is a radical difference between the *suffering in the other*, where it is unforgivable to *me*, solicits me and calls me, and suffering *in me*, my own experience of suffering, whose constitutional uselessness can take on meaning, the only one of which suffering is capable, in becoming a suffering for the suffering (inexorable though it may be) of someone else.[28]

This central distinction, between the suffering of the other and the suffering that I myself undergo, which bestows the only possible meaning in the midst of the unavoidable absurdity of suffering precisely in the incessant demand that the appeal of the other places upon me, is for Levinas the only supreme ethical principle — the only one, that is, which is impossible to question. Attention to the suffering of the other is, moreover, what Levinas considers to be the very nexus of human subjectivity — the truest fulfillment of the self's own human identity. This suffering alone, the suffering for the suffering of the other, is perhaps the only way that we can begin to face the unfathomable cruelties of the past century. For it is the suffering face of the other, in its very nakedness, weakness, and vulnerability, that alone can empower us to face the challenge that lies ahead, daring as we do to turn the last page of the last theodicy.

THE END OF THEODICY

Levinas's insistence that the suffering of the other, as willingly borne in the self's own suffering, is the only possible condition for any meaning, brings the question of suffering securely into the interhuman realm. The most human theodicy is not speculative, from either philosophical or theological stances, but practical, as an ethical imperative calling for nonindifference of the one to the other. As such, the call to the side of the suffering one before me is, at the same time, an indictment against all those traditional theodicies that, as mere academic brainteasers, fail to prompt an adequate human response.

We could linger on the word "human" just used: it is very much the key to understanding Levinas's objection to two of the most troublesome preoccupations in the history of Western thought — its priority of ontology and its need for (philosophical) theodicies. Here again arises Levinas's awareness of the limitations of any philosophy (read Heidegger) that, failing to go beyond Being, is rendered incapable of confronting evil. To understand this critique, we must delve deeper into Levinas's characterization of evil.

Richard Bernstein identifies three moments in Levinas's phenomenology of evil treated explicitly in "Transcendence and Evil."[29] In contemplating the problem of evil, Levinas observes evil's excessiveness, its seeming intentionality, and the horror that accompanies it in order to demonstrate that the "something" that lies beyond the realm of Being is the difference between good and evil. In brief, the excessiveness of evil refers to its inability to be integrated into our categories of understanding reason. We cannot adequately comprehend evil because evil is "not only nonintegratable, it is also the nonintegratability of the nonintegratable.' Evil is a malignant sublime."[30] Theodicy, on the other hand, is grounded in the presupposition that there does exist a way to integrate evil into a balanced economy of meaning. Bernstein observes that Levinas's reasoning here on the excess of evil parallels his critiques of totality and the dialectic of the same and the other whenever Being and ontology are given priority:

> Just as infinity *ruptures* totality, so too evil *ruptures* totality. . . . It is *because* of the "transcendence" of evil, *because* it cannot in any way be integrated or (strictly speaking) comprehended that the *only* adequate response to the malignancy of evil is a response that is "commensurate" with this transcendence of evil. This is precisely the ethical response that recognizes that the otherness of the other can never be comprehended, that I am infinitely responsible for the other person whose suffering is ethically more important to me than my own suffering.[31]

It is only within the realm of the ethical, specifically, our assymetrical, nonreciprocal responsibility, that one can respond with equal force to the (transcendent) nonintegratability of evil. Theodicy, according to Levinas, is a misguided and naïve attempt to domesticate that which essentially remains unbearable.

The second and third moments of evil in Levinas's phenomenology likewise point to the priority of the ethical over the ontological. Evil is experienced as if it seeks out its victim. It does not come to its victim as if by random, but rather seems to bear its own intentionality, "as if there were an aim behind the ill lot that pursues me, as though someone were against me, as though there were malice, as though there were someone."[32] The temptation toward theodicy is especially obvious here: the victim of evil in turn reckons that there must be some reason for the suffering of evil. But, as Bernstein explains, it is precisely evil that once again leads us to the primacy of ethics: "Indeed, the transcendence of evil leads me to realize that the *first* metaphysical question (*pace* Leibniz and Heidegger) is not 'why is there something rather than nothing?' but rather 'why is there evil rather than good.'"[33]

Finally, Levinas's third observation is as clear a defense for ethical priority as the first and second: one's very experience of evil as horrible and horrifying, and the hatred of evil that always accompanies it, attests to one's association with the good. Once again, the temptation arises to presuppose an economy of relationships by thinking that this horror of evil might be counterbalanced by a good, as if good were simply the dialectical negation of evil.[34] But Levinas is clear: "There can be no passage from Evil to the Good through the attraction of contraries. That would make but one more theodicy."[35] For Levinas, the only way to perceive the good as more than the mere dialectical negation of evil — as that which goes beyond the order of being, with its *conatus essendi,* its "law of being" forever driving me toward self-preservation — is by finding it in the transcendence that shines forth in the face of the other.

> This is no longer a transcendence absorbed by my knowing. The face puts into question the sufficiency of my identity as an ego; it binds me to an infinite responsibility with regard to the other. The original transcendence signifies in the concreteness, from the first ethical, of the face. That in the evil that pursues me the evil suffered by the other man afflicts me, that it touches me, putting into question my resting on myself and my *conatus essendi,* as though before lamenting over my evil here below, I had to answer for the other — is not that a breakthrough of the Good in the "intention" of which I am in my woe so exclusively aimed at? . . . The horror of evil that aims at me becomes horror over the evil in the other man. Here is a breakthrough of the Good which is not a simple inversion of Evil but an elevation. This good does not please, but commands and prescribes.[36]

Bernstein elaborates the central importance of Levinas's point about the horror of evil: "If we restrict ourselves to the horizon of Being, or if we limit ourselves to the *said* rather than to the *saying,* then we cannot adequately respond to the non-integratable evil that we *concretely* encounter, but which nevertheless transcends all categories of comprehension."[37] And, augmenting our overall stress on the notion of the unavoidable concreteness of evil, he continues, "it is the very concreteness of the 'horror of evil' that calls forth the ethical response that ruptures Being. It is only by ethically responding to the evil inflicted on my fellow human beings that I *become* fully human."[38]

This emphasis on the other that initiates the human, that holds that the life of the other is more important than my own life, is, by Levinas's own admission, "unreasonable" in its opposition to the law of being, which would have me look after myself. But it is precisely in the *human* being that the rupture with being's own law takes place. "It is because we, as *human,* know what suffering is that we can have obligations not to cause needless suffering to other living creatures... to *become* a human being is to transcend my own 'law of being,' and ethically respond to the non-integratable evil that afflicts my neighbor."[39] Likewise, any justification of the neighbor's pain must certainly be the source of immorality.[40]

For Levinas, living after Auschwitz is at the same time living after the end of theodicy. Many who cite their own problems with theodicy would not mourn its loss. Terrence Tilley, for instance, demonstrates convincingly how the practice of constructing theodicies became possible only in the context of the Enlightenment, especially in the midst of the rise of modern thought against the greater cultural crisis of authority that characterized that period.[41] This crisis of authority led to the use of autonomous reason to settle not only philosophical questions but also religious ones, since the credibility of religious authorities was under fire. Many thinkers would ponder the existence of evil and disharmony against the background of the Newtonian universe conceived as a self-regulating, perfect mechanism. In this context, it was becoming increasingly difficult to believe in providence: "God's design of the world, no longer evident to all, must be demonstrated."[42] Most importantly, this situation required that evil become "a theoretical term abstracted from specific instances of sin, suffering, and violence."[43] Evil would remain an abstraction in the discourse of philosophical theism even though in the great theological discourses it had not been treated as a single problem to be solved but rather as an aspect of various issues.[44]

Theodicy as an Enlightenment project is a discourse practice that attempts to respond to the problem of evil wherein the theodicist, bearing the burden of proof that it is not improbable that God exists, attempts to prove how the evil in the world is consistent with an accepted belief in God, and/or how such belief is plausible in the face of the evidence of suffering in the world.[45] This response is fundamentally "impractical":

> It is a purely theoretical practice responding to theoretical problems, not a practical theory responding to actual problems in religious practice. Theodicies do not respond to complaints or laments. They are not addressed to people who sin and suffer. They are addressed to abstract intellects which have purely theoretical problems of understanding evil.[46]

Theodicies are also fundamentally anthropocentric. Enlightenment thinkers faced with the burden of explaining evil without divine intervention shifted the "problem of evil" from God to humanity itself. As Kenneth Surin claims, "The intellectual thrust of the Enlightenment was . . . to secularize this 'problem,' to transform theodicy (properly so-called) into 'anthropodicy.'"[47]

Highlighting the Enlightenment roots of theodicy raises important questions for contemporary theodicies, such as John Hick's, which claim a patrimony beyond the Enlightenment, specifically to the two great strains of theodical thinking found in the works of Augustine and Irenaeus. In a careful historical analysis, Surin challenges the very foundational assertion that Augustine and Irenaeus were themselves theodicists. His attentiveness to the *Sitz-im-Leben* of these early theologians is of particular note here, since an undeniable *ahistoricity* characterizes the unfortunate legacy of (theoretical) theodicies so keen on employing philosophical abstractions of evil.

With regard to the so-called Augustinian tradition of theodicy, the so-called "free will defense," it is crucial to recall that the appropriate context of Augustine's consideration of evil is *conversion* — the soul's assent to God. Augustine treats evil in explicitly psychological terms that have little or no connection to the metaphysical or ontological stratagems that are typically employed by modern theodicists. For Augustine, the intractable nature of evil is the result of the stranglehold of habit (*consuetude*) as enhanced by memory (*memoria*). The way to blessedness is more a matter of the creature's utter dependence on the will of a gracious God through Jesus Christ. Thus it is only in conversion, which occurs when the human will cooperates with divine grace, that the "problem of evil" is solved.[48] The philosophical musings of modern theodicists have very little to say in such a psycho-spiritual context. Moreover, we can do justice to Augustine's treatment of evil only when we consider the historically contingent religious and cultural milieu from which it arose, namely, from within the newly liberated church of the post-Constantinian/Theodosian era, where the enemies of the soul were no longer external, in the form of persecutors, but internal, in the form of sin and doubt. Church and world were now in the position to accommodate each other, and Augustine's reflections are intended for the spiritually damaged subject in search of healing that can come about *only* through the soul's acquiescence to God.[49] This is a decidedly different subject from the one presupposed by post-Leibnizian theodicies, which are essentially rational and theoretical enterprises offering no practical strategies to overcome evil. Such a subject is "the putatively rational and autonomous individual who confines herself to the entirely *worldly* discipline of 'evidencing' and 'justifying' cognitive formations, formations which, moreover, are restrictively derived from reason and sense-experience."[50]

Clearly, the forms and presuppositions that underlie Augustine's treatment of evil are crucially different from those employed by modern theodicists. Their use of Augustine, therefore, is highly problematic:

> What we have here is not only a vivid example of the metaphysical theodicist's inability to confront modes of thinking and doing prevalent in the very culture whose intellectual legacy provides the linguistic and conceptual resources that make modern theodicy possible, but also a salutary reminder of how themes and ideas, when abstracted from their historically particular intellectual contexts, will merge into a discourse of free-floating abstractions, the kind of discourse which the post-Leibnizian metaphysical theodicy is in constant danger of becoming.[51]

Surin's historically sensitive critical analysis is also useful for an investigation of the so-called "soul-making" theodicies, which purportedly trace their roots to Irenaeus. As was outlined a bit earlier, such a theodicy rests on the notion of a pedagogy of salvation involving the slow progression of the human creature toward his or her creator. Here, the salient features of the *Sitz-im-Leben* of the early church, with its concern for the transmission of the primitive apostolic faith in all its purity and wholeness, come to the fore. Sound catechesis thus became the major concern in a context where gnosticism provided a constant threat to the integrity of that faith. Typical of many strains of Christian gnosticism was the emphasis placed on the sharp distinction between creation and redemption, which often led to the positing of two separate gods: an inferior Demiurge responsible for creation, the God of the Old Testament, and the supreme God responsible for its redemption, the God of the New. This heterodox formulation resulted in the problematic discontinuity between the two covenants, which led to a denial of the value of the Jewish dispensation in the economy of salvation.[52]

Once again, sensitivity to the historical situation proves to be the lynchpin of the argument. "The theologian who (like Irenaeus) wanted to combat this Gnostic heresy would therefore find himself confronted with the task of having to define *both* the differences *and* the continuity of the two Testaments. It was precisely to break the back of the Gnostic antinomy of the two testaments that Irenaeus invoked the doctrine of the progressive education of the human race towards salvation."[53]

Furthermore, Irenaeus's catechetical intentions must be situated within his own theology of history, which has as its key the incarnation of Christ, who recapitulates all things, including humanity, in himself. The incarnate one, who is the very *image* of God, effects a restoration in humanity of God's true *likeness*.[54] However, there is another case of historical inattentiveness among those modern theodicists who invoke Irenaeus as father of their soul-making theodicies. For Irenaeus's theology of history as catechesis had as its proper subject the individual who was in the process of being won over from *false* belief, not the skeptic or nonbeliever posited by the post-Enlightenment theodicy that holds that evil is "logically" necessary for the moral and spiritual perfection of souls as they advance in their relationship with their Creator.[55] For Irenaeus, the problem of evil has something to do with the very real and recurring problem of the pretense of knowledge which afflicts the searching one and provides the danger through which "by subtle questions and hair-splitting expressions he should fall into impiety."[56] Clearly Irenaeus and the modern theodicist are working out of radically different presuppositions flowing from quite incommensurable intellectual contexts.

By now we have come to see some of the very real dangers that lie embedded in the modern theodical enterprise, most especially its tendency to reduce a truly vigorous Christian response to concrete evils to a more rationalistic and theoretical exercise involving the accumulation of sufficient evidence for the construction of convincing justifications of God's existence and moral perfection. The presumed subject is always the capable individual possessing the necessary skills to make adequate judgments regarding the veracity and falsity of truth claims. We should note just how solitary an endeavor theodicy becomes in this vein. It seems best suited to the tranquility of the theodicist's study where in quiet isolation the theodicist can coolly withhold judgment until proper evidence is gleaned to support impending judgments.[57] In this rarefied environment, where theodicy is tooled from cognition, evil is conceived in abstraction, with the dangerous though unintended result of sanctioning a myriad of evils.[58] Since all theological and philosophical reflection inevitably mediates a certain social and political praxis, we have the responsibility to question just what kind of practices might result from such an esoteric and detached reflection that ponders evil in pure abstraction. When we consider the horrendous evils occurring in the twentieth century now behind us, we encounter evil in its most concrete and visible forms — the gassing shower rooms of Auschwitz, the killing fields in Cambodia, the blood-stained soil of Rwanda.

> A theodicist who, intentionally or inadvertently, formulates doctrines which occlude the radical and ruthless particularity of human evil, is by implication, mediating a social and political practice which averts its gaze from the cruelties that exist in the world. The theodicist...cannot propound views that promote serenity in a heartless world.[59]

There is yet another significant objection to the post-Enlightenment theodicies under consideration that is particularly relevant to the themes that are to be developed in a forthcoming chapter of the present study. The God presupposed in modern theodicies is very much a remnant of a philosophical, providential theism whose unipersonal God looks nothing like the triune God of Christianity.[60] What is most troubling here is the misguided approach, typical of so many contemporary theodicies, that posits a single, basic, divine entity who is essentially omnipotent, omniscient, and eternal and who comprises the core of a bland, all-purpose theism upon which can be appended various confessional additives (e.g., trinity, incarnation, atonement).[61] The confusion here suggests the mistaken view that it is somehow not essential for the theist to understand divinity in an irreducibly Trinitarian way. At this point in our investigation, we can finally see how it is possible to make the important distinction between theoretical theodicists (those to whom Surin has given the label "post-Leibnizians") and those who might be considered "practical" theodicists, for whom the Trinitarian God is more than just an incidental. Among these are Dorothee Sölle and Jürgen Moltmann, two of the more renowned proponents of the theology of the cross. Each shares the idea of God as co-sufferer; the denial that God is impassable, and the insistence that the crucial question of any theodicy is not the intelligibility of God, but of God's salvific activity to overcome evil.[62] Although the confines of our own outline prohibit a more in-depth examination of Sölle's *Suffering* and Moltmann's *The Crucified God*, for our purposes, what is most important is that these are practical theodicies that have at their base the experience of a Trinitarian God.[63]

We have already been introduced to Metz's insistence that all theology after Auschwitz must be theodicy-sensitive. It is clearer now which kind of theodicy is ruled out — the kind that treats evil in abstraction, ahistorically and theoretically, and culminates in a response of resignation, and which kind should remain — one sensitive to the memory of actual (historical) suffering, one insistent on remaining in the practical (protesting) realm, and one done in the presence of the Christian (Trinitarian) God.

If, for now, we can bring some resolution and closure to the present discussion on theodicy, perhaps it can only come with a strong plea to take suffering as seriously as we possibly can. This means to courageously face suffering and evil in all of their horribly concrete manifestations, avoiding specious abstraction and the temptation to give in to facile theoretical solutions. From a Christian perspective this plea may very well include an Augustinian and Irenaean call to personal conversion and holiness. But it entails our moving the theodicy question into another, quite different, theological context — one that, as Surin claims, comes under the rubric of a socially rooted redemption.[64]

We can bring closure to the question of the value of theodicies (post-Leibnizian, Enlightenment) for our time by briefly reviewing the convincing reasons for their rejection. As we have seen, traditional theodicy, with its habit of considering evil in abstraction, supplies a false comfort to sufferers (and thereby exacerbates the experience of suffering) by overlooking the unavoidable particularity of actual, concrete manifestations of evil, and blinds us all to the idea of just how complicit we are in allowing evil to flourish in our midst. Moreover, theodicies distort a truly Christian anthropology in that they are mostly derived from sustained academic reflection resulting from the theodicist's solitude and separation from others, in particular from their experience of actual suffering. Finally, Christian theology is distorted in the presupposition of a unipersonal God, rather than the triune God of Christian tradition and experience.

CHAPTER FOUR

Probing Evil

Evil and Suffering in the Twentieth Century
Third Reflection

As we have seen, the impetus behind much theodical activity is the human impulse toward problem solving.[1] While there is nothing wrong with strategizing to alleviate suffering and eliminate occurrences of evil and violence in our midst, evil (usually considered in the abstract) is, in the end, not simply a problem to be intellectually solved. The question of the existence of a God of love in a world of horrific suffering arises from a perennial doubt that characterizes the human journey throughout life, one that will last as long as history lasts. As Schillebeeckx insists:

> There is an excess of suffering and evil in our history. There is a barbarous "too much" that defies every explanation and interpretation. It is philosophically and theologically unplaceable in any system which contemplates life. There is too much innocent and senseless suffering to be able to rationalize the calamity ethically, hermeneutically or ontologically.... Suffering and evil can cause scandal, nevertheless they are not a problem, but an impenetrable, theoretically unreachable *mystery.* One can objectivize a problem, placing it at a distance from oneself so that a detached explanation is possible. But the suffering and evil of our human history are also *my* suffering, *my* evil, *my* agony and death. They cannot be objectivized.[2]

This is no endorsement of defeatism, much less a call for a passive quietism, which would compel us to refrain from rising up in protest and activism whenever and wherever this dark mystery reveals itself in bitter suffering. It is simply a humble acknowledgment that human reason can neither accuse nor justify God. It is, in addition, a call for a renewed appreciation for solidarity in suffering, where the suffering of the other and indeed all others is, in a very real sense, my very own.

With that said, we continue to take up the challenge of actively pursuing, with eyes wide open, the concrete manifestations — patterns, systems, occurrences — of the presence of evil as they are actually encountered in the world.

THE QUEST FOR PURE IDENTITY

Once again, we assert that our decision to highlight one genocidal episode for investigation should in no way imply that other recent catastrophes are not themselves instructive for study. Here we aim to probe one dynamic that has already been explored in the context of Auschwitz but that can be detected in the occurrence of a number of attempts to exterminate whole peoples — the quest for pure identity.

Having already considered the significant contribution of Levinas with respect to the importance of the other in establishing one's humanity, we are in a better position to describe the evil of genocide. Alexander Laban Hinton detects in genocides "a process of 'othering' in which boundaries of an imagined community are reshaped in such a manner that a previously 'included' group (albeit often included only tangentially) is ideologically recast (almost always in dehumanizing rhetoric) as being outside the community, as a threatening and dangerous 'other' — whether racial, political, ethical, religious, economic, and so on — that must be annihilated."[3] The key concept here is the intentional "reshaping" of the community's composition so as to exclude the segment that offends by its distinctiveness and difference.

Hinton insists that genocides are intimately linked to modernity, as we have already noted, which sets him in agreement with the position of Zygmunt Bauman already explored. But Hinton also insists that genocides are inescapably *local* and require experience-near understanding, that is, the mediation of local knowledge.[4] In both Nazi Germany and Cambodia, for example, it is clear that genocide was structured by the typical overarching schemes of modernity — social engineering, progress, the elimination of the impure, and were aided by the employment of certain conceptual binary oppositions: us/them, good/evil, progress/degeneration, order/chaos, belonging/alien, purity/contamination. But the meaning of such categories always takes on distinct local forms and expressions.[5] For example, the Khmer Rouge actualized their own project of social engineering in terms of Marxist-Leninist "science" that intended to enable a sanctioned leadership to construct a new society free of contaminating elements by employing ideology that defines the "impure" in terms of agrarian metaphors and Buddhist notions of (pure) order and (impure) fragmentation.[6] In Rwanda, the violence perpetrated invoked traditional conceptions of the body structured in terms of (orderly) flow and (disorderly) blockage. Acts of violence manifested such metaphors: the severing of Achilles tendons, breast oblation, the construction of roadblocks that served as execution sites, bodies being stuffed into latrines.[7] According to Christopher Taylor, in Hutu cultural discourse, Tutsis were conceived to be the ultimate agents of blockage. Rwandan rivers were used to exemplify both the blocking potency of the Tutsis and the expelling powers of the nation. Victims' bodies were first mutilated and then dumped into rivers and canals and onto roads and transportation arteries.

> It is no accident, then, that in the months of June, July, and August of 1994, when allegations of a massive genocide in Rwanda were just beginning to be taken seriously in the international media, thousands of bodies began washing up on the shores of Lake Victoria — bodies that had been carried there by the Nybarongo and then the Akagera rivers. So many Rwandan corpses accumulated in Lake Victoria that consumers in Kenya, Tanzania, and Uganda avoided buying fish taken from Victoria's waters, and the lake's important fishing industry was seriously jeopardized.[8]

We see, then, that the forms in which various genocidal episodes actualize this typical quest for pure identity through modern meta-narratives of progress and social engineering do indeed feed upon the various local specificities of particular cultural entities.

ENVY AND SCAPEGOATING

Any investigation of evil and the problem of violence would remain seriously deficient without a consideration of the work of René Girard. Girard's study of evil, within the category of anthropology of religion, is rooted in his understanding of envy, mimetic rivalry, and the conflict of the scapegoat. Although his interests include a vast and highly developed study of the genesis of myth and the function of ritual,[9] for our purposes, we limit our analysis to his work on the topics of human mimesis, the function of sacrifice and the role of the scapegoat in restoring peace, and the relationship of this process to continual occurrences of outbreaks of violence. Girard's analysis provides a helpful key for understanding human complicity in evil.

Girard's understanding of the origin and contagion of human violence is rooted in an anthropology of desire that he claims is the Bible's very own. Specifically, Girard's is an anthropology of *mimetic* desire, which holds that human beings (like animals) are imitators.[10] Indeed, Girard stresses the fundamental anteriority of desire in his preference for the word "mimesis" over the more familiar "imitation": the latter bearing a connotation of a more exterior and conscious type of imitation, along the lines of impersonation (such as when one dresses in imitation of another, or emulates that other's style or mannerisms). But for Girard, mimesis points to something interior to our make-up, the way we are essentially constituted as human beings and through which we receive the fundamentals of memory, language, consciousness, and a sense of being. Mimesis thus assures both the cohesion of the social tissue and the relative autonomy of the members who compose it. "Desire is what we call the movement by which mimesis gives autonomy and individuality to humans."[11]

In addition, mimetic theory posits a human "self" which is an unstable and changeable structure — a human being that is truly a human becoming. Accordingly, J.-M. Oughourlian, co-author with Girard of *Things Hidden since the Foundation of the World*, employs the term "holon" to refer to this *moi-du-désir*, this self constituted by desire. "Holon" denotes a structure constantly becoming according to its continuous exchanges with similar structures.[12] And for both Girard and Oughourlian, it is desire that brings the sense of self into existence, a desire that is itself mimetic in character.

Mimetic desire, then, is not a simple linear desire, following a direct subject-to-object pattern (e.g., "I want _____"; "I desire to be _____"). Instead, mimetic desire is *triangular* in structure (i.e., "I want _____ because you want it too"). The importance of this matter of the primacy of mimetic desire in the construction of the "me," the self, is clear: in some ways similar to Levinas's ethical observation of the priority of the other, that is, his understanding of the genesis of the human as arising in the event of "facing" the other, so too here do we see that the psychogenesis of the self is established with respect to the other, specifically, through the mechanism of mimetic desire. "We have a psychosocial being who is not only genetically the fruit of reproduction, but is, in the make-up of his or her consciousness as well, utterly *other*-dependent. It is the draw, mimesis, that precedes consciousness and makes it possible. It is the force by which each of us is drawn into the relational systems of the human race."[13] As with Levinas, the self-other dynamic is central to the Girardian conception of the self becoming human (although this dynamic plays a different role in each thinker's philosophy). Accordingly, the view that any one of us is, strictly speaking, autonomous, the idea that my own identity is something crafted and cultivated apart from others, under my own scrutiny and control, is simply delusional.

In addition to its depiction of the dialogical construction of selves, the mimetic theory allows us to identify the roots of violence embedded within the triangular structure of desire, once again, that we desire according to the desire of another. All desire is prompted by a mediator who acts as a model. But a climate of mutual and gradually antagonistic desiring develops, forcing the other into the role of rival. Mimetic desire leads to conflicts which escalate into violence unless acted upon in some decisive, extinguishing way.

For Girard, there is a "fundamental truth about violence: if left unappeased, violence will accumulate until it overflows its confines and floods the surrounding area."[14] Here is the "contagion" of violence that Girard stresses:

> Inevitably the moment comes when violence can only be countered by more violence. Whether we fail or succeed in our effort to subdue it, the real victor is always violence itself. The *mimetic* attributes of violence are extraordinary — sometimes direct and positive, at other times indirect and negative. The more men strive to curb their violent impulses, the more these impulses seem to prosper. The very weapons used to combat violence are turned against their users. Violence is like a raging fire that feeds on the very objects intended to smother its flames.[15]

According to Girard, the conflict follows a progression involving different modalities of mimesis. *Acquisitive* mimesis describes this first stage, where one imitates the desire of another for an object, thereby establishing the initial rivalry; this in turn sets group members against each other, giving way to *antagonistic* mimesis, which binds together members of a community at the expense of a victim. *Conflictual* mimesis arises when the importance of the original desire for the object is forgotten, and mimetic activity begins to manifest itself in the unification of rivals against some arbitrary other. According to Girard, this is the *sacrificial process* whereby the appointment and elimination of a victim aims at dissipating societal conflict and containing violence about to run amok.[16]

> Sacrifice plays a very real role in these [primitive] societies and the problem of substitution concerns the entire community. The victim is not a substitute for some particularly bloodthirsty temperament. Rather, it is

a substitute for all the members of the community from *its own violence;* it prompts the entire community to choose victims outside itself. The elements of dissension scattered throughout the community are drawn to the person of the sacrificial victim and eliminated, at least temporarily, by its sacrifices.[17]

There are key elements to the sacrificial process. Although chosen arbitrarily, the victim must resemble to some extent the object that it is intended to replace; otherwise the violent impulse would remain unsatisfied. The procedure thus requires a certain degree of misunderstanding — a concealment — if it is to be effective.[18] And yet there must be on some level some recognition that substitution has taken place. Moreover, sacrificial catharsis can occur, that is, the participants can dispose of their violence efficiently, only if they regard the violent act as a necessity imposed from without, such as by divine decree, and not as emanating from within themselves.[19] Conflictual mimesis works itself out in the elimination of the unanimously appointed *scapegoat;* the mob finds a victim that is liminal (an outsider), someone who is too prominent or has a physical disability.[20] The victim is expelled or sacrificed. Everyone agrees that their problems were due to the victim. His expulsion produces peace, the foundation of a new social order. Now it is seen that the victim brought the peace precisely because it is generally blamed for the disturbance prior to the killing. The group has to believe that the victim is guilty. Because the victim brought peace, it is now sacralized.[21]

Now social prohibitions and rituals are employed to maintain social order. Myths, too, are generated that are always about the foundational murder but that are intended to conceal the truth of the innocence of the victim. Life continues until there is a breakdown in the new order due to the inefficiency of the rituals and prohibitions. Violence again becomes a threat whose potential must be quelled; the scapegoating process is reinitiated, leading to further sacrifices with new myths, rituals, and prohibitions.

The role of religion in these primitive societies cannot be separated from the problem of violence and vengeance.

In primitive societies the risk of unleashed violence is so great and the cure so problematic that the emphasis naturally falls on prevention. The preventative measures naturally fall within the domain of religion, where they can on occasion assume a violent character. Violence and the sacred are inseparable. But the covert appropriation by sacrifice of certain properties of violence — particularly the ability of violence to move from one object to another — is hidden from sight by the awesome machinery of ritual.[22]

The subject of the role of ritual and myth in primitive religions is a complex topic that cannot be pursued here, given the confines of the present study's scope, which is, with regard to Girard, an attempt to identify the roots of violence embedded within the triangular structure of desire. In brief, what is important in Girard's analysis of primitive religion is its function to subdue violence in order to keep its contagion from spreading. In fact, he claims that in its broadest sense, religion is another term for that obscurity that surrounds human efforts at protecting itself from its own violence, through curative or preventative measures.[23]

There is a final comment that deserves mention in the context of the role of religion in staving off violence, even if its proper development must be delayed until a forthcoming chapter.[24] In some ways, it is strange to mention it here, at the end of this brief exploration of Girard's analysis of mimetic desire, violence, and the scapegoat mechanism, since its discovery for him was more of an initiating event: a moment of illumination at the beginning that structured the subsequent development of his oeuvre. Girard's analysis of primitive myths prompted the revelation of a glaring contrast: while myths are always told from the perspective of the lynchers, only the biblical myths, and especially Christianity, are unique in telling the story from the perspective of the victim. The sacrificial process, necessarily concealed in all other primitive mythology, is demystified by the Hebrew/Christian texts — the victim is innocent and only arbitrarily chosen. In fact, Girard goes so far as to claim that on the whole, this phenomenon is what the Bible is all about — undoing the old lie.[25]

DOMINATION SYSTEMS

Having investigated the contagion of violence spurred from competitive desire we turn now to a reflection on the topic of power. Just as Girard's understanding of mimetic desire and victim-making is based on his juxtaposed reading of biblical and other primitive myths, so too do we turn to a biblical investigation of domination systems, as interpreted by Walter Wink.[26] As always, our interest in the idea of the "powers" in the New Testament pertains to its usefulness today as a lens through which we can locate and reflect upon evils in our own time.

Wink's treatment of the powers leads us away from those religious interpretations of the "powers" that smack of gross literalism on the one hand, and those that dismiss altogether their potency for meaning in our day on the other. A more informed and balanced approach begins with the biblical perception that there do exist spiritual forces that impinge upon and influence our lives. Wink points out, for example, that in the second and third chapters of the book of Revelation, the seven letters contained therein are addressed not to a congregation, as in Paul's letters, but to an angel, or, more accurately, to the congregation through an angel. "The angel seemed to be the corporate personality of the church, its ethos or spirit or essence."[27] The angel is presented neither as a distinct spiritual entity, nor as a simple personification. Rather, the angel of a church was apparently the spirituality of a particular church. In *Naming the Powers: The Language of Power in the New Testament,* Wink asserts that the language of power pervades the New Testament in its entirety.[28] The powers should not be thought of as simply equivalent to institutions and structures. They seem to refer more specifically to the core spiritualities of those institutions and structures, "the inner aspect of material or tangible manifestations of power."[29] Accordingly, Wink acknowledges that if we want to change corrupt systems and dehumanizing structures, we must only address not their outer forms, but also their inner spiritual dimensions.

> It means that every business, corporation, school, denomination, bureaucracy, sports team — indeed, social reality in all its forms — is a combination of both visible and invisible, outer and inner, physical and spiritual. Right at the heart of the most materialistic institutions in society we find spirit. IBM and General Motors each have a unique spirituality, as does a league for the spread of atheism. Materialistic scientists belong to universities or research labs that have their own corporate personalities and pecking orders.[30]

Acknowledging both the outer and inner dimensions of structures and institutions does not get us far. What is crucial is a critical appraisal of these spiritualities in order to determine their relative health or pathology. Here Wink stresses the value of the Bible's approach in evaluating the powers. While the competency of modern sociology in treating these inner realities extends only as far as their ability to analyze what an institution is, only the biblical perspective can allow a judgment of an institution's spirituality — its angel — according to its divine vocation.[31] The challenge in our day is to regard corporations and governments as "creatures" whose purpose is to serve the general welfare.

We have already been introduced to the notion of systemic or structural evil. According to Wink, when an entire network of powers becomes integrated around idolatrous values and behaviors, we end up with what can be called the *domination system.* A domination system is characterized by unjust economic relations, and oppressive political relations, biased race relations, as well as patriarchal gender relations, hierarchical power relations, and the use of violence to maintain them all.[32] The relevance of our discussion of the powers and domination systems for an understanding of evil is clear. Evil is not only personal but structural and spiritual. We should not think of evil as simply the sum total of individual human actions, but the consequence of huge systems over which no individual has complete control. Personal redemption cannot be achieved apart from the concerted effort to redeem the social structure. Moreover, "only by confronting the spirituality of an institution *and* its physical manifestations can the total structure be transformed. Any attempt to transform a social system without addressing both spirituality and its outer forms is doomed to failure."[33]

DEMONIZING

Girard would probably concur with Wink's analysis of systemic evils and, in particular, would share Wink's appreciation for the usefulness and relevance of identifying the evils that exist in modern-day domination systems. Importantly, Girard, like Wink, stresses the necessity of astutely judging the powers of our time. "We cannot call the powers simply 'diabolical,' and we should not, under the pretext that they are 'evil,' systematically disobey them. It is the transcendence on which they are based that is diabolical. The powers are never strangers to Satan, it's true, but we cannot condemn them blindly."[34]

Girard's statement above introduces terminology — "diabolical," "Satan" — that, as of yet, we have not included in the present discussion on probing evil in our time. We do well to consider them in the present context of abusive powers. Both Wink and Girard draw heavily from the descriptive imagery and terminology of evil found in the New Testament. According to Wink, when corporations and governments fail in their divine vocation by refusing to serve the general welfare, "their spirituality becomes diseased. They become demonic."[35] "Demons" are "the psychic or spiritual powers emanated by organizations or individuals or sub-aspects of individuals whose energies are bent on overpowering others."[36] Girard identifies Satan as "mimetic contagion at its most secret power, the creation of the false gods out of the midst of which Christianity emerged," and explains that the gospels' use of the term in reference to the mimetic cycle allowed early Christianity to say or suggest many things about religions perceived to be "false, deceptive, and illusory."[37]

How evil is discussed — language used, imageries employed — is of great importance to our understanding of the reality of evil today. The ancient worldview of the Old Testament attests to a basic conviction of the goodness of the powers as created by God as well as of their fallen status. In the ancient biblical mind-set, Israel's misfortunes were too great to ascribe purely to human evil, and thus:

> The ancient myth of the fall of the "sons of God" in Genesis 6:1–4 was enlisted to explain the presence of an evil that emanates not from humanity alone but from something higher as well: not divine, but transcendent, suprahuman, that persists through time, is opposed to God and human faithfulness, and seeks our destruction, damnation, illness, and death.[38]

The idea of the existence of Satan as an actual personification of the force of evil is ancient as well, although its gradual influence on Jewish and later Christian theology developed unevenly and problematically. Exilic exposure to ancient Zoroastrianism while under Persian rule (536–331 B.C.E.) is possibly the main source of this dualistic influence.[39] For our purposes, what is more important is the persistence today of this tendency of thinking whereby Satan is readily identified and located in individuals and groups.[40] We have already explored, in our investigation of Auschwitz, the devastating and dehumanizing ends that result from this kind of perception. The present discussion of the New Testament powers may help us to understand the actual mechanisms implicit in this destructive activity. In his analysis of the scapegoating process, Girard has certainly demonstrated the human proclivity toward locating all evil outside of ourselves. Wink's description of the evils that characterize domination systems is at the same time a plea for *transforming* those powers, a goal that can be achieved precisely because the powers are not intrinsically evil. Redemption as liberation from the oppression of the powers first requires our seeing that the powers can and should be redeemed. The powers are Godly as well as fallen, good and evil. "If we acknowledge that the powers are good and evil we will not demonize."[41] Wink stresses the importance of acknowledging that the powers themselves are "inextricably locked" into God's system and as such are redeemable because they are answerable to God.

No subsystem that attempts to rival the status of God's system itself can last very long. The story of Satan's rebellion and expulsion from heaven symbolically depicts the fate of any creature that lusts after ultimate power and authority. By acknowledging that the powers are good, bad and salvageable — all at once — we are freed from the temptation to demonize those who do evil. We can love our enemies or nation or church or school, not blindly, but critically, calling them back time and again to their highest self-professed ideal and identities.[42]

Dehumanization and demonization are extreme forms of stereotyping that are especially functional in reminding members to maintain the enemy in the enemy role. These strategies lead to the justification of inflicting evil on others by instilling the belief that we are dealing with a demon, someone less than human, and that this subhuman demon is a threat to us, which requires that we attack and even eliminate this enemy in self-defense. In his investigation of violent identity conflicts, Rafael Moses observes: "The aggressor initiated use of the following collective psychic mechanisms: the demonization of the enemy; projection that ascribes to the antagonist all our evils so that we can view ourselves as good and pure; scapegoating and polarization that blames the enemy for faults that are our own and paints the world in black and white, with no gray allowed."[43]

As we have seen, demonizing as a habit, tendency, or outright strategy between enemies has certainly been a dangerous and all too common phenomenon in the past century.

BUILDING ON WEAK CATEGORIES

At this point in our investigation, an effort to revisit the topic of theodicy may seem redundant or even counterproductive: we have already examined the state of that question from a number of critical perspectives. Theodicies have been found to be deficient in their objective to supply a "reasoned" justification for the existence of evil in God's world created in love. As we have seen, theodicy has too often approached this abiding human dilemma in terms of an academic problem that could be solved with a winning argument in abstraction. Moreover, doing theodicy, as we have known it, has seemed to show itself a solitary activity, suited more to the lone thinker rather than to the solidarity of sufferers. Quite problematically, in such a scenario, the God invoked as one of the key terms in most theodical thinking is not even recognizably the God of Christianity, that is, a personal God, a Trinitarian God.

And yet the theology of Johann Baptist Metz — like the philosophy of Levinas, an unavoidably post-Auschwitz theology — is one that anchors the theodicy question about God and human suffering precisely in the center of discussion. Metz is not interested in solving the theodicy problem; rather, he is committed to elaborating a post-idealist "theology of interruptions" that allows the cries of suffering humanity to be heard in all their terrifying realism, a political theology with an apocalyptic vision, one founded not on metaphysics and abstract reasoning, but on what he calls the "weak" categories of memory and narrative, "weak" because these existentials stand on their own without the buttressing of a formal philosophical system of being that hovers over history. In short, it is a theology that throws the theodicy question back unto God.

Metz makes a plea for a theology that incorporates humanity's histories of suffering. Indeed, theology has too often glossed over tragedies and catastrophes in favor of an overemphasis on Being, a theology too subjectless, too situationless. In fact, in Metz's case, it was his consternation over so much astonishing apathy and denial with regard to Auschwitz that set his theology firmly on a political course.

> Auschwitz represents a horror that is beyond all the familiar theologies, a horror that makes every situationless talk about God show up as empty and blind. Is there . . . a God whom one can worship with back turned to Auschwitz? And can any theology worthy of the name keep on talking about God and about human beings after such a catastrophe, as if the presumed innocence of our human words would not have to be scrutinized in the face of such catastrophe?[44]

It is impossible to engage meaningfully in theology with eyes closed to catastrophe. Like Levinas, Metz is influenced by the Bible's vision of the human person, seen in terms of covenant and justice not primarily as "neighbor to Being," but rather as neighbor to the person, in particular, the stranger who suffers. "That way of thinking would urge not ontological but eschatological differences."[45] This is the basis for theology in political garb: concern for the unjust suffering of others which must be the first theological agendum in the wake of Auschwitz. Metz insists that theology is about God as the salvation of others, of those who suffer unjustly.

For discourse about God is either about a vision and promise of universal justice, touching even the sufferings of the past, or it is empty and void of promise, even for those alive today. The question immanent to this discourse about God is first and foremost the question about the salvation of those who suffer unjustly. The truth that guides it is known only in committed resistance against every form of injustice that creates suffering.[46]

Thus, theology after Auschwitz heightens (or should have heightened) our sensitivity to the suffering other, a disposition that makes us (or should have made us) responsible for alleviating the distressful cries all around us.[47] After Auschwitz, we can no longer be concerned about our own personal salvation without at the same time being concerned with that of the other. All of this points to the truth of Metz's observation about theology's woeful reluctance to remain mindful of catastrophe, a point that resounds with urgency in our time. For a theology that ignores the human history of suffering can only accelerate and intensify that history. A theology that attempts to reconcile the unreconcilable by glossing over the incontestable interruptions that our histories of suffering represent will only result in the multiplication of further catastrophes. Any theology that muffles the cries of victims with abstract rationales for the existence of suffering will only end up increasing the volume of those cries. For these reasons, and in keeping with the unabashedly eschatological framework of the Bible, our theologies must turn suffering back to God. For Metz, this means theology as theodicy must work out the concept of "a temporally charged expectation that God will justify himself in his own time."[48] This amounts to a restoration of the unavoidably apocalyptic vision of the Bible that challenges us to really believe in the God of the biblical tradition.

Do we believe in God? Or do we believe in our beliefs in God and, in so doing, perhaps really believe only in ourselves or in what we would like to think about ourselves? Consider, however, a faith that does not believe only in itself, but really believes in God. In this world of ours, however, does not such a faith necessarily take the form of a continual questioning in a temporally charged expectation?[49]

Metz's theodicy is directed back to God within a temporally charged expectation that God will "justify" God's self in God's own time in the face of this history of suffering, which inescapably points to the presence of "the unreconciled" in Christianity. It is the call for a renewed perception of expectation and parousia in our actual lives. Theology must facilitate our continual questioning in the presence of human suffering and in light of this biblical sense of temporally charged expectation.

This also points to the function of the Christian community in maintaining such an *eschatological proviso:* "The Church is to safeguard the openness of historical processes from the endemic human temptation to freeze them into ideological absolutes that then underwrite the kind of violence so horrifically characteristic of the twentieth century. It does so by means of an insistence on the sovereignty of the God of the future, which relativizes every particular human project in history."[50]

We must have the courage to bring our memories of unreconciled suffering into theology. We must also have the courage to hope, for hope arises from this imminent expectation as "a struggle for forgotten time." Hope is also that force which prompts us to do something about the predicament of the suffering one in our midst. "Christian hope is stressed in order to bring Christian praxis—the imitation of Christ—within the scope of time."[51]

This call to hope resounds all the more for those who live an apathetic, empty existence, as so many seem to be living today. But such despair is only the obvious outcome of a worldview that overlooks the Bible's awareness of finality, of God who brings to an end. It isn't a sense of the apocalyptic that causes such fatalism; it is rather a sense of the endlessness of evolution that instills feelings of resignation. Time is conceived as an empty process reaching toward infinity and leaving no room for expectation.

> We can see man's consciousness of catastrophe as expressed in the apocalyptic vision basically as a consciousness of time, not a consciousness of the time of catastrophe, but a consciousness of the catastrophic nature of time itself, of the character of discontinuity and the end of time. This catastrophic nature of time calls the future into question.[52]

Furthermore, it is only in tandem with such an apocalyptic vision that the Christian notion of imitation makes any realistic sense. For Metz, it is not possible to imitate Jesus radically if time is not shortened. Discipleship is imitation in imminent expectation: "Jesus' call: 'Follow me! And the call of Christians: 'Come, Lord Jesus!' are inseparable."[53]

There is a case to be made for a renewed appreciation of apocalypticism as an indispensable theological conceptual strategy, especially in light of what appears to be a growing apocalyptic sentiment in the broader post-Christian, cultural environment of our time.[54] Like Metz, Lieven Boeve believes that the softening or outright purging of the apocalyptic from the Christian tradition represents a distortion of that tradition, a process that "has introduced a *perception of time* that makes it impossible, in principle, to authentically conceptualise the radicality of the Christian faith."[55]

> Philosophically speaking, the apocalyptic understanding of time does not interface well with the Greek-Platonic perception thereof which remains virtually unquestioned in Christian theology. It is also incompatible with modern evolutionary theories of history that prevail up to the present day. Ideological exploitation of the phenomenon is far from alien to the political world, not only with respect to Nazism, for example, but also with respect to modern-day right-wing conservative cultural criticism, the formation of sects, terrorism, the legitimisation of violence, and so forth."[56]

Theology after Auschwitz can no longer cling to a blind and bland metaphysics of salvation. The question is urgent: "Must not the metaphysical *a priori* of suffering finally be acknowledged for every theological truth claim? And must theology 'after Auschwitz' not finally take leave of its trust in being (*Sein*) that is embedded in the forgetfulness of suffering and mythical dreams?"[57]

Indeed, forgetfulness becomes a considerable threat to a political theology that is sensitive to theodicy properly conceived. But memory in and of itself is only neutral. What matters is the judicious use of memory. Tzvetan Todorov warns against the sacralization of the past to the point where it becomes completely isolated from the present. To the other extreme, however, we can trivialize the past by seeing the present exclusively through its lens. Here, Todorov is searching for a way that events of the past can be deemed singular without their being set apart as sacred. This matter is of particular concern to our study of the Holocaust. For if it is understood to be without relation to all other past, present, or future events, it would at the same time prevent us from learning any lessons from it.

> It would be paradoxical, to say the least, if we asserted that the past should be a lesson for the present, and at the same time that it has no connection with the present. Things that are sanctified in this way are not much use to us in our real lives. The sanctified past may be kept in quarantine if we so wish it, it can remain a memory that guides us in our actions,

but to adopt that approach does not allow the past to make its proper contribution to an understanding of the human race of its future.[58]

So that catastrophes such as Auschwitz are not tragically repeated, it is imperative that Christians learn to develop an anamnestic culture, a culture that remembers.[59] According to Metz such an accent on memory amounts to a retrieval of the Jewish spirit of memory and complaint, invoking Israel's defenselessness and its ability to be mindful of itself in the remembrance of God. It is a plea for the cultivation of the memory of suffering.[60]

In a "post-idealist" theology, it is, once again, the "weak" categories of memory and narrative that serve as the foundation for Metz's agenda. This is a theology no longer permitted or expected to present its explanations of the world and its interpretations of human existence, in closed, a-situational systems. Temporality is key here: identity is rooted in time, which makes it weak and vulnerable — actually more like a nonidentity when compared to a metaphysics "strongly" rooted in ideas.[61]

The twentieth century has seen the gradual erosion of Enlightenment certainties such as the autonomy of the individual, the inevitability of progress, and the self-sufficiency and independent reality of the world. With the emergence of new modes of perceiving the world and constructing meaning, there is a renewed interest in the category of narrative as a foundation for theology. Terrence Tilley, for example, highlights the importance of narrative as a mode for teaching the primary metaphors of Christian faith: "Key Christian ideas are metaphors which have been contextualized by inclusion in prototypical narratives. These metaphors thereby become canonical and bear the content of faith. The key concepts of Christian faith — creation, fall, incarnation, atonement, church, eternal life, trinity — are all metaphors at rest, metaphors which have become Christian doctrines."[62] A strictly propositional theology treats such metaphors by analyzing, transforming, and systematizing them. Tilley does not attempt to dismiss the propositional, which can be useful in guiding and criticizing those stories anew, but it has a tendency to rob these central Christian metaphors of their power to transmit new insight. Narrative, on the other hand, leaves metaphors open-ended, and provides room for an account of the role of faith in the lives of believers.

Narrative also allows theology to incorporate human crisis in a meaningful way. The liberation theologian Juan Luis Segundo contrasts two languages of (really approaches to) theology — the *digital,* that language characteristic of scientific formulas, which seeks to define or clarify precisely and concisely a bit of information in crystallized, almost computerized forms; and the *iconic,* the figurative, suggestive, and imaginative style of language that conveys the actual existential predicament of the human person by preserving the element of crisis. For Segundo, this is the language that characterizes much of the Bible, but it is also the language that fosters the perpetuation of meaningful theology. The iconic is the language of stories, and story renders dogma *believable* because it enables us to see the rationality behind the transcendent data of faith. With narrative theology, questions that arise from crisis cannot be ignored. "In its very expression of the response the iconic points unmistakably to the question."[63] Faith needs to be rooted in history, in real life and human activity — in the very reasons for which one lives. Iconic language helps to raise the questions that prompt the deepest answers, and this is its greatest service to theology.

Narrative is fundamental to identity formation and as such is indispensable to ethics inasmuch as it shapes our very understanding of good and evil. As Darrell Fasching notes, "The choices we make, even the options we think we have, are governed by the kind of story we think we are in and the role we see ourselves playing in it."[64] Narrative is not just a means of communication, but a distinctive mode of reflection. As explained by Stanley Hauerwas, the leading theological proponent of narrative ethics, narrative is crucial in allowing new ways of seeing the world.

> It is exactly the category of narrative that helps us to see that we are not forced to choose between some universal standpoint and the subjectivistic appeals to our own experience. For our experiences always come in the form of narratives. . . . I cannot make my behavior mean anything I want it to mean, for I have learned to understand my life from the stories I have learned from others.[65]

Although Metz has lamented the neglect of recognition of the Auschwitz catastrophe in much contemporary theology, there are indications that narrative has opened the way to meaningful theological reflection and integration, even though, for both Jewish and Christian consciousness, Auschwitz remains a hermeneutical rupture, a crisis in the interpretation of meaning.[66]

Fasching, for example, acknowledges the relevance of the book of Job as a post-Holocaust parable on the relation of Jews and Christians. The Bible depicts Job as refusing to sacrifice his integrity in order to make God appear just, in stubborn opposition to the position held by his supposed "comforters," who insist on Job's guilt and on the honor of God who never allows an innocent to perish (Job 4:7). For Fasching, this is precisely the logic that Christians have used to explain, justify, and even induce the sufferings of the Jews throughout history. The Jews suffer (must suffer) as proof of their guilt before God and as a negative testimony to the truth of Christianity. It is only in the final chapter where God vindicates Job and excoriates his comforters (42:7–8) that we are able to see a new insight for the post-Holocaust world.

> Allegorically transposed by the event of the Shoah, the dialogue of Job and the comforters becomes the historical dialogue between Jews and Christians. Christians have claimed that the historical sufferings of Jews were a divine punishment and a sure sign of Jewish guilt for the rejection and death of the messiah. Jews have steadfastly and rightly maintained their innocence of any such guilt. In a post-Holocaust world, and under the impact of critical historical consciousness, Christians too are now admitting the dubiousness of such charges. They are, perhaps for the first time, ready to hear: "You have not told truth of me, as did...my servant."[67]

Fasching's reinterpretation of Job in a post-Auschwitz key resonates with Metz's call for building a theology upon the "weak" but eminently human categories of memory and narrative. The culture of memory, of cultivating a memory of suffering for ourselves and our posterity, is a task to which we must all remain committed. Only such theodicy-sensitive theology can clear a space for the memory of suffering so that it can irritate us, and thereby move us to hope, to resistance and reform.

CHAPTER FIVE

An Anatomy of Revenge

In many ways, everything that has preceded this closing chapter on revenge—our reflections on suffering and evil, the disappearance and persistence of theodicy, the contagion of violence and the scapegoating dynamic, even the call for memory and narrative—all of these considerations have come by way of preparation for this anatomy of revenge. If this is so, then what is offered below should serve as an apt summation of all that we have tried to convey thus far. We could justly subtitle this first part on 9/10, "The Deadly Automatism of Revenge"—and immediately bring to mind, in clever Volf-esque form, a sense of the problem at the heart of the matter: there is something about the reality of revenge that implies a disturbing lack of freedom, a drive that prevents the breakthrough of anything new or different. There is no possibility for a new beginning, for hopeful initiatives, for change. There is no sense of risk implied in revenge because there is no chance for the exercise of creativity. Likewise, because it frustrates any attempt at re-visioning the future, revenge seems to require a certain degree of *un*thinking in order to indulge its fascination with the allure of its own perception of the past and to maintain its proper focus on the resentments that first took root there. Revenge is a stultifying, life-draining, perpetuation of the self-same. It allows no interruptions. It is the condition of being *imprisoned*. Revenge is a lock.

RETURNING EVIL FOR EVIL

Our inspection of the problem of violence has revealed that violence is a chain. Girard's analysis of the origin of sacrifice and sacrificial rites bespeaks primitive societies' awareness and fear of the contagion of violence. As we have seen, sacrifice, as a preventative measure, regulated from within the domain of religion, is thought to keep vengeance in check. In time and with the advent of judicial systems, the safeguarding device against revenge is shifted to legal prohibitions and punitive measures. The threat of an escalating, all-consuming revenge remains, however, as more links are added to the deadly chain.

Why does the spirit of revenge, wherever it breaks out, constitute such an intolerable menace? Perhaps because the only satisfactory revenge for spilled blood is spilling the blood of the killer; and in the blood feud there is no clear distinction between the act for which the killer is being punished and the punishment itself. Vengeance professes to be an act of reprisal, and every reprisal calls for another reprisal. The crime to which the act of vengeance addresses itself is almost never an unprecedented offense; in almost every case it has been committed in revenge for some prior crime.... Vengeance, then, is an interminable, infinitely repetitive process. Every time it turns up in some part of the community, it threatens to involve the whole social body.[1]

Miroslav Volf describes two "predicaments" that characterize the endless spiral of vengeance wherein violence and revenge feed relentlessly upon each other. The "predicament of partiality" refers to the inability of parties locked in opposition to agree on the moral significance of their actions: "When one party sees itself as simply seeking justice or even settling for less than justice, the other may perceive the same action as taking revenge or perpetuating injustice ... a just revenge leads to a just counter-revenge."[2] Vengeance thrives on such a disparity in perspective between social actors. The second predicament is one that Volf adopts from Hannah Arendt. The "predicament of irreversibility" is simply an observation of the temporal sequence that characterizes human acts. We are unable to undo what we have done, even though we did not or could not have known what we were doing at the time. In other words, if our actions could be undone, the need for vengeance would diminish or even disappear altogether. But actions are irreversible, making vengeance all too often irrepressible.[3]

Another force that perpetuates the instigation of violence and vengeance is a cultural factor both widespread and enduring. The myth of redemptive violence is an insidious feature of social indoctrination involving a most simplistic, irrational, and yet titillating view of evil. The myth encourages the perception that evil can be located entirely over "there" (never in "here") fostering the illusion of the necessity of the "good guys" fighting the "bad." Such a black-and-white portrayal of good and evil lends itself to the easy justification of the use of violence against "them." In many cultures, indoctrination into this mind-set begins at a very early age, inspiring an incentive toward a false heroism through depictions of an uncomplicated and thorough triumph of good over evil. What seems like a healthy satisfaction with seeing the evil of violence finally subdued becomes in reality the sadistic enjoyment of violence itself. Literature, film, and even cartoons are enlisted to help bring home the point. In his helpful analysis of domination systems, Walter Wink observes:

> Once children have been indoctrinated into the expectations of a domi-
> nator society, they may never outgrow the need to locate all evil outside
> themselves. Even as adults they tend to scapegoat others (the Commies,
> the Americans, the gays, the straights, the blacks, the whites, the liberals,
> the conservatives) for all that is wrong in the world.[4]

As Wink points out, the supreme danger of the myth of redemptive violence is that it all too often leads to violence as an end in itself: security through
strength; peace through war. In this way the myth serves as the spirituality of
militarism; the state permits itself to utilize violence as if by divine decree and
always for the purest of intentions. "The name of God—any god, the Christian God included—can be invoked as having especially blessed and favored
the supremacy of the chosen nation and its ruling caste."[5] Beyond armies and
defense departments, however, lies the equally destructive potential that aims
at whole populations. In the end the myth of redemptive violence prompts
another dangerous myth: salvation through simple identification with the
powerful. The allure of vicarious invincibility is sometimes satisfying enough
to those who have never known empowerment themselves. Tragically and all
too often, it is the oppressed, duped by the desperation of their own disenfran-
chisement, that keep the oppressors thriving in power. "Everything depends
on victory, where one has the thrill of belonging to a nation capable of imposing its will on other nations. For the alternative — ownership of one's evil
and acknowledgment of God in the enemy — is for many simply too alien a
concept."[6]

In some ways, because the dynamics of retaliation seem so straightforward,
we could be tempted to think that there must exist some simple resolution to
it. Others hurt us. We suffer. The desire for revenge presents itself as an egress
of easy access—a way out of the pain of passio back into self-control. In this
way, revenge appears to be a normal, natural human response. We have already
examined a number of the problems and dangers that invariably accompany
the quest for revenge: the potential for escalation into an endless cycle of violence, the tendency to be seduced into thinking that the other is entirely evil,
our failure to see that our own acts may have inspired hatred, the allure of the
myth of redemptive violence that leads to uncontrollable and disproportion-
ate harm. At some point, we do need to consider what happens to our own

humanity when we seek to do harm to another. The question remains: Does revenge deliver the intended satisfaction that it promises? Does the anticipated joy resulting from the knowledge of having returned evil for evil received ever really materialize? As Etty Hillesum pondered from within the brutal confines of the concentration camp, vengeance is reprehensible simply because it makes us no different from those on whom we wish to avenge ourselves?[7] We are left to ask whether vengeance is the only way to recover a sense of self-esteem and to reassert one's power.

In *Forgiveness and Revenge,* Trudy Govier explores the important difference between the words "vindictiveness" and "vindication," both of which have a common Latin root (*vindicare*), but only a superficial similarity. "A person who is *vindictive* bears a grudge, is spiteful, or seeks revenge, whereas one who is *vindicative* is one who tends to vindicate (justify) someone (himself or another)."[8] The distinction between the two underlines the importance of the need to correct or "put right" the wrongdoing committed against the victim who all the while did not deserve such mistreatment. One way of seeking to vindicate oneself is by attempting to damage and diminish the other; another way, an infinitely more human way, is by aiming to restore oneself. Govier decides: "Better and more promising than vindictive actions that would put the other *down,* are vindicating actions that bring the victim *up,* through self-development and worthwhile accomplishments."[9] The victim does not have to cultivate hatred against the victimizer. In fact, the victim may pursue self-justification and the restoration of dignity and honor through education, through devotion to others, and through dedication to worthy humanitarian causes. The victim may also achieve vindication by working to insure that further acts of the same injustice and wrongdoing never aggrieve future victims.

VICTIMS AND VICTIMIZERS

Our attempt to investigate the anatomy of revenge has thus far employed rather clear-cut delineations between perpetrators and victims. While this may be helpful in examining issues on a more theoretical level, on the practical level, such a stark demarcation may only obfuscate the real picture. In an era such as ours where so many strive to claim the "authoritative" status of victim, the matter begs serious consideration. Can we honestly say that blame can be apportioned to only one side?

To what extent in a given situation can we insist upon the integrity of innocence? Obviously, there are instances when some take advantage of others, and others are violated through no fault of their own. But even if such could be proven the case, how long would the innocent retain their innocence, especially after the violation? For example, hasn't our investigation of evil, especially the evil of domination systems, revealed the ease and even willingness in which all parties can be drawn into conflicts unawares?

> People often find themselves sucked into a long history of wrongdoing in which yesterday's victims are today's perpetrators and today's perpetrators tomorrow's victims. Is there innocence within such a history? With the horns of small and large social groups locked, will not the "innocent" be cast aside and proclaimed "guilty" precisely because they seek to be "innocent"? The fiercer the battle gets the more it is governed by the rule "Whoever is not fighting with you is struggling against you." Can victims sustain innocence in a world of violence?[10]

Perhaps the myth of our own lily-white innocence is exposed by our secret desire to see our victimizers suffer the same fate that they have inflicted upon us. Self-deception may very well prove to be the ultimate culprit in antagonisms great and small. We have already learned, from Levinas, that there is no absolute vantage point from which human beings can make absolute judgments. Human beings are incapable of occupying that rarefied space that might render them qualified to make judgments about corruption and innocence. Rather than indulging in "us" versus "them," "pure" versus "corrupt" thinking, what is needed is a humble acknowledgment of the universality of sin, of our solidarity as sinners.

> Solidarity in sin underscores that no salvation can be expected from an approach that rests fundamentally on the moral assignment of blame and innocence. The question cannot be how to locate "innocence" either on the intellectual or social map and work our way toward it. Rather, the question is how to live with integrity and bring healing to a world of inescapable noninnocence that often parades as its opposite.[11]

Is such a recommendation likely to be implemented? Realistically, can we acknowledge our own sinfulness even as we ourselves are being sinned against?[12] Maybe the more urgent question resounds from our earlier consideration of catastrophe as catalyst. That is to say, perhaps the only question that really matters is the one that too often remains unasked. How much more suffering — of Auschwitz proportions — can humanity endure?

ISRAEL AND PALESTINE

This last section of our anatomy may be a prime example of "biting off more than one can chew." Indeed, there are probably far too many historical instances of "the deadly automatism of revenge" than we would care to recollect. One hesitates to approach any of them, in fear of trivializing the complexity of longstanding hostilities. Indeed, even the attempt to sketch a historical account draws one precariously close to the uneasy judgment seat that we have just acknowledged does not and cannot exist. All we can do is strive to remain aware of our universal membership in the solidarity of sin.

Such a humble admission is evident in the words of Rabbi Michael Lerner, co-chair of the Tikkun community, the international organization committed to social healing and transformation:

> But from the standpoint of the Palestinian people, the pain they suffered at our hands was very real. Yet, because we are still so traumatized by our own pain, we Jews still have difficulty acknowledging that we have caused any pain to the Palestinians, just as Palestinians continue to be unable to acknowledge the pain they cause to the Jewish people when it was we who were the powerless and the homeless.[13]

Acknowledging the pain of the other. We began part 1 with Metz's claim that the *memoria passionis* is the only universal category of humanity left open to us. We see now that what is crucial in this memory is not just the recollection of my own suffering, but a recognition of the suffering of the other, indeed, of all others. Only then can we ever expect to move beyond the terrifying confines of September 9–10.

The following reflections, springing from memory and leaning toward narrative, represent a number of links in the chain of ongoing violence locked by revenge. The chain is not necessarily forged by simple chronology; each passage demonstrates a different historical aspect of the same perpetuating mechanism of vengeance. Confusion resulting from the indistinguishability of victim and victimizer is entirely to the point.

> The political impact of the Holocaust on Jewish consciousness went into opposite directions. For some, the horror of racism and genocide led to a deep commitment to never again allow any people to face this kind of horrible reality.... Many — perhaps most — other Jews, however, drew a quite opposite set of conclusions. 'We Jews cared about everything else, but no one cared about us, no one protected us, and no one ever will. We

are alone in the world, and we can't count on anyone but ourselves, so we need to focus all our energies on protecting ourselves to ensure that it will never happen to us again. (54)

The Arabs believed that they were being asked to pay the price for the pain Jews suffered during the Holocaust. Why, they wondered, shouldn't the Jews be given a portion of Germany or some other country that had actually persecuted them, rather than part of the Arabs' homeland? And if Jews didn't want to be a minority in a Palestinian state, why should Palestinians have to be a minority within a Jewish state? (57)

Listening to the actual language being used by those engaged in violence, it would be hard to deny that anti-Semitic themes on the Arab side and anti-Arab prejudices on the Jewish side played into the willingness of both to believe a set of rumors about the other side's having already massacred people which provided 'justification' for more violence.... For centuries a small group of religious Jews had prayed and lived near the Machpelah in Hebron, the traditional burial site of Abraham and Sarah (and, in some accounts, of Adam and Eve). It was on this site sacred to Jews that Muslims had chosen to erect a mosque, and so it became for many years a shared site of holiness. The Arab mobs who murdered dozens of religious Jews in Hebron in 1929 left a scar on the memory of some Jews that would resurface in the eventual establishment there in the late twentieth century by fundamentalists who recall this earlier massacre to justify their hatred of Palestinians. (46)

Deir Yassin stands out in the memory of the Palestinians because of the atrocities committed there against Palestinian civilians, as men, women, and children were massacred by the IZL and Lehi troops (Jewish terrorist groups). Benny Morris quotes an Israeli commander who reported on April 12: "The conquest of the village was carried out with great cruelty. Whole families — women, old people, children — were killed, and there were piles of dead." In a report the next day, this same Hagannah commander reported, "Lehi members tell of the barbaric behavior of the IZL toward the prisoners and the dead. They also relate that the IZL men raped a number of Arab girls and murdered them afterward." (60)

Imagine the rage you would feel at having your worst fantasies confirmed: that the Zionist enterprise was in fact causing you to lose your homeland. You would hardly be able to believe your ears and eyes that the Zionists were now going to keep your house or apartment, forbid you to return to your village (if, indeed, it even existed anymore), and were rejecting resolutions calling for the return of refugees (Resolution 194) from the very United Nations whose vote had been used to legitimate the State of Israel in the first place. At such a moment, talk of acknowledging past errors, repudiating their leadership, or pleading for another chance with the State of Israel would have been perceived as utopian foolishness. (75)

Theology with Open Eyes

The challenge of 9/10 has been to articulate a theology of suffering sensitive to the theodicy question, in line with Metz's appeal, while avoiding the numerous problems that have called the theodicy tradition into question as a viable option for meaningful theologizing in our time. As we have seen, theodicy is more the offspring of Enlightenment philosophy's quest for reasonable proof of a benign rational order than of biblical theology's tradition of urgent questions and dire complaints in the wake of the ruptures of catastrophe. Especially now, at the turning of a century already marked by violence and revenge, our theology must be time-sensitive, that is, both aware of the limits of time and awake before the tragic interruptions of time.

We have seen that one of the more troubling aspects of the theodical option is its tendency to consider evil in abstraction, that is, evil detached from the historical, in order to function as a postulate for the metaphysical. Our decision to situate the question of God and suffering as part of a reflection on the twentieth century's dismal history of atrocity resulted in the recognition of the importance of praxis-centered approaches aimed at uncovering the actual dynamics of evil. By focusing our investigation on the catastrophe of Auschwitz we have highlighted the co-occurrence of the dehumanization of victims and the inner fragmentation of victimizers. We have seen that the evil of exclusion has a root in the problem of identity formation, specifically the attempt to establish it in opposition to the "other," the stranger, the one not like us who is among us. Purity, virtue, and wholesomeness begin their alignment on one side — always *our* side — so that the undesirable can stand handily in relief on the other. A path, then, is easily cleared for the oppression of that stranger-other; if blame is in the air, and especially if the memory of violence lingers there, then the eventual elimination of the scapegoated-other comes next. Particularly troubling in the scenario is the chilling ease with which it is all effected. The evil of 9/10 operates as a well-oiled machine, with advanced technology and anonymous bureaucracy employed in its service. Then it isn't questioned. It isn't even noticed. It becomes business as usual.

Metz has said that prayer after Auschwitz is possible only because there was prayer in Auschwitz. Perhaps we can also claim that we can do theology after Auschwitz, indeed after all the catastrophes of "9/10," only if we have remembered those who have suffered, by giving their "dangerous memory" a place in our theology. The memory is dangerous because it "calls into question our tightly-sealed up identities . . . it makes one rather 'weak,' it creates an open flank. It is a remembrance that does not use suffering to make us aggressive, but reflects on others who suffer."[1] Only in this way can memory help to overcome violence and revenge. And it is only in this way that we can approach 9/11 — with prayer reverently closing our eyes, and theology keeping them open.

PART TWO

9/11

A DISTURBING FIGURE reappears at the opening of part 2. It is Primo Levi's representative of the impossible witness to suffering — the *muselmann* — mute and lifeless victim of the death camps, the walking-dead whose testimony to atrocity persists in a silence that will not stop screaming. In a bizarre and unsettling way, the term can now be rendered literally: in its origin, *muselmann* actually means Muslim, an unfortunate allusion to an old stereotype for the oppressed Arab — submissive, powerless, prostrate in unthinking resignation.

In an important way, this vestige of the *muselmann* highlights the main theme of our investigation in part 2 — the memory of violence, the unrelenting cycle of vengeance and the relation of these to the incidence of terrorism in our time. The *muselmann* has become emblematic of the persistence of the memory of suffering and atrocity, a mute witness that demands to be faced.[1] The question remains: Are our eyes opened wide enough to see him? Does our theology even allow us to look in his direction?

We have already stated in the general introduction the main motivation for the present work: we aim at articulating a response, at encouraging a particular Christian response to an act of unfathomable cruelty resulting in incalculable suffering. How then are we as Christians to respond to such evil and suffering endured? We have determined some of the shortcomings of traditional theodicy: as an essentially rationalistic and theoretical exercise, it offers no implications for any practical strategies to overcome evil and diminish suffering. It considers evil in abstraction, pulling the theodicist away from the arena of suffering and into a safe and rarefied solitude. It thus supplies false comfort to sufferers and ultimately worsens the experience of suffering by passing over the particularity of actual evil, while blinding us to our own complicity in its flourishing. Furthermore, the God that theodicy presupposes and that it seeks to justify is far from the Trinitarian God revealed in the Bible, whose salvific activity to overcome evil is so pronounced.

At the same time, this rejection of theodicy hints at the direction that needs to be taken in attempting to deal with the problem of the suffering of evil. Such an option musters both the courage needed to face evil in its concrete and particular manifestations, so as to better understand those mechanisms that often bring it about, and the compassion with which Christians are called to respond whenever they encounter the human face of the suffering Christ in their midst. We are opting for an existential model of evil to make possible a more pastoral approach.

We need a practical theological perspective to guide us in our own reflection on God's presence "within" the 9/11 tragedy. As always we reject any attempt to attach meaning to catastrophe by seeking to justify the suffering that results from it — what for Maurice Blanchot would amount to the worst kind of "wisdom" — the kind that attempts to get around the anger, the pain, and the protest by domesticating the devastation: "To assign catastrophe a 'meaning' is to do no more than to prescribe an anodyne; for, in a way, an explanation is a certain kind of escape."[2] By refusing to consider this evil in abstraction, we find ourselves drawn to the site of the suffering itself. There, the concreteness of the tragedy maintains our focus on the real. We are challenged to look at the problem of suffering through as wide-angled a moral lens as possible, one that can capture both the subject and the shadow — the conspicuous atrocity as well as the hidden machinations that lie behind it. We thus begin our investigation with the assertion that the only adequate theology of suffering for us is the one that leads to Ground Zero. We allow ourselves a sustained look at the face of useless suffering until, hopefully, we can begin to detect the universal features of that suffering face. At Ground Zero, we are called to discover our co-humanity.

Our investigation of the catastrophe at Auschwitz resulted in the identification of certain dynamics of the evil that occurred there, and these we bear in mind as we turn our thoughts toward 9/11: evil's proclivity toward dualistic reductionism, its tendency to demonize the other, its bolstering through impersonal bureaucratic structures and technological innovation, its concealment in faceless domination systems, its disguise in the banal. We have also examined how these tendencies relate to the problem of exclusion of the other where an attempted purity of identity is established apart from or against the other. As we have seen, the predicament all too often leads to violence and a search for scapegoats, culminating in the vicious, all-consuming cycle of revenge. Such was the hallmark of 9/10. On 9/11, we additionally learn how shared participation in sin implies shared responsibility for all of the suffering. Again, this is not an attempt to assign some transcendent meaning to yet another catastrophe. For our purposes, "9/11" represents an urgent call to pay attention, and perhaps we can think of terrorism as just that kind of *wake-up* call. In our solidarity of sin and suffering we may finally learn that forgiveness is the only way to break the vicious cycle of hatred and revenge. For as Pope John Paul II insisted, "it is within our grasp to see that a century of tears, the 20th century, is followed in the 21st century by a 'springtime of the human spirit.'"³ This, the realm of hope, may be the lasting character of 9/12 — the growing reign of peace through relationships of kenotic self-donation, which is a share in the life of the Trinitarian God who is the God of peace. But for now, in the setting of 9/11, we are charged to open our eyes to the suffering that exists on all sides and to see ourselves and the embrace of our God in the midst of it.

CHAPTER SIX

The Attack

The idea is to remain focused in the realm of the real. Accordingly, we include the real names of actual people and places to further make the point that it is essential to ground any serious analysis of evil and suffering in the historical. We outline the main facts of the destruction to lay a foundation for the theological reflection that follows.

TWO HOURS OF DESTRUCTION

According to *The 9/11 Commission Report,* the devastating terrorist attacks of September 11, 2001, directly involved four transcontinental flights and nineteen terrorist hijackers.[1] On that morning, two men, Mohamed Atta and Abdul al Omari, met Satam al Auqami, Wail al Sherhri, and Waleed al Sherhri at Logan International Airport in Boston. The five men checked in and boarded American Airlines Flight 11 bound for Los Angeles, scheduled to depart at 7:45 a.m. Also at Logan, five additional men, Marwan al Shehhi, Fayez Bankhammad, Mohan al Sherhi, Ahmed al Ghamdi, and Hamza al Chamdi, checked in for their L.A. bound flight, United Airlines Flight 175, scheduled to depart at 8:00 a.m. At roughly the same time, at Dulles International Airport in Washington, D.C., five more men prepared to take off: Khalid al Mihdhar and Majed Moqed checked in at the American Airlines ticket counter for Flight 77, also bound for L.A. They were joined by Hani Hanjour, Nawaf al Hazmi, and Salem al Hazmi. Finally, at Newark International Airport in northeastern New Jersey, four men checked in for their flight, United 93, again L.A. bound: Saeed al Ghamdi, Ahmed al Nami, Ahmad al Haznawi, and Ziad Jarrah.

By 8:10, on the morning of September 11, 2001, the aforementioned nineteen individuals had managed to bypass successfully all security measures established for the prevention of hijacking. Their precisely planned mission, near-perfectly executed, involved commandeering all four of these passenger planes, transforming them into live guided missiles loaded with up to 11,400 gallons of jet fuel, and directing them into highly symbolic, densely populated targets.

The Hijacking of American Airlines Flight 11

Captain John Ogonowski and First Officer Thomas McGuiness piloted the Boeing 767. Carrying its full capacity of nine flight attendants, the plane was boarded by an additional eighty-one passengers, including the five hijackers. American 11 took off at 7:59 a.m. By 8:14 it had climbed to twenty-six thousand feet, at which time or shortly thereafter, the hijacking commenced. Betty Ong and Madeline "Amy" Sweeney, two of the flight attendants, reported that two of the hijackers, most likely the Shehris, who were seated in row two in first class, stabbed two unarmed flight attendants who were preparing for cabin service.[2] Shortly after, Atta, the only terrorist trained to fly a jet, and a second hijacker, probably Omari, broke into the cockpit. At the same time, one of the hijackers, probably Satam al Suqami, stabbed passenger Daniel Lewin, who was seated directly in front of him. It is supposed that Lewin may have made an attempt to stop the hijackers in front of him without knowing that another hijacker was seated directly behind him.[3] The five hijackers then gained control of the plane. They sprayed mace, pepper spray, or some other irritant in first class in order to force all of the passengers and attendants toward the back of the plane. Five minutes later, Betty Ong, using one of the airphones in coach, called the American Airlines Southeastern Reservations Office in Cary, North Carolina, to report the emergency. This call lasted about twenty-five minutes as she relayed information about events. It is clear that at 8:25 the hijackers had made an attempt to communicate with the passengers, because the following message, obviously intended for the cabin's public address channel, was inadvertently broadcast over air traffic control: "Nobody move. Everything will be okay. If you try to make any moves, you'll endanger yourself and the airplane. Just stay quiet."[4] Meanwhile, using another airphone, Amy Sweeney contacted the American Flight Services Office in Boston. At 8:26, Ong reported that the plane was "flying erratically." One minute later the plane turned south. Sweeney reported on her line that the plane had been hijacked, that a man in first class had had his throat slashed, and that two flight attendants had been stabbed. At 8:41, American's operations center, having officially declared AA 11 a hijacking, supposed that the plane was now headed for JFK airport in New York City and began to make preparations there for its landing. At 8:44, Sweeney, still in contact with the Boston office, relayed: "Something is wrong. We are in a rapid descent...we are all over the place." Michael Woodward, flight services manager, then asked Sweeney to look out the window to try to identify their location. Sweeney responded: "We are flying low. We are flying very, very low. We are flying way too low." Seconds later she added, "Oh my God we are way too low." Then the phone call ended. At 8:46, American 11 crashed into the North Tower of the World Trade Center in New York City. All on board, along with an unknown number of people in the tower, were killed instantly.[5]

The Hijacking of United Airlines Flight 175

Captain Victor Saracini, First Officer Michael Horrocks, seven flight attendants and fifty-six passengers boarded the Boeing 767 and departed Logan airport at 8:14 a.m. By 8:33 the plane had reached its cruising altitude of thirty-one thousand feet. Thus, UA 175 was taking off just as AA 11 was being hijacked. At 8:42 the United flight crew had just completed their report on a "suspicious transmission" overheard from another plane, which turned out to be AA 11. This was to be United 175's last communication with the ground. The hijackers made their first attack sometime between 8:42 and 8:46. According to eyewitness accounts made from a phone in the rear of the plane from passengers who had originally been seated in the front, the hijackers used knives (as reported by one flight attendant and two passengers), mace (reported by one passenger), and the threat of a bomb (reported by the same passenger). They stabbed members of the flight crew (reported by one flight attendant and one passenger). Thus the tactics were similar on both flights. At 8:47, the aircraft changed beacon codes twice within one minute, and at 8:51, the flight deviated from its assigned altitude. At 8:52, in Easton, Connecticut, Lee Hanson received a phone call from his son Peter, a passenger: "I think they've taken over the cockpit — an attendant has been stabbed — and someone else up front may have been killed. The plane is making strange moves. Call United Airlines — tell them it's Flight 175 Boston to L.A." Lee Hanson then called the Easton Police Department and replayed what he had heard. At 8:58 the flight began to head toward New York City. At 8:59 passenger Brian David Sweeney tried to call his wife, Julie. He left a message on the answering machine that the plane had been hijacked. Then he called his mother, Louise, and told her that the passengers were thinking about storming the cockpit to take control of the plane away from the hijackers. At 9:00 Lee Hanson received a second call from his son Peter: "It's getting bad, Dad. A stewardess was stabbed. They seem to have knives and mace — They said they have a bomb — It's getting very bad on the plane — Passengers are throwing up and getting sick — The plane is making jerking movements — I don't think the pilot is flying the plane — I think we are going down — I think they intend to go to Chicago or someplace and fly into a building — Don't worry, Dad — If it happens, it'll be very fast — My God, my God."[6] The call ended abruptly. Lee Hanson had heard a woman scream just before it cut off. At 9:03, United Flight 175 struck the South Tower of the World Trade Center. All on board, along with an unknown number of people in the tower, were instantly killed.[7]

The Hijacking of American Airlines Flight 77

American 77 was a Boeing 757 piloted by Charles F. Burlingame and First Officer David Charlebois. Four flight attendants served fifty-eight passengers. The flight departed from Dulles Airport in Washington, D.C., at 8:20, and by 8:46 it had reached its assigned cruising altitude of thirty-five thousand feet. At 8:51 the flight finished transmitting its last routine radio communication. The hijacking began at some point between 8:51 and 8:54. According to passenger and flight attendant accounts, the hijackers moved all the passengers to the back of the plane. Again, knives were used, but in this case, these were identified by one passenger as box cutters. At 8:54 the aircraft deviated from its assigned course turning south. Indianapolis Air Traffic Control tried reaching the aircraft but was unsuccessful. At 9:12 passenger Renee May called her mother, Nancy May, in Las Vegas, informing her of the hijacking and asking her to alert American Airlines. Between 9:16 and 9:26 Barbara Olson called her husband, Solicitor General of the United States Ted Olson. She told him what had happened and that the hijackers were unaware of her phone call. A minute later the phone call was cut off. Ted Olson tried unsuccessfully to reach Attorney General John Ashcroft. Later, Barbara reached her husband again. Ted asked for her location and she informed him that the plane was flying over houses. Another passenger told her that they were traveling northeast. He told her of the other hijackings. She remained calm. Then the second call was cut off. At 9:29, the autopilot on AA 77 was disengaged. The aircraft was flying at seven thousand feet and approximately thirty-eight miles from the Pentagon. At 9:34, Ronald Reagan Washington National Airport advised the Secret Service of an unknown aircraft heading in the direction of the White House. American 77 was then five miles west-southwest of the Pentagon and began a 330-degree turn. At the end of the turn the plane, now pointed toward the Pentagon and downtown Washington, descended twenty-two hundred feet. The hijacker pilot then advanced the throttles to maximum power and dove toward the Pentagon at 9:37. AA 77 crashed into the Pentagon at a speed of 530 miles per hour. All on board as well as many civilian and military personnel in the building were killed.[8]

The Battle for United Airlines Flight 93

UA 93 departed from Newark at 8:42 bound for San Francisco. Captain Jason Dahl and First Officer Leroy Homer piloted the Boeing 757; there were five flight attendants and thirty-seven passengers. The first forty-six minutes of the flight proceeded routinely. At 9:19 a United Airlines flight dispatcher began transmitting the warning: "Beware any cockpit intrusion — Two aircraft hit World Trade Center." UA 93 did receive this message, but it was not transmitted until 9:23. At 9:26, pilot Jason Dahl responded with a note of puzzlement: "Ed, confirm latest message, please." The four hijackers attacked at 9:28.[9] While traveling thirty-five thousand feet above eastern Ohio, the plane suddenly dropped seven hundred feet. The FAA air traffic controller in Cleveland received the first of two radio transmissions from the aircraft. The captain and first officer could be heard declaring "Mayday" amid the sounds of a physical struggle in the cockpit. The second message transmitted thirty-five seconds later indicated that the flight was continuing. The captain or first officer could be heard shouting: "Hey, get out of here — get out of here — get out of here." At 9:32 Jarrah made the following announcement: "Ladies and gentlemen, here the captain. Please sit down. Keep remaining sitting. We have a bomb on board. So, sit." The flight data recorder, which was later recovered, indicated that Jarrah then instructed the plane's autopilot to turn the aircraft around and head east. The cockpit voice recorder also indicated that a woman was being held captive in the cockpit. She struggled with one of the hijackers who killed or otherwise silenced her. Shortly thereafter the passengers and flight crew began a series of calls to family, friends, and colleagues from CTE airphones, and cellular phones which lasted until the end of the flight. At least ten passengers and two flight attendants made calls. Again, the hijackers wielded knives and claimed to have a bomb. Again they forced everyone to the back of the plane. At 9:57 the passenger assaults began. Several passengers had terminated phone calls with loved ones in order to join the counterattack. The recorder captured the sounds of the passenger assault muffled by the intervening cockpit door. The assault was sustained. In response, Jarrah immediately began to roll the aircraft from left to right, but the assault continued. At 9:59 Jarrah changed tactics and pitched the nose of the plane up and down to disrupt the assault. The recorder captured sounds of loud thumps, crashes, shouts, and breaking glasses and plates. At 10:00 Jarrah stabilized the plane. Five seconds later, Jarrah asked, "Is that it? Shall we finish it off?" The sounds of fighting continued outside the cockpit. Again Jarrah pitched the nose of the aircraft up and down. A passenger in the background was heard instructing: "Into the cockpit. If we don't we'll die!" Sixteen seconds later a passenger yelled, "Roll it!" Jarrah stopped the violent maneuvers at about 10:01, and said, "Allah is the greatest! Allah is the greatest!" He then asked another hijacker in the cockpit, "Is that it? I mean, shall we put it down?" to which the other replied, "Yes, put it in it, and pull it down." The passengers continued their assault, and at 10:02 a hijacker repeated, "Pull it down! Pull it down!" The hijackers were still at the controls but must have judged that the passengers were only seconds from overcoming them. The airplane headed down; the control wheel was turned hard to the right. The airplane rolled onto its back, and one of the hijackers began shouting "Allah is the greatest! Allah is the greatest!" With the sounds of the passenger revolt continuing, the aircraft plowed into an empty field in Shanksville, Pennsylvania at 580 miles per hour, about twenty minutes flying time from Washington, D.C. Jarrah's objective was to crash UA 93 into one of the symbols of the American republic — the Capitol or the White House.[10]

AFTERMATH

At 3:15 p.m. on September 11, President George W. Bush began a secure video teleconference meeting with his principal advisors with the words, "We're at War."[11] At 8:30 that evening, the president addressed the nation from the White House. According to *The 9/11 Commission Report,* he emphasized as first priority the task of helping the injured and protecting against any further attacks. He then added: "We will make no distinction between the terrorists who committed these acts and those who harbor them." He quoted Psalm 23: "though I walk through the valley of the shadow of death...." "No American," he said, "will ever forget this day."[12]

Rescue, Reaction, and Response

The sudden and drastic nature of terrorist violence resists theodicy's detached reflection on evil in abstraction. Nearly three thousand people were killed in the 9/11 terrorist attacks: 2,605 who died in the collapsing World Trade Towers; 147 who were passengers on the planes flown into the towers; 184 who died in the Pentagon crash, including those particular plane passengers; 40 who perished in the field in western Pennsylvania, plus the 19 hijackers.[13]

The attack on America was truly an international tragedy, as not only U.S. citizens but also large numbers of British, German, Belgian, South Korean, and Japanese were killed.

Of particular note to us here is that a number of the dead referred to above died while attempting to save others, including a large number of firefighters, police officers, and medical personnel who had responded to the rescue effort.

> After the South Tower collapsed, some firefighters on the streets neighboring the North Tower remained where they were or came closer to the North Tower. Some of these firefighters did not know that the South Tower had collapsed, but many chose despite that knowledge to remain in an attempt to save additional lives. According to one such firefighter, a chief who was preparing to mount a search-and-rescue mission in the Marriott, "I would never think of myself as a leader of men if I had headed north on West Street after [the] South Tower collapsed."[14]

Rowan Williams describes this "heroism of routine" that points to the everyday, "invisible" acts of courage that are necessary for a community's welfare and security and that come to be noticed and properly valued only in times of crisis. "Some people... practice living in the presence of death; not courting dramatic immortality through a cause, but as part of what will or may be necessary to serve the social body. They are often likely to be ignored or belittled by articulate people, they lack the romance of those who take risks for the sake of giving their lives 'meaning....' In one way, we have been reacquainted with a local and unexciting heroism that we have ignored in our restless passion for drama."[15]

Williams's observation of the quotidian nature of so many courageous acts of self-sacrifice prompts further consideration here. It calls to mind the objection made earlier to the tendency to philosophize over the problem of suffering rather than actively engage in solutions that might alleviate the plight of those suffering. Furthermore, it directs our attention to the arena of the ordinary whenever we search for good in our midst, a kind of counterexample to Arendt's well known description of the banality of evil. The question that arises has to do with our attentiveness to the good and, on another level, with those societal forces that influence what is noticed. The point is made clear in a sermon preached a few days after the attacks at St. Thomas Church, Fifth Avenue, in New York City. The homilist moves beyond the typical questions.

Jesus has taught us that God is both almighty and good; why God permits evil of this kind is a mystery. And as we know from the horrible scene
a few miles downtown, evil can be destructive and malicious beyond
our capacity to imagine. On the other hand, no one asks, Why does
good happen? Do you know, that is a deep mystery too? Goodness is a
mystery.[16]

There is no question that great acts of magnanimity followed in the wake of
the attack. As we reflect on the various responses to the destruction, we must
acknowledge, from the start, the occurrence of countless acts of irrefutable
goodness: that, for example, when faced with the inevitability of their own
deaths brought about by the terrorists, so many victims trapped in the towers
and planes attempted to contact loved ones with assurances of love.[17] In his
remarks at the National Day of Prayer and Remembrance Service, held on
September 14, 2001, and broadcast across the nation and beyond, President
George W. Bush described the "national character" in terms of the great acts
of sacrifice witnessed in the wake of the devastation. "Inside the World Trade
Center, one man who could have saved himself stayed until the end at the
side of his quadriplegic friend.[18] A beloved priest died giving the last rites
to a firefighter. Two office workers, finding a disabled stranger, carried her
down sixty-eight floors to safety. A group of men drove through the night from
Dallas to Washington to bring skin grafts for burn victims."[19] The point we
are introducing here, one to which we will return, has to do with the visibility
of goodness and the human propensity to diminish its significance.

The occurrence of certain acts of courage, however, should not take away
from the pervasive sense of trauma that afflicted millions after the attack. The
matter is especially important when we consider the prevailing tendency to
measure calamities by a simple tally of casualties. In the case of the World
Trade Center, far more survivors made it out of the Twin Towers than were
killed in them. Six months after the tragedy, the *Washington Post* observed
that "in the triage of national empathy, grief for the dead has overwhelmed
concerns for the merely traumatized." The traumatized "inhabit a space somewhere between those who died and everyone else."[20] One aspect of this trauma
is what can be called a "catastrophic style of thinking," the obsessive drive
to gather information about worst case scenarios in an effort to manage the
panic.[21] For many individuals the experience of trauma after the terrorist
attack represented a reawakening of past instances of fear and anxiety, which,
according to grief counselor Frank Geer, attest to the pattern-detecting and

pattern-shaping instinct of a meaning-driven humanity.[22] Significant, here, in times of traumatic loss, is the role that religion can play as a provider of time-tested patterns of meaning that ground individuals in a common pursuit of meaning.[23] Nancy Ammerman describes the importance of congregations and partnerships as contributors to the kind of "social capital" that could bring together diverse groups around common causes.[24] After September 11, that need for bridging and bonding was glaringly apparent as many individuals expressed the need to engage constructively in helping efforts.[25]

> A healthy society depends on there being places where relationships of trust are formed, where a sense of identity is nurtured. These relationships of trust are social capital in its most basic form. They facilitate communication and coordination of activities, and they provide basic well-being to the participants. Both individuals and society as a whole are healthier for the simple fact of belonging. After September 11 many in the U.S. seemed to sense exactly this. To be well, they needed to gather, and many chose to gather in communities of faith.[26]

Some spoke of the attack as a great equalizer, bridging many racial and socioeconomic barriers, resulting in a great community of grief. Indeed, some of the barriers bypassed were national, as a September 12 editorial in *Le Monde* made clear: "In this tragic time when words seem unable to describe the shock we are feeling, the first thing that comes to mind is this: We are all Americans! We are all New Yorkers."[27] This solidarity of suffering enabled a real transformation from shock and terror to prayer. The call to prayer reverberated from pulpits throughout the United States and the world:

> We need to pray fervently today for the thousands who have suffered the loss or injury of loved ones. We pray for caregivers, those who even now work to save those trapped and those who will need to provide ongoing care to those scarred in body and spirit. We pray that the hardened hearts of those responsible for — and supportive of — such acts be softened and reformed by the love that comes only from the God who cherishes and models reconciliation. We pray for swift justice, but a justice tempered by appropriate restraint. We pray for shalom — God's peace — in our broken world.[28]

It must be noted that a sincere plea for restraint was characteristic of many prayer services held in the days following the attack. An important interfaith response to terror was signed six days after the attacks by a broad spectrum of

Roman Catholic, Protestant, and Orthodox Christians as well as Muslim and Jewish leaders; it included heads of denominational, national, and regional organizations, local pastors and rabbis, and theologians from across the nation. The document is an honest and eloquent expression of the recently victimized still striving to uphold their humanity:

> We offer a word of sober restraint as our nation discerns what its response will be. We share the deep anger toward those who so callously and massively destroy innocent lives, no matter what the grievance or injustices invoked. In the name of God, we too demand that those responsible for these utterly evil acts be found and brought to justice. But we must not, out of anger and vengeance, indiscriminately retaliate in ways that bring on even more loss of innocent life.... The terrorists have offered us a stark view of the world they would like to create, where the remedy to every human grievance and injustice is a resort to the random and cowardly violence of revenge — even against the most innocent.... But we can deny them their victory by refusing to submit to a world created in their image. Terrorism inflicts not only death and destruction but also emotional oppression to further its aims. We must not allow this terror to drive us away from being the people God has called us to be.[29]

Although responses varied throughout the injured nation, we must not overlook the existence of the widespread call for restraint shared by so many of the victimized.

Scapegoating and Blame

Two days after the terrorist attacks, the American Jewish Committee issued a terse and prescient statement: "The catastrophic terror inflicted on American soil must not become an occasion for stereotyping or scapegoating. Jewish history makes us painfully aware that, too often, times of crisis provide opportunities for expressions of bigotry. An entire people or religion should never be implicated because of the heinous crimes committed by some of its members."[30] Not long after the attacks a number of incidents of "hate crime" were reported throughout the United States and beyond. According to an Amnesty International Report dated October 4, 2001, the Council on American-Islamic relations received reports of over 540 attacks on Arab Americans in just the first week following the hijackings, and many of these were directed at school children."[31] In an Associated Press exposé dated September 5, 2002, a number of such incidents were divulged: one day after the terrorist attacks bricks were thrown through the front windows of Almaeedah Market in Quincy, Massachusetts, a store owned and operated by Iranian-born Mohammed Saadat; in the same report, former Iraqi Majed Baddai claimed to have lost his job due to prejudice in the days immediately following the attacks.[32] Rhonda Roumani, an American Muslim living in New York City at the time of the attacks, acknowledged her own grave concerns:

> I feel afraid, not only for America at large, but for a specific group, American Muslims. Because I am one. I'm not really worried about myself. I blend in with most others in the street. I don't look particularly "ethnic," since I'm fairly light-skinned and I don't wear a head scarf. But one of my close friends here in New York wears *hijab* [the Islamic head dress], and she's afraid to walk outside today.... As I was walking the streets of New York the day of the attacks, I could hear the words "Muslims" and "Islam" being whispered. One person even said that this was a time for "extermination." There are reports that Muslims and mosques are being targeted.[33]

Members of Arab and Muslim communities were not the only victims of the scapegoating reflex. In a notorious press release issued by Pat Robertson, president of the Christian Broadcasting Network, the dualist's tendency to apportion blame was more than apparent: "Don't ask why did it happen. It happened because people are evil. It also happened because God is lifting His protection from this nation and we must pray and ask Him for revival so that once again we will be His people, the planting of His righteousness, so that He will come to our defense and protect us as a nation."[34] The "evil" people referred to by Rev. Roberston were more explicitly identified by Rev. Jerry Falwell on a September 13 airing of Roberston's popular television show, *The 700 Club*. During the program the two agreed that the terrorist attacks should be understood theologically as God's judgment on American society because of the secularization wrought by "the pagans, the abortionists, the feminists, the gays and lesbians ... the ACLU [American Civil Liberties Union]." "I point the finger in their face and say, 'You helped this happen.'"[35] Four days later, Falwell apologized publicly for the statement, redirecting the blame without reserve to the hijackers and terrorists, though still acknowledging that if the attacks of 9/11 did reflect the judgment of God, "that judgment is on all of America."[36] For the most part, however, the scapegoating that did occur did so at the expense of Muslims. What is remarkable in this regard, however, is that the rush to scapegoat the Muslim *other* seemed to necessitate a complete repression of the still recent memory of the Oklahoma City bomber, Timothy McVeigh, native son of the Christian Bible Belt.

We can make use of Girard's thesis of the scapegoat as we strive to interpret those acts of violence that did occur against Arab American and Muslim individuals in the wake of 9/11, notwithstanding the many calls for peace and restraint that echoed in those days following the attack. Isolated and collective acts of persecution against scapegoats spread and intensify in violent contagion especially when bolstered by public opinion. For Girard, these objects of persecution help to solidify the character of the dominant culture by virtue of their visible and distinct otherness. As we have seen,

> human beings learn through mimesis, an imitation that can produce pathological greed. Someone who looks, acts, or thinks differently, and is vulnerable, often ends up being the focus of a group's consolidated effort to define themselves and those deemed other by turning their own pursuit of power against those who cannot react. September 11 created a milieu of us "patriots" against them "foreign aliens." Thus a group (the really "real Americans") established itself by psychologically or physically eliminating or ousting the ones who are different (Arab Americans, including darker-skinned non-Arabs who wore turbans and were Hindu). Lynching (or stoning to death in the ancient world) and acts of terrorism are classic acts of collective violence, of scapegoating—familiar fare during World Wars I and II.[37]

Clearly, those widespread calls for peace and restraint after the attacks were more than mere pious platitudes. They were serious pleas to avoid a spiral of violence and revenge, symptoms of which were already detectable in more than a few demonstrations of the scapegoating impulse.

The 9/11 World

A catastrophe-sensitive theology would be justified in inquiring about the long-term effects of the disaster on our perceptions and beliefs; this, however, is something that only history can fully determine. We may ponder the question of uniqueness, as the passage of time allowed in the case of Auschwitz. We can consider, if only tentatively, whether 9/11 represents something really "new." Philosopher Jürgen Habermas, for instance, has considered the aspect of "intangibility" as the possibly "new" of 9/11.

One never really knows who one's enemy is. Osama bin Laden, the person, more likely serves the function of a stand-in.... Partisans fight on familiar territory with professed political objectives in order to conquer power. This is what distinguishes them from terrorists who are scattered around the globe and networked in the fashion of secret services. They allow their religious motives of a fundamentalist kind to be known, though they do not pursue a program that goes beyond the engineering of destruction and insecurity.[38]

According to Jacques Derrida, the "new" of 9/11 cannot be assessed in terms of the magnitude of the disaster, since other terrorist attacks in the past have resulted in greater devastation; nor can newness be established by the fact of the weapons utilized, since planes have been used before to destroy buildings full of civilians.[39] What is new here, as suggested by Derrida, is akin to the insight of Susan Neiman (first introduced in our investigation of Auschwitz in chapter 2) with regard to the loss of conceptual resources that had hitherto allowed people to make sense of the world, even, to some extent, its tragedies. Derrida's observation leads us to consider the unique role of the United States as the world's sole superpower at the close of the twentieth century, and, as such, its role as principal guardian of the prevailing world order, according to its own world of meaning and value. When such a powerful entity as the United States is attacked, the devastation cannot be measured simply on a physical scale alone.[40]

Is, then, what was touched, wounded, or traumatized by this double *crash* only some particular thing or other, a "what" or a "who," buildings, strategic urban structures, symbols of political, military, or capitalist power, or a considerable number of people of many different origins living on the body of a national territory that had remained untouched for so long? No, it was not *only* all that but perhaps especially, through all that, the conceptual, semantic, and one could even say hermeneutic apparatus that might have allowed one to see coming, to comprehend, interpret, describe, speak of, and name "September 11" — and in so doing to neutralize the traumatism and come to terms with it through a "work of mourning."[41]

We shall return to the question of conceptual devastation as we resume our investigation of the problem of power, indeed, *superpower,* and domination systems.

HISTORICAL AND CONJUNCTURAL CAUSES

A flood of analyses soon appeared after the attacks of 9/11, offering various explanations for the destructive acts. For our purposes, we turn to the socio-political analysis offered by Middle Eastern political specialist Fred Halliday, professor of international relations at the London School of Economics. A survey of the salient features of his perspectives on 9/11 is presented below for the purpose of theological engagement later in the chapter.

Halliday begins with a distinction between the historical and more immediate, "conjunctural" causes. With regard to the former, Halliday cites certain long-term antecedents as well as more recent historical contexts for September 11. In particular, certain unresolved issues pertaining to the history of colonialism and the Cold War have produced in the Middle East a generalized resentment toward the West, magnified by their confrontation with the inequalities associated with globalization.[42] Halliday highlights the destruction of Afghanistan from 1978 onward, and the West's support of transnational Islamist militias associated with Osama bin Laden against the local forces of the left, the People's Democratic Party of Afghanistan (PDPA). "There is an intimate relation between the rise of the armed Islamists and the crushing of the Left in the Cold War."[43] Also troubling here is the denial of responsibility on the parts of both East and West, that is, on the Arab world, for their failure to counter the dangerous demagogy of the Islamists, and on the West for having helped promote the terrorism that eventually culminated in the Taliban and in al-Qaeda for the sake of the West's own political interests, as well as for having subsequently abandoned Afghanistan once those interests seemed secured.[44]

Halliday also acknowledges the more immediate and conjunctural causes of the attacks. In particular, he describes the greater "West Asian" crisis — the nurturing of a culture of violence and religious demagogy that has been developing in certain countries such as Afghanistan and Yemen ("West Asian" refers to the vast area that includes the Arab world, Iran, Afghanistan, and Pakistan) wherever state power has weakened or altogether collapsed. Halliday observes here a pattern of linkages, real though to some degree rhetorical, between hitherto separate conflicts (e.g., Palestine and the Gulf).[45] The objective to portray the cause of resistance to the West as one unified movement is for the purpose of mobilizing support and momentum in pursuing what Halliday believes is the chief aim of the fundamentalist and militant movements throughout the West Asian region: to take power away from those who control states and to hold on to it.[46] Halliday makes the point adamantly: the goal of these movements is not religious, in the sense of faith, nor cultural, in the sense of values, but political:[47]

> The main target of September 11 is not US power or a somewhat care-lessly defined "civilized" or "democratic" world, but the states of the Middle East themselves. Osama bin Laden, with his regressive social and political ideals, particularly hostile to women and Shi'ite Muslims, is above all a threat to them. Suffice it to say that it is this goal, a clear political one, that determines what fundamentalists, including al-Qa'ida and others, do.[48]

And yet the political nature of the militants' goals is not enough to explain the devastation that took place on 9/11 in New York, Washington, and western Pennsylvania. For Halliday, the rise of *Islamism* is another significant, conjunctural cause of the attacks, "a political current within the Middle East and elsewhere, that aims to establish a state and society based on religious principles... [in] response to the modern challenges faced by these societies."[49] The roots of Islamism date back to the 1920s, but it did not really achieve force as a movement until the Iranian revolution of 1979. Even then, that Islamist uprising led to a questioning among the Iranian people of the cost and purpose of revolution. In other places, however, such as Afghanistan, Islamist fervor lacked grounding in the great Islamist program, needing to resort more and more to violence: "divorced from any established institutions or leaderships, basing themselves even more on terror, this second generation of Islamists became a force without strategy or limit, caught in a cycle of violence."[50]

Our brief outline of Halliday's analysis makes clear the complex background to the 9/11 attacks, which includes the longer-term antecedents of post–Cold War conflicts as well as the more immediate, what Halliday calls outstanding "conjunctural" causes that include the linkage of previously distinct Middle Eastern problems, the question of state sponsorship in militant activity, and the rise of Islamist violence. Once again, these sociopolitical observations are, of necessity, presented here in cursory fashion for the purpose of providing a foundation for a deeper critical investigation from a more theological and anthropological perspective below.

CHAPTER SEVEN

Apocalyptic Symbols
A Meditation

Chapter 4's treatment of apocalypse pertained to the necessity of maintaining in our theology a sharpened apocalyptic vision in keeping with the Bible's own sense of expectation. As we have seen, for Metz, true apocalypse does not have to do with a neurotic obsession to calculate the end of time, but rather it is a perception of the world in light of the knowledge of its end. Proper eschatology, true to the biblical spirit, has an apocalyptic intensity that should not be overlooked.

It is worth pursuing the apocalyptic theme again in the context of our investigation of the 9/11 tragedy. It should come as no surprise that the terrorist attacks roused the apocalyptic sensibilities of a pop culture that Hollywood has been nourishing with its own understanding of the term. Terror seizes the imagination and sharpens its focus on imminent and cataclysmic endings. That the attacks occurred in the year 2001 only heightened the impassioned overtones of millennial speculation. "Lord, we know that we are living in the last days, and all that is happening is what you have already warned us about through your holy word; I pray that we will all be prepared to meet you and stand before you."[1]

The apocalyptic imagination thrives in an age of the image such as ours. Filmed footage of the destruction of the World Trade Center was so graphic and, through the barrage of televised replay, so familiar that it seemed more a staged production than a horrible reality actually happening. "The city was like a movie set and we were just waiting for the director to yell 'cut' . . . and go back to Normal. . . . Are we ever going back to NORMAL?"[2]

That question, left on an online message board later in the day of the attacks, still waits to be answered. Catastrophe lingers elusively, erratically, in both private memory and in the collective psyche. No standardized map exists to lead the traumatized out of injury, no maps to take us back to the land of "normal." There does come a point when the return to the comfortable routine of daily life helps to hasten the healing process. But what happens to the memory of catastrophe, and the wisdom that can spring from memory, if the healing process itself has been hijacked, cut short by a powerful longing for the life we once knew?

Not long after the attacks that September, President Bush encouraged the nation to hasten the return of the normal by investing in the economy. In essence, Americans were encouraged to grieve by shopping. And Wall Street, still covered in dust and ash, lost no time in advising ordinary citizens to withdraw from their life savings in order to invest in the stock market—a risk most large corporations refused to take. In his brief reflection on 9/11, *The Terrorism Trap,* Michael Parenti quotes the head of the private banking division of J. P. Morgan that manages the fortunes of families with an average wealth of $100 million: "Since our clients were rich, our number one concern was their staying rich."[3]

Suffering is always an exorbitant tuition. Was the rush to return to the normal routine of getting and spending worth jeopardizing anything valuable we could have learned from this tragedy? Does that rush to return to the normal itself suggest something of the dark reality of evil that prefers concealment to revelation? These questions get to the heart of this second reflection on apocalypse.

The word, from the Greek *apocalypsis,* means unveiling. If we are to take seriously the true apocalyptic sense of the moment, we are going to have to remain committed to the kind of seeing that comes from sustained reflection on newly revealed realities. We will have to go beyond the special effects of doomsday imaginings, which would have us see 9/11 in terms of an Armageddon between forces of good and evil. We must linger with the unsettling uncertainties of this opened wound, long enough to behold what has only recently been unveiled. As is often the case, symbols may help us to see.

TOWERS

As a symbol for progress, the tower finds an interesting biblical antecedent in the ancient story of Babel (Gen. 11:1–9). Rabbi Jonathan Sacks considers the Genesis episode an apt parable for our time. The tower of Babel is "the first global project," that is, the first human attempt to impose an artificial unity on divinely created diversity.[4] Towers concentrate energies vertically, discouraging horizontal co-mingling. "Come, let us build ourselves a city, and a tower with its top in the heavens, and let us make a name for ourselves; otherwise we shall be scattered abroad upon the face of the whole earth" (Gen. 11:4). The temptation of hubris, of seizing the power of the gods, still accompanies the gift of technological prowess in the form of a certain mind-set in which universalism towers over particularity and uniformity smothers difference.

Giant towers cast long shadows. Stratford Caldecott comments on the obvious significance of the World Trade Towers and the Pentagon as the preeminent symbols of the hegemony of Western power:

> At a subliminal level, the symbolic power of these buildings was some-how magnified by their geometry, reminiscent of the Platonic solids. The buildings were the shadows or projections of archetypal objects: the ter-rorists had succeeded in attacking America and Western civilization not on the surface but at a deeper, much more primal level.[5]

It is precisely this deeper level that needs to be explored. We may be able to perceive a hidden aspect of the darker side of progress in the complex phenom-enon known as globalization — the exchange of people, products and ideas that first took root in the era of exploration and colonization, but that took off wildly with the technological advances in transportation and communications of the last twenty-five years, as well as with the emergence of fundamentalist free-market governments in the 1980s and the deregulation of world finan-cial markets.[6] That globalization is a mixed blessing is by now a well-worn commonplace. The benefits reaped by the entanglement of economies are overwhelmingly lopsided in favor of richer nations. Lenders to poor countries employ programs of "structural adjustment" to insure repayment, an innocu-ous sounding term for the nefarious demand of governments to cut spending on vital services such as health care and education.

> In Africa, external debt has ballooned by 400 per cent since the [World] Bank and the IMF began managing national economies through struc-tural adjustment. Today in Ethiopia a hundred thousand children die annually from easily preventable diseases, while debt repayments are four times more than public spending on healthcare. In Tanzania, where 40 percent of people die before the age of 35, debt payments are 6 times greater than spending on healthcare.[7]

In addition to the glaring issue of economic injustice, a further threaten-ing aspect of globalization becomes evident when we notice that the supposed "exchange" of global resources leaves in its wake an oppressive monoculture

that often stifles originality and diversity. This particular feature of globalization, this blanketing cultural hegemony, has likewise become so ingrained, so
institutionalized, that it now seems an inescapable fact of life, unmistakable
in pop music, fast food, in even the lay of the land. "Traditional architecture
is bulldozed to be replaced by featureless brickworks, multi-lane roads, shopping malls, hotels and fast food joints. Most cities in the more affluent parts
of the Third World either look like Dallas or theme-parked extensions of Los
Angeles."[8]

According to Jean Baudrillard, we do well to reflect upon the very architecture of the World Trade Towers, pondering the triumph of the self-same that
seemed symbolically captured there. The showcase of competitive capitalism
long epitomized in the varying verticalities of Manhattan's skyline was forever
changed when the World Trade Towers were completed in 1973.

> The effigy of the system was no longer the obelisk and the pyramid, but
> the punch card and the statistical graph. This architectural graphism is
> the embodiment of a system that is no longer competitive, but digital
> and countable, and from which competition has disappeared in favour
> of networks and monopoly. Perfect parallelepipeds, standing 1,300 feet
> tall, on a square base. . . . The fact that there were two of them signifies
> the end of any original reference. If there had been only one, monopoly
> would not have been perfectly embodied. Only the doubling of the sign
> truly puts and end to what it designates.[9]

Baudrillard's architectural critique seems extreme, but it does supply a very
sobering analysis of what is at stake with globalization. The faceless towers
closed themselves off from the world in perfect replication of each other, aptly
representing the faceless, impersonal, economic world system that they had
come to embody. The "unveiling" of the violence of a system writ large in its
very architecture needs to be pondered in what we might call the apocalyptic
resonance of the post-9/11 era.

DUST AND ASHES

The present study began with a meditation on dust. Ashes and dust covered
lower Manhattan, blanketing the streets as with a strange, ghastly snow. We
are, of course, reminded that we, too, are dust, that our lives are marked by
an impermanence that we would just as soon completely ignore. It is easy to
identify with the words of one pastor called to the horrifying scene: "I was

worried that I would be exposed to sights that I just didn't want to see. When I arrived at the site, many of my fears were realized. Part of it was the acrid, electrical, ozone smell. Part of it was the smell of death, from which we are usually insulated in our society."[10]

Death is the great mystery we would rather forget. When it is literally "in the air" it can no longer be avoided. In his Pulitzer Prize winning *The Denial of Death*, Ernest Becker explored "the universality of the fear of death, or 'terror'...in order to convey how all-consuming it is when we look it full in the face."[11] We are right, especially in this post-9/11 period, to consider those societal influences that tend to hinder our ability to integrate the reality of death more readily and fruitfully into our consciousness. We are also right to suspect that the common understanding of apocalypse, the one that antici-pates violent destruction couched in phantasmagorical imagery, may point to the problem. It is a shallow surrogate for the deeper acceptance of the reality of death that Christians are called to embrace in peace. Lieven Boeve has explored this form of contemporary apocalyptic sensitivity and sees as one of its specific characteristics a fear of the judgment of humanity's delusions of grandeur:

> In most instances, the apocalyptic imagination expresses the awareness
> that we are no longer in command of things, that we have created mon-
> sters we can no longer control. Humanity has seriously over-estimated
> itself, both at the level of planning the perfect society (with the large-scale
> abuse of human rights as one consequence) and in the implementation
> of a functionalistic and technological view of the world: the reduction of
> nature and the environment to that which fulfills our needs and sustains
> our designs.[12]

This fear of impending judgment may be one aspect of the death-denying dimension of much contemporary culture. Hyper-consumerism itself along with an obsession with affluent lifestyle may also be an attempt to stave off what could otherwise be a healthy integration of the reality of death in many lives.[13] But what is as troubling in this scenario is the fact that it is not only our own deaths that seem easy to ignore. We maintain a convenient blindness to the harsh reality of the daily suffering and the exorbitant death rates of those countless others outside of our own protected, privileged societies, let alone of those who live on the other side of the globe. For Mark Slouka, the cultural denial of death goes far in explaining the depths of trauma experienced by Americans on September 11.

It simultaneously exposed and challenged the myth of our own uniqueness. A myth most visible, perhaps, in our age-old denial of death. Consider it. Here in the New Canaan, in the land of perpetual beginnings and second chances, where identity could be sloughed and sloughed again and history was someone else's problem, death had never been welcome. Death was a foreigner — radical, disturbing, smelling of musty books and brimstone. We wanted no part of him. And now death had come calling. That troubled brother, so long forgotten, so successfully erased, was standing on our porch in his steel-toed boots, grinning. He'd made it across the ocean, passed like a ghost through the gates of our own chosen community. We had denied him his due and his graveyards, watered down his deeds, buried him with things. Yet here he was. He reminded us of something unpleasant.[14]

For Slouka, 9/11 was not just a terrorist attack. "This was an act of metaphysical trespass."[15]

SMOKE

Smoke billowed from the wounded sides of the towers, sending dark plumes into the atmosphere and signaling for miles the state of emergency lurking below. Liturgically, smoke is the ancient symbol of sacrifice to God. But on the morning of September 11, 2001, a small group of Islamic terrorists poisoned the clear, blue sky with the ungodly offering of nearly three thousand innocent victims.

Smoke filled the sky over Manhattan and thus alerted distant onlookers of a danger still unknown to them. But smoke also hides and conceals. The term "smoke screen" is used to signify something purposely designed to obscure, confuse, or mislead. Indeed, there are some who would find smoke an apt metaphor for the obscuring of truth in the U.S. response to 9/11 as a "war on terror."

Terrorism feeds on fear, but the events that followed the 9/11 attacks suggest that counterterrorism can likewise play on and indeed intensify fear, manipulating it to the point of irrational hysteria. The writers of *Hijacking Catastrophe,* a collection of interviews with leading political thinkers, share the view that in many ways the Bush administration has exploited fear and anxiety to advance a controversial neo-conservative agenda of maintaining global supremacy under the guise of the war on terrorism.[16] Noam Chomsky asserts that the manipulation of fear is a familiar tactic among governments.

> The United States is extreme, and it's extremely important because of its enormous power, but just about every power system in the world exploited 9/11 as a technique of repression.... Across the board, the more democratic countries, almost all of them, developed some kind of repressive legislation to discipline their own populations. Here, it was called the Patriot Act. They don't have much to do with terror — maybe nothing to do with it — but they have a lot to do with disciplining your own population. Power systems will exploit their opportunities.[17]

Chomsky is not alone in his critique of the fear factor. Benjamin Barber criticizes the U.S. government's decision to employ daily color-coded terrorist warnings, claiming that they "actually play right into the terrorists' goal of trying to incite fear."[18] Michael Eric Dyson claims that such fear-mongering is tantamount to a rejection of the very civil liberties that are at the heart of American democracy.[19] Margot Pepper even insists that such manipulation of fear is a form of brainwashing not unlike the massive propaganda campaigns employed by the despotic regimes of the twentieth century.[20]

Perhaps the decision to wage a "war" on terrorism is itself a glaring act of deception, since war usually presupposes a personal enemy that, through the contest of battle, could be defeated. The enormity of the deception is compounded when we consider that a declaration of war always aims at a patriotic response, which in turn culminates in the large-scale sacrifice of lives.

The foregoing reflection on symbols provides a hermeneutic for understanding the blatant evil of the terrorists' deeds. Although the towers and Pentagon were clear and obvious symbols of American economic and military domination, these structures, nonetheless, contained living people, and as Rowan Williams explains, living people can never be reduced to symbols. "It is always people who suffer and are killed, not symbols. When we strike out at a symbol such as a flag, we hurt nothing except perhaps the self-esteem of those who use the language of which it's a part. When we decide to treat people as symbols, the story is different."[21] Excerpts from the *New York Times*'s "Portraits of Grief," a daily column that first appeared three days after the attacks, brings home the point. Instead of featuring notices of the deaths in usual obituary format, the publishers of the newspaper chose to present them as stories, "snapshots of lives interrupted as they were being lived."[22]

JAMES E. POTORTI, *"Je t'aime, Jim"*

Paris, 1988. Nikki Stern is napping and the new love in her life, James E. Potorti, a sweet soul with penetrating eyes, is painting. For days they have been exploring Paris and discovering each other in its art galleries, cafes and, inevitably, the Eifel Tower. Now, as she sleeps, he arranges fresh oranges and grapes in a bowl, and he paints his simple still life with a purpose made clear by the inscription on his canvas, "Paris à Nikki — Je t'aime, Jim." "That," Ms. Stern recalled with a warm laugh, "is when I knew I had him."

Cayuga Lake, N.Y., 2001. It is Labor Day weekend, and Mr. Potorti, fifty-two, is kayaking side-by-side with Ms. Stern, his wife of ten years. They bought kayaks this spring, took lessons together, and now, on a clear, cool day, they are exploring Cayuga Lake, and discovering each other. Near the middle of the lake they drift for a moment, basking in the intimacy of being so alone, and so together. Ms. Stern reaches for her husband's hand. He leans close to her. They kiss. "The best day of my life," Ms. Stern said. These words came through tears. Mr. Potorti, a vice-president at Marsh & McLennan, who worked on the ninety-sixth floor at One World Trade Center, has left behind a wife who loved the way they ignored birthdays, Christmas and Valentine's Day because they much preferred surprising each other with gifts throughout the year. What does she miss most? "I definitely miss his physical presence," she said, again with that warm laugh. "We were close that way."[23]

PAUL FIORI, *the Gift of Gab*

Paul Fiori was a talker. "He would talk your ear off, and he would talk to anybody," says his wife, Lynda Fiori. He talked so much to the guys working at the Mobil station where he got gas that he befriended them. After it was reported he was missing, his friends there, six of whom attended his memorial service, wrote his wife a letter, "telling me he would help them make coffee, give people directions and always talk about his two daughters....One year ago, Mr. Fiori, then thirty, left his high school teaching position in Hawthorne, New York, for the equities desk of Cantor Fitzgerald so his young family could be more financially secure. On Sept. 11, their second child, Adriana, was only three months old. Their oldest, Debbi, two, now kisses Daddy's picture every day.[24]

MADELINE AMY SWEENEY, *the Final Call*

Madeline Amy Sweeney never went looking for fame, but fame found her on September 11. Her fifteen minutes were the last of her life. Mrs. Sweeney, known as Amy, was a flight attendant aboard American Airlines Flight 11, the first plane to strike the trade center. She called a ground supervisor by air phone and relayed information about the hijackers that gave the F.B.I. a head start on the investigation. Mrs. Sweeney's grace under pressure did not surprise her husband, Michael Sweeney, of Acton, Massachusetts. "She would have said she was just doing her job," he said.[25]

JOHN PATRICK TIERNEY, *Dedicated to Firefighting*

On Father's Day 2001, as Helen Tierney heard the news that three firefighters in Queens had been killed on the job, her heart broke. For the men who died, she cried. For her son John Patrick Tierney, 27, a probationary firefighter training in Queens at the time, she rejoiced that he had had that day off. "He always said, 'Don't worry, Ma. Everything will be fine.'" And it was. So, on September 11, when his unit, Ladder Company 9 in Manhattan, was called to the World Trade Center, she clung once again to her youngest son's words. Her prayer was that he had headed home to Staten Island that morning. But Mr. Tierney had hopped a fire truck so crowded that he was forced to sit in a colleague's lap. "The other guys told him he didn't have to come," Mrs. Tierney said. "But from the first day he went to probie school, he worked hard, he really wanted to be part of the Fire Department." And he was, for six weeks.[26]

There are close to three thousand other stories to be read, stories of real lives cut short, stories of innocents massacred. These are the victims of 9/11 who perished to prove someone else's point, whose lives were sacrificed in the service of making a vengeful, though highly symbolic statement. "The idea of fighting with God in an apocalyptic final battle against the devil plainly takes away every normal human restraint against killing, heightens the ecstasy of power and transforms suicide, combined with mass murder, into worship. The Islamic suicide bombers felt themselves to have become like God who annihilates the godless."[27]

APOCALYPSE *RIGHT* NOW

Paul Ricoeur has stressed the lingering significance of the symbols of apocalyptic mythology for contemporary reflection on evil.[28] We have chosen three symbols of our own — towers, ashes, and smoke — to guide us in this chapter's reflection on the meaning of apocalypse as unveiling. In this way, in this post-9/11 time, thinking apocalyptically suggests a commitment to seeing things anew, perhaps even allowing ourselves to see certain disturbing realities unveiled to us in this tragedy for the first time. The instinct for recovery after injury may itself be a sign of hope, but persevering in a state of vulnerable uncertainty about old verities, including cherished self-images and notions of innocence, may be a sign of that kind of wisdom that is born only to pain.

Rowan Williams describes something of what we are getting at in his poignant interpretation of the well-known story of Jesus and the woman caught in adultery in John 8. In the epilogue to his brief reflection on 9/11, Williams suggests one way of understanding John's puzzling description of Jesus "writing in the dust," even as the mob of angry accusers surrounds them. According to Williams, "He hesitates. He does not draw a line, fix an interpretation, tell the woman who she is and what her fate should be. He allows a moment, a longish moment, in which people are given time to see themselves differently precisely because he refuses to make the sense they want."[29]

If we allow ourselves to linger in such a "longish moment" we may come to understand that valuing the true meaning of apocalypse necessarily results in a change in perspective. One way to regard this transformation is to see it, with Lieven Boeve, as characteristic of the passage from *catastrophe* thinking to *crisis* thinking, i.e., from an obsession with disaster against the background of uninterrupted and unreconciled time, to a hopeful cry of trust wherein God is viewed as the boundary who interrupts time and judges it.[30]

> A neutral attitude at this juncture is no longer appropriate. Interruption, as the revelation of God, provokes us [to] assume a position: we can no longer maintain an indifferent stance to what is going on. What is called for is a critical praxis of hope. Etymologically speaking, the word "crisis" also implies "judgement." A Christian perspective on time thus requires submission to God's judgement and God's promise for the world and for humanity as revealed in Jesus Christ.[31]

In other words, an apocalyptic awareness of time in this post-9/11 era necessarily points to the fruitfulness of a crisis moment, which compels us to see and think, judge, and act anew. We are challenged to "put on the mind of Christ," since time, from beginning to end, belongs to God. And that end is coming with judgment.[32] We experience a greater sense of urgency that breaks the monotony of vacant time — one that will "provide a foundation for the seriousness of a liberating praxis and emphasise the urgent and critical character of human responsibility."[33]

Boeve's use of the word "foundation" is particularly thought-provoking in the context of our reflection on 9/11. Construction on the new "Freedom" tower at the World Trade site has begun and will continue to an impressive and patriotic 1776 feet, penetrating the skies that only shortly before contained such terror. If we are to take seriously the apocalyptic potential of this crisis moment, ought we not to consider the foundations upon which we build our empires, the power and domination systems that continue to victimize the forgotten or ignored "others"? Will that soaring height be sufficient to allow for a panorama that includes the miserable faces of the suffering others outside of the comfortable worlds of our own making? Or, tragically, will it be said, as it most certainly has been said so often in the past, that "in vain do the builders labor"?

The foundation that is needed is solidarity. It is the recognition of our long neglected solidarity in sin and of our long overlooked solidarity in suffering. We keep these in mind as we turn to a deeper investigation of the evil of 9/11.

CHAPTER EIGHT

Probing Evil 9/11

The pursuit of an existential model of evil in the first part (9/10) has yielded a helpful lens for the investigation of evil 9/11 now at hand. In particular, we recall three key characteristics of evil's manifestation in our time: the problem of exclusion, and specifically, that exclusion that results from the quest to achieve a purity of identity based on the elimination of difference; the problem of dualistic thinking, which culminates in a Manichean conception of the world in terms of good versus evil, and ultimately "us" versus "them"; and finally the very nature of violence itself, which, as we have seen, acts as a viral contagion that perpetuates an endless cycle of revenge. This last dynamic of evil, which has darkened so many pages of twentieth-century history, is first to be considered.

REVENGE AS "BLOWBACK"

It is pointless to engage in an analysis of 9/11 without first acknowledging the centrality of the connection between terrorism and the cycle of violence and revenge. Terrorism, however, is a particular form of revenge that needs to be analyzed in its own right. Further analysis of terrorism will build upon these introductory comments.

Preliminary Notes on Terrorism

We confront a serious challenge from the outset: the seemingly straightforward task of defining terrorism. It seems strange to suggest that something associated with such obvious devastation in the actual, concrete realm could be so elusive and non-self-evidential in the theoretical. Terrorism resists attempts at facile explanation and ready definition.

One reason for the difficulty is summed up familiarly: "One man's terrorist is another man's freedom fighter." Put in question form, we could ask further, how does one gain the kind of objectivity and detached eye needed to judge the difference? The line may thus be blurred, but as Liam Harte avers, this does not make the freedom fighter less of a terrorist, nor the terrorist more of a freedom fighter.[1] Accordingly, it is not surprising that the label "terrorist" is rarely if ever adopted voluntarily by a particular individual or group. That label is applied to them by others.

It is interesting to note that the word "terrorism," coming from the Latin *terrere*, means "to cause to tremble." That means that the term that has come to signify the most threatening kind of violent behavior in our time, first employed as such during the Reign of Terror at the close of the French Revolution,[2] actually describes not a particular act itself but the intended effect that the act provokes, the response to the violence: the trembling of fear. "The definition of a terrorist act is provided by us, the witnesses, the ones terrified — and not by the party committing the act."[3]

That simple fact already points to two significant characteristics of terrorism: fear and publicity. In an even deeper way, and getting more to the heart of the central themes of the present analysis, the observation points to something ineluctably social about the reality of terror, or, restated, terrorism itself points to the ineluctable sociability of our lives. Furthermore, the rise in incidence of what has been called international terrorism demonstrates another obvious but significant reality of our interconnectedness. Terrorism affects everyone, everywhere. For many Americans the events of 9/11 have proved a wake-up call to that harsh reality that many people living in unstable regions of the world have long known.

Beyond its inherent imprecision, the challenge of defining terrorism comes down to the ability to distinguish such behavior from other military and criminal acts and the qualification of not only individual and group but also state terrorism. Official definitions often cited by U.S. governmental agencies, such as that of the Immigration and Nationality Act, for example, begin by defining terrorist activity as "any activity which is unlawful under the laws of the place where it is committed." It then goes on to list certain delimiting actions, including hijacking or sabotage; seizing or detaining; threatening to kill or injure; assassination; the use of biological, chemical, or nuclear weapons; the use of explosives or firearms with intent to endanger.[4] Borradori correctly observes a lack of rigor in such definitions that are loose enough to include a great number of crimes. "One can no longer see the difference between a nonterrorist crime and a terrorist one, national terrorism and international terrorism, an act of war and an act of terrorism, military, and civilian."[5] Still, it is important to note that most people have in mind a basic idea of terrorism that includes violence and threats of violence against innocent civilians for political ends. But even such stripped-down versions of terrorist essentials leave open key problems such as identifying "innocent civilians." Charles Townshend comments on the futile attempt to transfer the notion from the international law of war to the study of terrorism: "innocence is another relative, unstable property."[6]

Without further belaboring the pursuit of a perfect definition, we offer the thoughtful and critical attempt made by political philosopher Michael Baur. The definition includes eight necessary elements:

> Terrorism is (1) the systematic use (2) of actual or threatened violence (3) against persons or against the vital interests of persons (i.e., against the terrorist's direct target) (4) in the pursuit of political, ideological, religious, social, economic, financial, and/or territorial objectives, (5) whereby the violence is sufficiently random or indiscriminate (6) so as to cause fear among members of the terrorist's indirect target group, (7) thus creating a generalized climate of fear, distrust, or instability within certain sectors of society or within society at large, (8) the ultimate aim of which is to influence popular opinion or governmental policy in a manner that serves the terrorist's objectives.[7]

Baur's definition is sensitive to philosopher Haig Khatchadourian's observation that terrorism is essentially "bifocal" in intent, specifically, in its direct targets — those victims who are killed, wounded, or maimed in terrorist attacks, and in its indirect targets — the observers of the violence who are the intended recipients of the message of fear.[8] That distinction is critical, as terrorism cannot be understood apart from the elements of fear and alienation that are its chief hallmarks. Any act of terroristic violence, therefore, for it to qualify as such, has to be accompanied by a message of intimidation. Likewise, in considering the victims of terrorist acts, one cannot overlook those many members of the wider audience among whom the fear was intended to spread and, therefore, the role that publicity plays in enabling terrorists to accomplish their intended mission. With its ultimate end of spreading fear, then, it is easy to see why terrorism, as Baur observes, has been called the "poor man's answer" to modern warfare — since it really takes only a small-scale effort of violence and destruction to bring about a large-scale response of fear.[9] Accordingly, the terrorist aims at taking hostage of society at large.

We should take seriously the comparison of terrorism to warfare. In *The Body in Pain,* Elaine Scarry defines war as a contest of "out-injuring," which aims not only to determine a winner and loser, but also to provide an arena in which injuries can be inflicted.[10] In reading Scarry's description of war's demonstrative function, it is easy to see how terrorism is warfare with limited economic means:

> The dispute that leads to the war involves a process by which each side calls into question the legitimacy and thereby erodes the reality of the other country's issues, beliefs, ideas, self-conception. Dispute leads relentlessly to war not only because war is an extension and intensification of dispute but because it is a correction and reversal of it. That is, the injuring not only provides a means of choosing between disputants but also provides, by its massive opening of human bodies, a way of reconnecting the derealized and disembodied beliefs with the force and power of the material world.[11]

In short, both warfare and terrorism exist in order to create "bodies in pain." Both have a validating function — soldiers and terrorists in effect serve to reconfirm "the truth."

Baur further identifies two essential components of the terrorist's violence, neither of which has to do with the terrorist's own explicit ideological aims or commitments: the *randomness* and indiscriminate character of the attack, with respect to the selection of victims and in some cases venues, or self-presentation of the perpetrators, and the way in which that randomness is *systematically* effected.[12] In this way the terrorist gains access to victims in any unexpected locale: busses, trains, planes, shopping malls, etc., and can thereby spread fear throughout a society. Needless to say, the terrorist does not abide by any rules of armed conflict, which, in effect, means that the terrorist implicitly refuses to recognize the very means by which an eventual truce could ever be reached. "This refusal, in turn, reveals that the terrorist *qua* terrorist is implicitly committed to the principle of uncontained and perpetual war, that is, to the kind of war that can never end through mutual recognition or a negotiated truce, but only through the ongoing suppression or complete obliteration of the adversary."[13] Baur concludes that it is this predicament of unending violence and perpetual conflict that points to what is distinctively wrong with terrorism. When we consider Girard's insistence that violence itself is contagious because we ourselves are imitators, then what results is truly a predicament of terror — unstoppable vengeance, an unceasing, infinitely repetitive process of annihilation.

Nothing New

As we have seen, there is something about vengeance that implies a deadly automatism — an enslavement, a forceful urge preventing the breakthrough of anything different or new. With revenge there is no possibility for a new beginning, for hopeful initiatives, for change. And because it frustrates any attempt at re-visioning the future, revenge seems to require a certain degree of *un*-thinking. Rather than seeing the promise of the future, those caught up in the cycle of revenge prefer to indulge the allure of their own perception of the past, specifically concentrating on the resentments that first took root there. Revenge is the stultifying, life-draining perpetuation of the self-same. It allows no interruptions. It is nothing new.

As Girard has shown, "the crime to which the act of vengeance addresses itself is almost never an unprecedented offense; in almost every case it has been committed in revenge for some prior crime."[14] With regard to 9/11, a specific name for the old problem of revenge emerges. "Blowback," a term first coined by the Central Intelligence Agency (CIA) as far back as 1953, refers to the unintended consequences of American foreign policy. According to Chalmers Johnson, "blowback" is another way of saying that a nation reaps what it sows.[15]

Johnson asserts that the actions that instigate blowback require a certain secrecy from the general public.[16] In our own pursuit of an existential model of evil, it is difficult not to acknowledge the reappearance of the word "secrecy": it is likewise key to the workings of the scapegoat mechanism, although in the latter case it is secrecy in terms of blindness to the truth rather than the deceitful repression of it. In the case of blowback such secrecy might suggest that as a concept it is more easily understood in circumstances of blatant acts of American aggression and militaristic intervention. But Johnson's investigation of the phenomenon reveals that it likewise pertains to ongoing conflicts that encourage resentment, such as economic and cultural domination, or duplicity with regard to the integrity of American intentions. Both acute and chronic demonstrations of domination and aggression can encourage the resentment-fed retaliation known as blowback.[17]

Perhaps the best-known critic of American imperialist self-interest is Noam Chomsky. In an interview conducted on September 22, 2001, Chomsky responded to a concern over possible acts of revenge on the part of the United States, spurred by televised images of Middle Easterners rejoicing upon hearing of the attacks:

A U.S.-backed army took control in Indonesia in 1965, organizing the slaughter of hundreds of thousands of people, mostly landless peasants, in a massacre that the CIA compared to the crimes of Hitler, Stalin, and Mao. The massacre, accurately reported, elicited uncontrolled euphoria in the West, in the national media and elsewhere. Indonesian peasants had not harmed us in any way. When Nicaragua finally succumbed to the U.S. assault, the mainstream press lauded the success of the methods adopted to "wreck the economy and prosecute a long and deadly proxy war until the exhausted natives overthrow the unwanted government themselves," with a cost to us that is "minimal," leaving the victims with "wrecked bridges, sabotaged power stations, and ruined farms," and thus providing the U.S. candidate with a "winning issue": ending the "impoverishment of the people of Nicaragua."[18]

It is difficult to isolate one episode of American aggression abroad that could directly account for the blowback witnessed on 9/11. In fact, it is more likely a chain of events that best explains the cultivation of hostilities in the Middle East. The U.S. entanglement in Afghanistan, in the waning years of the Cold War, is singled out by many political analysts as the clearest example of blowback. As was mentioned in our investigation of Halliday's analysis, in 1979, Soviet forces invaded Afghanistan, threatening U.S. dominance in the gulf region. U.S. Presidents Carter and Reagan responded by supporting covert operations to undermine the new Soviet-backed regime, assisting in the training of anti-Soviet *Mujahideen* — Islamist militants bent on purifying the Muslim world, among whose leaders numbered Osama bin Laden. In brief, once the Soviet threat had been extinguished, bin Laden and other militants continued plotting, fighting, and recruiting, an effort that would one day culminate in the emergence of al-Qaeda. Thus, the United States nurtured the very same Islamic military networks that would later be responsible for its own devastation on September 11, 2001.[19]

Blowback stemming from American involvement in Afghanistan cannot be understood apart from the greater U.S. interest in Saudi Arabia, specifically in its vast oil reserves.[20] The partnership between the two nations provided the United States with privileged access to Saudi oil reserves in exchange for American military protection against its internal and external enemies. Before 9/11, the United States had steadily increased its military presence in Saudi Arabia, a necessity in part to protect the enormous wealth of Saudi princes.

The vast and highly conspicuous accumulation of wealth by the royal family has alienated it from the larger Saudi population and led to charges of systemic corruption. In response, the regime has outlawed all forms of political debate in the kingdom (there is no parliament, no free speech, no political party, no right of assembly) and used its U.S.-trained security forces to quash overt expressions of dissent. All these effects have generated covert opposition to the regime and occasional acts of violence — and it is from this underground milieu that Osama bin Laden has drawn his inspiration and many of his top lieutenants.[21]

Thus, even when we attempt to identify this single instance of blowback, it is clear that other factors soon emerge to compound what had appeared to be only an isolated resentment. But as we have seen, it is the nature of domination systems to conceal hidden motives that might otherwise reveal a fuller depiction of the truth. As the American dissident Edward Herman has said, "It is the function of the experts, and the mainstream media, to normalize the unthinkable for the general public."[22]

An additional point on revenge, first introduced in part 1, should be recalled in this examination of the blowback phenomenon. It has to do with the ease with which we find ourselves employing the categories of "victim" and "perpetrator," especially in situations such as 9/11, where an obvious act of atrocity has occurred. If this exploration on revenge as blowback has revealed anything, it is should be clear that we cannot afford to reflect on evil by employing the myth of innocence.

The reality of a violent world calls for a recognition of our solidarity in sinfulness. Self-deception may very well prove to be the ultimate culprit in antagonisms great and small. Those who perished in the 9/11 attacks were clearly victims of evil and unjustified acts. Of course, it is they and their bereaved survivors who are the first victims to be remembered. But there are other victims in the background of this picture, and their forgotten status as victims has much to do with the recent victimization of those in the foreground. The suffering of these forgotten victims also needs to be investigated.

Richard Hughes explores the myth of American innocence and concludes that for most of the twentieth century — the "9/10" of violence and revenge — the mainstream of American life had little doubt that the ultimate meaning of their nation was one that represented good against evil, democracy against tyranny, and virtue against vice.[23] The historical development of this self-perception is complex — the spiritually upbeat, "can-do" attitude of nineteenth-century revivals, for example, grafted a confident Arminian branch onto the sterner trunk of the American Calvinist tree[24] — but Hughes identifies two factors that played a particularly important role in the formation of America's myth of innocence. The first stems from the U.S. role in fighting Nazism in World War II, a clear and obvious evil threatening the world, which fostered an equal and opposite view that Americans themselves were fundamentally good. The second is a mix of other ancillary myths, which Hughes also investigates, that together culminated in the myth of innocence. Among these are "the myth of nature's nation" — that is, the gradual recognition that the vast, untouched American wilderness resembled a veritable "New Eden," and therefore a new and purifying opportunity for the human race, and "the myth of the millennial nation" — which fostered the conviction that America stood apart from normal history, leading the world into a golden age of perfection.

> By identifying itself so completely with these mythic periods of perfection, America lifted itself, as it were, above the plane of ordinary human existence. America became, as the Great Seal of the United States so clearly states, a *novus ordo saeculorum,* a new order of the ages. Other nations were mired in the bog of human history, but not the United States. Other nations had inherited the taint of human history, but not the United States. . . . In this way, America emerged, as it were, as an innocent child among the nations of the world, without spot or wrinkle, unmarred and unblemished by the finite dimensions of human history.[25]

According to Hughes's analysis, America had secured a self-image bolstered by an understanding of its own exceptional time and exceptional place in the world. And although America's self-confidence in its virtuous ideals have undoubtedly contributed to the protection and promotion of "life, liberty, and the pursuit of happiness," its presumption of innocence and virtue, and denial of greed and imperialist intent, have prevented the realization of those values for countless "others" who find themselves excluded from the "American way." Clearly, the view of a "national" identity, established on an uncritical view of its own exceptional virtue, is another version of the dangerous tendency to establish identity by exclusion, which we have already considered. We can say that 9/11 unveiled, for those who would see it, the evil of identity by exception.

    This consideration of blowback, of revenge and 9/11, necessarily brings us back to those moments directly following the terrorist attacks and to the

questions and concerns always prompted by the experience of suffering resulting from violation and treachery. What now? What comes next? Will it bring
hope? Or will it be nothing new?

DUALISM AS FUNDAMENTALISM

This reflection on 9/11 brings us to a further examination of the problem of
dualistic thinking. The tendency to see the world in binary terms — good/evil,
right/wrong, pure/impure — is characteristic of the evil of exclusion, which, as
Volf has cautioned, can lead to an intensified outcome of violence, especially in
situations of rivalry and where a sense of identity feels threatened from external forces. In the context of 9/11 we see that dualism is especially related to
fundamentalism, which itself can take on many forms.

The Collision and Collusion of Fundamentalisms

Use of the term "fundamentalism" could be problematic without a consideration of the varied ways in which its meaning has shifted over the years.[26] Its
origins are in American Protestantism, dating back to the Deep South of 1920,
but the term has come to refer to the radicalism that is found in all kinds of
extremist groups. It was first used to describe the hard-line Protestant believer
who, faced with the threat of encroaching liberalism on the certainty of Christian tradition, was "willing to do battle royal for the Fundamentals" of the
faith.[27] Such a siege mentality has characterized most fundamentalisms before
and since the appearance of the term, from the onset of the Christian crusades
at the close of the eleventh century to the fall of most of the last tottering fascist
and communist regimes at the close of the twentieth.

Fundamentalist fervor peaks during periods of sustained cultural crisis and
change, when the authority of old and familiar value systems seems threatened
by new and foreign elements that instill uncertainty, discomfort, and fear. Stuart Sim adds that, along with the desire to retain traditional value and belief
systems, fundamentalism also reflects a search for power and an attempt to
accentuate self-definition in situations of multiculturalism. "Going 'back to
basics' is an attempt, however misguided, to hold radical change at bay and,
if possible, to turn back the clock to a time when the world, apparently at
least, conformed to your value system. In religion, to a time when all were
believers of the same creed and theocracy was in force; in politics and nation-
alism, to a society before pluralism and multiculturalism became complicating

features on the cultural landscape."[28] This nostalgic harkening backward, however, is rarely recollected accurately; simplicity and contentment are most often injected into the faded picture.

The fundamentalist mind-set does not like difference. It prefers uniformity and cultural homogeneity to the diversity and dimensionality of typically liberal democratic societies. Accordingly, it resides uncomfortably within the postmodern milieu of contrasting opinions and worldviews. The fundamentalist thus favors strict conformity over the freedom to question and experiment. Fundamentalism opts for uncritical adherence to authority and complete submission to tradition as defined by the legitimate authorities.

Fundamentalists possess an essentially Manichean worldview in which good and evil are forces set in diametrical opposition and which remain in constant battle on a universal scale. Such a black-and-white conception of good and evil, right and wrong gives the fundamentalist a particularly keen sensitivity to matters of purity: purity of vision, purity of virtue, and in particular a pure and uncorrupted sense of purpose and mission in fighting the multifarious representatives of evil in the world. There is never any doubt with regard to God's approval of fundamentalist objectives: God is always on "our side." Accordingly, in the fundamentalist's world, "us" and "them" are the only two kinds of people.

Most pertinent to our characterization of the fundamentalist mind-set is the observation that the tendency toward fundamentalism is one that resides in every human person. It exists at least latently as a disposition that could arise in any segment of any population given the proper environmental conditions, e.g., the experience of oppressive economic policies or a perceived threat to longstanding, traditional belief and value systems.[29] Sim, for one, acknowledges that the fundamentalist mentality is a part of human nature and insists that that is precisely why we should be so perspicacious in monitoring it. "The disposition towards authoritarianism and dogmatism may lurk within us, but that's no reason for allowing it to dominate and thus set the tone, and the values of our society."[30]

That last observation points to the call for an increased awareness of our solidarity in sin. Indeed, whenever we can see, with uncannily clear precision, the depravity that lurks solely in the other, the evil *over there*, chances are it is we ourselves who are seeing with the eyes of the fundamentalist. This becomes especially worrisome when we are speaking of fanatical religious fundamentalists, where all too often the conviction of being right comes with the entitlement to destroy those who are wrong.

It cannot be denied that religious fundamentalism has proven a very fertile context for inciting the escalation of terrorist activity occurring throughout the world at this time. Brian Jenkins notes the basic change in terrorist motives since the last decade, which has resulted in larger-scaled spectacles of attack with higher shock value and casualties of epic proportions, such as 9/11. Whereas terrorist attacks of the 1970s and 1980s were chiefly fueled by nationalist ideologies, often with separatist aims and with the intention of making a persuasive political statement, since the 1990s most terrorist acts have been influenced by religious motivations. "Those convinced that they have a mandate of God to kill their foes have fewer moral qualms about mass murder and care less about constituents.... And in the minds of the devout, death in God's cause brings reward in the afterlife."[31]

Fundamentalism of the Islamic variety is undoubtedly in the position to offer a number of cases in point. And yet this does not imply that fundamentalist extremism is a violence endemic to Islam alone. The numerous bombings of abortion clinics throughout the United States over the past decades, the rise of extreme right-wing white supremacist churches, as well as the entire notorious history of the Ku Klux Klan demonstrate all too convincingly that radical Christian fundamentalism is vulnerable to violent extremism. As'ad AbuKhalil writes, "In reality, the fundamentalists of the three faiths are quite similar in outlook and objective: they all are intolerant, misogynist, obscurantist, homophobic, puritanical, armed, and willing to use violence to advance their causes."[32] A careful reading of the letter written to one of the 9/11 terrorist hijackers, Muhammad Atta, which was discovered shortly after the attacks, demonstrates how religious discourse is used to construe mass murder as a devout religious practice. The letter instructs the terrorists to meditate on *surahs* eight and nine of the Qur'an, the war chapters that command the followers of the Prophet to strike terror into "the enemy of God and your enemy" and remind them that they have been promised "gardens of bliss where they shall dwell forever, and that the 'women of paradise are waiting, calling out, "*Come hither, friend of God*." They are further instructed to pray Qur'anic verses into their hands and then to rub their hands on their clothes, knives, and passports to bless them, and to shout *"Allahu Akbar!"* (God is great!) when the hijacking begins, in order to strike fear into the hearts of the nonbelievers. They are finally instructed "to end their own lives by praying in the seconds before the target.... 'There is no God but God, and Muhammad is His messenger.'"[33] The part of the letter detailing the steps of the actual killings of the first victims on board the plane are supported by two arguments for the justification of the violence: the first, an account of the prophet Mohammad's own military practices as a legitimating model, and the second, the likening of those victims (i.e., the flight attendants) to sacrificial beasts, whose throats would be slit in ritual fashion.[34] Islamic cultural historian Malise Ruthven comments on the profound solipsism evident in the message, which, in its attempt to frustrate possible moral misgivings, appears devoid of any sense of human compassion save for a concern for the would-be martyr's soul. "The actor who undertakes an apocalyptic mission identifies his action with the will of God; by doing so he leaves to God the moral consequences of his act."[35]

The conflation of religious discourse and legitimated violence is similarly blatant in the text of the speech given by Osama bin Laden less than a month after the 9/11 attacks. In it, the al Qaeda leader exults in the knowledge of a besieged America "struck by God Almighty in one of its vital organs, so that its greatest buildings are destroyed." He goes on to describe the attack in terms of God's blessing on "a group of vanguard Muslims, the forefront of Islam, to destroy America. May God bless them and allot them a supreme place in heaven, for he is the only one capable and entitled to do so." America is described as the "camp of the infidels" and "the modern world's symbol of paganism." He states that 9/11 has produced a radical division between the pagan American camp and the camp of the faithful. Bin Laden concludes with the declaration: "God is the greatest and glory be to Islam."[36]

Bin Laden's disturbing speech was actually composed a bit earlier than it was aired. It was delayed so that it could serve as a prompt riposte to U.S. president George W. Bush's speech to the nation that was televised on October 7, 2001, on the occasion of the first air strikes against al Qaeda training camps and Taliban military installations in Afghanistan. President Bush's speech, by comparison, is much more reserved in overall religious tenor. In it he confesses that a commander-in-chief commits troops to battle only after "great care and a lot of prayer." The only reference to God in the entire address comes at its close: "May God continue to bless America."[37]

But a careful reading of Bush's speech does suggest certain features of the fundamentalist's mind-set. Just as Bin Laden makes reference to the two rival camps of the post-9/11 world, so too does Bush depict in stark terms a cosmic struggle between forces of good and evil: "In this conflict there is no neutral ground. If any government sponsors the outlaws and killers of innocents, they have become outlaws and murderers, themselves. And they will take that lonely path at their own peril."[38] Bush, like bin Laden, carries out his dualistic conception of the world through the use of similar binary structures:

"good/evil," "heroes/villains," "us/them." Moreover, both Bush and bin Laden clearly allude to purity and innocence in their references to children: for bin Laden, it is those children deprived of food and medical supplies due to the American embargo of Iraq at the time; for Bush, it is those children who starve under the oppressive Taliban regime, as well as an American fourth grade girl, reluctant but willing to offer her father for military service in his war on evil. As Bruce Lincoln observes: "By the time he [Bush] was finished, he had positioned the United States as champion of freedom throughout the globe, hedge against darkness, and protector of the weak."[39]

Of course, highlighting what appears to be a certain shared tendency toward dualistic thinking is not the same as implying that Bush and bin Laden also share a similar character, or system of values, or moral fabric. What we are interested in asserting, however, is the notion that fundamentalism exists as a dangerous and widespread tendency, one found among peoples of drastically varying backgrounds, a tendency which, if unchecked, can lead to dangerous, even terrifying consequences anywhere. What is proving indispensable in the present climate of escalating political and cultural conflicts is the ability to detect, not only in our foes but in ourselves, this all too human proclivity toward fundamentalist reductionism. This task becomes especially crucial when the particular fundamentalism at work is emboldened by the deluded religious claim that "God is on our side."

With a growing intensity after 9/11, President Bush consistently portrayed the international scene in terms of a conflict between good and evil. In his January 29, 2002, State of the Union address, Bush declared that the nations of Iraq, Iran, and North Korea comprised an "axis of evil," and on numerous occasions after that warned of "the evil ones" and "the servants of evil." Using categories clearly borrowed from the Bible's apocalyptic tradition, he urged all people of good will to "call evil by its name," and "to fight evil" everywhere.[40] Clearly, Bush's terminology suggests that he saw terrorism not so much in terms of a problem that is endemic to modern society — one demanding multilateral cooperation for lasting economic improvement among developing nations, sensible restraint as well as adamant resolve — but in terms of an apocalyptic struggle between the ultimate forces of evil and good, darkness and light. Certainly the decision to invade Iraq smacks of this same cosmic dualism. As Peter Singer observes, "It seems probable that it was not faith in general that gave Bush and his aides a misplaced confidence that they knew the answers. It was the idea that Saddam was evil. Writing in *Newsweek* on how Bush justified going to war with Iraq, Howard Fineman observed, 'He decided that Saddam was evil, and everything flowed from that.' "[41]

It is interesting to note the way in which various types of fundamentalisms interact, sometimes in collusion, other times in collision, in all times leading to disaster. Here the various brands of American fundamentalisms offer a disturbing case in point. Stuart Sim and Malise Ruthven paint convincing portrayals of the intersection of Christian right-wing, political, and market fundamentalisms evident on the current American scene. It is no secret that a large portion of the Bush Republican constituency was comprised of Christian conservatives, many of whom labeled themselves fundamentalists, some of whom are fairly assessed to be extremist in their views and positions. Bush received enormous support from Jerry Falwell and Pat Robertson, the famous televangelists who, as we have noted above, attributed the 9/11 attacks to God's punishing hand on gays, lesbians, abortionists, and feminists in American society (before being pressured to recant). Falwell and Robertson, like many American Evangelicals and Christian fundamentalists, adhere to the pre-millenial belief, based on literalistic readings of the Bible, that a fully restored State of Israel will signal the beginning of Christ's thousand-year reign on earth, an event featuring the conversion of (righteous) Jews to Christianity. A withdrawal by Israel from the Palestinian territories it gained and has occupied since 1967, the beginning signs of which have already been accomplished, does, in the view of many Evangelicals, impede God's design for Christian victory over sin and disbelief.[42] This is especially instructive with regard to the resentment nurtured by many in the Arab world over the perception that America has been lopsided in its condemnation of terrorist atrocities in the Middle East in favor of Israel.

Sim's analysis of fundamentalisms in conflict includes an excellent exposé of American imperialist fundamentalism against the background claims of Francis Fukuyama's well-know assertion, though nuanced of late, that in the wake of the fall of communism, we are now living at the "end of history" with nothing left to oppose triumphant Western liberal democracy. The problem, of course, is that the triumph of the West has left the rest of the world without any substantial political alternative around which to organize.[43] It is worthwhile to consider the oppressive effects of what Sim has called market, corporate, and global fundamentalisms, in which American culture has typically played a starring role. We should recall that what is common to the fundamentalist ethos in general is the desire to eliminate difference and control individual behavior while presenting itself as the path to self-fulfillment. As we have seen in part 1, idolatrous domination systems have an inner spiritual dimension that must be challenged if sinful structures are ever to be transformed. U.K. cultural critics Ziauddin Sardar and Merryl Wyn Davies, who have labeled the United States the world's only "hyper power," stress as crucial the necessity to see beyond the American media's tendency to gloss euphemistically over the ulterior motives of many U.S. economic policies:

> "Free markets" is simply a euphemism for free mobility of American capital, unrestrained expansion of American corporations, and free (uni-directional) movement of goods and services from America to the rest of the world. The US dollar is the world's main reserve currency, the medium that everyone needs to pay for their foreign imports, and there is no restraint on the US's ability to print its own currency to finance its trade deficits with the rest of the world. Since international lending is carried out in dollars, crisis-ridden borrowing countries saddled with trade deficits always have to take on dollar debt burdens greater than their capacity to repay. Couple this with the US control of international financial institutions such as the IMF, World Bank and WTO, and we see how the world economy functions to marginalize the less-developed world.[44]

What we discover is the selling of globalization "as if it were the answer to all the planet's social and political problems: the only possible way to reach economic salvation" . . . alongside "the assumption of the world's largest corporations (multinationals or transnationals as they are usually referred to) that they have the right to monopolise the global economy, even to the extent of dictating terms to national governments."[45] Such cooperating fundamentalisms can and do combine to present an awesome and antagonizing front to those of differing cultural traditions. What we see is not so much the "clash of civilizations," Samuel Huntington's well-known articulation of what appear to be mutually hostile civilizations defined regionally,[46] but what might be better called *a collision of fundamentalisms,* wherein certain complementary varieties of fundamentalist strategies function symbiotically and, in turn, create a similar momentum of oppositional force in response. Ruthven draws the astute conclusion that the evidence of clashing is found not between civilizations but within individuals, "in which uneducated religiosity combines with rage, utopianism, social anomie and technical sophistication."[47] This means that for the suicide bomber (or pilot), the violence and terror of such clashing had already turned him into a walking bomb long before he chose to don a vest of explosives (or commandeer a jetliner and fly it into a towering office build-ing). What is truly terrifying here is that for the suicide terrorist, the decision to "self-detonate" is not irrational.

> A range of social and economic factors combine to create a situation in which suicide terrorists emerge because there's a demand for their sac-rifice, and the individuals concerned can see the logic of that demand. Suicide bombing is part of a political campaign … and it's rational in terms of the objectives sought: the destabilization of the enemy such that they are forced to negotiate with the revolutionary organization directing the suicide attacks, or at the very least to reconsider their policy towards them. 9/11 was a carefully calculated exercise in which all the partici-pants had a clearly defined role to play: it was no mere nihilistic gesture on the part of some psychologically disturbed individuals. … The ter-rorists see advantages both for themselves and for their families in the sacrifice they make for the cause. They are guaranteed a place of hon-our in the history of their people, no small matter in such traditionalist cultures, and even promised a place in heaven.[48]

It is clear that in the case of 9/11, fundamentalisms both colluded and col-lided. It is also clear that the tendency to entrench oneself in dualistic structures of thought is a tendency more universal than perhaps we are ready to admit. Although we have considered here a number of fundamentalisms that are less frequently discussed under the label, such as market, political, and global fun-damentalisms, it is still certain that religious fundamentalism played a pivotal role in the attacks. The question of religion and terrorism is a topic that calls for further inspection.

Violence in the Name of God

9/11 prompted widespread interest in the topic of religiously motivated acts of terrorism. We are right to consider the compelling question: Is religion inher-ently violent? The concern is a longstanding one, although it has taken on a new urgency in recent decades, which have witnessed a rise in such violence conditioned by religion.[49]

For our purposes, however, the question regarding the inherent violence of religion must be distinguished from the more pertinent question of the relationship between religion and, specifically, terrorism, as it is the latter phenomenon that specifies the present investigation.

For Oliver McTernan, the core of the problem lies in the way that faith-inspired terrorists perceive their religion and, in particular, how they understand the process of revelation that lies behind their sacred texts.[50] We have already examined the fundamentalist's quest for inerrancy, which is plainly reflected in the view that foundational texts are the product of divine dictation and are therefore beyond interpretation. What we must pursue now is a consideration of some factors that explain the appeal that religion holds for those drawn to participate in terrorist activity. In the case of 9/11 this matter is crucial, for it is difficult to understand the terrorists' deeds apart from the sense of higher mission that clearly served as their motivating force.

McTernan's analysis of 9/11 rests on the claim that religiously motivated terrorism is not a new phenomenon. "To accept the common assumption that the hijackers were driven solely by a fanatical hatred rather than the sense of a higher mission is to lose sight of the fact that people were killing in God's name before the coming of modernity, secularism, globalization, cosmopolitanism and even the founding of the United States of America."[51] Accordingly, McTernan objects to the oft-heard question posed by many Americans in the wake of 9/11, "Why do they hate us?" a preoccupation suggesting that grievance and envy were really the driving motivations behind the attacks. In his address to the nation three days after the attacks, President Bush insinuated as much by remarking, "In every generation, the world has produced enemies of human freedom. They have attacked America because we are freedom's home and defender."[52] McTernan contends that poverty, social injustice, and political repression certainly provide the "breeding ground" for the thriving of terrorism, but religious conviction should not be underestimated.[53] While this is clearly the case, we assert that without an honest accounting of these myriad grievances, we cannot interpret adequately the sense of empowerment that religion bestows on the aggrieved. Ignored grievances and mounting resentments can transform religion into a lethal weapon.

The work of sociologist of religion Mark Juergensmeyer is particularly helpful to our study. Juergensmeyer contends that religion bestows an enormous sense of power to terrorist endeavors chiefly through its symbolic currency and its cosmic war imagery.[54]

We have already considered the basic symbolic character of terrorist activity: how such events are not arranged for their practical value, such as could be measured by an optimum number of casualties, but for their symbolic value, resulting in a fear-inducing spectacle that makes for an unambiguous statement. They are intended "to illustrate or refer to something beyond their

immediate target: a grander conquest, for instance, or a struggle more awesome than meets the eye."[55] Juergensmeyer considers them theatrical forms of
violence:

> Such instances of exaggerated violence are constructed events: they are
> mind-numbing, mesmerizing theater. At center stage are the acts them-
> selves — stunning, abnormal, and outrageous murders carried out in a
> way that graphically displays the awful power of violence — set within
> grand scenarios of conflict and proclamation. Killing or maiming of any
> sort is violent, of course, but these acts surpass the wounds inflicted dur-
> ing warfare of death delivered through capital punishment, in large part
> because they have a secondary impact. By their demonstrative nature,
> they elicit feelings of revulsion and anger in those who witness them.[56]

Such dramatic events aimed at impressing on a symbolic plane make them
akin to the function of religious ritual: they are designed to have an affective
impact on witnesses, transforming them into a new consciousness. "Those
who witness the violence — even at a distance, via the news media — are
therefore a part of what occurs."[57] For Juergensmeyer acts of religious terrorism are both *performance* events, in their symbolic character, and *performative*
acts insofar as they aim at effecting a change. This dual dimension accounts,
to some degree, for the appeal that terrorist acts have on radical religious
enthusiasts.[58]

Juergensmeyer also explores the sense of symbolic empowerment that is
bestowed on "marginal men" in which the language and imagery of divine
warfare bestows a certain legitimacy and nobility to the terrorists' aims. "A
society provides an accepted — even heroic — social role for its citizens who
participate in great struggles and have been given the moral license to kill."[59] It
is easy to see how many religious radicals could identify themselves as soldiers
fighting the "good fight."

Examples of martial imagery and vocabulary are part of the heritage of most
religious traditions. Certainly the Islamic concept of struggle — *jihad* — has
been exploited by terrorists to allow for the use of physical force and destruction,[60] just as Christian patriots have justified violent acts sung to the tune of
"Onward Christian Soldiers." According to Juergensmeyer, "what makes religious violence particularly savage and relentless is that its perpetrators have
placed such religious images of divine struggle — cosmic war — in the service
of worldly political battles. For this reason, acts of religious terror serve not

only as tactics in a political strategy but also as evocations of a much larger spiritual confrontation."[61]

Much of the discussion on the topic of religion and violence has focused on those elements found in religious traditions that may of themselves be violence-inducing. This approach is helpful in drawing attention to those images and texts that, for example, justify and even glorify warfare. The work of Girard on the function of sacrificial rites is a notable example of this approach, which has as a starting point a particular aspect of religious tradition or practice and then moves on to a consideration of how these may function in perpetuating or discouraging problematic situations involving violence.[62] But in analyzing the topic of religion and terrorism, a different approach may also prove helpful, one that starts not with those characteristics of religion but with an examination of the kind of violent situations that tend to reach out for religious justification. Juergensmeyer appears to suggest that both approaches could act in a complementary way for a thorough investigation of religious terrorism. With regard to the latter approach, he cites three particularly volatile situations that reach out for religious justification: when the struggle is perceived as a defense of basic identity and dignity, when losing the struggle would be unthinkable, and when the struggle is blocked and cannot be won in real time or in real terms.[63] These predicaments form a most fitting segue to this next aspect of our investigation of evil 9/11.

EXCLUSION AS HUMILIATION

We recall that Miroslav Volf has named exclusion an objective evil of our time. We have seen how exclusion has often manifested itself in the futile attempt to establish identity as if the other did not exist. We have examined how this evil of exclusion has perpetuated the ongoing cycle of violence and revenge that has led to the irrefutable record of suffering in recent history. All of the aspects of evil 9/11 that we have investigated thus far seem to coalesce under the heading of exclusion. We turn now to a consideration of how exclusion, in the time/space of 9/11, can to some extent be interpreted as a problem of *humiliation*.

Passive Voice

The previous section on fundamentalisms made clear two basic starting points for a discussion on violence and religion, namely, that the problem reveals the violence inherent in religious texts themselves, and that the problem points to certain external factors, e.g., political, socioeconomic conflicts, which can make of those particular religious texts a volatile foundation for identity cohesion. Both McTernan and Juergensmeyer are aware of the need to examine the problem of religious terrorism in terms of the conjunction of both external and internal factors. Indeed, any attempt to understand the mind and motivation of the terrorist in abstraction from the exigencies of real life is futile and detrimental.

Of the two, McTernan seems to place less emphasis on external factors such as poverty and lack of education, which do not directly cause but serve only as a breeding ground for religious terrorist activity. Juergensmeyer, however, stresses one factor above all others — humiliation — in his understanding of the problem of religious terrorism. This phenomenon, we agree, cannot be overlooked. For when issues of honor and pride are at stake, revenge is often triggered as an almost visceral response to the experienced humiliation.

> Revenge is retaliation designed to subject another to a similar humiliation as that which he has imposed on one or, perhaps preferably, a worse shame. This will nearly inevitably elicit, in its turn, a violent response, and so a cycle of revenge is set in train. . . . The problem is that although revenge is essentially "paying someone back" for what he has done to one, there is no measure of what constitutes fair payment. . . . For each party puts a higher estimate upon themselves, than those who injure them do. So what seems like getting even to the injured, seems disproportionate to the injurer, and the cycle goes on.[64]

Humiliation, then, plays an especially catalytic function in instigating the cycle of revenge.

It is instructive to consider the etymology of the term. In English the word "humiliate," which comes from the late Latin *humiliare*, is based on *humilis*, the word for "humble." By the mid-sixteenth century, humiliate had begun to mean "made low," so that by the eighteenth century, standard usage, still current today, had come to suggest the passive voice — "make (someone) feel ashamed and foolish by injuring their dignity and self-respect, especially publicly."[65] We recall that the Latin word for suffering, *passio*, suggests something of its meaning: suffering makes us passive. Humiliation is a real suffering.

We have already considered a number of political, economic, and cultural factors connected to the 9/11 tragedy. What needs to be explored further in this theological investigation is how those factors have led to the real experience of injury to "dignity and self-respect," and this "especially publicly," given our world-made-global village.

It would be easy to underestimate the experience of humiliation as a serious motivating factor in acts of religious terrorism, if we were to make the mistake of equating it with the familiar feeling of awkwardness or embarrassment. Humiliation includes but runs deeper than the experience of shame. Likewise, it would be wrong to conclude that humiliation could be ameliorated by a typically modern approach to problem-solving, some socioeconomic intervention aimed at providing desperately needed goods and services. But we are not simply speaking of a human reflex that occurs automatically wherever abject poverty or oppression exists. Indeed, the biographies of the nineteen terrorists involved in the 9/11 attacks suggest that poverty or lack of education were not compelling motivating factors for their deeds.

Juergensmeyer has shown convincingly how the desperate can perceive both religion and violence as antidotes to humiliation. As the political head of the Hamas movement confided: "To die in this way [suicide bombings] is better than to die daily in frustration and humiliation."[66]

The truly disturbing reality is that the sentiment expressed above is one that has echoed among many of the humiliated throughout the Middle East. It directs our attention to the "other" side of the terrible tragedy of 9/11, where it becomes clear that for many people, those "others" outside of our comfort zones, becoming a terrorist seems to promise hope.

> Perpetrating acts of terrorism is one of several ways to symbolically express power over oppressive forces and regain some nobility in the perpetrator's personal life. Those who have been part of cultures of violence and who have participated in acts of empowerment — even vicariously — have experienced the exuberance of the hope that the tide of history will eventually turn their way. Such performances of power have provided the anticipation that victory is at hand. Alas, the experience has often been fleeting. Sadder still, it has been purchased at an awful cost.[67]

When humiliation, understood as an assault on basic human dignity, is taken seriously as a dimension of the evil of exclusion, then it becomes imperative to consider the ways in which we ourselves have contributed to its flourishing. What is needed is a kind of phenomenology of humiliation through which we can perceive the suffering of others who have been *made* low, made to live their lives in the passive voice.

We must proceed with care and precision when discussing passivity in this context. In *Oneself as Another,* Paul Ricoeur explores a "triad of passivities" through which the *otherness* that is at the very heart of selfhood is experienced. This variety of experiences of passivity is intertwined in multiple ways in human action: the experience of one's own body as the mediator between the self and the world, the relation of the self to the foreign, the "other (than) self" inherent in the relation of intersubjectivity, and the relation of the self to itself which is conscience.[68] However, distinct from these senses of passivity is the passivity of suffering. "Undergoing and enduring are, in a sense, revealed in their complete passive dimension when they become suffering."[69] In this respect, with passivity as "the decrease of the power of *acting,* experienced as a decrease of the effort of *existing,* the reign of suffering, properly speaking, commences."[70] Among the descriptions of suffering that Ricoeur pursues, one seems particularly useful for our own reflection on humiliation. Ricoeur has explored what he calls "narrative identity" in which he examines how narrative joins together agents and patients in the "entangling of multiple life histories." Here he considers what he himself calls "more deeply concealed forms of suffering: the incapacity to tell a story, the refusal to recount, the insistence of the untellable — phenomena that go far beyond mishaps and adventures, which can always be made meaningful through the strategy of emplotment."[71] In other words, we are proposing to consider one aspect of the phenomenon of humiliation in terms of the muting of the self-constructing voice of narrative. It is impossible to avoid the terrible vision of the *muselmann* standing at the end of this road.

Along with Ricoeur's understanding of the passivity of suffering with regard to narrative, another way to approach the phenomenon of humiliation is by recalling Volf's own understanding of God's creative work as depicted in Genesis, a process of "differentiation" that results in patterns of interdependence, or, using the terms employed by Cornelius Plantinga, a process of "separating" and "binding together" that we first introduced in part 1.[72]

> The account of creation as "separating-and-binding" rather than simply "separating" suggests that "identity" includes connection, difference, heterogeneity. The human self is formed not through a simple rejection of the other — through a binary logic of opposition and negation — but through a complex process of "taking in" *and* "keeping out." We are who we are not because we are separate from the others who are next to us, but because we are *both* separate *and* connected, *both* distinct *and* related; the boundaries that mark our identities are both barriers and bridges.[73]

Understanding humiliation along these lines, we can see that an obstruction to either pole of differentiation, that is, to the separation side or to the connection side of the creative process, can result in exclusion as humiliation.

Our succinct review of the "historical and conjunctural" causes of 9/11 offered by Halliday revealed that a pattern of linkages of previously unrelated conflicts had begun to develop in the Middle East for the purpose of harnessing the momentum of frustration and mobilizing support in the fundamentalists' quest for political power. One such conflict listed earlier, but that is now better positioned for consideration in the context of exclusion as humiliation, is the Israeli/Palestinian conflict. We recall that part 1 closed with a reflection on that same conflict, focusing especially on two main points: the ease with which we can discern an unbroken cycle of violence and revenge, and the difficulty implied in distinguishing between victims and perpetrators. Here we are concerned with humiliation that comes from a breakdown in the differentiation that is key to our created identity of interconnectedness. Disintegration in both functions, in binding together and in separating, can be discerned.

In the first place, exclusion is a transgression against "binding together." It is a severing of the bonds that keep the self properly connected to the other and prevent it from assuming a position of sovereign independence: "The other then emerges as an enemy that must be pushed away from the self and driven out of its space or as a nonentity — a superfluous being — that can be disregarded and abandoned."[74] Humiliation in this context is the predicament of finding oneself cut off from the veritable lifelines that are creation, an assault on the integrity of the other's rightful place in the God-ordained network of interconnectedness.

With regard to the integrity of the function of binding in the context of the Israeli/Palestinian conflict, it is important to review the earliest encounters with modernity in the Middle East. Noam Chomsky explores how the Jewish national movement, Zionism, very much an offshoot of European "civilization," first brought economic development to the Palestinian region in the early part of the twentieth century, but at a considerable cost to Palestinian Arabs, who through zealous policies of land purchase and boycotting, were displaced from land and livelihood.

The motives for the latter policies were complex. In part, they can be traced to chauvinism and an "exclusivist" ideology, but in part they also reflected the dilemmas of socialists who hoped to build an egalitarian society with a Jewish working class, not a society of wealthy

Jewish planters exploiting the natives. The Yishuv [Jewish settlement] was thus faced with a profound, never resolved contradiction. The most advanced socialist forms in existence, the germs of a just and egalitarian society, were constructed on lands purchased by the Jewish National Fund, from which Arabs were excluded in principle, lands that were in many instances purchased from absentee landlords with little regard for the peasants who lived and worked on them.[75]

The problems of this foundational contradiction have multiplied exponentially since the foundation of the Jewish state in 1948, as tales of reciprocal terrorism in the last fifty years make clear.

For our analysis, what is most important is the history of obstacles that have been set up in the path of Palestinian progress toward modern ideals of self-determination and — improvement. Applying Volf's differentiation schema, this is exclusion resulting from a transgression against "separating," which entails the erasure of the distinctive otherness of the other, thereby ignoring that the other belongs to the same pattern of interdependence. "The other then emerges as an inferior being who must either be assimilated by being made like the self or be subjugated to the self."[76] What we are calling humiliation is the result of this "having been made" to exist apart from the interconnectedness that distinguishes the true order of creation as made by God. The other, then, is not just "made" to live (the passive voice) a disruption of the dignity of difference, but is actually "remade" according to an image and likeness other than God's own.

In spite of the award of the 1994 Nobel Peace Prize to two Israelis, Rabin and Peres, and to the Palestinian Arafat, in reality very little by way of lasting peace was achieved. According to Edward Said, the "lopsided" award of two-to-one was a telling indication of the lopsidedness of the results of the "peace" proposals embodied in the Declaration of Principles and the Gaza-Jericho agreements that the prize ostensibly celebrates. An inspection of the terms reveals little that indicates the sure peace that only justice secures. Said critically inspects the areas of limited autonomy and early empowerment returned to the Palestinians, and describes the destroyed infrastructure there resulting from twenty-seven years of Israeli occupation.

In principle this meant that far from vacating the Occupied Territories the Israelis were forcing the Palestinians to comply with continued occupation and, more important, to condone past Israeli practices without reparations. To take a relatively small example, the over 2,000 Palestinian houses that were destroyed by the Israeli military during the *intifada* were not accounted for. Gaza, which the American economist Sara Roy has characterized as an area purposely de-developed by the Israelis, its population pauperized, its sanitation, health, educational, residential, and commercial services reduced to nothing by them, was dumped in Arafat's lap to rule even though they had made the place impossible to sustain.[77]

We are right to question the integrity of any "peace" that perpetuates the humiliation of a subjugated people. Using Volf's analysis of sin as a breakdown in the binding together and separating aspects of differentiation, it is clear that the Palestinian people, deprived of full participation in the goods of modernity, have been cut off from the network of relationships that is the healthy flourishing of the created order. As Tanya Reinhart claims, "During the four decades of occupation, Israel has enforced a total dependence of the Palestinian economy on Israel."[78]

And yet, as our earlier consideration of the Israeli-Palestinian conflict exposed, it is difficult to see clearly the exact boundaries of hostilities in the chaotic flux generated by the endless cycle of revenge. We can, for instance, consider the *fatwa* issued in 1996 by the Palestinian Mufti banning the sale of Arab and Muslim property to Jews. According to Mitchell Bard, the decree demanded the killing of anyone who violated it, and, in fact, seven land dealers were executed that year by operatives working for the Palestinian Authority's General Intelligence Service in the West Bank.[79] In addition, on May 5, 1997, "PA Justice Minister Freih Abu Middein announced that the death penalty would be imposed on anyone convicted of ceding 'one inch' to Israel. Later that month, two Arab land dealers were killed."[80] What is blatant here is the transgression against binding, but in this instance on the part of the Palestinian people against Israelis.[81] An examination of population statistics for Jews in Arab countries between 1948 and 2001 indicates that the problem exists on a huge scale throughout the Arab world. For example, in Iraq there were 150,000 Jews in 1948, but only 100 in 2001. Similarly, of the 265,000 Jews in Morocco in 1948, only 5,700 remained in 2001.[82]

It is also clear that transgressions against separating — in failing to allow Jews to maintain their culture — have also been apparent in the Middle East. The situation in Syria provides an especially clear example. Since its independence from France, the Syrian government has enacted many measures impinging upon Jewish life, such as restricting the teaching of Hebrew in Jewish schools and promoting boycotts against Jewish businesses. During the 1980s and early 1990s, the transgression against separation was particularly acute.

> For years, the Jews in Syria lived in extreme fear. The Jewish Quarter in Damascus was under the constant surveillance of the secret police, who were present at synagogue services, weddings, bar-mitzvahs and other Jewish gatherings. Contact with foreigners was closely monitored. Travel abroad was permitted in exceptional cases, but only if a bond of $300–$1,000 was left behind, along with family members who served as hostages.[83]

Particularly noteworthy here is the fact that the "other" is forced to remain in a society that denies him or her the freedom that separation allows, namely, the freedom to practice his or her distinctive culture "out loud," that is, by actively living the freedom to be oneself. Instead, it appears that a strange value is itself derived in subjugating the other, forcing him or her to live out the passivity of humiliation.

Self-Donating

This final section of chapter 8 leaves us with the stark contrast of two forms of the same concept. The first example of self-donation is the one that has been under inspection throughout this chapter, one that we will bring to conclusion below; the second is the subject of part 3 in its entirety, a different way of understanding what we mean by the same words "self-donating," or giving of oneself.

Here, however, is self-donation in the context of terrorism. In the era of 9/11, self-donation may call to mind the activity of certain terrorist strategies, namely, those that employ the contribution of suicide bombers. Thus, in a literal sense, terrorists donate themselves, that is, their very lives, for the cause that compels them.

We have considered the complexity of factors that contribute to the making of a terrorist. That "complexity," it must be stressed, makes it impossible to reduce the problem of terrorism by employing a simple mathematical style to problem solving. We cannot, for example, assert that wherever factors of humiliation, alienation, and desperation exist and are added to other factors — religious extremism and the problem of the persistence of the memory of violence — then these necessarily lead to a tidy sum that we can conveniently label terrorist activity. There is always something in our attempts to understand evil that necessarily halts before its mystery, always the something beyond, something that doesn't add up. And yet we can ill afford to simplify in the other direction by failing to attend to the concrete factors — those recurrences and patterns of evil that so often bring about horror and inhumanity. There is no one answer to the problem of terrorism. Psychologists[84] and sociologists[85] of various specializations and schools, political experts and cultural theorists all add needed perspectives on this complexity we cannot get beyond. Theologians, too, have something to say. For notwithstanding all that can and must be said about terrorists, they are, to the last one, human persons. And the human person, essentially, the human person in relation — to God, to others, to the world — is the proper concern of the theologian.

Here the human person before us is a suicide bomber. It is difficult even to arrange the terms "human" and "bomber" in the same sentence. And yet if we remain committed to avoiding the pitfalls of dualistic thinking — of setting evil over there and good over here, and of demonizing that other we have forced apart from us, then we may very well begin to perceive the unlikely vision of the suicide bomber's own humanity.

Our investigation thus far has yielded an understanding of evil in terms of a breakdown of the patterns of our interdependence and of the essential interconnectedness that is at the core of our human identity. As Volf has explained, the formation of identity involves *both* distinction from the other *and* internalization of the relationship to the other: "it arises out of the complex history of 'differentiation' in which both the self and the other take part by negotiating their identities in interaction with one another."[86] Accordingly, we are better positioned to articulate something definitive about the humanity of the terrorist we are trying to discern. For it is increasingly evident that one of the most disturbing realities about the problem of terrorism is our own involvement in the process. Given the inescapable bonds of our interconnectedness, we can begin to perceive our role as co-creators of the excluded and humiliated. That means that at least to some extent, we play a part in making our own terrorists.

Our aim is to set before us this human person (read, differentiated interconnectedness) *cum* suicide terrorist. According to Robert Pape's authoritative analysis of the 315 suicide bombing attacks that occurred throughout the globe between 1980 and 2003, suicide terrorism is the most aggressive form of terrorism because it is coercion without reserve that risks alienating even neutral audiences.

In principle, suicide terrorism could be used for demonstrative purposes or could be limited to targeted assassination. In practice, however,
recent suicide terrorists often seek simply to kill as many people as
they can. Although this maximizes the coercive leverage that can be
gained from terrorism, it does so at heavier costs than other forms of
terrorism. Maximizing the number of enemy killed alienates virtually
everyone in the target audience, including those who might otherwise
have been sympathetic to the terrorists' cause. In addition, the act of
suicide creates a debate and often loss of support among moderate segments of the terrorists' community, although it may also attract support
among radical elements. Thus, while coercion can be one of the aims
of any form of terrorism, coercion is the paramount objective of suicide
terrorism.[87]

Although September 11 was monstrous in scale, for Pape, it was not unique.
History has witnessed numerous examples of such terrorism where the attack-
ers either do not expect to survive or even employ a method that requires their
deaths. However, Pape notes that as a tool of political coercion suicide terrorism is increasing, as especially evidenced in the first years of the twenty-first
century not only in Sri Lanka, Israel, and the Persian Gulf, where these forms
of terrorism had for some time been occurring, but also in Chechnya, Kashmir,
and of course, on September 11, 2001, the United States.[88]

Pape's analysis is thoughtful and thorough. His extensive research supports
the claim that this troubling phenomenon cannot be facilely attributed to
single factors such as poverty or to psychological explanations, neither of which
can explain why suicide terrorism occurs only in certain societies and at certain
times, nor to a problem endemic to Islamic fundamentalism, since the greatest number of suicide terrorist acts have been perpetrated by members of the
anti-religious Tamil movement. By analyzing the strategic, social, and individual logic of suicide terrorists, Pape concludes that suicide terrorism is mainly a
response to foreign occupation. "Isolated incidents in other circumstances do
occur. Religion plays a role. However, modern suicide terrorism is best understood as an extreme strategy for national liberation against democracies with
troops that pose an imminent threat to control the territory the terrorists view
as their homeland."[89] Pape's findings, which basically concur with Halliday's
interpretation of the 9/11 attacks as primarily an issue of political influence,
thus point to at least two earlier observations made regarding the problem
of evil in our time, the existence of domination systems that indicate vast

imbalances of power, and identity antagonisms resulting from the experience of the threat of the foreign.

Pape explains that unlike military coercion used by states, with suicide terrorism the coercer is always the weaker actor and the target always the stronger. Moreover, in situations of foreign occupation, national identity becomes a particularly volatile factor, insofar as the identity of the foreign occupier is normally the most significant other to the occupied group. "When one country is in political control of another, the national identities of both communities usually include more negative images of the other than do the identities of the same two nations when they are at peace. The boundary between the nations hardens, as well."[90] This situation, in turn, brings religious difference to the forefront.

> The main mechanism is exclusivity. The harder the boundary between groups — the more exclusive are membership rules — the more extreme is the "us" versus "them" dichotomy. Religion is normally more exclusive than other national difference (except for race) under the conditions of an occupation and so often becomes the principal defining boundary between an occupier and the local community. People can learn the occupier's language without abandoning their own, and can even participate in many social practices associated with the occupier's society without rejecting their own, but a person cannot be a member of two religions at once, except under the rarest circumstances.... Even when members of the occupied community have no religious commitment at all, religious difference tells them that they and other members of their society are not part of the occupier's society, while the need for national cohesion for resistance to an occupation intensifies this sense of difference between the two communities.[91]

Pape's important study also includes an excellent exposé of the background biographies of three suicide terrorists, including that of Mohammad Atta, the leader of the group of terrorists involved in the 9/11 attacks. His intention is to show that Atta, like many suicide terrorists today, is far from the image of a bloodthirsty monster or crazed fanatic bent on nihilism. Indeed, Atta, who was raised in a middle-class family in a respectable neighborhood in Cairo, the son of a lawyer and brother to one sister who is an M.D. and another who is a university professor, was himself intelligent, mild-mannered, and dutiful, a good student who had completed with impressive results a graduate program in engineering at a university in Hamburg, Germany. According to Pape's research, Atta was a devout Muslim who lived conscientiously the dictates of his faith but who in no way showed signs of religious fanaticism as a youth or younger man.[92]

Pape's consideration of Atta's biographical background is helpful in our attempts to come to terms with this particular human person who, in spite of what appear to be healthy family origins with even some degree of social privilege, did end up killing himself in order to kill others. One apparent lacuna, however, does present problems. Pape devotes scant attention to Atta's experience of living outside of his native Arabic culture, that time spent in northern Europe as a young graduate student. In his attempt to account for the drastic change that took place in the life of Atta, Pape cites the pivotal experience of his *haj* to Mecca in 1995. Since Atta would have at least been aware of the U.S. military presence in the Arabian peninsula, the assertion seems to underscore both aspects of his basic theory of suicide terrorism, namely, that it occurs as a response to a perceived threat to national identity sharpened by the experience of religious difference. While Pape's conclusions on identity issues are certainly enlightening and of value to our present study, it is unfortunate that he underestimates the significance of the fact that before embarking on his pilgrimage, Atta had been living, for some time, in a foreign culture that may have seemed to him to be inimical to his own national or ethnic or religious identity. This is of paramount importance since it is beyond doubt that, like Atta, many of the key hijackers or al-Qaeda agents associated with 9/11 shared the experience of living on the fringes of European society. For most of these individuals, it was there, and not in an Arab homeland, much less in Mecca, where radicalization was bred by Islamist elements. As Professor Adrian Karatnycky points out, "Not all the terrorists who attacked America on September 11 were the products of the Islamic Middle East and South Asia. Many became extremists while living in the West, sustained by fanatical mullahs and organizations that operate openly in our midst."[93]

Thomas Friedman, political analyst and noted columnist of the *New York Times,* posed the question in an op-ed piece on January 27, 2002: "Who were the guys in the middle — the killer pilots who went beyond passive support to become suicidal mass murderers?"[94] For him, the personal encounter between these young men and Europe is key to understanding the motives of the suicidal terrorists of 9/11.

According to Friedman, two factors especially need to be considered with regard to the Islamic diaspora in the United States and Europe. The first is the fact that, for a great number of young Muslims living abroad, the exposure to Western society brings with it a barrage of uncertainties. As an Arab friend confided to Friedman, "Suddenly they are thrown into Europe, and there are a whole different set of social rules that shakes their core. They don't know how to adapt because they've never had to, so they become more insular and hold on to their [Islamic] core even more."[95] The second factor points to the fact that Muslim immigrants are often considered perennial outsiders in Europe:

> In America, Muslims can enjoy a fairly rapid transition to citizenship, but in Europe there is no melting pot. "Our problem in Belgium is that there is Islamophobia," said Nordin Maloujahmoum, president of the Muslim Executive Council of Belgium. "Some 54 percent of the population here say they don't believe non-Belgian ethnic groups could ever be real Belgians. A woman wearing a veil here finds it impossible to get a job." What radicalized the September 11 terrorists was not that they suffered from a poverty of food; it was that they suffered from a poverty of dignity. Frustrated by the low standing of Muslim countries in the world, compared with Europe or the United States, and the low standing in which they were personally held where they were living, they were easy pickings for militant preachers who knew how to direct their rage.[96]

The "poverty of dignity" is what we mean when we consider the problem of exclusion in the form of humiliation. It is a reality that is all too evident when we consider the full biographical data of the suicide terrorists of 9/11, and when we acknowledge our own participation in those social structures that foster alienation over integration.

Theology in Big Letters

The story goes that Flannery O'Connor, the great American Catholic fiction writer, was once confronted by a perplexed reader who asked the author why all of her stories seemed to rely so heavily on grotesque and violent imagery. It is said that O'Connor, in her characteristically soft, Southern drawl, replied: "For the almost blind you draw in large and startling figures."[1]

As we have seen, terrorism is clearly the challenge "writ large" for our times. Perhaps what is most terrifying is to imagine a wake-up call written in letters bigger than the figures 9/11.

Part 2 has attempted to investigate the terrorist attacks from many perspectives; it must be remembered, however, that this was all in the service of formulating an appropriate response to those evil acts that brought such suffering to so many innocent people. It is important to recall that intention here, as it could be easy to expect, after these pages, some kind of remedy to the problem, or at least some definitive explanation for why terrorism occurs when and where it does. No such easy answer or explanation is available.

What part 2 does offer is a theological reflection on the human toll of suffering related to the catastrophe by attempting to look at the full picture of the terrorism involved. As was mentioned, one of the first difficulties encountered in analyzing terrorism is the problem of definition, namely, *whose* definition to use? Who decides what constitutes terrorist behavior? While it is utterly clear to anyone with eyes that the terrorism of 9/11 involved planes, buildings, and thousands of innocent lives, what is less apparent are other forms of terrorism that likewise played a part in the destruction of lives: the terrorism involving exclusion that is experienced as humiliation, that can contribute to the dying of the self long before an explosives vest is detonated or a passenger plane is transformed into a live bomb. This does not diminish the severity of the evil perpetrated by the nineteen hijackers and the hundreds of others involved in masterminding the plot to attack the United States. It does, however, indicate that evil is not so easily apportioned all on one side, and, indeed, points to the evil endemic to the view that it can ever be so. Such dualistic thinking in the form of a myriad of fundamentalisms was undeniably present on more than one front. Moreover, a reflection on the historical factors lurking in the background revealed the age-old cycle of violence and revenge, here offering a new way of looking at the problem: revenge as the violence that *blows back* to the earlier offender.

Seeing the fuller picture has been the challenge of part 2. If we heed that challenge, then 9/11 revealed more than could have been seen, over and over again, in the barrage of televised replays of the towers collapsing. And this "more" is indeed a "revelation." Our reflection on the true apocalyptic significance of the day led us away from the cataclysmic imagery of destruction and its attendant fascination with the end times, to the "unveiling" of the sobering reality of our own participation in the violent system of victimization.[2]

What remains, then, if we have truly seen the "big letters" of September 11, 2001, is an awareness of our solidarity in sin. And using the lens that Volf has provided, we can see that this sin in which we share is the putting asunder of what God has joined, the breaking of our created bonds of interconnectedness.

But there is another solidarity that marks our existence, which was also highlighted by 9/11. It is the undeniable solidarity of suffering, which, if we recognize the truth of the other solidarity, is hard to dismiss. We recall that Metz has wondered if suffering may be the only universal category left open to us in our day. Could it be, then, that the Christian response to 9/11 that we are pursuing begins at least in the recognition of the reality of our own interconnectedness which, when sinned against, registers as pain in every human person?

To bring home the point, we recall at the end of part 2 the same disturbing figure who opened it: the *musselman,* the walking dead figure that roamed the confines of the death camps, and we consider here, once again, the meaning of the term. At Auschwitz, the word for the Jewish prisoner completely broken by suffering was "Muslim."

PART THREE

9/12

T HIS FINAL PART is called 9/12. The name seems to indicate an actual point in time, but as was the case with part 1 (9/10) and part 2 (9/11), part 3 is not a single calendar day. It does, however, suggest a time that one day might come. 9/12 points to the promise of the future and, as such, attempts to make a contribution to existing theologies of hope. Thus we can think of the reflections that follow as an articulation of a much needed theology of hope in an age of terror. Hope dispels the fear that settles, dust-like, on the Ground Zeroes of our world with a light that promises a new day and a future securely grounded in the love that is God. Such hope is crucial in the aftermath of catastrophe, when despair seems an easier alternative and the enormity of suffering seems more than we can bear.

> We have already — in the World Wars, in the Holocaust, in famine and genocide, and, less drastically, in the destruction of families and environments — seen more devastation than we can easily cope with. We are losing the capacity to "mourn," to draw on reserves of compassion that help us to reaffirm values, feeling the enormity of pain and death and violence, and feeling it because we have a richer and better hope for men and women. When there is no time or energy to mourn because there is too much to mourn for, hopelessness takes over, accompanied by the lack of a sense of responsibility.[1]

It is apparent from the start, then, that the 9/12 to be investigated in this final part is easily distinguished from the other, more infamous 9/12, which hijacked the world's hopes and trumped up its fears — the violence and retaliation that characterized a chiefly militaristic response in Afghanistan and that later culminated in the invasion and occupation of Iraq. This, sadly, was the 9/12 that commandeered the world's attention. Accordingly, the 9/12 of our investigation, the 9/12 of our hope, is at the same time a call to repentance for this and all those other "days after" that attempt to bypass the true peace of Christ in ways that end up only fortifying the vicious cycle of violence and revenge.

> In the face of denials of guilt and fantasies of innocence, the gospel tells us that we have to repent, to take responsibility for what we have made of our world and beg for vision and strength to do better. In the face of apathy and fatalism, the gospel requires us to ask where difference can be made and what precisely our part might be in realizing this. In the face of obsessions about security and control, the gospel reminds us that we are made in dependence on each other and on our creator.[2]

In brief, it is the Gospel that makes this particular relationship explicit and clear: "For I was hungry and you gave me food, I was thirsty and you gave me something to drink, I was a stranger and you welcomed me, I was naked and you gave me clothing, I was sick and you took care of me, I was in prison and you visited me. . . . Truly I tell you, just as you did it to one of the least of these who are members of my family, you did it to me" (Matt. 25:35–36, 40).

It is a practical, pastoral response to suffering that concerns us. Theologian Daniel J. Louw draws a compelling argument for the recovery of the unique identity of pastoral care as a theological discipline. "In addressing the reality of evil, pastoral care reinterprets divine power as compassionate and creative empowerment, the basis for hopeful activity."[3] With respect to the task of theologizing on catastrophe, Louw insists that we must move away from the explanatory model of the metaphysical paradigm, which attempts to safeguard God's honor in the face of evil, to a more existential and hermeneutical one that aims at a response to tragedy that more abundantly embodies God's presence in the context of human suffering. The matter is clear: "On the 11th of September, 2001, Americans encountered the reality of evil not as a theoretical principle but as a threatening existential reality."[4]

Two main theses guide the investigations that comprise part 3. The first accompanies our consideration of some of the social implications of the Christian doctrine of the Trinity and, specifically, the assertion that a most lasting and authentic Christian response to terrorism cannot rest merely on the notion of our awareness of the Trinity but rather in an understanding of our participation in it.[5] The second claim centers on the theme of forgiveness, specifically, that the call to forgive after 9/11 follows from the recognition of the integrity of our created bonds of interconnectedness, which, when neglected or denied, foster identity formation based on the dualism of "us against them."

CHAPTER NINE

Hope in an Age of Terror

Having already introduced the topics of eschatology and apocalypse in part 2, especially with regard to the ease with which end-of-the-world scenarios are sometimes dangerously misconstrued toward violence, we can see that the category of hope to which we give the label "9/12" is very much a courageous and yet careful hope. We must opt for a "disciplined hope" that, as Kevin Hughes explains, avoids saying too much, risking ideology, or too little, risking despair.[1] We have seen the extreme of overstatement in our investigation of various fundamentalisms. Hope that overstates its case by claiming to know too much is not hope at all but ideological wish fulfillment. We are making a plea for the *apophatic* tradition, which appreciates the infinite mystery that is God, through which "eschatology may learn to speak of hope without overdetermination."[2] The other extreme that a disciplined hope must avoid is the tendency of saying too little. Hughes himself critiques certain postmodern approaches that culminate in variations of "faith without faith" — a deconstructive "hope without hope" arising out of the belief that any concrete hope already contains the threat of violence: "Such a strategy may succeed in removing the violent consequences of certain fundamentalist accounts of hope, but it also seems to erase hope itself altogether."[3] Thus, the disciplined hope we are considering cannot protect itself from saying too much by refusing to say anything at all.

GOD AT GROUND ZERO
AND THE *GROUND ZEROING* OF GOD

We recall the assertion carefully posed in part 1 that catastrophe has sometimes served as a catalyst for more meaningful theological reflection. In an effort to avoid the use of theodical abstractions of evil in our examination of "Glimpses of God" at Auschwitz, we reflected on the words of actual witnesses in their desperate struggle to encounter the living God. But the point of a more existential approach to the problem of evil is actually to *pay attention* to those voices whose echo can still be discerned and to integrate the authority of their witness into our own profound struggles. Only in this way can we claim to be a part of that same biblical tradition of staying faithful in crisis, that is, of remaining committed to the human task of struggling and striving, of searching and sometimes finding.

9/11 happened after Auschwitz. Indeed, living after Auschwitz, if we have integrated that memory, means living in the aftermath of the questions raised at and after that catastrophe. The absent God, the abusive God, the suffering God — these and other impressions of God had to have had some influence on the tenor of our God questioning since that time. Living after Auschwitz means remembering their questions.

In asking *"Wo war Gott am 11 September?"* Michael Albus reminds us that the history of the use of the name of God has been a history of misuse, in New York on 9/11 on the lips of the suicide bombers, as it was in the case of the "God with us" inscribed on the buckles of German soldiers in the last century; because of this "brittleness" of our talk of God, of our religious language, we should watch what we say: "All of their formulas, all of their creeds, all of their sayings, especially when they are so ancient and so worthy, have gone flat on the morning of September 11, 2001. Silence is golden."[4]

Where was God on September 11? For the writers of *Faith and Doubt at Ground Zero,* "what made September 11th different from other dark nights was that so many Americans came away from it asking these fundamental questions at the same time, not only those who witnessed the slaughter at Ground Zero but those who watched in horror at a distance."[5] Some answers bring to mind the familiar torment:

God the Barbarian

I really can't see the purpose why all these people had to die. I can't accept this. Right now, God's not giving me that comfort. We're a community in mourning.... It might sound crazy, but I cursed him. I damned him. I think God could have just ended this all.... I didn't have any love for God the weeks that followed September 11th. It was really hatred. I can't accept this unless I can have an answer as to why it all occurred.... It was too barbaric. It was too barbaric, the way the lives were taken. That wasn't mercy. So I look at him now as a barbarian, and I probably will. And it's a sad situation. I think I'm a good Christian, but I have a different view and image of him now, and I can't replace it with the old image. I can't replace it with the old image.[6]

The Blank Face

The face of God for me was one that was strong, secure, consistent, a face that while at times seemed distant, could more or less be counted on to be there, who kept things in order — the sun would come up, the sun would go down — who'd provide, could be counted on. After September 11th, the face of God was a blank slate for me. God couldn't be counted on in the way I thought God could be counted on. That's what I felt as I stood on Ground Zero. God seemed absent. And it was frightening because the attributes that I had depended upon had all been stripped away. And I was left with nothing but that thing we call faith. But faith in what? I wasn't sure.[7]

God Left Hanging

Since September 11th, people keep asking me, "Where was God?" And they think because I'm a rabbi, I have answers. And I actually think that my job as a rabbi is to help them live with those questions. If God's ways are mysterious, live with the mystery. It's upsetting. It's scary. It's painful. It's deep. And it's interesting. No plan. That's what mystery is. It's all of those things. You want plan? Then tell me about plan. But if you're going to tell me about how the plan saved you, you better also be able to explain how the plan killed them. And the test of that has to do with going and saying it to the person who just buried someone and look in their eyes and tell them God's plan was to blow your loved one apart. Look at them and tell them that God's plan was that their children should go to bed every night for the rest of their lives without a parent. And if you can say that, well, at least you're honest. I don't worship the same God, but that at least has integrity. It's just too easy. That's my problem with the answer. Not that I think they're being inauthentic when people say it or being dishonest, it's just too damn easy. It's easy because it gets God off the hook. And it's easy because it gets their religious beliefs off the hook. And right now, everything is on the hook.[8]

God the Un-American

I cling to a very noble image of God, a majestic God. Our anthems are basically hymns to this majestic God who blesses America with every-thing. But September 11th killed that God for me because there was no way to have a majestic God, a God who controlled everything. There was no way to have a God who understood reward and punishment, fair or unfair, who felt that America should be blessed above other nations because we were good people. There was a God on September 11th who didn't even mind that God's own name could be used as the final prayer of a suicide hijacker as he plowed into a building. We needed, and I know I needed, to have another God to turn to at that moment, or there was going to be no God.[9]

We have considered the limitations of a theology of suffering that attempts to justify God's goodness in the face of evil. And yet perhaps it can be said that something of the theodical impulse always remains, if only as a reflex, whenever horrendous suffering is encountered. Perhaps the question "Why, God?" necessarily characterizes the human experience of chaos and suffering as an immediate reaction, even though we have asked it before, and even though we may know better. Perhaps this "interruption" experience of suffering must always remain, if only in the form of a cry, even after our experiences of catastrophe can no longer sustain the belief of a God out there who should have known better, let alone of a God whose very name can be used to justify killing.

We began this study with a meditation on dust, calling it an apt symbol for the pervasiveness of death and destruction that infiltrated the atmosphere of Ground Zero. But there were other profound and unforgettable images of 9/11, and one in particular suggests itself as a kind of countersymbol to the dust that is death which has already been pondered.

One of the most impossible and memorable images of that day were people leaping out of the windows, being forced out by the fire behind them, driving them, herding them out the windows. And to see that image of two people — co-workers, strangers I had no idea, but that not knowing made it all the more poignant for me — reaching out for somebody's hand to take your last step, that you would end your life in the hands of a stranger, plummeting thousands of feet to your death.[10]

The sheer humanity of the scene keeps it from being mistaken for nihilism. We are referring here, in a jolting paradox, to an image that represents life. When facing the extreme, strangers reached out for one another. For them the final life-affirming act before the inevitable dust of death was embrace. For many of the passengers awaiting their deaths on hijacked planes, other forms of final embrace could only be made in the form of verbal goodbyes.

Until September 11, 2001, we had no sample of any size to tell us what people were like when they faced certain death. Now, however, we know, thanks to dozens of cell phone calls and beyond any doubt, what men and women do in these last seconds of their lives. They forget themselves as they think of those they love, their spouses and children, their parents and friends. They do not complain or bemoan their fate. Neither do they pray for miraculous deliverance or even for the forgiveness of their sins. They do not think about themselves as they speak their last words. They just want to tell others how much they love them, that they want them to be safe, that they want them to be happy, that their last will and their true testament is one of utter concern for those they cherish, that they break free of the grasp of death and judgment on their lives by giving themselves away so completely that, before time runs out, they are already immersed in the eternal.[11]

There is food here for theological thought. A brief sampling of glimpses of God at Ground Zero allowed us to consider the experience of God's absence in the wake of this catastrophe, just as surely it was done at Auschwitz and at all the many episodes of mass suffering that comprise the annals of enmity, the "9/10" of recent history. But do not these final, poignant images of embrace suggest that other intimations of God are available, those that speak just as much to God's presence and that further imply a kind of *ground-zeroing* of a particular understanding of God? As one rabbi reflects:

Since September 11th, this, for me, that there's something out there and that I'm here, no longer meant anything because every time I thought there was something out there, it turns into inevitably something opposed to me, something I have to define myself against, whether that's God or whether that's a Christian or whether that's a Muslim or whether that's a Buddhist. And that's not my experience. My genuine experience of life is that there is nothing out there, this is all there is. And when you see the seamlessness of it all, that's what I mean by God. Every tradition has that. Every morning three times a day since I'm six years old, five years old, I've been saying, "Hear O Israel, the Lord our God, the Lord is one." Right? It's one of our few creedal statements, right, the Shema. Three times a day since I'm six years old. And 9/11 — if you ask me what did 9/11 really do, it made me understand the truth of that, the truth that everything is one. Not that there's some guy hanging out there who has it all together, who we call One, but that it is all one. We all know it deep down!...We've all had those experiences when we recognize, "Whoa! We're much more connected here." That's

what those firemen had. They recognized. Now, they didn't have time to
think about it, right, because actually, if you think about it, you begin to
create separations. They didn't think about it. All they knew was we're
absolutely connected. We're absolutely connected to the 86th floor. Well,
that's where God is. . . . That's what we mean when we say God. And yet,
these insights of connectedness and oneness, which make us feel so at
home in the world, are so difficult to hold on to. And so inevitably, we
wind up living lives of isolation and loneliness.[12]

Does not this powerful testimony point to the fact that such acts of connection and love challenge and ultimately shatter the false gods of 9/11, the gods
that have been used to break the bonds of interconnection and to thwart the
creative process of differentiation? This includes the gods invoked by malevo-
lent interpretations of *jihad,* as well as by the very notion of crusade; the gods
behind the allure of heavenly reward, however religiously construed, and the
gods that encourage killing in order to collect it. In short, isn't the god that can
be so easily hijacked, the god of us against them, the god aligned to nation-
state or ethnicity or even to religion, isn't this the very god whose people we
can no longer afford to be?

The idea is not new. In the midst of that other catastrophe, Dietrich
Bonhoeffer pondered the possibility of a "religionless Christianity." For him
interpreting in a "religious" sense means to interpret metaphysically and
individualistically,[13] that is to say, to focus on the being question, with an eye
toward the "out there," for my own private spiritual gain "in here." But already
in 1944, Bonhoeffer could perceive that "neither of these is relevant to the biblical message or to the man of today."[14] What is most important for us here, as
Bonhoeffer ponders the question from within the confines of imprisonment,
is the question he asks about the nonreligious future of Christianity.

How do we speak of God — without religion, i.e., without the temporally conditioned presuppositions of metaphysics, inwardness, and so on?
How do we speak (or perhaps we cannot now even "speak" as we used
to) in a "secular" way about "God"? In what way are we "religionless-
secular" Christians, in what way are we the ἐκ-κλεσία, those who are
called forth, not regarding ourselves from a religious point of view as
specially favoured, but rather as belonging wholly to the world?[15]

Could it be that the enduring image of embrace before death that we have
seen at Ground Zero does in some way hint at the future of Christianity that

Bonhoeffer was beginning to see on the horizon? This does not suggest another round of a program of demythologization whereby Christian doctrines are merely updated for sophisticated believers. It rather points to a movement of these truths to the center of human existence, wherein they can be lived rather than merely held in the form of propositional truths. As we shall see, the doctrine of the Trinity, understood in this vein, may very well point to the foundational Christian praxis of living out our essential interconnectedness in a nonreligious way.

PORTRAITS OF *GRACE*

We recall that our investigation in part 2 included a reflection on several excerpts from the *New York Times*'s "Portraits of Grief," the long-running, daily columns commemorating the victims of the terrorist attacks that were presented, not as death notices, but as stories of lives cut short. Here now, other portraits.[16]

MARK BINGHAM, to his mother

> I want you to know I love you very much, and I'm calling you from the plane. We've been taken over.

MELISSA HARRINGTON HUGHES, to her father

> I love you too, Dad. You have to do me a favor. You have to call Sean and tell him where I am and tell him that I love him.

The message she left on Sean's answering machine

> Sean, it's me. I just wanted to let you know I love you and I'm stuck in this building in New York. A plane hit the building, or bomb went off. We don't know, but there's lots of smoke and I just wanted you to know that I love you always. Bye.

WELLES CROWTHER, to his mother

> Mom, this is Welles. I want you to know that I'm okay.

As told by those he rescued

> I see this incredible hero, running back and forth and saving the day. In his mind, he had a duty to do — to save people. (Judy Wein)

He's definitely my guardian angel — no ifs, ands or buts — because without him, we would be sitting there, waiting [until] the building came down. (Ling Young)

NICK GERSTLE, *on rescuing*

I was scared, but at the same time there was so much camaraderie you didn't feel the fear. You're under the rubble, you hear the [police officers] saying, "Don't let us die, don't let us die." I'm thinking, "I'm down here with you. If you go, we all go."

YVETTE WASHINGTON-MONTAGNE, *a 911 operator on 9/11*

You had people begging you to save them. The pleas became more and more intense, with men crying and begging you to tell them what you should do.

Sgt. William Butler, on Yvette Washington-Montagne

After listening to the calls she handled that day, the way she handled herself and cared for the people on the other end of the phone, I'm just struck by [how] compassionate and kind she was to people.

ISAAC HO'OPI'I, *Pentagon cop*

If you can hear me, head toward my voice. If you can hear me, head toward my voice.

William "Wayne" Sinclair, on Isaac Ho'opi'i

He kept saying that over and over. And that is what guided us out of the smoke and fire.

EDGAR EMERY

"If you can finish chemo, then you can get down those steps," Mr. Emery told an exhausted Ms. Foodim, who had just completed a round of chemotherapy. When they finally reached a packed elevator on the 78th floor, Mr. Emery made sure everyone got aboard. He squeezed Ms. Foodim's shoulder and let the door close in front of him.[17]

EDMUND MCNALLY

Edmund McNally, director of technology for Fiduciary, called his wife, Liz, as the floor began buckling. Mr. McNally hastily recited his life insurance policies and employee bonus programs. "He said that I meant the world to him and he loved me," Mrs. McNally said, and they exchanged what they thought were their last goodbyes.

Then Mrs. McNally's phone rang again. Her husband sheepishly reported that he had booked them on a trip to Rome for her 40th birthday. He said, "Liz, you have to cancel that," Mrs. McNally said.[18]

LINDA PERRY THORPE

(Eric Thorpe managed to get a call to his wife, Linda Perry Thorpe, who was waiting to hear from him at a neighbor's apartment. No one spoke from the tower. Instead Ms. Thorpe and the neighbor listened to the ambient noise.)

One man went berserk, screaming. I couldn't understand that he was saying anything. He just lost it. I heard another person soothing him, saying, "It's O.K., it'll be O.K."[19]

TOM MCGINNIS, to his wife, Iliana

"Are you O.K., yes or no?" she demanded.

"We're on the 92nd floor in a room we can't get out of," Mr. McGinnis said. . . . "I love you," Mr. McGinnis said. "Take care of Caitlin."

Mrs. McGinnis was not ready to hear a farewell. "Don't lose your cool," she urged. "You guys are so tough, you're resourceful. You guys are going to get out of there."

"You don't understand," Mr. McGinnis said. "There are people jumping from the floors above us."

It was 10:25. The fire raged along the west side of the 92nd floor. People fell from windows. Mr. McGinnis again told her he loved her and their daughter, Caitlin.

"Don't hang up," Mrs. McGinnis pleaded.

"I got to get down on the floor," Mr. McGinnis said.[20]

MYCHAL JUDGE, O.F.M.

Death certificate # 0001:
the first official casualty of the World Trade Center

(On September 10, less than twenty-four hours before he died, Judge happened to rededicate Fire Commissioner Von Essen's old firehouse in the Bronx. The department has the ceremony on videotape.)

"Good days, bad days," says Judge, clad in a bright white robe. "But never a boring day on this job. You do what God has called you to do. You show up, you put one foot in front of the other, and you do your job, which is a mystery and a surprise. You have no idea, when you get in that rig, what God is calling you to. But he needs you . . . *so keep going.* Keep supporting each other. Be kind to each other. Love each other. Work together. You love the job. We all do. What a blessing that is."[21]

Such portraits of grace represent practical responses to suffering. There are many more such portraits of quotidian courage and spontaneous self-donation that represent an actual living out of Christ's call to care for any "one of the least of these who are members of my family" (Matt. 25:40). This is a pastoral participation in the divine compassion — "and when he saw him, he was moved with pity" (Luke 10:33) — that comprises the real community of disciples in the world known as "the Body of Christ." God at Ground Zero was seen in those who spontaneously and graciously moved out of themselves in self-giving to suffering others.

THE END OF FAITH?

The title of this section questions the central claim made in a recent bestseller by the same name. In it, author Sam Harris argues that 9/11 has signaled the beginning of the end of faith. At first glance Harris's claim may seem to run parallel with Bonhoeffer's observation cited above. In actual fact, the two have quite dissimilar ideas of just what has, is, or needs to be coming to an end. Part of the problem is a confusion over terms. Harris seems to use interchangeably the words religion, belief, and faith, whereas Bonhoeffer, as we have seen, wanted to purify faith of religion's emphases on metaphysics and inwardness.

Harris is not a theologian. He is a neuroscientist whose interests lie in the neural basis of belief, disbelief, and uncertainty. His work is mentioned here only to comment on the popular reception it has enjoyed in certain circles,[22] and to better distinguish it from Bonhoeffer's similar sounding yet substantially different prediction.

Harris's thesis is familiar: much of the problem of violence in the world is due to the nonrational claims of the world's religions, which have fostered uncritical faith in dogma and literal interpretations of sacred texts. His analysis of religiously inspired violence becomes more extreme with his charge that it is precisely the liberal notion of religious tolerance that has effectively distanced religious truth claims from rational critique based on evidence. "The very ideal of religious tolerance — born of the notion that every human being should be free to believe whatever he wants about God — is one of the principal forces driving us toward the abyss."[23]

One problem with Harris's argument is that he fails to acknowledge that the move toward privatized beliefs of God in effect allowed the enlightened nation-state to reign supreme as a kind of "god" to which citizens owed their ultimate allegiance. As David Cunningham explains: "A generic portrait of God can easily be absorbed by the state, because — as the Enlightenment thinkers testified — it can be accepted by 'all rational people' (though of course they left the concept of *rationality* quite uninterrogated). But the triune God forms Christians into the Body of Christ, which is the only real rival to the dominant social body of the modern age — the state."[24]

Again, the objective here is not to engage the thought of Harris beyond its usefulness as an indicator of one particular response to the problem of terrorism in our time.[25] For our purposes, it is enough to acknowledge that Harris is representative of those who see, or at least hope to see in the future, the demise of faith-based religion and the coming of a time when humanity's quest for the sacred will more fully thrive in the form of a deeply rational spirituality.

Admittedly, a more nuanced usage of the terms "faith," "belief," and "religion" would probably soften the blow of Harris's total rejection of faith.[26] To be fair, in places Harris seems to be making observations that sound a great deal like Bonhoeffer's well-known critique of "stop-gap" faith. Harris writes, for instance, that "faith is what credulity becomes when it finally achieves escape velocity from the constraints of terrestrial discourse — constraints like reasonableness, internal coherence, civility, and candor."[27] Yet Bonhoeffer, we recall, was specifically interested in safeguarding the integrity of Christian faith so that it could allow Christ a central place in the lives of believers "come of age." His critique, made sixty years earlier, may actually offer more insight into the problem of religious-inspired violence in the context of terrorism.

Resituating Bonhoeffer's plea in the context of the current problem of terrorism is not such an outlandish proposition, especially if we consider some of his last writings. His collected prison letters include an "Outline for a Book," wherein he plans to explore in the first chapter a "stock-taking" of Christianity:

Nature was formerly conquered by spiritual means, with us by technical organization of all kinds. Our immediate environment is not nature, as formerly, but organization. But with this protection from nature's menace there arises a new one — through organization itself. But the spiritual force is lacking. The question is: What protects us against the menace of organization? Man is again thrown back on himself. He has managed to deal with everything, only not himself. He can insure against everything, only not against man. In the last resort it all turns on man.[28]

Certainly the same "immediate environment" that Bonhoeffer describes in terms of man-against-man is operative in the context of religiously inspired terrorism. But the more compelling observation arises when we consider this predicament in conjunction with his critique of religion's tendency, through its otherworldly focus and tendency toward inwardness, to weaken Christianity's spiritual vitality. It is clear that, for Bonhoeffer, religion that encounters God as an abstract belief has pushed God out of the realm of human affairs and into the realm of superfluity. That was the predicament in which Bonhoeffer found himself, and he risked asking the penetrating question of why Christianity was not making a real difference in his own world torn asunder by war and atrocity. Crucially, what we are asserting here is that it is precisely the superfluous God of abstraction that has been so often and easily "used" by fundamentalist terrorists and counterterrorists alike. What is so desperately needed, in our day as much as in his, is the courage to get to the heart of Christian faith for men and women "come of age." This necessitates asking the God question with urgency in our own time of suffering, while avoiding the allure of rational theodicy's easy answers.

Who is God? Not in the first place an abstract belief in God, in his omnipotence, etc. That is not a genuine experience of God, but a partial extension of the world. Encounter with Jesus Christ. The experience that a transformation of all human life is given in the fact that "Jesus is there only for others." His "being there for others" is the experience of transcendence. It is only the "being there for others," maintained till death, that is the ground of his omnipotence, omniscience, and omnipresence. Faith is participation in this being of Jesus (incarnation, cross, and resurrection). Our relation to God is not a "religious" relationship to the highest, most powerful and best Being imaginable — that is not authentic transcendence — but our relation to God is a new life in "existence for others" through participation in the being of Jesus.[29]

The key concept here is the notion of faith as *participation*.[30] Bonhoeffer is defining the experience of transcendence in terms of participating in the very being of Jesus, a reality whose real presence is manifest in the transformation of our existence, from self-centered to other-centered lives. Authentic transcendence is not a matter of aligning oneself on the side of the highest and most powerful God. It is rather a matter of participating in the lowly and most humble example of Jesus the foot-washer, God in human form. In the post-9/11 world wherein terrorism writes in big letters, Bonhoeffer's plea for religion-less Christianity cannot be so easily dismissed. For Christians, participation in the mystery of God has this unmistakable hallmark: the enhanced ability to love, which reveals a new dimension of what it means to be.

THEODICY REVISITED

Bearing in mind Bonhoeffer's call for authentic transcendence, characterized in terms of actual participation in the being of Jesus, we are justified in taking up again the theodicy question — not, of course, framed as a philosophical proof from within the metaphysical paradigm, but rather as an existential one situated within the framework of pastoral theology. As we have seen, the question of God and suffering never goes away, and, we have stressed, all theology must finally be answerable to it. We will always try to understand the reality and character of God in the face of evil and from the midst of our own anguish and suffering. Theology in our time must remain "theodicy-sensitive" in this broader sense, if it is to engage men and women in their most urgent concerns in a way that makes a real and salvific difference in their lives.

The topic of participation also allows us to take seriously the option of a more practical theology that attends to suffering people with a message of hope. Daniel Louw suggests that theology's rational and intellectual dimensions (*fides quaerens intellectum*) must be complemented by the aims of practical theology wherein faith seeks different ways of communicating and acting (*fides quaerens verbum et actum*) in order to be a faith that seeks to foster hope (*fides quaerens spem*).[31] Re-situating the theodicy question within a pastoral hermeneutics thus necessitates "the recovery of God's embodiment in concrete actions of care (*diakonia*), which aim at reconstruction and transformation in the face of violent acts whose purpose is to violate human dignity through hatred."[32] Practical and pastoral theology might well be understood as the discipline where religious belief, tradition, and practice meet contemporary experiences, questions, and actions to yield an imaginative interplay between idea and action.[33]

Such a practical approach to the persistent theodical question, focusing on concrete actions of care and service (of which there were countless examples in the tragedy of 9/11, as we have seen) elucidates Bonhoeffer's view of Christianity as participation in Christ. It is important to recall here that our given conceptions of God's power affect both our experience of and response to evil and suffering. In the hopeful time-space of 9/12, which allows for an understanding of our participation in the life of God, we are proposing a reinterpretation of the theistic conception of omnipotence, domination, and control in favor of one which highlights God's relationality, communality, and fidelity.[34] And the challenge to understand God's power in this way gets to the heart of the problem of violence.

> What nation, through power alone, can ensure world peace? There is no sword that can cut away all forms of danger and distress when relationships are involved. Where persons are concerned, both human and divine, the qualities of empathy, of compassion, and of persuasion are the forms of power that are finally transformative.[35]

Thus, in order to address the reality of evil, "pastoral care interprets divine power as compassionate and creative empowerment, the basis of hopeful activity."[36]

It is worth noting that the topic of pastoral theology is of considerable importance among many hermeneutical theologians today. Commenting on the papal office, Santiago Zabala offers an interesting challenge:

> If the Catholic Church is to have a future as an institution in the twenty-first century, it will require a papacy that is not above the world, as the head of the Church, but in the Church as, in the words of Pope Gregory the Great, "the servant of the servants of God." The Catholic Church no longer needs primacy in law and honor; it needs a constructive pastoral primacy, in the sense of a spiritual guide, concentrating on the duties required by the present.... An immeasurable number of Christians, in communities and groups throughout the world, are living out an authentic ecumenism centered on the gospel regardless of any resistance by the ecclesiastical hierarchy: the challenge of the future will be to convince the Church that charity must take the place of discipline.[37]

It is interesting to consider how a reconception of God's power in terms of compassionate relationality could actually affect the way that the church envisions and engages in its offices of power and administration. One wonders if the topic of collegial models of church governance, the subject of so much hopeful discussion at Vatican II, has receded in the wake of a resurgence of more traditional structures of control.

CHAPTER TEN

Pursuing the Personal

In rejecting the explanatory model of theodicy, variously called post-Leibnizian or Enlightenment theodicy, we observed that the God presupposed in such theodical endeavors is not Trinitarian, and therefore cannot be considered the God of Christian tradition. Any serious reflection on the problem of God and suffering and evil in the world must take heed of the foundational Christian experience and claim that God is Trinity and that God's relationality cannot be overlooked. The notion of participating in God is firmly rooted in the Christian awareness, *through experience,* of God as Trinity. Indeed, as Paul Fiddes explains, the ancient doctrine arose from the demands of actual experience and pastoral need.

> When the early church fathers developed the doctrine of the Trinity they were not painting by numbers; they were finding concepts to express an *experience.* That is, they were trying to articulate the richness of the personality of God that they had found in the story of salvation and in their own experience. It was not any longer sufficient to say "the Lord" when they spoke a blessing in worship (Num. 6:24–26); they must speak of the love of the Father, the grace of the Lord Jesus and the fellowship of the Holy Spirit (1 Cor. 13:14) [*sic*], although they knew that the ultimate demand on their lives must come from one Lord. They began with God at work in salvation, healing human life.[1]

That this foundational experience of salvation was bound up in the *personal* healing presence and activity of Jesus Christ meant that speaking of God — which would ultimately develop into the doctrine of the Trinity — employed the language of person. Indeed, it is a thoroughly Trinitarian Christology that allows for a most meaningful discussion on God and suffering. By pursuing the personal in our reflection on this problem, we cannot avoid the question of how God personally relates to those who are suffering and in need. As we have attempted to make clear, the answer to that question lies in the examples of countless acts of self-giving rescue and care that so convincingly embodied the love of God at Ground Zero.

It is interesting to acknowledge here, as we turn to a theological investigation of Trinitarian personhood, a further insight from Elaine Scarry, whose definition of war was so instructive in chapter 8. According to Scarry, violence against another person is both caused by and indicative of a failure to fully imagine the other as a real person:

> There exists a circular relation between the infliction of pain and the problem of "otherness." The difficulty of imagining others is both the cause of and the problem displayed by the action of injuring. The action of injuring occurs precisely because we have trouble believing in the reality of other persons. It displays our perceptual disability.[2]

Because our capacity to injure other people is greater than our capacity to imagine them, the solution to violence against others involves not only imagining others but also "disimagining ourselves."[3]

Reflection on God in the Christian tradition cannot ignore the centrality of the category of "person" in its theological formulations. One theologian whose work has focused on the essential importance of the concept of personhood in Christian theology is Orthodox systematic theologian John D. Zizioulas, Metropolitan of Pergamon in the Ecumenical Patriarchate of Constantinople. Zizioulas's insights are particularly relevant to our study because he takes seriously the condition of enmity in a world where otherness and communion do not coexist.

ZIZIOULAS AND THE CAPPADOCIAN CONTRIBUTION

Zizioulas insists that Trinity is not about accepting a theoretical proposition about God; rather, it describes something profound about the dynamic relationship that exists between human beings, indeed, between all of creation and the living God.[4] Central to this thinking is the concept of "person," the notion that gets to the heart of Zizioulas's Trinitarian theology.

Zizioulas explores the influence of the Cappadocian fathers — Basil the Great, bishop of Caesarea (c. 330–79); Gregory of Nazianzus, bishop of Sassima, and later archbishop of Constantinople (c. 330–89/90); and the younger brother of Basil, Gregory, bishop of Nyssa (c. 335–94), and their friend, Amphilochius, bishop of Iconium (340/45–?) in the development of the doctrine of the Trinity in order to highlight how the concept of person became an ontological category. This contribution, in Zizioulas's estimation, stands as the greatest philosophical achievement in patristic thought.[5] In essence, the momentous achievement of the fathers came in their confrontation with the problem of the ancient ontological monism of Plato on the one hand, and the problem of the gulf between God and the material world of the Gnostic world-view on the other. The answer to the problem of how to know God came from pastoral theology: the bishops[6] approached God "ecclesially," that is, from the eucharistic experience of the ecclesial community — *ecclesial being*. That is to say, they understood that God is known through personal relationships and love. Eventually, this eucharistic experience of ecclesial being would lead them to conceive of God's being in terms of the primacy of personhood.[7]

> It would be unthinkable to speak of the "one God" before speaking of the God who is "communion," that is to say, of the Holy Trinity. The Holy Trinity is a *primordial* ontological concept and not a notion which is added to the divine substance or rather which follows it.... The substance of God, "God," has no ontological content, no true being, apart from communion.[8]

It was the biblical understanding of creation that provided the Cappadocians with the conceptual language needed to distinguish their views of nature from that of classical Greek thought, chiefly the Platonic understanding of human nature as an ideal humanity, of which every human being is an image, or the Aristotelian view, understood in terms of the substratum of the human species from which various human beings emerge.[9] Of course, the Cappadocians stressed the biblical position that human existence is a *created* existence, that is, one with a beginning, and should therefore not be made into a metaphysical principle.[10]

Zizioulas explores the contrast between the experience of ecclesial being and the limitations set by this Greek understanding of being as one[11] — specifically the impossibility of attaining the freedom to become one's own person (and consequently, the impossibility of acknowledging the integrity of difference) — which prevented the concept of personhood from taking on unique permanence.[12] The genius of the theologian pastors lies in their ability to have united freedom and ontology, that is, in their ability to join the biblical view of *creatio ex nihilo* with the Greek understanding of the *being* of man understood in terms of his abiding essence. In so doing they articulated the conception of person with its absolute and ontological content, a notion, once again, "born historically from the endeavor of the Church to give ontological expression to its faith in the Triune God."[13] As Patricia Fox explains: "Within a biblical world view, being is caused by *someone*. And the personal causation of all being means that particularity can be understood as causative and not derivative in ontology."[14] Thus for the Cappadocian fathers the particular was not secondary to being; the particular was free, and they could understand it this way because the world's being was contingent on the freedom of a person — God. For patristic thought *freedom* is the "cause" of being:

> The Cappadocian Fathers for the first time in history introduced into the being of God the concept of cause (*aition*), in order to attach it significantly not to the "one" (God's nature) — but to a *person*, the Father. By distinguishing carefully and persistently between the nature of God and God as the Father they thought that *what causes God to be is the Person of the Father,* not the one divine substance. By so doing they gave to the person ontological priority, and thus freed existence from the logical necessity of substance, of the "self-existent."[15]

This most critical point of patristic theology, namely, that God exists on account of a person, the Father, and not on account of a substance, and that the Father is the cause of personhood in God's being, has profound anthropological consequences, and it is these with which we are most concerned in the present investigation. Freedom, and not necessity to substance, constitutes true being, for ourselves as for God. But this means that our freedom, like God's, is the freedom to love. "True being comes only from the free person, from the person who loves freely — that is, who freely affirms his being, his identity, by means of an event of communion with other persons."[16] Thus, patristic thought affirms two foundational theses with regard to the being of God: that there is no true being without communion, and, that true communion must come from a free and concrete person (*hypostasis*) and lead to free and concrete persons (*hypostases*). This points to the fact that God, "as Father and not as substance, perpetually confirms through 'being' His free will to exist. And it is precisely His Trinitarian existence that constitutes this confirmation: the Father out of love — that is, freely — begets the Son and brings forth the Spirit."[17] For us, this makes a powerful statement with regard to the *imago Dei,* what it means to be created in the image and likeness of God whose freedom is grounded in the priority of personhood over substance, that is, the priority of the Father who is the cause (love in freedom) of both the generation of the Son and the procession of the Spirit.

The basis of ontology is the person: just as God "is" what He is in His nature, "perfect God," only as person, so too man in Christ is "perfect man" only as hypostasis, as person, that is, as freedom and love. The perfect man is consequently only he who is authentically a person, that is, he who subsists, who possesses a "mode of existence" which is constituted as being, *in precisely the manner in which God also subsists as being* — in the language of human existence this is what a "hypostatic union" signifies.[18]

This amounts to the Christological proclamation to humanity that human nature can be assumed and hypostasized similarly in terms of a relationship with God. "Thanks to Christ man can henceforth himself 'subsist,' can affirm his existence as personal not on the basis of the immutable laws of his nature, but on the basis of a relationship with God which is identified with what Christ in freedom and love possesses as Son of God with the Father."[19] The freedom that results from this hypostasis of the person is precisely a freedom from those conditions that result from the ontological necessity of biological hypostasis — individualism and death.[20] It is, moreover, freedom that is love, inasmuch as love hypostasizes God.

> It thus becomes evident that the only exercise of freedom in an ontological manner is *love*. The expression "God is love" (1 John 4:16) signifies that God "subsists" as Trinity, that is, as person and not as substance. Love is not an emanation or "property" of the substance of God . . . but is *constitutive* of His substance, i.e., it is that which makes God what He is, the one God. Thus love ceases to be a qualifying — i.e., secondary — property of being and becomes *the supreme ontological predicate*. Love as God's mode of existence "hypostasizes" God, *constitutes* His being.[21]

Zizioulas elaborates on an important anthropological implication of the patristic claim that the Father is the cause of personhood in God's being and that love is constitutive of God's being. It is impossible to conceive of personal existence as self-existent, self-sufficient, or self-explicable.

> A person is always *a gift from someone*. It is demonic to attribute one's own personal identity to oneself or to an a-personal something. The notion of self-existence is a substantialist notion, not a personal one. Persons have a "cause," because they are the outcome of love and freedom, and they owe their being who they are, their distinctive otherness as persons, to another

person. Ontologically, persons are givers and recipients of personal identity. Causality in Trinitarian existence reveals to us a personhood which
is constituted by love.[22]

OTHERNESS *AND* RELATION

Further anthropological consequences come to the fore in our consideration
of Trinity on 9/12. These not only get to the heart of Zizioulas's enthusiastic
endorsement of the Greek fathers' insistence on the ontological priority of
personhood but also further explicate this answer with regard to the theological
foundation we are articulating for the gracious and spontaneous acts of self-
giving that alone serve as the most adequate Christian response to 9/11. In
addition, by briefly considering these consequences, we may be able to discern
a useful interpretive key through which we may better comprehend some of
the complexities of the disturbing reality of enmity that have been explored in
parts 1 and 2.

The considerations that follow are rooted in the understanding, central to
patristic theology and to this study, that we must be careful always to allow
God's way of being to reveal to us true personhood and not the other way
around — the latter approach, according to Zizioulas, typifying more the tendency of existential philosophy, which is helpful only in pointing out the tragic
experience of personhood: that we as human beings are discontent with who
we are and long for true personhood. "It is precisely because we realize the
tragedy of our personal existence that we cannot transpose our concept of person to the being of God."[23] We thus conceive of our personhood in the light of
our faith in the triune God. This is the proper direction implied by the *imago
Dei,* namely, that we derive a right notion of the person from our experience
of God's presence: "personal presence *qua presence* is something that *cannot
be extrapolated from created existence.* It is a presence that seems to come to
us from outside this world — which makes the notion of person, if properly
understood, perhaps the only notion that can be applied to God without the
danger of anthropomorphism."[24]

It is fair to note a certain resonance here between Zizioulas and Levinas with
regard to the primacy of otherness. In fact, Zizioulas directly credits Levinas
as being one thinker in the past century who takes seriously enough the category of otherness and the necessity to safeguard absolute alterity in defending
constitutive otherness in the face of totalizing sameness in ontology.[25] As we
have seen, for Levinas, consciousness of the other — because consciousness is

always at the same time consciousness of something — is itself a process of turning the other into an object. "Levinas insists on the departure from the *Il y a,* that is, being in general, which is the equivalent of "substance" and which enslaves the Other."[26] The absolute alterity of the other precludes the "same" from attempting to integrate every other into itself as a totality: the other has priority even over consciousness because it is the other that provokes consciousness to begin with. "The identity of the same in the *ego* (*je*) comes to it despite itself from the outside, as an election or an inspiration, in the form of the uniqueness of someone assigned."[27]

But one significant difference between Zizioulas and Levinas does remain. As Zizioulas points out, with Levinas there is no way to reconcile otherness with communion. Indeed, Levinas rejects the notion of communion because it is a threat to otherness by sameness and generality. Communion, for Levinas, is tantamount to the subjection of otherness to unity. In place of comprehension and communion, Levinas regards expression, invocation, prayer, and ethics as meeting points with the other.

> Levinas tried to escape from the totalitarianism of Being with the help of a metaphysic of transcendence expressed with the term *Infini:* in the face of the Other the "I" experiences or realizes or undergoes a transcendence towards the infinite through an adventure into the unknown (*aller sans savoir ou*). Being is thus replaced with *Desire,* which is distinguished from *Need* (*Besoin*) in that, as infinite, it knows of no satisfaction.[28]

But a desire that cannot be satisfied begs the question of whether or not the other does actually serve as the ultimate destination of desire. As Zizioulas rightly points out, for Levinas, the other, which is never a "term" and is never capable of stopping the movement of desire, is not the destination of desire — the desire itself is. "For Levinas the ultimate destination of Desire is not the Other but the Desire of the Other."

> Since the Other we infinitely desire is not a particular being, in whom our Desire would ultimately rest, what we are left with in the end is nothing but our own Desire. Given that the Other we infinitely desire is one who attracts our Desire but does not himself desire us or any other, otherness finally evaporates in a Desire without the Other.[29]

For the Greek fathers, however, God is the ultimate destination of desire because God is both the term of the desire and the cause of the desire. "For the Fathers, therefore, God, as the Other *par excellence,* is the 'object' of endless desire — a desire that knows no satiety — but at the same time the ultimate destination of Desire, its rest (στάσις)."[30] As the Greek fathers understood it, at the very heart of otherness there exists an event of communion. Though Levinas rejects relational otherness for fear of totalizing reduction, which is itself an instance of violence, patristic thought avoids that danger by proposing a relational otherness that is caused by the other and rests in the other.

> The otherness of the Other does not dissolve in sameness through communion, because relations do not take place at the level of the *logos of being* (= substance), but at the level of the *mode of being* (= personhood). . . . If otherness is conceived in terms of personhood, it does not involve distance, rupture and secession or "deconstruction." By being "other" and at the same time relational, the person differentiates by affirming rather than rejecting the "other." In personhood there is no "self," for in it every "self" exists only in being affirmed as "other" by an "other," not by *contrasting* itself with some "other."[31]

Such patristic views have enormous ramifications for a theology of hope on 9/12. Through this investigation of the Greek fathers,[32] we have come to appreciate the centrality of the idea of the personal causation of all being, that is, that being is caused by someone and not derived from the necessity of substance. As a result, freedom constitutes true being, in ourselves as in God, but, as in God, our freedom must be the freedom to love. But love here is not a disposition of the self toward an "other." Love, rather, is a gift — one that comes "from the 'other' as an affirmation of one's uniqueness in an indispensable relation through which one's particularity is secured ontologically."[33] This means that there is no true being without communion because far from threatening otherness, relation in love generates otherness. As with God, true communion comes from a person and leads to persons. Fear of the other — the enmity, exclusion, expulsion, and even elimination of the other that are the long days of 9/10 and 9/11 — is overcome only by love — that is, by "acceptance and affirmation by the Other and of the Other as indispensable for our own otherness."[34] Thus, if "perfect love casts out fear" (1 John 4:18), then no "other," not even the terrorist other, can ultimately exist as my enemy.

The challenge of deriving an adequate understanding of "person" through this investigation of God's personhood in Trinity calls to mind another term for which definition proved to be something of a challenge — "terrorism." In fact, the notion of person we have before us may end up pointing to additional nuances of meaning that were absent from the more legalistic definition of terrorism provided in part 2. Thus, what we know about person from the foregoing patristic perceptions of God's personhood — one who is *other* and at the same time *relational,* and therefore one who differentiates by *affirming* rather than *rejecting* the other — may cast some light upon further insights into the experience of terror. We can say that terror is *the condition of isolation from others resulting in the loss of freedom to be fully other, which is a distortion of the created communion and otherness of personhood that may result in the wholly ungodly desire to destroy the other.*

PARTICIPATING IN GOD

It is a thoroughly participative model of Trinity that best secures the hope envisioned as 9/12. "The point of Trinitarian language," Paul Fiddes observes, "is not to provide an example to copy but to draw us into participation in God, out of which human life can be transformed."[35] Zizioulas's exposition of Trinitarian personhood allows for this view of engagement in God because his theological anthropology culminates in ecclesiology, the two merging in his understanding of ultimate reality as "ecclesial being." Since God's being is an "event of communion," "ecclesial being is bound to the very being of God."[36] In brief, for Zizioulas, the Trinity is revealed only in the Church — the reality wherein sonship in the Spirit is practiced, that is, "the constant movement of filial grace from the Father, giving his Son to us in the Spirit, and as a return of this by us, 'giving grace' to him by offering back to him his Son in his incarnate, sacrificial and risen state as the head of a body comprising all of us and all that exists (τά πάντα)."[37] The church ethos is where the Trinity is seen; this is more than ethics — it is an entire ethos of new life initiated in baptism and renewed in Eucharist.[38]

A concern regarding Zizioulas's notion of ecclesial being calls for consideration. In terms of our focus on the problems of enmity and violence, Zizioulas does provide a helpful and thought-provoking interpretation of sin understood primarily as a breakdown of our created interconnectedness, a living out of our innate fear of the other that leads to the affirmation of the self through the rejection of the other.[39] We are right to wonder, however, whether or not this view of theological anthropology provides an adequate doctrine of sin, one that sufficiently takes heed of the true gravity of evil and the enormity of suffering in our lives. In other words, what other factors — physical, social, economic — play a part in distorting personhood other than "fear of the other"? What of those dimensions of evil probed in part 1 — the evil of Auschwitz: those corporate structures of evil, for example, that could produce the *muselmann* who has appeared and reappeared in this present study? What of disease, human frailty, and mental illness, or the unrelenting trauma of natural disaster and man-made catastrophe? Edward Russell criticizes Zizioulas for undervaluing our createdness, the very physicality of existence, which also must be incorporated into theological anthropology, most likely through nontheological factors such as the role of narrative and the sociohistorical situatedness of personhood.[40] Russell also correctly points out that such weak doctrines of sin often end up underestimating the brokenness or rupture of the cross. Although baptism is the great symbol of the cross and resurrection, he charges Zizioulas with focusing too much "on the signifier and not the thing signified."[41] In spite of the fact that Zizioulas's concerns are chiefly ecclesiological, as Russell acknowledges, we must agree that a view of ecclesial being that does not make room for the real rupture of the cross of Jesus Christ does not seem compelling in the face of the hard realities of suffering. Volf reminds that the "offense of the cross" lies deeper than the theology of the cross, since "the very nature of the triune God is reflected on the cross of Christ."[42] But bearing in mind the importance of a recovery of a Trinitarian understanding of God's power in terms of willing acceptance, participation, and transformation, we see that a theology of the cross is in no way a theology of impotence.

> Suffering is real and can never be expunged; the loss is real and can never be recovered. Everything will not come out "all right," as if the anguish were justified or amounted to nothing in the end. But everything can be resurrected through the power of God in the life of God to become new life. That is not resignation; nor is it denial; nor is it escape. That is conquest from within, a gentle might working to transform suffering into a new creation.[43]

Russell makes an important point in insisting that Zizioulas's theological anthropology of ecclesial being must integrate the reality of suffering and the brokenness of the cross. At the same time, it is difficult to give the cross its due centrality apart from what it means for the life of the church in terms of the quality of relationality that is lived. "Every community of faith mirrors who its God is. That the Triune God is compassionate, righteous, and just is to be known by the character, life, and praxis of the community of faith."[44] David Cunningham calls the church the "school for peace," not only because the church is witness to the ethical teachings of Jesus on peacemaking, but also because peacemaking is a Trinitarian practice.[45] "The Triune God is a God of peace; and God's peace, through the grace of the Living Water poured out upon us, nourishes and strengthens us to participate in the practice of peacemaking. In so doing, we are taken up into the peace of God, restored to the image of the God of peace."[46]

Certainly the cross characterizes Christian relationships in terms of solidarity with victims. But Volf insists, in the name of none other than Jon Sobrino, that a Trinitarian theology of the cross demands that solidarity must be considered a subtheme of the overarching theme of self-giving love. "Especially when solidarity refers to 'struggling on the side of,' rather than simply to 'suffering together with,' solidarity may not be severed from self-donation."[47]

We have already considered the idea of "self-donation" as a negative manifestation in the horrible contrast example of suicide bombers.[48] In the coming section we will consider how Trinitarian self-donation serves as the theological foundation for the hope we are calling 9/12.

PERSPECTIVES ON *PERICHORESIS*

We must acknowledge that, in itself, relationality is a neutral concept. Relationships can be superficial, abusive, and mutually destructive; as Cunningham stresses, "we cannot simply value our relationality in the abstract; we have to think about the character of our relationships."[49] A Trinitarian theology of the cross indicates that the character of Christian relationships we are examining is defined by God's life of self-giving and other-receiving love. Self-emptying[50] ("he emptied himself and took the form of a slave," Phil. 2:7) and mutual indwelling ("The Father is in me and I am in the Father," John 10:38) specify the distinctive Christian relationality that provides hope in a world of enmity and violence.[51]

The Greek term *perichoresis* refers to the mutual indwelling, or, as Volf prefers, "mutual interiority"[52] of the persons of the Trinity — "the permeation of each person by the other, their coinherence without confusion."[53] Two Latin translations were used that together expressed well the meaning of the Greek term: *circuminsessio,* preferred by Thomas Aquinas, a term expressing a state of being, means that one person is present in the other, and *circumincessio,* preferred by Bonaventure, a more dynamic term conveying a sense of "moving in and through the other."[54]

This ancient understanding of mutual indwelling expressed by the term *perichoresis* can render different models of interpretation when the Trinitarian persons are taken to be individual subjects, in line with Volf's more social Trinitarian perspective, or as subsistent relations, as is found among more traditional approaches. Whether helpful or not, it has become somewhat customary to employ, almost as a shortcut, a basic distinction in Trinitarian theology that claims that typically Eastern perspectives on Trinity begin with the three and move to the one, whereas typically Western (Latin) views begin with God's oneness (of nature) and then move to a consideration of the three persons. Our aim is not to determine which of the two perspectives is the most historically accurate. As Volf notes, "Each model is inadequate to the extent to which it fails to accommodate the truth of the other."[55] Our aim is rather to examine how a participatory approach to Trinitarian theology, our engagement in the life of God, is accessible via a particular understanding of the subsistent relations of God.

Although the Greek word *perichoresis* is not actually derived from *perichoreuo,* "to dance around," the play on words that results ends up stressing the dynamic sense of movement that is central to the ancient understanding of mutual indwelling.[56] This concept of movement is key to our understanding of participation as the point of Trinitarian language, a notion that supports the claim that the hope of 9/12 is not only a call to imitate the triune life but an invitation to share in it.

Participating in the movement of God calls to mind what Thomas Aquinas meant by the term "subsistent relations" — "a divine person signifies a relation as subsisting"[57] — since Aquinas begins his discussion by focusing on actions in God — the two processions of *begetting* and *breathing forth,* which correspond to the missions of God in the created world of incarnation and inspiration.[58]

In keeping with Aquinas's strategy of emphasizing movements of relationship, we can speak of God as "three movements of relationship subsisting in one event."[59] It is clear that such language is not that of a spectator but of a participant: "It only makes sense in terms of our involvement in the network of relationships in which God happens."[60] Such participation is already demonstrated in the New Testament pattern of prayer, which is directed *to* the Father *through* the Son and *in* the Spirit.

> This means that when we pray to God as Father, we find our address fitting into a movement like that of speech between a son and father, our response of "yes" ("Amen") leaning upon a child-like "yes" of humble obedience that is already there, glorifying the Father. At the same

time, we find ourselves involved in a movement of self-giving like that of a father sending forth a son, a movement which the early theologians called "eternal generation" and which we experience in the mission of God in history. To pray "in the event of Golgotha" means that these movements of response and mission are undergirded by movements of suffering, like the painful longing of a forsaken son towards a father and of a desolate father towards a lost son. Simultaneously, these two directions of movement are interwoven by a third, as we find that they are continually being opened up to new depths of relationship and to new possibilities of the future by a movement that we can only call "Spirit."[61]

The "Anatomy of Revenge" presented in part 1 examined the cyclical nature of violence and vengeance resulting from the problem of exclusion, an apt term for the "us versus them" polarity at the root of human enmity. Volf offers a model of *embrace* as a symbol of "God's reception of hostile humanity into divine communion," a model for how human beings should relate to each other.[62] Embrace, which represents more than the "mutual indwelling" aspect of love, is Volf's metonym for restored communion: he traces the movement from exclusion to embrace through four essential moments: repentance, forgiveness, making space in oneself for the other, and healing of memory.[63]

What is most important with Volf's model is that embrace serves as a reminder that forgiveness itself is not the terminus of the divine activity. God's love is such that forgiveness properly ends in *reconciliation* — the reuniting of those formerly divided. The model of embrace is especially enlightening as a metaphor for what is taking place on the level of individual identity with respect to the other in the process of reconciliation between former enemies. Volf pursues a "phenomenology of embrace" to illustrate the "making space for the other" taking place. He identifies four structural elements in the movement of embrace: (1) opening the arms, (2) waiting, (3) closing the arms, and (4) opening the arms again.[64]

> For embrace to happen, all four must be there and they must follow one another on an unbroken timeline; stopping with the first two (opening the arms and waiting) would abort the embrace, and stopping with the third (closing the arms) would pervert it from an act of love to an act of oppression and, paradoxically, exclusion. The four elements are then the four essential steps of an integrated movement.[65]

According to Volf, the first step — opening the arms — signifies that there is desire for the other, but more than that, it is a sign that "I have *created space* in myself for the other to come in and that I have made a movement out of myself so as to enter the space created by the other." Opening the arms is a gesture of invitation. The next step — waiting — shows that this invitation is not an act of invasion: "the self has 'postponed' desire and halted at the boundary of the other." For Volf, such waiting signifies both that the other cannot be coerced into embrace but also that only the other can complete the act of embrace through reciprocity. The third movement — closing the arms — the actual goal of the embrace, can take place only via a "soft touch," as it were, so as not to assimilate the other or lose the self in some kind of other- or self-destructive act of abnegation. "The embrace itself depends on success in resisting the vortex of de-differentiation through active or passive assimilation, yet without retreating into self-insulation." Finally, opening the arms again signifies that the mutual indwelling of the selves in embrace does not have, as its end, the disappearance of distinctive identity. This "opening of the arms underlines that, though the other may be inscribed into the self, the alterity of the other may not be neutralized by merging both into an undifferentiated 'we. . . .' The other must be let go," and in so doing, the embrace ends as it began, in openness: "Though embrace itself is not terminal, the movement of the self to the other and back has no end."[66]

Volf's embrace model is helpful in illustrating how "self-giving" and "other-receiving" — the two dimensions of God's perichoretic love — encourage us toward envisioning and co-creating a more hopeful future.

CHAPTER ELEVEN

An Anatomy of Forgiveness

As we have seen, every deliberate act of terror aims at making a statement. That statement, we recall, comes down to a word—fear. Through acts of violence that are intentionally calculated to maximize the apparent randomness of their occurrence, terrorists aim at inciting fear in as large an audience of witnesses as possible. Our investigation of exclusion has revealed that fear of the other is the basis of so much of the long history of enmity that remains locked within the cycle of violence and vengeance. In an age of terror and counter-terror, of trumped-up fear and suspicion, the full statement reads: *otherness and communion cannot coexist.*

God has also made a statement in the world. Indeed, as we have considered, the whole world as created by God through "separating and binding together" *is* God's statement. This statement also comes down to a word — *the Word* — of perfect self-giving and mutual indwelling, who "became flesh and dwelt among us" (John 1:14). The witnesses of this word have come to see the truth of his full statement: *Do not be afraid.* "On that day you will know that I am in my Father, and you in me, and I in you" (John 14:20).

Perhaps the central task of discerning the most Christian response to 9/11 and to understanding how best to find God in the midst of our suffering comes down to a matter of hearing — and to those two statements: "fear" and "fear not." At the same time, we do not want to run the risk of making it sound simple: in a time of terror, when "self-donation" conjures up images of suicide terrorists, it is actually very easy to be afraid.

And after 9/11, it is very difficult to bring up the word "forgiveness." To forgive is especially challenging because it is so often misconstrued to mean "to accept," or "to look the other way," as the phrase "forgive and forget" seems to imply. But one cannot forgive if one forgets. In fact, as Volf insists, forgiveness always entails blame. "To offer forgiveness is at the same time to condemn the deed and accuse the doer; to receive forgiveness is at the same time to admit to the deed and accept the blame."[1] Forgiveness is a much more active form of responding than such passive options indicate, which is of particular importance when we recall the passive connotation of suffering that the Latin term — *passio* — implies so well. Accordingly, forgiveness needs to be understood as a healing option that restores the victim-made-passive in suffering to the activity of true subjectivity. This accent on the activity of forgiveness further underscores the participatory way of knowing God.

In attempting to discern the most adequate Christian understanding of forgiveness, it is necessary to avoid those preconceived notions that tend toward passivity or escape or that look upon forgiveness merely in terms of a private decision to absolve an offender from guilt. Forgiveness cannot be understood apart from its central purpose of restoring communion. Likewise, forgiveness is best understood as an ongoing practice of the church, and a "costly" one at that. For Bonhoeffer, it is the essence of true discipleship: "To confess and testify to the truth of Jesus, and at the same time to love the enemies of truth, his enemies and ours, and to love them with the infinite love of Jesus Christ, is indeed a narrow way."[2]

THE JOURNEY INTO THE EXPERIENCE OF THE OTHER

Paul Fiddes provides a helpful metaphor for forgiveness interpreted as a journey into the experience of the other — a costly journey of empathy and identification that attests to the creative power of suffering, not its passivity. "The *voyage* of forgiveness has the power that flows from participation. It points to the transforming effect of sharing the experience and feelings of another."[3] Although Fiddes has clearly compiled his thoughts on forgiveness with the scenario in mind of enmity existing between two individuals, his insights on the necessity of making an empathetic journey into the experience of the other may also be instructive, to some degree, for this investigation of forgiveness on 9/12.

We recall the point made earlier regarding the difficulty of clearly distinguishing in an absolute sense between victims and victimizers, observing that it is the nature of human relationships, indeed the nature of persons understood in terms of interrelationship, that no one is entirely innocent. Forgiveness thus implies that a change takes place on both sides of the grievance, even where it is clear that one side is most grievously culpable. It is a recognition that, given the reality of the bonds of our created interconnectedness, forgiveness brings about a change in both parties, both for the one offering forgiveness and for the one seeking it.

The journey of forgiveness, a two-staged journey as Fiddes explains, begins with the *voyage of discovery* wherein the forgiver has to *think himself or herself into the mind of the offender*. This is truly a voyage — a movement from one place to another — as the forgiver, still suffering the pain of the offense, must figuratively leave behind what feels like a right to pursue just recriminations in order to meet the other in the other's experience and attempt to understand why the offender may have acted as he or she did. It is interesting to note that Bonhoeffer spoke of the suffering of forgiveness in this very sense: the forgiver suffering not only from the original offense but also from the suppression of the rightful claims to restoration resulting from that offense.[4] As Fiddes explains, it is only when this costly leg of the journey has been made — of empathetic identification with the offending other, an experience that shapes the offended one's approach to the offender — that the offended one is able to say, "I forgive you." It is important to see how the words themselves enact judgment: to say the word "forgiveness" is a reminder of the wrong and the hurt that has taken place. "Now the offender must embark upon his own voyage of discovery; he has been shaken into awareness of what he has done, and there can be no healing unless it is faced up to and sorrowed over."[5] Volf makes a similar point about forgiveness as judgment that justice has not been done. But it is a transcendence of the simple claims of strict justice. "By forgiving we affirm the claims of justice in the very act of not letting them count against the one whom we forgive."[6]

The next stage of the journey of forgiveness is the *voyage of endurance*. This is the more passive phase of the journey because the forgiver must submit to the consequences of having brought to light the committed offense which the offender prefers to keep in the dark. "The forgiver must absorb the hostility of the other, to bear it and receive it into herself. By offering the word of forgiveness she has taken the first step across the guilt which separates the two who are apart, and so she has exposed herself to attack. She has made herself vulnerable, laying herself open to aggressive reactions."[7]

The words "I forgive you" have evoked anger in the offender; indeed, the offender is possessed and driven by anger. Key to this stage is the forgiver's willingness to avoid self-justification and other-accusation. The forgiver must "bear patiently the hostility of the other" . . . and neutralize the hostility by sub-missively bearing with the other in love."[8] Thus, Fiddes draws our attention to the *transformative* effect that the journey of forgiveness has had on both parties: on the forgiver who has been shaped by the journey of empathetic identifica-tion with the other, and on the offender whose own hostility and anger have been minimized so that they no longer obstruct the path toward reunion. For our purposes, what is most important is that Fiddes has described a model for forgiveness that recommends something *to do,* an active engagement that utilizes the creative power of suffering to avoid the passive dimension of the *passio* that is our suffering. This experience of forgiveness in human relationships also provides an opportunity for us to interpret God's gift of forgiveness of human beings as a creative endeavor that brings about a new situation universally. This would represent a departure from those legalistic views of salvation understood in terms of satisfactory atonement. "The *voyage* of forgiveness points to atonement as having the power that flows from participation. It points to the transforming effect of sharing the experience and feelings of another."[9]

But we are justified in questioning the extent to which this active engagement, as outlined by Fiddes, can be appropriated as a viable path on which to journey on 9/12. As mentioned already, Fiddes is writing to illuminate the path of forgiveness toward reconciliation between *individuals* set against each other by transgression. Surely there are a number of legitimate disqualifications that arise when the journey of forgiveness is applied to September 11, 2001. The enormous scale of destruction wrought by the terrorist attacks can hardly be contained by the notions of "transgression" or "offense." The names of nearly three thousand innocent victims whose lives were taken that morning render these words and all their synonyms meaningless. Likewise, how are we to discern roles of "offender" and "forgiver" for this journey when thousands upon thousands of other names qualify for each of those roles? Furthermore, can it be said that, on the other hand, anyone living can rightly claim either of those roles since the direct "offenders," the nineteen hijackers, eliminated themselves in the process of eliminating the nearly three thousand who alone could initiate forgiveness?

These are difficult questions and all of them fair. The present study opened with an investigation of the violence and revenge that marred so much of twentieth-century history, by focusing on the "catastrophe" or "atrocity" associated with the name *Auschwitz;* those words themselves, we determined, proved inadequate to the task of containing the horror, as they probably do when applied to 9/11. The point is not to compare tragedies, but to acknowledge, once again, that before the enormity of mass-scale evil, human language appears frail. No words seem adequate. And yet struggling with the limitations of language, we realize that the only human thing left to do is to use the words within our reach, and to maybe even utilize catastrophe as a catalyst toward "wording" more meaningful theologies. Certainly this was the case after Auschwitz. The experience of evil associated with the catastrophe of 9/11 presented itself, on some level and to some degree, as a *personal* attack and hence as a personal offense to millions of people, not only to the immediate survivors, though in the first place to them — the family and friends of those lost — but also to countless others associated with them. The tragedy of 9/11 itself highlighted the reality of personal interconnectedness: it seemed everyone knew someone who knew someone who knew someone. Because of our created bonds of interconnectedness, the suffering of every "other" is, to some extent, my own. Catastrophes attest to the reality of the solidarity of our suffering. And to that end, words like "transgression" and "offense" may actually help to maintain our focus on the level of personal relationship when assessing the devastation. As we shall see, the notion of Trinitarian personhood itself thus provides something of an answer to the question "Who forgives?"

Thus, in attempting to articulate the most Christian response to the terror of 9/11, we identify the forgiver as the one wounded, and that *one* is necessarily a corporate reality. We are not naming this one the "United States" or the "American" people. But this is not to say that nations cannot forgive and that forgiveness cannot be an integral part of public policy, as was made clear by the "National Unity and Reconciliation Act" of July 26, 1995, which established the "Truth and Reconciliation Commission" in South Africa.[10]

The journey into the experience of the other is the heart of Christian forgiveness. Certainly this movement of identification is characteristic of Jesus' entire other-centered life of service, as he enters into the experience of estranged humanity and endures utter forsakenness in his death. "The various words of Christ from the cross which the Evangelists place in their narratives interpret the event: the plea 'Father, forgive them,' does not conflict with the awful cry 'My God, why have you forsaken me?' but brings out its meaning since forgiveness is nothing less than a voyage into the dark void of another's guilty life."[11] This example of Christ's voyage serves as the point of embarkation for our own voyages of forgiveness. By pointing out the direction in which to travel — *toward* the sinner — the path of forgiveness represents a decisive redirection of the "turning *away* from" that is characteristic of the sinful predicament of "us against them."

Still, we are right to wonder whether this discussion of forgiveness, understood in terms of the journey of empathy aiming toward restored relationship, applies in situations such as 9/11, where anonymous killers, never in personal relationship with their victims to begin with, are in any case disqualified from the possibility of reconciliation by the fact of their own deaths. Is there any good that can come from pursuing forgiveness where there is no possibility of reconciliation? One way to approach this problem is to remember that by participating in God we are participating in God's own time, that is, beyond the confines of our own life spans and into the eternity of God's love. God's time is the eschatological promise of the reconciliation of all humanity in restored relationship. Until that fullness of time is revealed, however, forgiveness, it can be said, is also good for the forgiver.

> The one who forgives can still set out in spirit and imagination on the path of empathy towards the other, so becoming the kind of person who is freed from the chains of the past. The forgiver can still benefit himself or herself from the attitude of forgiveness, "moving on" from the prison of bitterness and resentment, even where this does not reach destination and closure in reconciliation. Moreover, because we make this movement *in God*... it can have incalculable effects in the lives of others. The journey of our forgiveness becomes part of God's journey, and so has persuasive power in creating reconciliation in the world; we cannot know what this will achieve, either in the one with whom we desire to be reconciled, or in others who need to be reconciled and of whom we are quite unaware.[12]

In this way, too, we emphasize the eschatological significance of our efforts toward forgiveness that do not immediately culminate in the desired restoration of communion. We "respond to God's forgiveness by 'preparing the way' for the final, ultimate word of God's forgiveness."[13]

REMEMBERING RIGHTLY

L. Gregory Jones emphasizes that Christians learn to "embody" forgiveness as members of a baptismal community who participate in the practice of Christian forgiveness. "The new life of holiness signified by baptism is found and lived in communities of God's kingdom: People learn to embody forgiveness by becoming part of Christ's Body."[14] Importantly, he emphasizes that it is through participation in the church that we learn what to do with our painful memories of the past:

> As they are initiated into the practices of God's Kingdom, the forgiving grace of Jesus Christ gives people a new perspective on their histories of sin and evil, of their betrayals and their being betrayed, of their vicious

cycles of being caught as victimizers and victims, so that they can bear to remember the past well in hope for a new future.[15]

Remembering well is critical on 9/12. From that day on, the many who were traumatized by the attacks or who felt on any level injured joined in the rally cry, "We shall never forget." But if never forgetting is to avoid the temptation of vengeful retaliation, remembering rightly becomes a crucial moral obligation.

Volf comments on the fickleness of memory built into the very nature of the act of recollection — the temporal distance between the present self and the former seeing. "That temporal gap and the work of memory needed to bridge it leave space for falsehood to slip in, for imagination to supply what memory is lacking."[16] Likewise, when we remember we do so always from particular perspectives that are unavoidable due to our inescapable spatial and temporal limitations. Accordingly, "we fail to perceive fully what preceded any given event, what in the past contributed to its making; and we are mainly in the dark about the effects it will have in the future."[17] But these limits endemic to human remembering do not suggest that we cannot speak meaningfully of truthful memories. We, of course, have a moral obligation to remember truthfully, to "not bear false witness" (Exod. 20:16), albeit provisionally, due to our inherent cognitive limitations. But from a Christian perspective, remembering truthfully can never be separated from the larger obligation of caring for the other, indeed, loving neighbors as Christ loves them. "The purpose of truthful memory is not simply to name acts of injustice, and certainly not to hold an unalterable past forever fixed in the forefront of a person's mind. Instead, the highest aim of lovingly truthful memory seeks to bring about the repentance, forgiveness, and transformation of wrongdoers, and reconciliation between wrongdoers and their victims."[18]

The question of remembering truthfully in love is especially crucial when we consider how deeply what we remember affects what we *do*. With reference to the terrorist attacks, remembering in love has much to do with the path that will ultimately take shape on 9/12:

· If we are concerned primarily with *ourselves* as we remember wrongs suffered, we may remember in order to avoid getting into similarly injurious situations again; try to restore some measure of inner well-being disturbed by the traumatic event; adjust our expectations about the future; gain moral capital or draw economic and political advantage as victims; or withdraw into ourselves and nurse our wounds. If we are concerned primarily with *offenders* as we remember wrongs suffered, we may remember in order to exact revenge on culprits and keep them shamed, guilt-ridden, morally inferior, politically controllable, or economically exploitable. Or, if we are inclined to show grace to the offenders, we may remember so as to forgive their misdeeds, so as to release them from guilt and shame and from the just consequences of their actions.[19]

Again, memory, and how we use it, has much to do with the retrieval of hope after 9/11. This is our point in pursuing the main lines of Volf's reflection on remembering rightly in his recent work, *The End of Memory.* He asserts that "we may hope that even the meaninglessness of horrendous wrongs cannot ultimately shatter the wholeness of our lives. Even if some segments of our lives remain irredeemable, we ourselves can and will be redeemed."[20] But on this point, are we not right to wonder whether Volf's optimism borders on that same theodical urge to hold together a gravely broken world with a positive attitude? He does, for example, recommend that if we conceive of our lives as stories, we can integrate remembered wrongdoing by giving it a positive *meaning* within that story: even horrendous wrongs can be *labeled* "senseless segments of our life-story."[21] Does this take seriously enough the rift of suffering in a world torn asunder by sin? If Volf avoids the charge of glossing over the dark reality, it will be because of his insistence that ultimately our hope is secured, not so much in life's ultimate meaning as an integral story, but in the actual reality of the new identity that the Christian receives in Christ. Only this identity, divinely bestowed, provides the healing of wounded selves that is our hope.

> We remember wrongs suffered as people with identities defined by God, not by wrongdoer's evil deeds and their echo in our memory. True, sometimes that echo is so powerful that it drowns out all other voices. Still, behind the unbearable noise of wrongdoing suffered, we can hear in faith, the divinely composed music of our true identity. When this happens memories of mistreatment lose much of their defining power. They have been dislodged from the place they have usurped at the center of the self and pushed to its periphery. They may live in us, but they no longer occupy us; they may cause pain, but they no longer exhaustingly define. We are more than what we have suffered, and that is the reason we can do something with our memory of it.... We may be able to embark, maybe at first haltingly, upon a journey of reconciliation with those who have wounded us.[22]

In fact, this new identity, of self-giving and other-receiving, bestowed on us in Christ, means that although forgiveness without reconciliation is better than no forgiveness, the completion of healing comes about only in the restoration of the relationship. "Reconciliation with the wrongdoer completes the healing of the person who suffered the wrong."[23] Indeed, remembering rightly now is a matter of memory serving reconciliation. But, interestingly, remembering rightly now also has the aim of proper *forgetting*. This is truly the eschatological forgetting of our sins on the part of God. Here, Volf considers the rationale of Paul in his letter to the Romans as a kind of "anti-theodicy": "I consider that the sufferings of this present time are not worth comparing with the glory about to be revealed to us" (8:18). We note the simplicity of the logic: "If something is not worth comparing, then it will not be compared, and if it will not be compared then it will not have been remembered. For how would one fail to compare suffering with glory if one remembered the suffering while experiencing the glory."[24] Such an interpretation of Paul's insight suggests that integral to the glory of our salvation is the final grace of *nonremembering*. There will be no need to remember the suffering of wrongdoing. This eschatological forgetting does not mean that we should give up our memories of inhumanity now: to do so would be to dishonor the memory of those who have suffered and to pave the way for further deeds of inhumanity. But our remembering now must be guided by the vision of our hope in that day when remembering will no longer be necessary.

> We remember now in order that we may forget then; and we will forget then in order that we may love without reservation. Though we would be unwise to drop the shield of memory from our hands before the dawn of the new age, we may be able to move it cautiously to the side by opening our arms to embrace the other, even the former enemy.[25]

Forgiveness, learned and practiced in the Christian community, and re-membering rightly, that is, exercising memory in love that aims toward reconciliation, are the true hallmarks of a hope-filled 9/12. That day is long— mercifully so, since these Christian ideals cannot be abruptly coerced before their time. But the day is long also because it is God's day, and, as the psalmist understands, "a day in your courts is better than a thousand elsewhere" (84:10).

A CALL TO ARMS

One particular virtue of Volf's embrace model is the emphasis it places on rec-onciliation as the end and purpose of forgiveness. Too often it is easy to think that the Christian response to transgression culminates in the act of forgiving, but it is fair to say that if restored relationship is not the goal, then forgiveness could begin to approximate the legal concept of "pardon," that is, a kind of dismissal of due punishment that brings a case of injury to a close. Such a view, however, departs from the Christian view of the centrality of personal relationship and, moreover, deprives the forgiver of the option of active participation in the kind of creative suffering that opens up closed relationship to future life. A truly hope-filled view of forgiveness cannot merely make a statement in the present about the status of a transgression committed in the past: it must also say something about the potential and promise of the future. Without restored relationship, past grievances, even those that seem to have been put to rest by acts of pardon, all too easily become fodder for future acts of revenge and retaliation.

This accent on reconciliation, an active engagement with the offending other that seeks to restore a future to broken relationship, is characterized by a willingness on the part of the forgiver to readjust his or her own identity. Specifically, Volf argues that reconciliation with the other will succeed "only if the self, guided by the narrative of the triune God, is ready to receive the other into itself and undertake a readjustment of its identity in light of the other's alterity."[26] Part 1's investigation of enmity as exclusion revealed the view wherein the other's alterity is determined to be a problem that must be resolved through strategies of suppression or elimination. Reconciliation, we note, looks upon the other's distinctive otherness as a necessary component of God's own narrative of forgiveness. In the hope of 9/12 the model of embrace serves as a "call to arms" that is especially discernable in three dimensions of God's narrative of love.

The Embracing Arms of the Prodigal's Father

Volf acknowledges that it is Luke's story of the Prodigal Son (15:11–32) that originally prompted the idea of a theological model of embrace. The two main features of the story — the father's giving himself to the estranged son and his receiving that son back into his household — exemplify the important matter of how identities need to be constituted if broken relationships are to be restored.[27] Volf aims at exploring the social significance of the well-known parable of a younger son who attempts to "un-son" himself by cutting himself off from the relationships that define his very identity, a father who never lets go of the relationship between them, and an older brother who, resenting the forgiving father's refusal to follow the basic rules of inclusion and exclu-sion, proves himself to have become in the process a "non-brother." For our purposes, Volf's examination of the story yields three important insights for the topic of reconciliation after 9/11. The first is the fact that the Lucan story depicts the son's "memory of sonship" as preceding his repentance and jour-ney back to his father's house, indeed, that it is the memory of belonging that makes repentance possible. Accordingly, the son's confession of wrongdoing upon his journey home, an essential point in the drama, *follows* the father's act of accepting him back, even though the son's original plan of return entailed his *leading* with confession. Secondly, the son's attempt to "un-son" himself and the father's refusal to let go of his memory has meant that the father has had to renegotiate his own identity: "Since he would not give the departed son up, he became a father of the 'lost' son, of the 'dead' son (v. 24)" and would become by the story's end a father of the "son-that-was-dead-and-is-alive-again."[28] The father's priority of relationship has necessitated a readjustment of his own iden-tity. Finally, the father's same priority of relationship, which has welcomed the wayward son back into the household, has meant that he could reorder the older brother's traditional order of "follow the rules or you're out." Here, rela-tionship is prior to moral rules. Transgression affects relationship, but it does not terminate it.[29]

> Guided by the indestructible love which makes space in the self for others in their alterity, which invites the others who have transgressed to return, which creates hospitable conditions for their confession, and rejoices over their presence, the father keeps re-configuring the order without destroying it so as to maintain it as an order of embrace rather than exclusion.[30]

Volf explores various approaches to relating forgiveness, reconciliation, and justice, and these are appropriate to consider in the context of this reflection on the arms of love. The first approach is to opt for forgiveness outside of the quest for justice, that is, to plead for reconciliation and peace before the present injustices have been removed. Volf rejects this option as "cheap reconciliation" in which justice and peace are set up against each other as alternatives. "To pursue cheap reconciliation means to give up on the struggle for freedom, to renounce the pursuit of justice and to put up with oppression."[31] This is the "never mind" approach of acting toward the perpetrator *as if the sin were not there,* which is tantamount to a betrayal of all those who suffer injustice and violence. In its weakening of the prophetic voice, it stands as an aberration of the Christian tradition's struggle against injustice. Volf recommends watchfulness particularly here: "For the imperative of justice, severed from the overarching framework of grace within which it is properly situated and from the obligation to nonviolence, underlies much of the Christian faith's misuse by religiously legitimized violence."[32]

A second way of conceiving the place of justice in the pursuit of forgiveness and reconciliation is the "first justice, then reconciliation" approach. Volf also rejects this option of the pursuit of peace because it is impossible to carry out: especially in protracted conflicts, what constitutes "justice" is almost always contested by each party's rivals. We recall this same predicament described in part 1's "Anatomy of Revenge," wherein each side sees itself as the victim and the other as the victimizer. The impossibility of this approach, however, extends further: the pursuit of strict justice cannot succeed in a finite world of conflicting perceptions, nor is it really desirable. Though it may settle the score, it does not erase hostility. What is desirable, as Volf insists, reflects the interrelatedness of our personal identities, which, as we have seen, "are not defined simply from within an individual or a group, apart from relationships with their near and distant neighbors. We are who we are not simply as autonomous and self-constituting entities but essentially also as related and other-determined."[33] Thus, this option, which implies that forgiveness be withheld until the demands of justice have been satisfied, is deemed inadequate, not only because it is impractical, but because it does not lead to the healing that is desired as an extension of our created interconnectedness.

Thus, as Volf makes clear, efforts to secure forgiveness and reconciliation *outside* of and *after* justice are to be rejected. To find their proper relationship, Volf draws our attention to the narrative of the cross, where we find the very character of God.

The Outstretched Arms of the Crucified for the Godless

Christ's words on the cross — "Father, forgive them, for they do not know what they are doing" (Luke 23:34) — means that "the passion of Christ is the agony of a tortured soul and wrecked body offered as *a prayer for the forgiveness of the torturers*."[34] Once again, true peace is not just forgiveness but the reconciliation of former enemies. For Volf, the cross is central because it stands as Christ's refusal to give up on the sinful other who has set out to be an enemy. "The arms of the crucified are open — a sign of a space in God's self and an invitation for the enemy to come in."[35] Christ does not imitate the violence done unto him, but as victim he acts as true judge: "by offering to embrace the offenders, he judges both the initial wrongdoing of the perpetrators and the reactive wrongdoing of many victims. Enmity toward enmity... *transforms* the relation between the victim and the perpetrator."[36]

> On the cross, God is manifest as the God who, though in no way indifferent toward the distinction between good and evil, nonetheless lets the sun shine on both the good and the evil (cf. Matt. 5:45); as the God of indiscriminate love who died for the ungodly to bring them into the divine communion (cf. Rom. 5:8); as the God who offers grace... to the vilest evildoer.[37]

There is no way to conceive of the connection of justice and forgiveness/ reconciliation outside of God's own *transformative* sense of justice, which seeks out the sinner in loving embrace. Accordingly, Volf stresses four essential claims about the relationship between justice and the peace that comes about through authentic forgiveness and reconciliation. First, the primacy of the will to embrace the other is prior to any judgment about the other, since our struggle for peace is not caught up in the effort to distinguish good from evil forces, but in the pursuit of transforming the world. Second, that will to embrace can culminate in actual and true embrace only insofar as it is also a struggle for justice: "The will to embrace includes the will to rectify the wrongs that have been done, and it includes the will to reshape the relationships to correspond to justice."[38] Third, the will to embrace must provide the framework itself for the search for justice. That is to say, only the will to embrace can allow us to be able to properly evaluate injustice in the first place. It clarifies our perception of wrongs and lights the path of our greater struggle for justice. Finally, healing relationships must always be regarded as the proper *telos* of the struggle for justice. Without that vision, other insufficient goals may appear to suffice, such as the mere determination of the right and "winning" side. Taking these four points together, Volf provides a decidedly "utopian" concept of reconciliation that aims at the creation of authentic communion upheld in the embrace of self-giving and other-receiving love. But it is more than a vision. In a world of strife, where reconciliation can never be coerced, "it translates into the shaping of cultural sensibilities that help people live in a humane way in the absence of the final harmony."[39] Indeed, this visionary model was in fact realized in the reconciliatory activity of a number of survivors of the victims of the 9/11 tragedy, as we shall see.

The Open Arms of Trinitarian Perichoresis

What we see on the cross — self-giving and other-receiving love — is what we believe to be the very life of God.[40]

> The one divine person is not that person only, but includes the other divine persons in itself; it is what it is only through the indwelling of the others. The Son is the Son because the Father and the Spirit indwell him; without this interiority of the Father and the Spirit, there would be no Son. Every divine person *is* the other persons, but he is the other persons in his own particular way.[41]

We have already investigated the patristic notion of perichoresis among the Trinitarian persons. But further, Volf stresses that that same love which characterizes the internal self-giving and other-receiving of the Trinity characterizes God's love for humanity. "We, the others — we, the enemies — are embraced by the divine persons who love us with the same love with which they love each other and therefore make space for us within their own eternal embrace."[42] Volf, like Zizioulas, understands the Eucharist as the ritual celebration of this divine love that makes space for the other. Like Zizioulas's emphasis on the notion of "ecclesial person," Volf also emphasizes the transformative aspect of the celebration. "Inscribed on the very heart of God's grace is the rule that we can be its recipients only if we do not resist being made into its agents; what happens to us must be done by us. Having been embraced by God, we must make space for others in ourselves and invite them in — even our enemies."[43]

Volf's social Trinitarian perspective is a final response to claims that belief in God's oneness has fostered much of the violence in our world by creating an "us" who know the one true God versus a "them" who do not. At this point in our investigation it is clear that Trinitarian monotheism implies a universalism that does not construct such a wall of enmity. Once again,

> to believe that the one God is the Father, the Son, and the Spirit is to believe that the identity of the "Father" cannot be understood apart from the "Son" and the "Spirit." To be the divine "Father" is from the start to have one's identity defined by another and therefore not to be undifferentiated

and self-enclosed. Moreover, the divine persons as non-self-enclosed identities are understood by Christians to form a perfect communion of love;
the persons give themselves to each other and receive themselves from
each other in love.[44]

With Volf, we assert that this understanding of God's oneness has implications
for our lives together here and now. For, notwithstanding the appearance of
book titles calling for "the end of faith" (to quote one of them) after the violence of 9/11, Christian faith grounds its hopes for peace in the very being of
the God of peace.

Theology That Re-members

An interesting film project was initiated shortly after the 9/11 terrorist attacks. Ten 35mm time-lapse motion picture cameras were set up in and around Ground Zero, in New York City, to capture on film the complete rebuilding of the World Trade Center. Called *Project Rebirth*,[1] the cameras are shooting one frame of film every five minutes, round the clock and calendar, for the duration of the rebuilding process. They began shooting six months after the attacks and will continue shooting until the historical reconstruction is completed, some five years hence. The production will yield a twenty-minute film chronicle of the entire rebuilding process.

In a sense the various themes in this work also amount to the challenge of rebuilding after 9/11. To some extent we have all been engaged in reconstructing our lives after this catastrophe, even with the same aim of one day viewing our rebirth from the happy perspective of all the progress we have made. But if judging how far we have come is ever to lead us to a better place than from where we began, our rebuilding will have to involve more than the clearing away of debris and the construction of ever taller and more shock-absorbing towers. We have to look deeply for the signs of change that attest to our openness to the progression of God's spirit in our lives. As we have considered, such change involves a renewed vision of the human person as created in the image of the Trinitarian God's own self-giving and other-receiving personhood.

Such a renewed conception of personhood is far from idle theological speculation. Recalling Hannah Arendt's observation, we can judge for ourselves just what is at stake: if by "banality" we mean the tendency to trivialize even the most heinous of evil acts, then what word aptly characterizes the mindless repetition of such horrific acts? The *automatism* of evil? If after Auschwitz, as Irving Greenberg insists, all statements, theological and otherwise, must be made "in the presence of the burning children," then what kind of judgment is rightly passed on those theological statements by the horrendous sacrifice of still more burning children?

Insurgents detonated a bomb in a car with two children in it after using the children...as decoys to get through a military checkpoint in Baghdad, an American general said Tuesday.... "Children in the back seat lower suspicion," he said, according to the transcript. "We let it move through. They parked the vehicle. The adults run out and detonate it with the children in back."[2]

Although we cannot establish a simple causal link between such horrendous acts and the failure of theology to engage a broken, violent world, the memory of still more suffering innocents compels us to evaluate the efficacy of our theological responses. Having to say "never again" *over and over again* means that we are no longer in the realm of mere banality.

Theologizing after 9/11, like theologizing after Auschwitz, means taking heed of the catastrophes—Metz's unrelenting "interruptions"—that are supposed to disturb the comfort and security of our already learned, well-rehearsed explanations. More than ever, theology cannot afford to settle for pat answers or mere logical consistency. This means that theology must remain committed to facing the scandal of suffering without resorting to formal theodicies or even the very real theodical tendencies that lurk behind our theological agendas—what could be called the *distraction of abstraction*. Does something like a hierarchy of exigencies need to accompany the notion of a "hierarchy of truths" to insure that theology prioritizes its proper interests and pursuits?[3] In a time of terror, when the "statements" of terrorists are emphatically concrete, to say the least, should not theology draw our attention to the same concrete realm where the statement of God's self-revelation in Christ is made? One of Bonhoeffer's last writings from the Tegel military prison underscores the importance of the point: "Our speech must be truthful, not in principle, but concretely. A truthfulness which is not concrete is not truthful before God. 'Telling the truth,' therefore, is not solely a matter of moral character; it is also a matter of correct appreciation of real situations and serious reflection upon them."[4]

As we have seen, because evil threatens as an existential reality and not as a theoretical principle, the appropriate response to the suffering of evil is likewise a practical one. Daniel Louw points us in the right direction toward approaching the problem of God and suffering:

The why-question becomes meaningful apart from the necessity of finding a logical answer or rational solution. God no longer functions as an explanation. On the contrary, God is where questions of suffering and evil can be addressed by means of lamentation. It becomes even possible to accuse God and to express our human anger by means of faith.... In this respect, God becomes our friend and covenantal partner in our suffering: This "friendship of God" is the practical outcome of divine faithfulness.[5]

From a Christian perspective, we cannot even approach the question of God and suffering without recognizing God's relationality. And the kind of relationship that is the living God of the Christian tradition — the Trinitarian God of kenotic mutual indwelling, of self-giving and other-receiving love — means that God acts to overcome evil with the sacrificial action of love: "God 'overcomes' all enemies not by annihilating them but by loving them."[6] Only this God, whose love is constructive and transformative, can insure that the rebuilding efforts at Ground Zero are securely grounded in a hope that is concrete. The God who makes "all things new" is the final rebuilder-in-chief after this and every catastrophe. As we have seen, the "portraits of grief" were many afer 9/11. But so, too, were the "portraits of grace."

The construction site at Ground Zero is also an appropriate setting for calling to mind the notion of "epistemological crisis," as developed by Alasdair MacIntyre.[7] Simply put, epistemological crises occur when our basic cultural assumptions, the historically founded standards by which we derive meaning, are thrown into question. "Every tradition, whether it recognizes the fact or not, confronts the possibility that at some future time it will fall into a state of epistemological crisis, recognizable as such by its own standards of rational justification."[8] MacIntyre insists that we could find ample evidence of such crises occurring throughout history, but most interestingly, he highlights the Trinitarian controversies in the fourth century as understood by John Henry Newman.

> Newman's own central example was of the way in which in the 4th century the definition of the Catholic doctrine of the Trinity resolved the controversies arising out of competing interpretations of scripture by a use of philosophical and theological concepts whose understanding had itself issued from debates rationally unresolved up to that point. Thus that doctrine provided for the later Augustinian tradition a paradigm of how the three requirements for the resolution of an epistemological crisis could be met.[9]

In many ways, the foregoing study has been proposing this very same notion of a Trinitarian resolution as capable of shedding much needed light on the current predicament of enmity in which we live. Can we, in fact, look upon the vicious cycle of violence and vengeance in this time of terror as indicative of an insufficient or incomplete integration of the doctrine of God as Trinity *into our own understanding of ourselves?* In this way, we can think of Trinity as crisis resolution in two distinct but mutually dependent acts: the first involving how the doctrine of the Trinity enabled Christians to think more adequately about God; and the second (the potential of which, we are asserting, has not been sufficiently contemplated) wherein the Trinity enables us to think adequately about ourselves — which is to say, in a way that enables the flourishing of the greater human community. As we have seen, a perspective that divides the world into "us" versus "them" is one that has not taken seriously the implications of God's personhood for our own. If it is true that the distinctly Western tradition of regarding the person in terms of isolated, self-enclosed entities is showing signs of having entered into a state of epistemological crisis, then perhaps a more robust confidence in the Christian claim of God as Trinity will further illumine our paths toward peace and promise. It is the challenge of this clash — the clash of perspectives on person — that must be faced before we can set out to resolve any purported "clash of civilizations."

We are thus provided with a key for interpreting the question of God and suffering that avoids the trap of abstracting theodicies. The eminently practical doctrine of the Trinity culminates in our living out of its truth: in our embodying the created interconnectedness that defines our personhood in God's image. The coexistence of otherness and communion in God implies that our suffering is therefore profoundly social — the breakdown of that created wholesomeness.

This also means that it is appropriate to theologically consider human suffering in light of the doctrine of creation and not just the doctrine of the Fall. As L. Gregory Jones observes: "We find it difficult to accept our creatureliness, following a will-to-power, a will-to-self-obliteration, or perhaps despairing amid the struggle to sustain identities in the face of the awesome forces of annihilation. In each case, the reality of communion collapses into a series of isolated and divided individuals obsessively concerned with preserving or sustaining a sense of 'self.'"[10] We should take seriously this idea of suffering understood in terms of the disruption of created interconnectedness, especially when we recall, once again, Metz's claim that suffering may very well be the last universal category left open to us. In a tragic way, a crucial but often overlooked aspect of suffering is that, because of the very brokenness of created interrelatedness at the heart of suffering, we often cannot even see the truth of that Metzian insight. When communion is disrupted suffering itself remains supremely self-ish; it cannot serve as a bridge of empathy, an occasion of love.

All of this means that rebuilding after 9/11 implies the resolution to avoid the dualistic appraisal of good and evil that, in a world of enmity, all too easily leads to the dangerous view that people themselves are either good or evil. Tzvetan Todorov correctly makes the plea: "A maxim for the twenty-first century might well be to start not by fighting evil in the name of good, but by attacking the certainties of people who claim always to know where good and evil are to be found."[11] The reality of interconnectedness means more than the simple awareness of the integrity of our created bonds; it also implies the inescapable co-responsibility that we bear for each other's lives, including the sinful aspects that we are too often inclined to view simplistically and in ways that maintain the illusion of our own purity and innocence. "We should struggle not against the devil himself but against what allows the devil to live— Manichaean thinking itself."[12]

The terrorist attacks of 9/11 constituted an act of gross inhumanity, an objective evil that no sane person can deny. But the reality of interconnectedness and the task of co-responsibility compel us to acknowledge our own involvement in the tragedy. In light of the discussion on interconnectedness, this means recognizing how the particular suffering of humiliation, which can be understood only in the context of the social, is a very real suffering. Just as the presence of the "oppressed" implies the existence of an "oppressor," the reality of humiliation presumes both active and passive participants. We could bicker about the degree of our culpability in this humiliation, but even more tellingly, we are often not even aware of our part in the humiliation of the other. That lack of awareness underscores the importance of understanding sin and suffering in terms of the breakdown of the bonds of created interconnectedness. Understanding the role of humiliation in this way suggests that in many situations of conflict, the aggrieved might actually play a role in raising up the very ones who would bring them down.

We are right to contrast the passive suffering of humiliation with the example of Christ's active *humility,* his kenotic self-emptying to make room for the other, even the sinful other. Answering the call to imitate or participate in the humility of Christ means clearing away the self so that the other is not ignored. There is no chance for humiliation when the other is truly a part of the self. "We must overturn so many idols, the idol of self, first of all, so that we can be humble, and only from our humility can we learn to be redeemers, can we learn to work together in a way the world really needs."[13] As Oscar Romero saw it, true humility is what makes genuine and lasting transformation possible.

Humility as self-emptying, other-receiving love is one way to understand the Christian imperative to forgive. Forgiveness aims at reconciliation. It is not simply the way to move beyond injury. It finds its proper end in the restoration of relationships that have been torn asunder by enmity. The call to forgiveness-to-reconciliation, therefore, should not be understood in terms of individual, isolated acts of debt cancellation. It is, rather, a call to participate in God's redemptive love of creation. In this way, we do not define the other according to his or her sinful deeds. We do not confine the other to his or her past. We know the other in terms of the promise of the future secured by God.

Another reason not to think of forgiveness in terms of individual, isolated acts apart from the greater work of reconciliation is that as such it is simply too hard to do. The tragedy of 9/11 is too enormous to be handled in individual terms. Its evil was vast, involving complex networks of planners, financiers, executors, etc. It stands in line with many other instances of large-scale, horrendous evil that simply exceed our moral categories of judgment and our emotional capacity to cope.

But there is yet another greater reason to resist thinking of forgiveness in terms of victimized individuals remitting the offenses of their perpetrators. From the Christian perspective, forgiveness is an essentially communitarian reality. No *one* can really effect genuine forgiveness on his or her own. As such, L. Gregory Jones observes how people *discover* forgiveness: through the richness of their communal practices, Christians learn how to be forgiven and how to forgive:

Learning to be forgiven and to forgive requires us also to learn to speak (and listen) truthfully, pray, heal, confess, and engage in mutual admonition.... What do such activities do? They focus attention on the abundant grace and love of God, the close interrelations of our bodies and souls, the power of language to destroy and to heal, and the central importance of acknowledging our own sin if we are to learn to forgive others faithfully rather than self-righteously.... We are to engage in practices that shape a way of life in which we learn to live with one another — even, perhaps especially — amid suffering, sickness, and sin. In so doing, they school us as citizens of God's kingdom, people capable of learning to live in faithful communion with God, with one another, and with the whole creation.[14]

Importantly, for Jones, we *discover* forgiveness in the character of changed relationships. Moreover, in living out these relationships wherein we learn how to ask for and receive forgiveness and learn how to forgive others who offend us, we learn something of the graciousness of forgiveness. To forgive and be forgiven is to give and receive a gift.

We have witnessed since 9/11 further tragedies of inhumanity, reminding us that the problem of enmity and fragmented community is not easily solved. One such tragedy, however, provides a striking example of the truth of the unavoidably communitarian dimension of Christian forgiveness. On October 2, 2006, in the small Amish schoolhouse in Nickel Mines, Pennsylvania, a gunman murdered five girls and wounded five others before killing himself. For many, the shock of that atrocity was matched by the shock of the Amish community's response: they decided to forgive the man and to extend compassion to his widow. According to Stephen Nolt, professor of theology at Goshen College in Indiana, the Amish practice of forgiveness — even incomprehensible instances of it such as witnessed here — is a central component of their Christian witness. "They have a 300-, 400-year history of responding to wrong in this way. They have examples, and they also do it as a community. They don't view forgiveness as the responsibility of the specific individuals who have been wronged. It's something that's shared by the entire community."[15] The point is that for a community that is so tightly knit, which implies a tradition of the kind of practices that Jones is addressing, it is perhaps easier to see how this practice of forgiveness could take place. The question we have to look at is how might forgiveness in its true communal sense be possible on a scale of tragedy like that of 9/11.

David Potorti lost his older brother, Jim, when American Airlines Flight 11 crashed into the North Tower and the offices of Marsh & McLennan, where Jim was a vice-president. Jim's "portrait of grief" was quoted in part 2. Rita Lasar lost her brother, Abe Zelmanowitz, in the collapse of that same tower. His act of courage in remaining with a quadriplegic friend who could not escape was likewise mentioned in part 2. Together with a number of other survivors of the nearly three thousand who perished in the attacks, David and Rita found themselves troubled by the violence that characterized the official U.S. response of retaliation and, in particular, by the way in which their loved ones' memories were invoked as justification for that response. "Those of us who lost family members that morning found ourselves in particularly painful positions. Our losses were not simple murders, but international incidents, symbols, and public events.... And whether we liked it or not, their deaths would become public property."[16] Out of a desire to make public a different response to their losses and to take up the duty of memory more honestly, several survivors came together to form "September 11th Families for Peaceful Tomorrows," a group seeking to promote nonviolent responses to the tragedy of 9/11.

> While September 11 remains for many the genesis of new fears, new suspicions, and a redoubling of efforts to secure themselves and their possessions, for us it was a day that demolished the belief that we could ever be truly independent of each other. It was a day when the walls came down, not up.... We refuse to believe in an us-versus-them world.[17]

This spirit of interdependence and commitment to nonviolence has sustained the group in many peace-building initiatives. In January 2002, a number of members traveled to Afghanistan, where they visited Afghani civilians who had been affected by the U.S. bombing campaign. In January 2003, a delegation of members journeyed to Iraq to witness for peace before the invasion took place. There they encountered the suffering of a population subjected to repeated wars and international sanctions. There, while they toured an overcrowded pediatric hospital lacking basic medical supplies, a physician told them, "Sanctions are the real weapons of mass destruction."[18] The group even developed a relationship with some of the survivors of the bombing of Hiroshima, staging exchange visits between survivors of the two catastrophes. Rita Lasar, invited to give keynote addresses at major peace conferences in Japan in the summer of 2002, remarked, "I came to Japan, having gone from one Ground Zero — lower Manhattan, in New York City — to a second Ground Zero — Afghanistan, and I am now on the original Ground Zero. So I suppose you might say that my perspective changed. I was adding atrocities to my consciousness, which in turn makes me more dedicated to pleading with my fellow humans to start thinking truly about non-violent responses to provocations."[19]

We should ponder her description of the "changed perspective" that comes about when human atrocities are actually faced openly and forthrightly. What is of particular interest for our own investigation is that this group's chief impetus was their commitment to engage properly and justly in the work of memory. They wanted to work for peace and in this way serve the demands of the memory of their loved ones.

Clearly then, the work of memory is indeed a matter of *re-membering*. St. Augustine spoke of memory in this sense of *recollecting*, but in terms of the actual dynamics of cogitation. In book 10 of his *Confessions*, he writes:

My memory holds a great number of facts . . . things which I have already discovered and . . . placed ready to hand. This is what is meant by saying that we have learnt them and know them. If, for a short space of time, I cease to give them my attention, they sink back and recede again into the more remote cells of my memory, so that I have to think them out again, like a fresh set of facts, if I am to know them. I have to shepherd them out again from their old lairs, because there is no other place where they can have gone. In other words, once they have been dispersed, I have to collect them again.[20]

In light of our insistence that the proper end of memory is the reconciliation of former enemies, we can see how something like this intellectual movement of recollecting within the person manifests itself on a social level among persons. For truly, God *re-members* us. That is to say, in our efforts toward establishing reconciliation, God is at work recollecting, making us members again of one human community. This is the foundation of Christian hope, even in a time of terror.

The desire to remember rightly led these victims of loss to practical involvement in the problem of suffering. "Re-membering rightly" continues to allow us to recognize that the work of forgiveness properly leads to the restoring of broken bonds of interconnectedness. Re-membering rightly highlights the importance of Christian community — where "all the members of the body, though many are one" (1 Cor. 12:12) — as the school of reconciliation wherein forgiveness is learned through the practice of genuine repentance.

Re-membering 9/11 means integrating the other's memory of suffering into our own — and recognizing there the depth of our true solidarity in suffering. Re-membering 9/11, furthermore, means seeing the futility and inhumanity of a primarily violent response to the attacks, which only intensified the entrenchment of the bitter cycle of violence and vengeance — and recognizing there the depth of our true solidarity in sin. Finally, but foremost, the work of re-membering is the justice of God, who continues to heal a world wounded by violence of all of its terrors and all of its fears — and who makes of its enemies, friends.

Afterword

Another figure of late antiquity, indeed, a contemporary of Augustine, wrote a *Confessio* of his own while living on the opposite reaches of the Roman Empire. However, more than a little legend intersects the hagiography of Patricius (Patrick, Pádraig, Irish), a Roman Briton who was captured by Irish raiders and brought to Ireland as a slave.[1] In his *Confessions,* Patrick writes that his faith grew while in captivity. In time, he escaped and returned to his family and formally entered the church in Britain. Later, however, Patrick returned as a missionary to Ireland, where he served until his death.

It is said that St. Patrick used a three-leaf clover to help the ancient Irish embrace the mystery of God's threeness in one. The humble clover may have proved helpful as a teaching aid. But an even more compelling sign of the reality of the Trinity was Patrick himself in his decision to return in service to the people who had once held him captive. Our lives, too, are called to be symbolic of the Trinity, bearing witness to the reality of divine love.

Patrick called his prayer a "breastplate." In it he seeks, almost desperately, divine protection in a hostile world.

> Christ be with me, Christ before me,
> Christ be after me, Christ within me,
> Christ beneath me, Christ above me,
> Christ at my right hand, Christ at my left,
> Christ at this side, Christ at that side,
> Christ at my back...
> Christ in the heart of every man who thinks of me,
> Christ in the mouth of everyone who speaks of me,
> Christ in every eye that sees me,
> Christ in every ear that hears me.

We could be tempted to disregard his prayer as simplistic and quaint, a superstitious bidding to a primitive warrior God. But Patrick lived in a violent and threatening world — one beset, like our own, with real, tangible dangers. The prayer suggests that in order to combat evil, he "armed" himself in God alone — the Trinity, his true "protection." In response to 9/11, we, too, are called to embody the mystery.

> I bind unto myself the name,
> The strong name of the Trinity;
> By invocation of the same,
> The three in one, the one in three,
> Of whom all nature hath creation;
> Eternal Father, Spirit, Word,
> Praise to the Lord of my salvation,
> Salvation is of Christ the Lord. Amen.

Notes

Introduction

1. W. H. Auden, "September 1, 1939" in *Selected Poems* (New York: Vintage Books, 1979), 88.

Part 1. 9/10

1. Johann Baptist Metz, preface to *Faith and the Future: Essays on Theology, Solidarity, and Modernity,* by J. B. Metz and Jürgen Moltmann (Maryknoll, N.Y.: Orbis Books, 1995), vii.

2. Francis Schüssler Fiorenza, introduction to Metz, *Faith and the Future,* xv.

3. Johann Baptist Metz, *A Passion for God: The Mystical-Political Dimension of Christianity,* ed. and trans. J. Matthew Ashley (New York: Paulist Press, 1998), 2.

4. Ekkehard Schuster and Reinhold Boschert-Kimmig, *Hope against Hope: Johann Baptist Metz and Elie Wiesel Speak Out on the Holocaust,* trans. J. Matthew Ashley. Studies in Judaism and Christianity (Mahwah, N.J.: Paulist Press, 1999), 33. Quotation from interview with Metz.

Chapter 1. The Question of God and Suffering

1. Abraham van de Beek, *Why? On Suffering, Sin, and God,* trans. John Vriend (Grand Rapids: Eerdmans, 1990), 19.

2. Ibid., 18.

3. Ibid., 21.

4. John H. Hick, *Evil and the God of Love* (New York: Harper and Row, 1966), 5. Epicurus's formulation is quoted as follows by Lactantius (c. 260–c. 340 C.E.): "God either wishes to take away evil, and is unable, or He is able, and is unwilling, or He is neither willing nor able, or He is both willing and able. If He is willing and unable, He is feeble, which is not in accordance with the character of God; if He is able and unwilling, He is envious, which is equally at variance with God. If He is neither willing nor able, He is both envious and feeble, and therefore not God; if He is both willing and able, which alone is suitable to God, from what source then are evils? Or why does He not remove them?" Cf. ibid., 6.

5. John H. Hick, *Philosophy of Religion,* 4th ed., Foundations of Philosophy Series (Englewood Cliffs, N.J.: Prentice Hall, 1990), 40. It is interesting to note that Leibniz's book entitled *Theodicy* (1710) was his only work published during his lifetime. This attempt to show that God is right and just needs to be situated against the broader framework of his philosophical agenda, in particular, his metaphysical system that posits the well-known claim that this world is the best of all possible worlds. This optimistic view flows from his understanding of reality as consisting fundamentally of nonmaterial substances called monads, each containing its own preassigned pattern created by an infinitely perfect being (God) who, from any number of possible worlds, created this one, which unfolds according to his own benevolent design. In other words, a perfectly good being must create the best world it can. According to Leibniz, the creation of a perfect world would simply be a duplication of God's very being, an impossibility since God is non-extensive spirit. The best of all possible worlds, then, is the one containing as much existence as possible combined with the greatest amount of perfection, a working out of a preestablished harmony known only to God. According to Donald Rutherford, Leibniz's metaphysics was designed to support his theodicy. For Leibniz, metaphysics is very much a rational science, and the fundamental category of being is substance. "The ground of Leibniz's belief in the doctrine of the best of all possible worlds is a thoroughgoing faith in the governing power of reason: reason as it directs the creative will of God, reason as it is subsequently realized in the intelligible order of the created world, and reason as it helps human minds discern and appreciate that order." Clearly, the pervasiveness of reason is the guiding force behind Leibniz's theodicy. Donald Rutherford, *Leibniz and the Rational Order of Nature* (Cambridge: Cambridge University Press, 1995), 12. For a critique, from the standpoint of Judeo-Christian religious ethics, of Leibniz's assumption that a perfectly good being must create the best world it can, see Robert Merrihew Adams, "Must God Create the Best?" in Rowe, *God and the Problem of Evil,* 24–37.

6. Hick, *Philosophy and Religion,* 40.

7. There are, as well, other major types of theodicy such as process theodicy, based on the process thought of Alfred North Whitehead (1860–1947) and Charles E. Hartshorne (1897–2000) and taken up notably by David Griffin in his works *God, Power and Evil* (1976 and 1990) and *Evil Revisited* (1991), as well as a number of other philosophical theodicies. These theodicies, however, are not typical of traditional Christian theologies of God and the problem of evil. Given the scope of the present study, space limitations preclude a fuller critique of Hick's analysis of the history of theodicy.

8. J. Patout Burns, trans. and ed., *Theological Anthropology,* Sources of Early Christian Thought (Philadelphia: Fortress, 1981), 14.

9. See Augustine, *De Genesi ad litteram,* Imperfectus liber, 1,3.

10. Hick, *Philosophy and Religion,* 42.

11. Cf. ibid., 43.

12. John H. Hick, "Soul-Making Theodicy," in Rowe, *God and the Problem of Evil,* 267. According to Hick, the Irenaean type of theodicy dates back to the early Hellenistic fathers of the church, particularly to St. Irenaeus who, without having worked out a formal theodicy of his own, was chief among those Greek fathers who did achieve a framework for the eventual development of a theodicy. The so-called Irenaean theodicy was further developed with greater notoriety by Friedrich Schleiermacher (1764–1834).

13. Hick, *Philosophy and Religion,* 44. See Irenaeus, *Against Heresies,* book 4, chapters 37 and 38.

14. Hick, *Philosophy and Religion,* 45. Hick comments elsewhere, "This [epistemic] distance consists, in the case of humans, in their existence within and as part of a world which functions as an autonomous system and from within which God is not overwhelmingly evident. It is a world, in Bonhoeffer's phrase, *etsi deus non daretur,* as if there were no God." See Hick, "Soul-Making Theodicy," 270.

15. Irenaeus, *Against Heresies,* book 4, chapter 38, trans. and ed. J. Patout Burns, *Theological Anthropology,* 26.

16. Hick, "Soul-Making Theodicy," 269.

17. Hick, *Philosophy and Religion,* 48.

18. Kristiaan Depoortere, *A Different God: A Christian View of Suffering,* Louvain Theological and Pastoral Monographs 17 (Louvain: Peeters Press, 1994), 21.

19. Susan Neiman, *Evil in Modern Thought: An Alternative History of Philosophy* (Princeton, N.J.: Princeton University Press, 2002).

20. Ibid., 2.

21. Ibid, 250.

Chapter 2. Auschwitz: Evil and Suffering in the Twentieth Century – First Reflection

1. Neiman, *Evil in Modern Thought,* 240.

2. Metz, *Hope against Hope,* 35.

3. Hannah Arendt, *Eichmann in Jerusalem: A Report on the Banality of Evil* (New York: Penguin, 1963), 273.

4. Joan Ringelheim, "The Strange and the Familiar," in Signer, *Humanity at the Limit,* 37.

5. According to Article II, 1948 United Nations Genocide Convention, genocide refers to any of the following acts committed with intent to destroy, in whole or in part: (1) killing members of a group; (2) causing serious bodily or mental harm to members of the group; (3) deliberately inflicting on the group conditions of life calculated to bring about its physical destruction in whole or in part; imposing measures intended to prevent births within the group; forcibly transferring children of the group to another group. Alexander Laban Hinton, ed., *Annihilating Difference: The Anthropology of Genocide* (Berkeley: University of California Press, 2002), 3.

6. Additionally, another 3 million Soviet prisoners of war were killed, along with 2 million Soviet civilians, over 1 million Polish civilians, over 1 million Yugoslav civilians, seventy thousand men, women, and children with mental and physical deficiencies, two hundred thousand Gypsies, and unknown numbers of political prisoners, resistance fighters, deportees, and homosexuals. Ibid., 3. By focusing our attention on the Jewish victims, we in no way intend to underestimate the horror of the deaths of millions of others who perished during these years. See also John Pawlikowski, "Uniqueness and Universality in the Holocaust: the Need for a New Language," in G. Jan Colijn and Marcia Sachs Littell, *Confronting the Holocaust: A Mandate for the 21st Century,* Studies in the Shoah 19 (Lanham, Md.: University Press of America, 1997), 51–62. Also see Gabrielle Tyrnauer, "Holocaust History and the Gypsies," in *The Ecumenist* 12 (September–October, 1988): 90–94; Ian Hancock, "Uniqueness, Gypsies and Jews," in Yehuda Bauer et al., *Remembering for the Future,* 2017–25; Robert Proctor, *Racial Hygiene: Medicine under the Nazis* (Cambridge, Mass.: Harvard University Press, 1988); Richard Plant, *The Pink Triangle: The Nazi War against Homosexuals* (New York: Henry Holt, 1986).

7. Rosemary Radford Ruether, "The Holocaust: Theological and Ethical Reflections," in Baum, *The Twentieth Century,* 76.

8. Ibid.

9. Holocaust historian Raul Hilberg sums up in three steps the centuries-long path to the genocide of the Jews. In brief, the process begins with Christianity's ghettoization of the Jews after failing to convert them; the second step traces the Jewish emergence from the ghetto, in secular Europe, when they are perceived as an economic threat; the final step is bolstered by the "scientific" theory of the Jews as racially inferior and menacing to the Aryan race. See Raul Hilberg, *The Destruction of European Jews,* 3 vols. (New York: Holmes & Meier, 1985).

10. Richard L. Rubenstein and John K. Roth, *Approaches to Auschwitz: The Legacy of the Holocaust* (London: SCM Press, 1987), 138.

11. Ibid., 139.

12. Ibid.

13. Ibid., 139–40.

14. Ibid., 147.

15. Steven T. Katz, "The Uniqueness of the Holocaust," in Cohn-Sherbok, *Holocaust Theology: A Reader,* 58. Regarding the uniqueness of the Jewish Holocaust event, Katz makes a distinction between the Nazi extermination of the Jews and that of the Gypsies, who are often cited as having suffered the same exact fate. However, "the Nazis did not ontologize the Gypsy into their metahistorical antithesis, nor did they make the elimination of all Gypsies from history a primal part of either their historic 'mission' or their metaphysical 'mythos'" (59).

16. For Bauer, the uniqueness lies in the Nazis' rebellion against the very civilization from which it was born. In this way, they were the "illegitimate" heirs of the Enlightenment,

of Western philosophy in general, and of German philosophy in particular. See Yehuda Bauer, "The Trauma of the Holocaust: Some Historical Perspectives," in Colijn and Littell, *Confronting the Holocaust,* 5.

17. Kenneth Seeskin rightly asks: "Did the bureaucrats who ordered the gas have the same intention as the people who turned it on? Did either have the same intention as the officers who designed the ingenious methods of torture, or the citizens who looked the other way?" Kenneth Seeskin, "What Philosophy Can and Cannot Say about Evil," in *A Holocaust Reader: Responses to the Nazi Extermination,* ed. Michael L. Morgan (New York: Oxford University Press, 2001), 327.

18. Rubenstein and Roth, *Approaches to Auschwitz,* 292.

19. Primo Levi, "Survival in Auschwitz," in Morgan, *A Holocaust Reader,* 27.

20. Rubenstein and Roth, *Approaches to Auschwitz,* 323.

21. Hannah Arendt, "The Concentration Camps," in Morgan, *A Holocaust Reader,* 56.

22. Ibid., 58.

23. Ibid., 59.

24. Tom Segev, *Soldiers of Evil: The Commandants of the Nazi Concentration Camps* (New York: Berkley Publishing Group, 1987), 80. Developmental psychologist Erik Erikson refers to the concept of "pseudospeciation" by which "people lose the sense of being one species and try to make other kinds of people into a different and mortally dangerous species, one that doesn't count, one that isn't human.... You can kill them without feeling that you have killed your own kind." Erik Erikson quoted in James Waller, *Becoming Evil: How Ordinary People Commit Genocide and Mass Killing* (New York: Oxford University Press, 2002), 244.

25. See Rubenstein and Roth, *Approaches to Auschwitz,* 322–23.

26. Quoted in Jonathan Glover, *Humanity: A Moral History of the Twentieth Century* (New Haven, Conn.: Yale University Press, 1999), 338–39.

27. *Hitler's Table Talk, 1941–1944,* intro. by Hugh Trevor-Roper (Oxford: Enigma, 1988), 332.

28. In *The Tower and the Abyss* (New York: George Braziller, 1957), Erich Kähler considered this characteristic Nazi split between cruelty and brutality on one hand and a sophisticated civilized sensibility on the other as indicative of a new kind of schizophrenia which, in its rudimentary and potential form, is widespread in modern civilization. See discussion in David Hirsch, "The Gray Zone, or the Banality of Evil," in Roth and Grob, *Ethics after the Holocaust,* 102–3.

29. Didier Pollefeyt, "The Holocaust and Evil," in Cohn-Sherbok, *Holocaust Theology: A Reader,* 166–67.

30. Ibid., 168. See Didier Pollefeyt, "Auschwitz, or How Good People Can Do Evil," in Colijn and Littell, *Confronting the Holocaust,* 101–2.

31. Omer Bartov, *Mirrors of Destruction: War, Genocide, and Modern Identity* (New York: Oxford University Press, 2000), 93.

32. Ibid. Bartov continues his analysis of identity and exclusion by tracing the historical evolution by which the Jews became the elusive enemy, problematic other, and scapegoat for all of Germany's cultural and political problems. At the beginning of World War I, largely through effective uses of propaganda, the enemy was easily and obviously identified as "those (outsiders) who threaten us" or, "that one who is fighting against me." Toward the end of the war, however, once the full-blown, visceral horrors of trench warfare had been experienced by soldiers on both sides, the identity of the enemy seemed to shift to those invisible forces who were responsible for so much suffering: those military strategists, politicians, industrialists, and those involved in the state's powers of mobilization and control, who seemed to perpetuate the unending cycles of battles and bloodshed from the rear. Oddly, a new kind of solidarity was being forged among soldiers of both sides who had experienced and survived the terrors of modern warfare. At the same time, the new modes of industrial killing also began to create a morbid fascination and sometimes even an overpowering intoxication with the horror of the battlefield. In the wake of the devastation of the fighting, postwar Germany was rife with bitter animosities, mutual blaming, violence and terror, all of which paved the way for the rise of the Nazi party. A new quest to identify those really responsible for the suffering and defeat had begun that would ultimately lead to accusations against the Jews for their alleged subversion and disloyalty (93–99). "Those on the lookout for domestic enemies needed a group that would be both sufficiently visible and more or less universally disliked, perceived as both all-powerful and numerically marginal so that its elimination from society would not have a major detrimental effect on the nation, both an easy target for victimization and generally accepted as the chief instigator of its persecutors' own victimhood. An enemy, that is, whose very persecution would serve to manifest the power and legitimacy of the victimizer, while simultaneously allowing the persecutor to claim the status of the 'true' (past, present, and potentially future) victim" (99).

33. Ibid., 105.

34. Hinton, *Annihilating Difference,* 14. Laban cites several factors that have contributed to modernity's tendency toward essentializing difference. Science itself, for example, is always in search of regularity as exemplified by its classification systems, theoretical laws, and quantitative measures. The notion of progress, especially manifest in modernity's project of social engineering, required a rational design which can be regulated from above. The modern nation-state, too, with its fixed territorial borders, centralized control of power, and impersonal, bureaucratic means of governance depends on a high degree of homogeneity for its "imagined community" of theoretically uniform citizens all of whom have the same needs, interests, duties, and rights. "This tendency frequently culminates in a naturalized identification between person and place, often expressed in origin myths and arborescent metaphors that physically 'root' nationals to their homeland and assert the identification of blood, soil, and nation (13). Laban asserts that modern anthropology itself arose as a discipline of difference in the colonial encounter with the

strange and primitive "other." An interesting study on how historical difference has been manufactured with the "evidence" of archeology is found in Bettina Arnold, "Justifying Genocide: Archeology and the Construction of Difference" in Laban, *Annihilating Difference,* 95–116.

35. Jean Améry, "On the Necessity and Impossibility of Being a Jew," in Morgan, *A Holocaust Reader,* 29.

36. See Waller, *Becoming Evil,* 236–44.

37. Ibid., 239.

38. Ibid. Waller bases his group-identification theories primarily on the separate studies of social psychologists Muzafer Sherif, Henri Tajfel, and Marilynn Brewer. See also M. Sherif, O. J. Harvey, B. J. White, W. R. Hood, and C. Sherif, *Intergroup Conflict and Cooperation: The Robbers' Cave Experiment* (Norman: Oklahoma Book Exchange, 1961); Henri Tajfel and John C. Turner, "An Integrative Theory of Intergroup Conflict," in Austin and S. Worchel, *The Social Psychology of Intergroup Relations;* and Marilynn B. Brewer, "The Psychology of Prejudice: Ingroup Love or Outgroup Hate?" *Journal of Social Issues* 55 (1999): 435.

39. Waller, *Becoming Evil,* 243. According to Waller, the process of social death that begins with us-them thinking is intensified by the subsequent steps of (1) dehumanization of the victims, followed by (2) blaming the victims, either for what they allegedly have done and even for what they could have done in order to resist persecution but failed to do (see 249–55).

40. Arendt, *Eichmann in Jerusalem,* 277.

41. Didier Pollefeyt, "Auschwitz, or How Good People Can Do Evil: An Ethical Interpretation of the Perpetrators and the Victims of the Holocaust in Light of the French Thinker Tzvetan Todorov," in Colijn and Littell, *Confronting the Holocaust,* 94–95.

42. Arendt's phrase, moreover, is associated with the binary debate among Holocaust scholars between "intentionalists," those who hold that the Nazi plan to exterminate European Jewry was something conceived as early as their ascendancy to power, and "functionalists," those who believe that the Holocaust was the result of an extended, sometimes haphazard, development of events that lasted over ten years. See Bardov, *Mirrors of Destruction,* 181ff. The intentionalist position, in some cases, maintains that the Holocaust could only have occurred in Germany and stresses the uniqueness of German anti-Semitism. An extreme form of the monocausal (anti-Semitic) approach is found in Daniel Jonah Goldhagen's *Hitler's Willing Executioners* (1996). However, for an insightful critique of Goldhagen, see also Franklin H. Littell, ed., *Hyping the Holocaust: Scholars Answer Goldhagen* (East Rockaway, N.Y.: Cummings & Hathaway, 1997), especially Didier Pollefeyt and G. Jan Colijn, "Leaving Evil in Germany: The Questionable Success of Goldhagen in the Low Countries," 3–18. Regarding the word "monster," David Hirsch points to the definition listed as substantive #4 in the *Oxford English Dictionary:* "A person of inhuman and horrible cruelty or wickedness." He asks a probing question: "Suppose the Israelis had

put Dr. Josef Mengele on trial, instead of Eichmann, would it then have been possible for Arendt to discover the same "banality of evil" in Mengele that she did in Eichmann?" (Hirsch, "The Gray Zone," 103).

43. Pollefeyt, "Auschwitz, or How Good People Can Do Evil," 96. Pollefeyt bases his analysis here on the thought of French thinker Tzvetan Todorov. See *Face à l'extrême,* first published in 1991 (Paris: Seuil/Collection La couler des idées) and later revised in 1994 (Paris: Seuil/Collection Points), 295.

44. Zygmunt Bauman, *Modernity and the Holocaust* (Cambridge: Polity Press, 1989). See also Richard L. Rubenstein, "Apocalyptic Rationality and the Shoah," in Jacobs, *The Holocaust Now: Contemporary Christian and Jewish Thought,* ed. Steven L. Jacobs (East Rockaway, N.Y.: Cummings & Hathaway, 1996).

45. Bauman, *Modernity and the Holocaust,* 61–62. Strictly speaking, racism needs to be analytically distinguished from more common and pervasive instances of *heterophobia,* in essence, fear of the different. In the heterophobic situation, the collective identity of the alien group is not so obvious or easily recognized and as such remains an obscure (but certain) threat in its boundary-blurring potency. It is the manifestation of the anxiety arising from the feeling that one has no control over the situation and therefore is unable to influence its outcome. Characteristic of heterophobia is the sense of the "enemy in our midst" which most often leads to a vehement frenzy of boundary-drawing in an attempt to locate the object toward which hostility can be directed and by which the anxiety of confusion can be eliminated and the familiar (right) way of life restored. Heterophobia must be further distinguished from *contestant enmity,* which is a more specific antagonism motivated by the need to separate from the clearly defined other in order to seek identity and draw boundaries. Hatred and resentment are the emotional appendages to the activity of separation itself. See Bauman, chapter 5.

46. Ibid., 65. Here we might recall Theodor Adorno's advice that in order to understand anti-Semitism one should analyze not the Jews but the anti-Semites. "It is they who should be made conscious of the mechanisms that provoke their racial prejudice." Theodor Adorno, Else Frenkel-Brunswik, Daniel Levinson, and R. Nevitt Sanford, *The Authoritarian Personality* (New York: Harper, 1950), 128.

47. Bauman, *Modernity and the Holocaust,* 68–72. The Nazi agenda of social engineering was horrifyingly extensive: "well before they built the gas chambers, the Nazis, on Hitler's orders, attempted to exterminate their own mentally insane or bodily impaired compatriots through 'mercy killing' (falsely nicknamed 'euthanasia') and to breed a superior race through the organized fertilization of racially superior women by racially superior men (eugenics). Like these attempts, the murder of Jews was an exercise in the rational management of society and a systematic attempt to deploy in its service the stance, the philosophy and the precepts of applied science" (72).

48. Haim Bresheeth, Stuart Clink Hood, and Litza Jansz, *The Holocaust for Beginners* (Cambridge: Icon Books, 2000), 88–97.

49. Rubenstein and Roth, *Approaches to Auschwitz,* 149.

50. Franklin Sherman, "Speaking of God after Auschwitz," in Morgan, *The Holocaust Reader,* 198.

51. Eliezer Berkovits, *Faith after the Holocaust* (New York: KTAV Publishing, 1973), 68. Berkovits distinguishes between an inauthentic quest (using the Holocaust to prove one's previously held disbelief in the living God) and an authentic quest (approaching the horrors within the faith of the living tradition). "Only the believer in the living God of Israel is involved in the crisis of faith of the death camps; only he can lose his faith on account of it."

52. Elie Wiesel, *Night* (London: Macgibbon & Kee, 1960), 88.

53. Neiman, *Evil in Modern Thought,* 2.

54. Wiesel, *Night,* 88. Wiesel recollects here the words of a Polish rabbi.

55. Rubenstein and Roth, *Approaches to Auschwitz,* 301.

56. Richard Rubenstein, *After Auschwitz: Radical Theology and Contemporary Judaism* (Indianapolis: Bobbs-Merrill, 1966), 69.

57. Emil Fackenheim, *God's Presence in History* (New York: Harper, 1970), 73.

58. The deafening silence of Auschwitz, God's silence, the silence of bystanders, the silence of utter bewilderment, continues to disturb. On his visit to Auschwitz on May 28, 2006, Pope Benedict XVI confessed: "In a place like this words fail; in the end, there can only be a dread silence — a silence which is itself a heartfelt cry to God: Why Lord, did you remain silent? How could you tolerate all this?" (Craig Whitlock, "Pope Prays at Auschwitz Death Camp," *Providence Journal,* May 29, 2006, A2).

59. Two radically different but, by now, classic answers to this central question are found in Ignaz Maybaum, *The Face of God after Auschwitz* (Amsterdam: Polak & Van Gennep, 1965), and Rubenstein, *After Auschwitz.*

60. Helmut Gollwitzer et al., eds., *Dying We Live: The Final Messages and Records of Some Germans Who Defied Hitler,* trans. Reinhard C. Kuhn (London: Havill Press, 1956), 76. The above is the testimony, written from his cell, of Carl Friedrich Goerdeler.

61. G. Baudler, "The Biblical God and Theodicy," *Theology Digest* 47, no. 2 (Summer 2000): 135.

62. Ibid.

63. The topic of the role of narrative is explored later in this first part. See also Anson Laytner, *Arguing with God: A Jewish Tradition* (Northvale, N.J.: Jason Aronson, 1990). See also David R. Blumenthal, *Facing the Abusing God: A Theology of Protest* (Louisville: Westminster John Knox, 1993).

64. Wiesel, *Night,* 62. Although this passage is quoted from Wiesel, the particular interpretation of a suffering God cannot necessarily be inferred from it. This interpretation is primarily derived from Jürgen Moltmann. See his *The Crucified God: The Cross of Christ as the Foundation and Criticism of Christian Theology,* trans. R. A. Wilson and J. Bowden (London: SCM Press, 1994), 274.

65. Colin Eimer, "Jewish and Christian Suffering" in Cohn-Sherbok, *Holocaust Theology: A Reader,* 135.

66. The idea of a suffering God is certainly not without its detractors. Most notably, in his recent work *Does God Suffer?* Thomas Weinandy answers his title question with an adamant and resounding "No!" He claims that those theologians who opt for the passibility of God, even after the calamity of Auschwitz, are merely buying into the Enlightenment tendency of needing to make mysteries not only clear but also comprehendible. Of course, Weinandy defends the notion that God is utterly passionate in his love, mercy, and compassion. It is only the notion that "God experiences inner emotional changes of state, either of comfort or discomfort, whether freely from within or by being acted upon from without" that he disputes (Thomas G. Weinandy, O.F.M. Cap., *Does God Suffer?* [Edinburgh: T. & T. Clark, 2000], 39). Interestingly, Weinandy admits early in the book that it was precisely the Auschwitz event that filled him with trepidation when deciding to take up his project of defending God's impassibility. And yet, after reading the book, one wonders if Weinandy really has meaningfully integrated that catastrophe into his project, as the book fails to engage the topic sufficiently, having included little more than a brief closing tribute to Edith Stein.

67. Dorothee Sölle, "God's Pain and Our Pain," in Maduro, *Judaism, Christianity, and Liberation,* 113.

68. Ibid., 113–14.

69. Ibid., 114. All the same, Johann Baptist Metz insists that "those who talk about a suffering and co-suffering God nonetheless presume a particular form of omnipotence, namely, the omnipotence and invincibility of God's love. For how could God be God, and continue to be God, how would God be anything other than the hopeless duplication of our own suffering and our own love, if God's love could itself founder in this suffering and co-suffering? In this case is there not something like a semantic sleight-of-hand going on, if (consciously or unconsciously) we talk about a suffering God that can never really break down, can never really collapse?" (Johann Baptist Metz, *Hope against Hope,* 47).

70. Paul Fiddes, *The Creative Suffering of God* (New York: Oxford University Press, 1988), 267. "But in the cross the encounter of God with death reaches its uttermost pitch, and so his suffering becomes most creative and persuasive."

71. Paul Fiddes, "The Holocaust and Divine Suffering," in Cohn-Sherbok, *Holocaust Theology: A Reader,* 128.

Chapter 3. Exclusion: Evil and Suffering in the Twentieth Century – Second Reflection

1. Miroslav Volf, *Exclusion and Embrace: A Theological Exploration of Identity, Otherness, and Reconciliation* (Nashville: Abingdon Press, 1996), 68.

2. Volf is indebted to Cornelius Plantinga for his understanding of the notion of God's creative "separating" and binding together" as depicted in the book of Genesis. See Cornelius Plantinga Jr., *Not the Way It's Supposed to Be: A Breviary of Sin* (Grand Rapids: Eerdmans, 1995).

3. Volf, *Exclusion and Embrace,* 66.

4. Ibid., 65.

5. Ibid., 67.

6. Vern Neufeld Redekop, *From Violence to Blessing: How an Understanding of Deep-Rooted Conflict Can Open Up Paths to Reconciliation* (Ottawa: Novalis, 2002), 23.

7. Ibid., 147.

8. Richard J. Bernstein, "Evil and the Temptation of Theodicy," in Critchley and Bernasconi, *The Cambridge Companion to Levinas,* 253.

9. Emmanuel Levinas, *Totality and Infinity: An Essay on Exteriority,* trans. Alphonso Lingis (Pittsburgh: Duquesne University Press, 1969), 21–22.

10. Ibid., 80.

11. Levinas, however, does find a different approach in the third of Descartes's *Metaphysical Meditations,* which analyzes the irreducibility of the "infinite," an idea itself that is found in human consciousness. Infinity prevents the Other from assimilation or absorption by the Same. See the editorial notes to *Transcendence and Height* [1962] in Emmanuel Levinas, *Basic Philosophical Writings,* ed. Adriaan T. Peperzak, Simon Critchley, and Robert Bernasconi (Bloomington: Indiana University Press, 1996), 11.

12. Simon Critchley, "Introduction," in *The Cambridge Companion to Levinas,* 13.

13. Emmanuel Levinas, *Ethics and Infinity: Conversations with Philippe Nemo,* trans. Richard A. Cohen (Pittsburgh: Duquesne University Press, 1985), 75.

14. This is precisely where Levinas parts company with Heidegger, to whom he is indebted for the latter's basic critique of the intellectualism of traditional metaphysics, but who must ultimately still comprehend the particular being with reference to the universal *eidos.* See Emmanuel Levinas, "Is Ontology Fundamental?" (1951) in Peperzak et al., *Basic Philosophical Writings,* 1. Of course, the fateful moment of Levinas's break with Heidegger coincided with the latter's political commitment to National Socialism and his appointment, in 1933, to the position of Rector of Freiburg University.

15. Levinas, *Ethics and Infinity,* 86. "The way in which the other presents himself, exceeding *the idea of the other in me,* we here name face. This *mode* does not consist in figuring as a theme under my gaze, in spreading itself forth as a set of qualities forming an image. The face of the Other at each moment destroys and overflows the plastic image it leaves me, the idea existing to my own measure and to the measure of its *ideatum* — the adequate idea. It does not manifest itself by these qualities but καθ αὐτό. It *expresses itself.* The face brings a notion of truth which, in contradistinction to contemporary ontology, is not the disclosure of an impersonal neuter, but *expression:* the existent breaks through all the envelopings and generalities of Being to spread out in its 'form' the totality of its 'content,'

finally abolishing the distinction between form and content. This is not achieved by some sort of modification of the knowledge that thematizes, but precisely by 'thematization' turning into conversation" (Levinas, *Totality and Infinity,* 51).

16. Levinas, *Ethics and Infinity,* 86.

17. Emmanuel Levinas, *Entre Nous: On Thinking-of-the-Other,* trans. Michael B. Smith and Barbara Harshav (New York: Columbia University Press, 1998), 192.

18. Levinas, *Ethics and Infinity,* 100.

19. Ibid., 101.

20. Jacques Haers, for one, is not convinced that obsession with the other from the other's place "on high" is in and of itself sufficient insurance against the pitfall of totalization. See Jacques Haers, "Defensor Vinculi et Conversationis: Connectedness and Conversation as a Challenge to Theology," in *Theology and Conversation: Towards a Relational Theology,* Bibliotheca Ephemeridum Theologicarum Lovaniensium 172, ed. Jacques Haers and Peter De Mey (Leuven: Leuven University Press–Peeters, 2003). For Haers, ethical priority can become as oppressive as ontological starting points if according to the former (using Levinasian terms) the other-defining-I still attempts to exhaust infinity, "an attempt to control the deep connectedness from the perspective of an ethical discourse. It would represent a grand narrative — be it an ethical one — and a perversion of the very connectedness that aims at overthrowing all grand narratives, as it objects to I-centered thought" (10). Citing the objections of Rudi Visker, Haers finds that Levinas's appeal of the Other as challenging the egoism of the I's *conatus essendi* makes him miss the complexity of this subject, which had already been decentered prior to the challenge of the face — the sense of the threatening "vague debt" points to this originary decentering that bespeaks of the subject's attachment to something to which it is denied access, the existence of which is made clear in the subject's encounter with the strangeness — the difference — of the other's own forms of expression through which he likewise expresses, defensively, his own indebtedness to that which tries to dethrone him. But Visker's "vague debt" is for Haers still too close to Levinas in indicating a sense of threat, here resulting from subversion of the subject affirmation in the subject, which in itself indicates I-centered thinking, insofar as it is viewed from the perspective of the I. Haers asks: "Would the original rootedness not represent something infinitely more positive, i.e., the connectedness to the whole of reality as the basis for the building of a subject or a self? Would not the evil (Levinas) and the threat (Visker) originate not in the connectedness itself, but in its articulation and as a consequence of competitive settled I's?" (12). See also Rudi Visker, *The Human Condition: Looking for Difference after Levinas and Heidegger,* Phaenomenologica 175 (Dordrecht: Kluwer Academic Publishers, 2004).

Haers makes a good point, and it finds support in an unusual source, Megumi Sakabe's discussion of the Japanese concept of human personhood. Specifically, Sakabe critically analyzes Tetsuro Watsuji's attempt to build an ethics upon the Japanese view of the priority of relationships: the same Japanese word *hito* means both "human being" and "other human being." He explains, "There is an implicit understanding that a human being can never be a human being without being situated beforehand in a relation to others, or, in other words, in the field of 'in-between' or 'between-ness.'" However, Sakabe notes the problems that arise with too easy a reliance on this notion of "in-between-ness" as a simple foundation for an ethical system. He finds evidence in recent Japanese history itself: "The priority of 'between-ness' or the intersubjective field over the individual subject entails, almost as its logical consequence, a tendency to conformism or even totalitarianism, to the suppression of the active manifestation of individuality or the rights of individuals.... There is in the Japanese mentality, as represented typically by Watsuji, a certain tolerance toward totalitarian tendencies. In fact, toward the end of World War II, Watsuji fell prey to just such tendencies" (Megumi Sakabe, "Surrealistic Distortion of Landscape and the Reason of the Milieu," in *Culture and Modernity: East-West Philosophic Perspectives,* ed. Eliot Deutsch [Honolulu: University of Hawaii Press, 1991], 347–48). Thus, this Eastern perspective seems to highlight the same misgivings that Haers expresses, namely, the mere fact of the priority of relationality does not guarantee against totalitarian tendencies. We will return to Levinas on otherness in the final part.

21. Levinas, *Ethics and Infinity,* 107.

22. Todd May, *Reconsidering Difference: Nancy, Derrida, Levinas, and Deleuze* (University Park: Pennsylvania State University Press, 1997), 139. And yet May does accuse Levinas of collapsing together the feeling of responsibility and the actual having of it. "We must first note that an experience, as such, cannot be justifying for any ethical claim. One might, for instance, experience another as vile or unworthy; surely that does not justify treating that person as vile or unworthy" (140). Indeed, May may be pointing to what seems to be an obvious challenge to Levinas's ethics of the face, namely, that seeing the face of a Jew *did not stop* a Nazi from killing him. All the same, does not this very discrepancy point to the importance of the quality of "otherness" in the other? Seeing the face cannot simply mean exposure to the face. Figuratively speaking, one could stare at a face and still never see it, that is, never experience the otherness there and, in this way, avoid the "Thou shalt not kill" altogether. Levinas is emphasizing the integrity of the experience: No one kills who has truly experienced the face of the other. The question inevitably becomes: what realities prevent us from truly encountering the other? Still, it is worth reflecting on how it ever could be that 6 million "faces" could escape being "seen."

23. Levinas, *Entre Nous,* 91.

24. Ibid., 92.

25. Van de Beek, *Why? On Suffering, Sin, and God,* see p. 11, n. 2.

26. Levinas, *Entre Nous,* 92.

27. Ibid.

28. Ibid., 96.

29. Emmanuel Levinas, "Transcendence and Evil," in *Collected Philosophical Papers,* trans. Alphonso Lingis (The Hague: Martinus Nijhoff, 1987).

30. Bernstein, "Evil and the Temptation of Theodicy," 260.

31. Ibid., 261.

32. Levinas, "Transcendence and Evil," in *Collected Philosophical Papers,* 159–60.

33. Bernstein, "Evil and the Temptation of Theodicy," 261.

34. Implied here is a critique of Augustine's and Thomas's notion of evil as *privatio bonae.*

35. Levinas, "Transcendence and Evil," in *Collected Philosophical Papers,* 161.

36. Ibid., 163–64. According to Bernstein, Levinas's use of the term *conatus essendi* derived primarily from Spinoza: "The law of being, the *conatus essendi,* is the drive of being to preserve itself — the effort to exist. We as human *beings* are, of course, beings. Consequently, qua *beings,* this law of beings is our law" (Bernstein, "Evil and the Temptation of Theodicy," 263–64).

37. Bernstein, "Evil and the Temptation of Theodicy," 262.

38. Ibid., 263.

39. Ibid. 265.

40. Levinas, "Useless Suffering," 163. Levinas is adamant in his insistence that we are now living in a time "after theodicy." His critique of theodicy is severe: "This is the kingdom of transcendent ends, willed by a benevolent wisdom, by the absolute goodness of a God who is in some way defined by this super-natural goodness in Nature and History, where it would command the paths which are, to be sure, painful, but which lead to the Good. Pain is henceforth meaningful, subordinated in one way or another to the metaphysical finality envisaged by faith or by a belief in progress.... The evil which fills the earth would be explained in a 'plan of the whole' " (160–61). We can no longer invoke a metaphysical realm to help us cope with suffering. The real question for Levinas has to do with the meaning of religiosity and morality after Auschwitz, since "the phenomenon of Auschwitz demands (if we are not duped by morality) that we conceive of 'the moral law' independently of the Happy End" (Bernstein, "Evil and the Temptation of Theodicy," 256).

41. Terrence W. Tilley, *The Evils of Theodicy* (Eugene, Ore.: Wipf & Stock, 2000), 221–23. Tilley examines the negative status of religion during that time where churches frequently supported wars and revolutions in the name of "true" religion and debated such religious doctrines as predestination, which many had come to see as belittling to human freedom. Likewise, the rise of Newtonian scientific theory seemed to undermine the authority of so much of Scripture and church tradition, the great medieval synthesis of Thomas and Aristotle. "The Churches ceased being effective witnesses to a god worth worshipping" (223).

42. Ibid., 224. "When God is seen as the 'creator and benevolent governor of the world,' and when the world God created seems hardly benevolent or well governed, the supporter of the design argument must address challenges about the adequacy of the foundation for religious thought."

43. Ibid. Tilley looks to the "classic" Enlightenment theodicy of Archbishop William King, the Anglican archbishop of Dublin, who, though writing directly after the tumultuous era of the Glorious Revolution, fails to mention the previous century of religious wars or the suffering and evils of that bellicose period (225).

44. Ibid. "For Aquinas, for instance, there is no single problem of evil. In the *Summa,* evil is an objection to the existence of God (*ST,* I qq. 47–49)."

45. Tilley, *The Evils of Theodicy,* 226.

46. Ibid., 229.

47. Kenneth Surin, *Theology and the Problem of Evil* (Oxford: Basil Blackwell, 1986), 43. Surin situates this process within the greater anthropocentric turn following Descartes's *cogito* and as described in the work of such influential Enlightenment thinkers as David Hume whereby the human individual becomes the pivot of his or her own thinking and doing in the world as a self-defining subject. "This self-defining subject regards the world, including the good and evil contained therein, as an object of control, of *productivity.*"

48. Ibid., 10–11.

49. Surin also treats Augustine's theology of history as both a work and sign of God's providence (the post-Leibnizian theodicist is not constrained to understand history as possessing any intrinsic meaning or importance) and his epistemology, influenced as it was by the neo-Platonic notion of the divine illumination of the human mind (12). According to Surin, modern, post-Leibnizian theodicies include the free will defense as formulated by Alvin Plantinga, the natural law theodicy of Richard Swinburne, process theodicy of A. N. Whitehead and Charles Hartshorne, and John Hick's soul-making theodicy.

50. Surin, *Theology and the Problem of Evil,* 13. Tilley concurs with Surin on this important point. An examination of Augustine's discourse practices (Tilley's theses in *The Evils of Theodicy* rely on his interesting treatment of discourse practices according to "speech-act" theory) reveals a defense (*Enchiridion*) and a confession. "Augustine did not write a theodicy, although theodicies can be constructed from his writings" (228).

51. Surin, *Theology and the Problem of Evil,* 14.

52. Ibid., 15.

53. Ibid. See the intricate analysis of Irenaeus's argument in Surin, *Theology and the Problem of Evil,* 16–18.

54. Ibid., 18–19.

55. Ibid., 18.

56. Irenaeus, *Against Heresies,* II, 26, 1, quoted in Surin, *Theology and the Problem of Evil,* 19.

57. Surin, *Theology and the Problem of Evil,* 20–21. See also Tilley: "theodicy has become a discourse with a home more in the academy than in the churches" (*The Evils of Theodicy,* 233).

58. Surin rightly speaks of theology and philosophy as "signifying practices" wherein the text fully participates in society, that is, the text provides a structured representation of social and historical reality, and its subjectivity is in turn modified by the specific arrangements of social and historical materiality (*Theology and the Problem of Evil*, 50).

59. Surin, *Theology and the Problem of Evil*, 51. Tilley concludes that Surin exaggerates the power of theodicy to have such an endorsing effect on the evils of the world, unless, that is, Surin is speaking of theodicy not simply as a discourse practice but as the performance of assertive declarations by which theodicists not only describe but declare what is evil. Still, in a caveat similar to Levinas's objection to totality, Tilley warns against judging theodicists too severely in this way since such a judgment would presuppose "an unobstructed vision . . . an Archimedean perspective from which theodicists can be declared evil" (Tilley, *The Evils of Theodicy*, 248). "However, if they [theodicists] fail to declare 'evil' what is truly evil, their declarations create a reality in which what is truly evil is not evil. If theodicists misdeclare evil, they create an inconsistent and finally destructive discourse" (235).

60. Olivier Boulnois examines the development of the notion of providence throughout history and concludes that in the New Testament, far from promising happiness and ease to those who enjoy God's favor, providence is really about what one must be willing to risk, all the while trusting in the presence of the Spirit who will allow us to give witness. "Divine goodness does not assure believers that they will be victors in this world. Providence is not to be understood from the perspective of an abstract and rationalistic God, but rather from the perspective of Christ, who is the model of all relationship to divine Providence. . . . It must therefore be read from a perspective that is at once christological and Trinitarian: the Providence experienced by the Son is clearly that of the Father, who knows our needs. It culminates with the gift of the Spirit" (Olivier Boulnois, "The Concept of God after Theodicy," *Communio* [Fall 2002]: 456).

61. Surin, *Theology and the Problem of Evil*, 5. Surin is particularly critical of the theodicy of Richard Swinburne but sees similarly troubling signs in the theodicies of Alvin Plantinga and, though to a much lesser extent, John Hick.

62. Ibid., 124.

63. This is not to suggest that either of these theologians of the cross escapes critical assessment with respect to the Trinity. For example, some have found it objectionable that Moltmann's effort to unite the economic and immanent trinities has the undesirable effect of ontologizing evil and suffering. "For if, as Moltmann avers, pain, anguish and death become entrenched in the divine being, it must be the case that they have a positive quality, that they must retain their *potency* in the divine being if they are to be what they are. The outcome is bound to be highly problematic, not only for the concept of God, but also for the claim, central to the Christian faith, that in Christ God acted decisively in history to deprive evil of its power over human beings" (Surin, *Theology and the Problem of Evil*, 131).

64. Ibid., 23. See also Sarah K. Pinnock, *Beyond Theodicy: Jewish and Christian Continental Thinkers Respond to the Holocaust* (Albany: State University of New York Press,

2002). Pinnock utilizes an analysis of the works of Martin Buber and Ernst Bloch, Gabriel Marcel and Johann Baptist Metz, to provide both an existential and political rejection of theoretical theodicies that fail to effectively confront the existence of evil in the world.

Chapter 4. Probing Evil: Evil and Suffering in the Twentieth Century – Third Reflection

1. The American poet Robert Frost examined the dilemma of man's addiction to reason in the "God's Speech to Job" portion of *A Masque of Reason:*

> I've had you on my mind a thousand years
> To thank you some day for the way you helped me
> Establish once for all the principle
> There's no connection man can reason out
> Between his just deserts and what he gets.
> Virtue may fail and wickedness succeed.
> 'Twas a great demonstration we put on.
> I should have spoken sooner had I found
> The word I wanted. You would have supposed
> One who in the beginning *was* the Word
> Would be in a position to command it.
> I have to wait for words like anyone.
> Too long I've owed you this apology
> For the apparently unmeaning sorrow
> You were afflicted with in those old days.
> But it was of the essence of the trial
> You shouldn't understand it at the time.
> It had to seem unmeaning to have meaning....
> (Robert Frost, "God's Speech to Job,"
> *One Hundred Modern Poems,* ed. Selden Rodman
> [New York: Mentor Books, 1949], 113–14).

2. Edward Schillebeeckx, "The Mystery of Injustice and the Mystery of Mercy: Questions Concerning Human Suffering," *Stauros Bulletin* 3 (1975): 10–11. Indeed, the very attempt to posit the so-called "best of all possible worlds" is itself dehumanizing: "In short, the Enlightenment theory of world-harmony devalues the human person, making it a means to a greater end, the Totality" (6). In unintentional though very tragic ways, Enlightenment theodicy seems to resemble some of the same totalitarian urges detected in National Socialism.

3. Alexander Laban Hinton, *Annihilating Difference: The Anthropology of Genocide.* California Series in Public Anthropology 3 (Berkeley: University of California Press, 2002), 6.

4. In fact, modernity and locality are linked in genocide. Hinton stresses that modernity is not one "thing" but refers to a number of interrelated processes that give rise to distinct local formations, or "modernities." "If genocide has frequently been motivated by and legitimated in terms of metanarratives of modernity, genocide, like modernity itself, is always a local process and cannot be fully comprehended without an experience-near understanding. Thus modernity and genocide both involve the essentialization of difference, but the ways in which such differences are constructed, manufactured, and viewed may vary considerably across time and place" (18).

5. Ibid. For example, the Nazis incorporated typically German notions of blood, soil, bodily aesthetics, genealogy, and anti-Semitism.

6. Ibid., 19.

7. Ibid.

8. Christopher C. Taylor, "The Rwandan Genocide of 1994," in Hinton, *Annihilating Difference,* 160.

9. In brief, Girard holds that violence is "the heart and secret soul of the sacred," and that the function of ritual is to purify violence by replacing bloody acts of violence with symbolic acts of violence. "Ritual is nothing more than the regular exercise of 'good' violence . . . some rites may seem to us nothing more than senseless inversions of prohibited acts" (René Girard, *Violence and the Sacred,* trans. Patrick Gregory [Baltimore: Johns Hopkins University Press, 1977], 37). See also chapter 4 of the same source ("The Origins of Myth and Ritual," 89–118), and especially Girard, *Things Hidden since the Foundation of the World,* trans. Stephen Bann and Michael Metteer (Stanford, Calif.: Stanford University Press, 1987). Also see René Girard, *Deceit, Desire, and the Novel: Self and Other in Literary Structure* (Baltimore: Johns Hopkins University Press, 1965). Space limitations prohibit any further examination of Girard's understanding of the roots of violence in the sacred, as well as his discussion on the Eucharist, specifically on the point of any co-responsibility on behalf of the church for perpetuating the scapegoat mechanism via the understanding of Eucharist as the renewed sacrifice of Christ.

10. James Alison, whose treatment of the doctrine of original sin has been shaped by the mimetic theory, defends Girard's anthropological starting point: "Desire is shown to be anterior to language (and thus reason), to will (and thus freedom), and to memory (and thus history)" (Alison, *The Joy of Being Wrong: Original Sin through Easter Eyes* [New York: Crossroad, 1998], 40).

11. Ibid., 29.

12. See J.-M. Oughourlian, *The Puppet of Desire: The Psychology of Hysteria, Possession, and Hypnosis* (Stanford, Calif.: Stanford University Press, 1991). "The true psychological fact, the center of interest, is the relation between two holons" (quoted in Alison, *The Joy of Being Wrong,* 31).

13. Alison, *The Joy of Being Wrong,* 29.

14. Girard, *Violence and the Sacred,* 10. Girard points out that in the New Testament the words that designate mimetic rivalry and its consequences are the noun *skandalon* and the verb *skandalizein.* "Like the Hebrew word that it translates, 'scandal' means, not one of those ordinary obstacles that we avoid easily after we run into it for the first time, but a paradoxical obstacle that is almost impossible to avoid: the more this obstacle, or scandal, repels us, the more it attracts us" (Girard, *I See Satan Fall like Lightning,* trans. James G. Williams [Maryknoll, N.Y.: Orbis Books, 2001], 45).

15. Girard, *Violence and the Sacred,* 31.

16. Girard develops the progression of the sacrificial process in *Violence and the Sacred,* in which he also differentiates his position on the role of sacrifice in primitive societies from that of other more formalistic traditional theorists, such as Henri Hubert and Marcel Mauss, who in *Sacrifice: Its Nature and Function* (Chicago: University of Chicago Press, 1964) uphold the view that sacrifice is an act of mediation between a sacrificer and a deity. "Because the very concept of a deity, much less a deity who receives blood sacrifice is relegated by most modern theorists to the realm of the imagination.... The approach of Hubert and Mauss leads to the judgment of Claude Lévi Strauss in *Pensée sauvage:* because sacrificial rites have no basis in reality, we have every reason to label them meaningless" (Girard, *Violence and the Sacred,* 7). In contrast, in his extensive study of rituals and myths in primitive societies Girard identifies a key feature that establishes the efficacy of all sacrifices. "This common denominator is internal violence — all the dissensions, rivalries, jealousies, and quarrels within the community that the sacrifices are designed to suppress. The purpose of the sacrifice is to restore harmony to the community to reinforce the social fabric" (8). For our purposes, we are less interested in this aspect of Girard's view than in his account of mimetic desire.

17. Girard, *Violence and the Sacred,* 8. "In a universe where the slightest dispute can lead to disaster — just as a slight cut can prove fatal to a hemophiliac — the rites of sacrifices serve to polarize the community's aggressive impulses and redirect them toward victims that may be actual or figurative, animate or inanimate, but they are always incapable of propagating further vengeance. The sacrificial process furnishes an outlet for those violent impulses that cannot be mastered by self-restraint; a partial outlet, to be sure, but always renewable, and one whose efficacy has been attested by an impressive number of reliable witnesses. The sacrificial process prevents the spread of violence by keeping vengeance in check" (18).

18. Ibid., 11.

19. Ibid., 14.

20. Girard claims that it is clearly mimetic contagion that explains the hatred of the masses for exceptional persons, including Jesus and all the prophets. He emphasizes that it is not a matter of ethnic or religious identity. "The Gospels suggest that a mimetic process of rejection exists in all communities and not only among the Jews. The prophets are the preferential victims of this process, a little like all *exceptional* persons, individuals who are

different. The reasons for exceptional status are diverse. The victims can be those who limp, the disabled, the poor, the disadvantaged, individuals who are mentally retarded, and also great religious figures who are inspired, like Jesus or the Jewish prophets, or now, in our day, great artists or thinkers" (Girard, *I See Satan Fall like Lightning,* 26).

21. Alison, *The Joy of Being Wrong,* 19.

22. Girard, *Violence and the Sacred,* 19. Girard emphasizes that in these primitive societies that predate the establishment of a working legal system, participants in the violence of the sacrificial process recognize the violence "only in an almost entirely dehumanized form; that is, under the deceptive guise of the *sacred*" (30).

23. Ibid., 23. Girard also notes that the same enigmatic quality pervades the judicial systems that evolved to replace the institution of sacrifice.

24. Girard warns of our contemporary incredulity toward the sacrificial process: "A unique generative force exists that we can qualify only as religious in a sense deeper than the theological one. It remains concealed and draws its strength from this concealment, even as its self-created shelter begins to crumble. The acknowledgment of such a force allows us to assess our modern ignorance — ignorance in regard to violence as well as religion.... As soon as the essential quality of transcendence — religious, humanistic, or whatever — is lost, there are no longer any terms by which to define the legitimate form of violence and to recognize it among the multitude of illicit forms. The definition of legitimate and illegitimate forms then becomes a matter of mere opinion, with each man free to reach his own decision.... Only the introduction of some transcendental quality that will persuade men of the fundamental difference between sacrifice and revenge, between a judicial system and vengeance, can succeed in bypassing violence. All this explains why our penetration and demystification of the system necessarily coincides with the disintegration of that system" (24).

25. Of course, in light of our reflection on evil and suffering at Auschwitz, the most heinous episode of illegitimate scapegoating in our time, we must acknowledge that throughout history the biblical texts themselves have been regularly used to conceal rather than reveal social victimage practices. See Girard, *The Scapegoat* (Baltimore: Johns Hopkins University Press, 1986).

26. For an interesting compendium of critical reviews on both Wink's overall biblical and hermeneutical perspectives in general and on his recent work on "Son of Man" Christology in particular, see Brin Stevens, ed., "Six Critics Review Walter Wink's *The Human Being: Jesus and the Enigma of the Son of the Man,*" in *Cross Currents* 53 (Summer 2003): 264–317.

27. Walter Wink, *The Powers That Be* (New York: Doubleday, 1998), 5.

28. Walter Wink, *Naming the Powers: The Language of Power in the New Testament* (Philadelphia: Fortress, 1984). Wink points out that the phrase *archai kai exousias* ("principalities and powers'") is but one of many paired expressions for power and should not be singled out as of unique significance. Other such pairs include: Rulers (*archontes*) and

great men (Matt. 20:25); those who supposedly rule (*hoi dokountes archein*) and great men (Mark 10:42); kings (*basileis*) and those in authority (*hoi exousianzontes*) (Luke 22:25); chief priests (*archiereis*) and rulers (*archontes*) (Luke 24:20); authorities (*archonton*) and Pharisees (John 7:48); angels and principalities (*archai*) (Rom. 8:38); power (*dynamei*) and name (*onomati*) (Acts 4:7); power (*dynamin*) and wisdom (*sophian*) (1 Cor. 1:24); Power (*dynamin*) and authority (*exousian*) (Luke 9:1; Rev. 17:13); authority (*exousias*) and commission (*epitropes*) (Acts 26:12); authority (*exousia*) and power (*dynamei*) (Luke 4:36). "The language of power in the New Testament is imprecise, liquid, interchangeable, and unsystematic" (7–9).

29. Ibid., 104. "The 'principalities and powers' are the inner or spiritual essence, or gestalt, of an institution or state or system." Moreover, "as the soul of systems, the Powers in their spiritual aspect are everywhere around us. Their presence is inescapable. The issue is not whether we 'believe' in them but whether we can learn to identify them in our actual everyday encounters. The apostle Paul called this the gift of discernment" (Wink, *The Powers That Be*, 29).

30. Wink, *The Powers That Be*, 4–5.

31. Ibid., 5.

32. Ibid., 40.

33. Ibid., 29.

34. Girard, *I See Satan Fall like Lightning*, 98. Girard facilitates the discussion of powers by turning to the anthropological theories of social life propounded by Emile Durkheim, especially with regard to the concept of "social transcendence": "The great sociologist found in primitive societies a fusion of the sacred and the social that comes quite close to the basic paradox of the powers and principalities. The union of these two words, 'social' and 'transcendence' has been much criticized" (100).

35. Wink, *The Powers That Be*, 5.

36. Wink, *Naming the Powers*, 104.

37. Girard, *I See Satan Fall like Lightning*, 70. For example, "Let us go back to the moment when the divided community, at the height of the mimetic process, reestablishes its unity against a single victim who becomes the supreme scandal because everyone, in a mimetic fervor, holds this one to be guilty. Satan is the violent contagion that persuades the entire community, which has become unanimous, that this guilt is real. He owes one of his most ancient and traditional names to this art of persuasion. He is the *accuser* of the hero of Job, before God and even more so before the people. In transforming a community of people with distinct identities and roles into a hysterical mass, Satan produces myths and is the principle of systematic accusation that bursts forth from the contagious imitation provoked by scandals. Once the unfortunate victim is completely isolated, deprived of defenders, nothing can protect her or him from the aroused crowd. Everyone can set upon the victim without having to fear the least reprisal" (35–36).

38. Wink, *Naming the Powers*, 23.

39. Peter Vardy and Julie Arliss, *The Thinker's Guide to Evil* (Alresford, U.K.: John Hunt Publishing, 2003), 68. Zoroastrianism, structured around the dualism of good and evil, continues today as a very small religion in the name of Parsiism. "By the time the Christian Scriptures were written there is an assumed knowledge about the devil/Satan. Belief about life after death, and the afterlife as a time for reward or punishment was accepted by many." Paul had already taken key steps toward "demythologizing" by means of the categories of sin, law, the flesh, and death. See Wink, *Naming the Powers,* 105. The Gospels refer to the evil personification by his Hebrew name, Satan, as well as by his Greek title, the devil (*diabolos*); both words refer to the one who accuses, slanders, denounces, and seduces (Girard, *I Saw Satan Fall like Lightning,* 32).

40. According to Elaine Pagels, the vision of cosmic struggle, originally derived from Jewish apocalyptic sources, was later taken up and developed by certain sectarian groups, such as the Essenes, as they defended themselves against antagonistic forces opposing them: "This split cosmology, radically revising earlier monotheism, simultaneously involved a split society, divided between 'sons of light,' allied with the angels, and 'sons of darkness,' in league with the power of evil. Followers of Jesus adopted the same pattern." This strategic vision continued as the Jesus movement spread to Gentile converts, and in later generations against other movements deemed heretical throughout the centuries and in other polemical periods such as the Reformation. Despite such Manichean semblances, Pagels reminds that the overall scenario is rooted in the proper Christian conviction of the victory of Christ over Satan (Elaine Pagels, *The Origin of Satan* [New York: Vintage Books, 1995], 179–80).

41. Wink, *The Powers That Be,* 34. For Girard, the devil's quintessential being is the violent contagion that has no substance to it. "The devil does not have a stable foundation; he has no *being....* He is totally mimetic, which amounts to saying *nonexistent as an individual self*" (Girard, *I See Satan Fall like Lightning,* 42).

42. Wink, *The Powers That Be,* 34.

43. Rafael Moses quoted in Redekop, *From Violence to Blessing,* 160.

44. Johann Baptist Metz, "Theology as Theodicy?" in *A Passion for God: The Mythical-Political Dimension of Christianity,* ed. and trans. J. Matthew Ashley (New York: Paulist Press, 1998), 54. That portion of this source was originally published as "Theologie als Theodizee?" by J. B. Metz in *Theodizee: Gott vor Gericht,* ed. Willi Oelmüller (Munich: Herder, 1990).

45. Ibid., 55.

46. Ibid.

47. Metz was concerned over the absence of a profound enough integration of the implications of the Holocaust catastrophe in the theology of his teacher, Karl Rahner. J. Matthew Ashley contends that we cannot really understand how Metz departs from Rahner in this regard without first considering the relationship between theology and spirituality: "The dramatic shift he [Metz] made in the 1960s can be fully understood only in light of his

embrace of elements of apocalyptic spirituality that he learned by reading certain (secularized, to be sure) Jewish thinkers who had turned to those same sorts of resources in Judaism." Ashley goes on to demonstrate how Rahner, who confronted the same historical challenges, "responded to them by rooting his theology *more deeply* in the spiritual tradition in which he already stood: a particular, primarily apophatic and Neoplatonic, rendering of Ignatian spirituality" (J. Matthew Ashley, *Interruptions: Mysticism, Politics, and Theology in the Work of Johann Baptist Metz* [Notre Dame, Ind.: University of Notre Dame Press, 1998], 26). Indeed, it is Metz's mystical stance "prior to theological articulation and conceptualization," an open-eyed mysticism "painfully aware of the suffering of the world, of the negativities of history," that influenced his mistrust of certain philosophies (e.g., Heidegger) that purport to a sensitivity to temporality (37). "Metz is worried about how Heidegger's understanding of the temporality of Dasein relates to concrete history. Metz explains Heidegger's understanding of the temporality of Dasein, and then adds that 'the more specific connections [between the ontological temporality of truth and being and ontic history] have remained up to this point unexplained, so that *a curious unhistoricity* [*Ungeschichtlichkeit*] and *artificiality* adheres to Heidegger's concept of history' " (63). Ashley points here to what he has called "one of the leitmotifs of Metz's thought: to what degree does a theoretically derived concept of humans' involvement in history really direct them to the concrete events of history?"

48. Metz, "Theology as Theodicy?" 56.

49. Ibid. Metz's call for a sharpened apocalyptic vision does not lead to crude biblicism. Loss of this sense of apocalyptically charged expectation is due in part to current hermeneutical approaches that attempt to dismiss the apocalyptic as a relic of an antiquated, mythical world view. Metz warns: "Let us be guided with the suspicion that the appeal to hermeneutics in theology can also serve to silence the provocation of the biblical discourse about God and gently disburden us of its scandal" (57). On this point, too, do we find a significant difference between Metz and Rahner, who, in his essay on the theological hermeneutic of eschatological assertions, wants to purify eschatology from the apocalyptic tendencies that seem to predefine the future and curtail the Christian's freedom. See also "Eschatology," in Karl Rahner and Herbert Vorgrimler, *Concise Theological Dictionary* (New York: Herder & Herder, 1965), 149–50. Metz avers that any kind of Judaism or Christianity that loses its sight of the end times has already come to an end. "The apocalypse in biblical traditions is not a neurotic or inquisitive calculation of the point of time at which the world will end; rather it is a perception of the world in light of the knowledge of its end. I think that an eschatology developed with apocalyptic intensity is the authentic, culturally understandable dowry of the biblical spirit" (Metz, *Hope against Hope,* 41).

50. J. Matthew Ashley, "Johann Baptist Metz," in *The Blackwell Companion to Political Theology,* ed. Peter Scott and William T. Cavanaugh (Oxford: Blackwell Publishing, 2004), 250.

51. Johann Baptist Metz, *Faith in History and Society: Toward a Practical Fundamental Theology,* trans. David Smith (New York: Crossroad, 1980), 169.

52. Ibid., 175–76. Metz places some of the blame for contemporary despair on the Nietzschean image of time as the eternal return of the same. See Metz, *Hope against Hope,* 42. For Moltmann, contemporary apathy is partly attributable to society's failure to see the connection between suffering and love. "Life becomes inhuman; it becomes superficial. Work and consumption have the effect of repressing suffering, one's own as well as the other's. And when suffering is repressed, so is love. Finally, with the loss of love comes the demise of interesting life. One walks over dead bodies and one becomes a living corpse" (Jürgen Moltmann, *The Experiment Hope,* trans. M. Douglas Meeks, repr. ed. [Eugene, Ore.: Wipf & Stock, 2003], 96).

53. Metz, *Faith in History and Society,* 176.

54. Lieven Boeve, "God Interrupts History: Apocalypticism as an Indispensable Theological Conceptual Strategy," *Louvain Studies* 26 (2001): 196. Boeve identifies three characteristics of this contemporary apocalyptic sensitivity: a fear of the judgment that one seems to have provoked oneself, catastrophe mania as the flip side of the culture of the "kick" and as a symptom of and response to growing insecurity (198–201).

55. Ibid., 202. Boeve points out that it was the existential interpretation of Rudolf Bultmann that really instigated the process of de-apocalypicism as a part of his greater program of de-mythologization.

56. Ibid., 208–9. Boeve contrasts the Jewish concept of time — a linear understanding with a beginning and an end and within which God intervenes, and the Greek — an asymmetric duality between time and eternity wherein time is only conceptualized in relation to eternity as a continuum. "Time has become a synonym for continuity and participation in eternity" (206).

57. Johann Baptist Metz, "Toward a Christology after Auschwitz," in *Theology Digest* 48 (Summer 2001): 104. Here Metz is practicing what he preaches: a post-Auschwitz Christology must be grounded in three convictions. It must be: sensitive to theodicy; apocalyptic in vision (otherwise it will more than likely deteriorate into an ideology of victory; Christology has traditionally been "the spearpoint of anti-Semitism"); and based on the synoptic paradigm (that is, it must be shaped not by ideas and systems that have no subject, but in the history of discipleship)" (106–7).

58. Tzvetan Todorov, *Hope and Memory: Reflections on the Twentieth Century,* trans. David Bellos (London: Atlantic Books, 2003), 162.

59. Metz, *Hope against Hope,* 15. Christian theology, heavily influenced by the apologetic intention of Augustine's doctrine of human freedom (a counterposition against Marcion gnosticism), developed a sensitivity to sin rather than to suffering. Suffering becomes all humanity's fault. The problem, as Metz points out, is that human freedom is posited by God; it is not autonomous but theonomous. "Augustine makes salvation paired with universal justice a matter of sin and guilt. [But] what about all the suffering that

cannot be traced back to sin or guilt? The God question, that is, God's justice, the eschatological question, is silenced. And what have been the consequences? Theology allowed
no questioning of God in the face of suffering and an exaggerated role of guilt" (Metz, *A
Passion for God,* 71).

60. Metz, *Hope against Hope,* 24.

61. Ibid., 12.

62. Terrence Tilley, *Story Theology* (Collegeville, Minn.: Liturgical Press, 1990), 30.

63. Juan Luis Segundo, S.J., *The Liberation of Dogma: Faith, Revelation, and Dogmatic
Teaching Authority,* trans. Phillip Berryman (Maryknoll, N.Y.: Orbis Books, 1992), 108.

64. Darrell J. Fasching, *Narrative Theology after Auschwitz: From Alienation to Ethics,*
South Florida Studies in the History of Judaism, ed. Jacob Neusner et al. (Atlanta: Scholars
Press, 1999), 89.

65. Hauerwas quoted in ibid., 93–94: "According to Hauerwas, narrative is the connected description of contingent events and human sufferings that captures the drama of
human life in a plot. The plot explains to us just what that drama is and thus what kinds of
responses might be appropriate" (93). See Stanley Hauerwas, Richard Bondi, and David B.
Burrell, *Truthfulness and Tragedy: Further Investigations in Christian Ethics* (Notre Dame,
Ind.: University of Notre Dame Press, 1977).

66. Fasching, *Narrative Theology after Auschwitz,* 22. Fasching examines the search for
even a way to name the event — *Holocaust* (burnt offering), *Shoah* (desolation) as evidence of the challenge the crisis has posed to the human need to find meaning in the wake
of tragedy. For Arthur Cohen, only the term *tremendum* does justice to the *caesura,* the hermeneutical rupture that ensued. For Richard Rubenstein, it was the *death of God.* For him,
after Auschwitz, religious explanations no longer seem adequate. For Elie Wiesel, it was
God, and not the Jews, we proved unfaithful. In the absence, Emil Fackenheim hears a new
revelation, a "commanding voice" that forbids Jews to hand Hitler a posthumous victory.
"Hence the agonizing dialogue goes on as the Jewish people seek to understand themselves
anew after the hermeneutical rupture of the Holocaust. Where it shall all lead is yet to be
decided" (22–23). For Christians, a further dimension of the crisis is the acknowledgment
of the church's complicity in anti-Semitism, as found in the age-old perpetuation of the
myth of supersession. In 1965, the Second Vatican Council's *Nostra aetate* represented a
radical break with the supersession myth: based on the Letter to the Romans, the document
portrays the church as a "wild shoot" grafted on the "well-cultivated olive tree" of Judaism.
And a 1973 joint Protestant-Catholic statement by a study group of the National Council
of Churches and the National Council of Catholic Bishops demonstrates succinctly the
reversal that Christian faith is undergoing: "In Christ the Church shares in Israel's election
without superseding it." See Helga Croner, ed., *Stepping Stones to Further Jewish-Christian
Relations* (New York: Stimulus Books, 1977), 152, as quoted in Fasching, *Narrative Theology after Auschwitz,* 24. The crisis of interpretation has allowed a new hermeneutical

principle that Fasching bases on Irving Greenberg's stark dictum that no statement, theological or otherwise, should be made that would not be credible in the presence of the burning children. "Greenberg reminds us that during the Holocaust the Nazis threw Jewish children alive in the crematoria fires. After Auschwitz, no theologian should ever write a sentence without spiritually descending in sympathy and imagination into those fires to submit his or her writings for the approval of those children. Never again should any theologian write anything that might even remotely reopen the path from supersession to genocide" (40).

67. Ibid., 38–39.

Chapter 5. An Anatomy of Revenge

1. Girard, *Violence and the Sacred,* 14. But even the judicial system, which of course is infinitely more effective than sacrifice and sacrificial rites, can operate successfully as a deterrent to retribution only in conjunction with a firmly established political power. Ibid., 23.

2. Volf, *Exclusion and Embrace,* 121.

3. Ibid. See Hannah Arendt, *The Human Condition: A Study of the Central Dilemmas Facing Modern Man* (Garden City, N.Y.: Doubleday, 1959), 212.

4. Wink, *The Powers That Be,* 54.

5. Ibid., 57.

6. Ibid., 60. The values and mores that once gave a sense of belonging to members of traditional cultures no longer have that binding effect. As a result, people are often powerfully swayed by the fads and trends of the communications media. "People live under the illusion that the views and feelings they have acquired by listening to the media are their own." Ibid.

7. See Etty Hillesum, *An Interrupted Life: The Diaries of Etty Hillesum,* trans. Arnold J. Pomerans (New York: Pantheon, 1984).

8. Trudy Govier, *Forgiveness and Revenge* (London and New York: Routledge, 2002), 20.

9. Ibid., 21.

10. Volf, *Exclusion and Embrace,* 80.

11. Ibid., 84.

12. This is not to imply that there is no legitimate differentiation between perpetrators and victims. As Primo Levi suggests in *The Drowned and the Saved,* human actions need to be considered on both a legal and an anthropological level: the latter suggests that we may all be capable of committing monstrous deeds; the former stresses that we are all free agents and therefore responsible for our own acts. "I do not know, and it does not much interest me to know, whether in my depths there lurks a murderer, but I do know that I was a guiltless victim and I was not a murderer. I know that the murderers existed, not only in Germany, and still exist, retired or on active duty, and that to confuse them with their

victims is a moral disease or an aesthetic affectation or a sinister sign of complicity; above all, it is precious service rendered (intentionally or not) to the negators of truth." Primo Levi, *The Drowned and the Saved,* trans. Raymond Rosenthal (London: Abacus, 1988), 32–33. Tzvetan Todorov commends Levi's humility: "He does not shout but speaks *sotto voce; . . .* he weighs up the pros and the cons, he recalls the exceptions, and seeks out the reasons for his own reactions. He neither gives shattering explanations of past history nor adopts the tone of a prophet with a direct line to the holy. Facing the Extreme, he remains human, all too human. And when he does speak of evil, the source of the offense, he does not point an accusing finger at others, but subjects himself to intense and never indulgent scrutiny." Todorov, *Hope and Memory,* 180.

13. Michael Lerner, *Healing Israel/Palestine: A Path to Peace and Reconciliation* (Berkeley, Calif.: Tikkun Books/North Atlantic Books, 2003), xii. The following reflections are excerpted from this source.

Conclusion to Part One. Theology with Open Eyes

1. Metz, *Hope against Hope,* 34.

Part Two. 9/11

1. Giorgio Agamben insists that the subject of testimony at Auschwitz is the one who bears witness to a desubjectification. "Testimony takes place where the speechless one makes the speaking one speak and where the one who speaks bears the impossibility of speaking in his own speech, such that the silent and the speaking, the inhuman and the human enter into a zone of indistinction in which it is impossible to establish the position of the subject, to identify the 'imagined substance' of the 'I' and, along with it, the true witness." Giorgio Agamben, *Remnants of Auschwitz: The Witness and the Archive,* trans. Daniel Heller-Roazen (New York: Zone Books, 1999), 120. According to Agamben, it is therefore the *muselmann* that ultimately refutes the deniers of Auschwitz. Slavoj Žižek holds that Agamben's thesis is a kind of ontological proof against revisionists: notions such as the *muselmann* are so intense that they could not have come about without the fact of its existence. According to Žižek, Agamben is saying, in reply to Levi's summation of the Nazis' rationale that what was done was so horrible, no one could ever believe it, "true, it is not possible to bear witness to the ultimate horror of Auschwitz — but what if *this impossibility itself is embodied in a survivor?* If, then, there is a subjectivity like that of the *muselmann,* a subjectivity brought to the extreme point of collapsing into objectivity, *such desubjectivized subjectivity could have emerged only in the conditions which are those of Auschwitz.*" Slavoj Žižek, *Welcome to the Desert of the Real: Five Essays on September 11 and Related Dates* (London: Verso, 2002), 140.

2. William Stacy Johnson, "Probing the 'Meaning' of September 11, 2001," *Princeton Seminary Bulletin,* new series (2002): 42. See Maurice Blanchot, *The Writing of the Disaster* (Lincoln: University of Nebraska Press, 1986).

3. John Paul II, "Pope's Address to New Ambassador to the Holy See," *America,* October 8, 2001, 6.

Chapter 6. The Attack

1. *The 9/11 Commission Report: Final Report of the National Commission on Terrorist Attacks upon the United States,* authorized edition (New York: W. W. Norton, 2004). Unless otherwise specified, details for the factual analysis of chapter 6 and its subdivisions are derived from this authoritative source.

2. Ibid., 4. Most of what is known about the hijacking of American 11 was detailed by Ong and Sweeney.

3. See *The 9/11 Commission Report,* 453, n. 27.

4. Ibid., 6.

5. Ibid., 7.

6. Ibid. See FBI report of investigation, interview with Lee Hanson, September 11, 2001, 454.

7. Ibid., 7–8.

8. Ibid., 8–10.

9. The other hijacking teams consisted of five men. The fifth operative in the UA 93 flight was most likely Mohamed al Kahtani, who had been refused entry by a suspicious immigration inspector at Florida's Orlando International Airport earlier in August. Ibid., 11.

10. *The 9/11 Commission Report,* 11–14.

11. Ibid., 326. The president's statement is derived from the White House transcript. See Rice interview with Bob Woodward of the *Washington Post,* October 24, 2001, 367.

12. Ibid. See Statement by the president in his address to the nation, September 11, 2001 (online at *www.whitehouse.gov/news/releases/2001/09/20010911–16.html*).

13. *USA Today,* reporting October 29, 2003. The figures represent the final tally.

14. *The 9/11 Commission Report,* 309.

15. Rowan Williams, *Writing in the Dust: Reflections on 11th September and Its Aftermath* (London: Hodder & Stoughton, 2002), 47–48.

16. Andrew C. Mead, sermon preached on September 16, 2001, in Farina, *Beauty for Ashes,* 114.

17. John Horgan and Rev. Frank Geer, *Where Was God on September 11? A Scientist Asks a Ground Zero Pastor* (San Francisco: Brown Trout, 2002), 66–68.

18. The remains of this man were not identified until over a year had passed and were then flown to Israel for burial. Abraham Zelmanowitz, an observant Jew, worked as a computer programmer; his quadriplegic co-worker, a Catholic named Edward Beyea, could not descend the stairs after the towers were hit, even with the assistance of his nurse's aide. Zelmanowitz told the aide to leave, for the sake of her own children and then stayed with

his friend, refusing to leave him, until eventually he died with him. John Harvey, "To War," *Commonweal,* September 13, 2002, 9.

19. George W. Bush, President's Address at National Day of Prayer and Remembrance Service, September 14, 2001, National Cathedral, Washington, D.C.

20. Dale Russakoff, "Memories Haunt WTC Survivors," March 9, 2002; available from *www.msnbc.com/news/721921.asp./*

21. Daphne Merkin, "Terror-Filled," *New York Times Magazine,* August 15, 2004, 42.

22. Horgan and Geer, *Where Was God on September 11?* 38.

23. "In the midst of doubt we can be reassured when we realize that the human community has more than economic resources, more than military resources. In times of crisis spiritual resources emerge. These resources can awaken and energize our own spirit, individually and collectively. We can draw from spiritual resources of the past, from traditions that flourished in prehistoric times and are preserved in the spiritual teachings of indigenous peoples and in the wisdom tradition of the great traditions that crystallized over two thousand years ago as the major world religions." Ewert Cousins, "A Meditation at the Site of the Destruction of the World Trade Center: October 11, 2001," *Chicago Studies* 41, no. 1 (Spring 2002): 7.

24. Nancy T. Ammerman, "Grieving Together: September 11 as a Measure of Social Capital in the U.S.," in Markham and Abu-Rabi, *September 11: Religious Perspectives on the Causes and Consequences,* 54.

25. See "Harnessing the Spirit of September 11," *New York Times,* November 5, 2001, A 16.

26. Ammerman, "Grieving Together," 62–63.

27. Jean-Marie Colombani, "Nous sommes tous Américains," *Le Monde,* September 12, 2001, trans. Mary-Alice Farina, in John Farina, ed., *Beauty for Ashes,* 5. The pledge of solidarity for victims of the terrorist attack came from all over the world. See also in the same source, "Palestinian Christians Grieve over U.S. Tragedy," 12; The United Nations' condemnation of terrorist attacks, 14–15; Michel Sabbah, Latin Patriarch of Jerusalem, Homily of the Mass for Peace and Remembrance of the Victims in the U.S.A., September 17, 2001, 31; Statement from the Middle East Council of Churches, September 15, 2001, 34. Joint Statement by U.K. Religious Leaders, Lambeth Palace, September 12, 2001, 36; American Jewish Committee, "Deny Intolerance," in Farina, *Beauty for Ashes,* 48.

28. Robert H. Roberts, "A Shameful Distortion of Justice," in Farina, *Beauty for Ashes,* 38. The response of prayer was immediate and widespread. On September 12, Pope John Paul II invited the world to join him in prayer for the victims, begging the Lord "that the spiral of hatred and violence will not prevail"; he stressed the same sentiment on the next day in his address to the new ambassador of the United States to the Holy See: "In the century now opening before us, humanity has the opportunity to make great strides against some of its traditional enemies: poverty, disease, violence." Pope John Paul II in Farina, *Beauty for Ashes,* 15–18.

29. National Council of Churches of Christ in the U.S.A., "Deny Them Their Victory: A Religious Response to Terrorism," *Midstream: The Ecumenical Movement Today* 41, no. 1 (January 2002): 75.

30. American Jewish Committee, "Deny Intolerance," 48.

31. Amnesty International Report, "The Backlash: Human Rights at Risk throughout the World," October 4, 2001, available online. "In the USA there was a wave of compassion for the victims of the attack, with many people rushing to help, some at the cost of their own lives. But the horror and fear triggered by the attack also unleashed a wave of bigotry across the country targeted at Muslims, Asians, and those of Middle Eastern appearance. Such sentiments were fueled by radio stations falsely reporting that Muslims in the USA were celebrating the attack."

32. Ken Maguire, "Muslims Reflect on How Their Lives Have Changed," September 5, 2002 (AP). See online: *www.boston.com/news/packages/sept11/anniversary/wire_stories/0905 _muslims.htm.* The Massachusetts attorney general brought four civil rights cases to court in September, 2001: On September 12, three teens from Somerset and Fall River threw a Molotov cocktail into a convenience store whose owner, an Indian man, was thought to be Arab; also on September 12, a Hanover man threatened to kill James J. Zogby, president of the Arab American Institute in Washington, D.C., and his family; on September 29, an Arlington man threatened to run over the Greek owner of a convenience store in Belmont; in Georgetown, a claim was filed by an Algerian-born man who claimed to no longer introduce himself by his last name. In addition, twenty people filed discrimination complains with the Massachusetts Commission against Discrimination.

33. Rhonda Roumani, "I'm an American Muslim — and I'm Afraid," in Beliefnet et al., *From the Ashes,* 147–48.

34. Pat Roberston, "God Almighty Is Lifting His Protection," in Farina, *Beauty for Ashes,* 124.

35. Jerry Falwell quoted in James Skillen "Not without Criticism," in Farina, *Beauty for Ashes,* 127.

36. Ibid.

37. Cheryl A. Kirk-Duggan, "Civil War, Civil Rights, World Trade Center," in *Strike Terror No More: Theology, Ethics and the New War,* ed. Jon L. Berquist (St. Louis: Chalice Press, 2002), 36.

38. Jürgen Habermas, interview by Giovanna Borradori in Giovanna Borradori, *Philosophy in a Time of Terror: Dialogues with Jürgen Habermas and Jacques Derrida* (Chicago: University of Chicago Press, 2003), 29. Habermas also considers as new the fact that a local tragedy was simultaneously transformed into a global event through the presence of television cameras capturing the destruction. "Perhaps September 11 could be called the first historic world event in the strictest sense: the impact, the explosion, the slow collapse — everything that was not Hollywood anymore but, rather, a gruesome reality, literally took place in front of the 'universal eyewitness' of a global public" (28).

39. Borradori, *Philosophy in a Time of Terror,* 92–93.

40. The physical damage was vast, with economic ramifications so enormous they can hardly be tallied. Some estimates: lost future income of those killed in New York City, $7.8 billion; cleanup, rebuilding, replacement of WTC, $18 billion; rebuilding of subways, utilities, $3.7 billion; lost wages in New York, $6.4 billion; repairs to the Pentagon, $700 million; net jobs lost, $1.3 million [sic]; decrease in gross domestic product, $150 billion; lost airline revenues, $11 billion; government bailout of two airlines that were bankrupted, $15 billion; new border security expenses (federal government), $38 billion; state expenses for homeland security, $1.3 billion; protective services paid by private companies, $33 billion. Burton M. Leiser, "The Catastrophe of September 11 and Its Aftermath," in Primoratz, *Terrorism: The Philosophical Issues,* 194.

41. Jacques Derrida, interview by Giovanna Borradori in *Philosophy in a Time of Terror,* 93.

42. Fred Halliday, *Two Hours That Shook the World: September 11, 2001: Causes and Consequences* (London: Saqi, 2002), 35. According to Halliday, these unresolved issues include the question of Palestine, the Kurdish issue, and the status of Kuwait, "and indeed the very sense of thwarted relations with the outside world."

43. Ibid., 36.

44. Although Halliday reminds that it was the Afghanis themselves and not the East or the West that prompted the explosion of Afghan society in the late 1970s. "The conflict began, and will end, as an Afghan civil war" and for this reason the PDPA must assume responsibility for provoking social unrest. "Afghanistan was an example even more extreme than anything seen in Iran, Algeria, Egypt or Turkey or a revolt against the modernizing secular state" (37).

45. Avi Shlaim similarly analyzes "linkage politics." See Avi Shlaim, "The United States and the Israeli-Palestinian Conflict," in Booth and Dunne, *Worlds in Collision* (Houndmills, Hampshire, U.K.: Palgrave Macmillan, 2002), 172–83.

46. Halliday, *Two Hours That Shook the World,* 38–40. State involvement in and support of many of these militant movements is a problem that, according to Halliday, will remain central to this conflict. See Halliday's chapter 3.

47. AbuKhalil, professor of political science at California State Stanislaus, concurs: "It is not theology that drives these clerics, but politics and economics. The climate in which the (mis)use of religion takes place is purely political." As'ad AbuKhalil, *Bin Laden, Islam, and America's New "War on Terrorism"* (New York: Seven Stories Press, 2002), 29. The author, in particular, stresses the problematic nature of the U.S. alliance with Israel and its negative effect on American foreign policies with other Middle Eastern nations. "The rise of pro-Soviet governments in Syria, Egypt, and Iraq at different times in the 1950s and 1960s, allowed Israel to align its wars against Arab states with America's Cold War strategies against the Soviets" (32).

48. Halliday, *Two Hours That Shook the World,* 40–41. While agreeing with Halliday's basic thesis emphasizing the political, Ruthven stresses other influential factors, claiming that the seeds of this terrorism were spread by Islamist movements supported by conservative Muslim states with participation of Pakistan and as a direct consequence of the CIA policies of the United States during and after the Reagan years. He especially emphasizes the Saudi export of the extreme form of Islam known as Wahhabism. See Malise Ruthven, *A Fury for God: The Islamist Attack on America* (London: Granta Books, 2002), 171–72.

49. Halliday, *Two Hours That Shook the World,* 43. According to Halliday, such modern challenges include colonial domination, the rise of mass parties of a secular character, and moves by certain modernizing states such as Turkey and Iran to introduce a secular realm of law, education, and politics.

50. Ibid., 44.

Chapter 7. Apocalyptic Symbols: A Meditation

1. Beliefnet message Board, 9/11/01, 1:24 p.m., in Beliefnet et al., *From the Ashes,* 147–48.

2. Ibid., 121.

3. Quoted in Michael Parenti, *The Terrorism Trap: September 11 and Beyond* (San Francisco: City Lights, 2002), 29.

4. Jonathan Sacks, *The Dignity of Difference: How to Avoid the Clash of Civilizations* (London: Continuum, 2002), 52. Sacks refers to Rabbi Naftali Zvi Yehuda Berlin's interpretation of Babel as the first totalitarianism. According to Sacks, "The men on the plain of Shinar make a technological discovery. They learn how to make bricks by drying clay. As after so many other technological advances, they immediately conclude that they now have the power of gods. They are no longer subject to nature. They have become its masters. They will storm the heavens. Their man-made environment — the city with its ziggurat or artificial mountain — will replicate the structure of the cosmos, but here they will rule, not God." Ibid.

5. Stratford Caldecott, "War without Boundaries," in Farina, *Beauty for Ashes,* 228.

6. Wayne Ellwood, *The No-Nonsense Guide to Globalization* (Oxford: New Internationalist Publications, 2001), 19–20.

7. Ibid., 51. Ellwood reports that on average African governments transfer four times more to Northern creditors in debt payments than they spend on the health and education of their citizens. Ibid.

8. Ziauddin Sardar and Merryl Wyn Davies, *Why Do People Hate America?* (Cambridge: Icon, 2002), 128. The authors claim that the real source of resentment toward America that many Saudis exhibit has less to do with the former American military presence in its Holy Sites — troops were located hundreds of miles to the north of Mecca and Medina — and more to do with the destruction of traditional Saudi life by the relentless

process of an Americanized, mass-produced monotony. "Saudi cities do not reflect the history, culture, tradition or values of the Arabian Peninsula — they sing solemn homilies to the American way of life." Ibid., 129.

9. Jean Baudrillard, *The Spirit of Terrorism and Requiem for the Twin Towers,* trans. Chris Turner (London: Verso, 2002), 42–43.

10. Horgan and Geer, *Where Was God on September 11?* 19.

11. Ernest Becker, *The Denial of Death* (New York: Free Press, 1973), 15. Becker explores this fear of death in relation to Rudolf Otto's understanding of the terror of the world in the face of creation, the *mysterium tremendum et fascinosum.* See pp. 49ff.

12. Boeve, "God Interrupts History," 199.

13. See Jessica Mitford, *The American Way of Death* (New York: Simon & Schuster, 1963).

14. Mark Slouka, "A Year Later: Notes on America's Intimations of Mortality," *Harper's Magazine* (September 2002): 36, quoted in Richard T. Hughes: *Myths America Lives By* (Urbana and Chicago: University of Illinois Press, 2004), 157–58.

15. Ibid., 158.

16. Sut Jhally and Jeremy Earp, eds., *Hijacking Catastrophe: 9/11, Fear and the Selling of American Empire* (Northampton, Mass.: Olive Branch Press, 2004).

17. Noam Chomsky in ibid., 42–43.

18. Benjamin Barber, in ibid., 18. Suspiciously, these daily warnings seemed to intensify according to the items in Bush's domestic agenda that needed to be emphasized or deemphasized.

19. Michael Eric Dyson, in ibid., 78.

20. Margot Pepper, "The Smell of Smoke," in *September 11 and the U.S. War: Beyond the Curtain of Smoke,* ed. Roger Burbach and Ben Clarke (San Francisco: City Lights and Freedom Voices, 2002), 79.

21. Williams, *Writing in the Dust,* 70.

22. Howell Raines, foreword to *Portraits: 9/11/01: The Collected "Portraits of Grief" from the New York Times* (New York: Times Books, 2002, 2003), vii. All excerpts are from this source.

23. Ibid., 481.

24. Ibid., 186.

25. Ibid., 586.

26. Ibid., 599.

27. Jürgen Moltmann, "Im Ende — der neue Anfang: Apocalyptischer Terror und christliche Hoffnung," in Kässmann, *Glauben nach Ground Zero,* 32. Translation of this excerpt and all others from the same source is my own.

28. See Paul Ricoeur, *The Symbolism of Evil* (New York: Harper & Row, 1967), 348.

29. Williams, *Writing in the Dust,* 81.

30. Boeve, "God Interrupts History," 210.

31. Ibid.

32. As such Boeve calls for the rediscovery of the *Naherwartung,* a restoration of the expectation of an imminent second coming. Ibid., 212.

33. Ibid.

Chapter 8. Probing Evil 9/11

1. Liam Harte, "A Taxonomy of Terrorism," in *Philosophy 9/11: Thinking about the War on Terrorism,* ed. Timothy Shanahan (Chicago: Open Court, 2005), 25.

2. A cursory investigation of the history of the term would yield a basic typology of terrorism. To that end, Charles Townshend's classification and historical overview are helpful. Charles Townshend, *Terrorism* (Oxford: Oxford University Press, 2002). The first use of the term dates to the closing years of the French Revolution, when in "Year II" (1793–94) the leaders of the French Republic were under threat from foreign invasion and internal rebellion. The National Assembly declared terror the order of the day to preserve the revolution against enemies, kings, and aristocrats. Specifically, the Committees of Public Safety and General Security, which pioneered representative democracy and equality before the law, were the first to call for the use of terror. The first dictionary definition of the word "terrorism" — "système, régime de la terreur" — was offered by the Académie française in 1798. Ibid., 36. Underlying these origins of state terrorism is the Enlightenment assumption that the social order can be changed by human agency. "For a long time, those who were prepared to defend the terrorists did so on the grounds that their action was rational because inevitable, in the circumstances." Ibid., 37. The distinct political logic is the notion that violence can change political attitudes. Townshend claims that the French Revolution's ruthless and systematic use of violence created a model for state powers for the application of terrorizing force for the next couple of centuries. This terrorism "from above" was usually in the form of repressive autocracies and despotisms, or radical revolutionary regimes such as the Bolsheviks during the Russian Civil War but also in times of crisis by constitutional states, such as in France during the crushing of the Paris Commune in 1871 and the June days of 1848. The United States tolerated, if not encouraged, the persistent systematic terrorization of Southern blacks by the Ku Klux Klan and the use of intimidating violence by employers against labor unions. "Free-range terrorism" is the name given to the instances of military or military-controlled regimes in Chile, Argentina, Peru, Uruguay, and elsewhere that unleashed full-blown systems of terror designed to paralyze all left-wing activity in the face of a socialist threat. "The keynotes of the systems, in which whole armies and police forces seem to have participated enthusiastically, were not just killing, but a perhaps more sinister and subversive structure of arbitrary imprisonment, torture, and 'disappearance.'" Ibid., 46. "Revolutionary terrorism" represents the customary way in which terrorism is traditionally conceived, i.e., as a strategy of assault on the state. This form emerged in the nineteenth century in the form of an increasingly well-defined strategy in which terror forms the central and even exclusive method — the "attempt to seize political power from

the established regime of a state, with the aim of causing fundamental political and social change." Ibid., 54. Finally, the 1970s seemed to be the age of the groupuscules — "tiny fissiparous radical activist groups which spread across Western Europe" (68).

3. Mark Juergensmeyer, *Terror in the Mind of God: The Global Rise of Religious Violence*, updated edition, Comparative Studies in Religion and Society 13 (Berkeley: University of California Press, 2000), 5.

4. Cited in Noam Chomsky, *9–11* (New York: Seven Stories Press, 2001), 123–24. See also Noam Chomsky, *Understanding Power: The Indispensable Chomsky*, ed. Peter R. Mitchell and John Schoeffel (New York: New Press, 2002), especially chapter 1.

5. Borradori, *Philosophy in a Time of Terror*, 190. "The definition given by the *United States Code Congressional and Administrative News,* 98th Cong., 2nd sess., Oct. 19, 1984, vol. 2, par. 3077, 98 STAT. 2707 [West, 1984] is shorter but essentially the same, with one important difference: it speaks of violent acts intended to intimidate or coerce a "civilian" population or intended to influence the policy of a government by intimidation or coercion. The "civilian" population is also named in the definition given by the FBI. And the international dimension is explicitly mentioned in the definitions published by the CIA and the Departments of State and Defense." Ibid.

6. Charles Townshend, *Terrorism,* 7. "It was, for instance, impossible for people fighting against Germany in the Second World War to accept that most German civilians (with the exception of the regime's political opponents who were in concentration camps) bore no responsibility at all for the existence and conduct of the Nazi regime." Ibid.

7. Michael Baur, "What Is Distinctive about Terrorism," in Shanahan, *Philosophy 9/11,* 13–14. Baur's definition points to the overall instrumental rationality of terrorists.

8. Ibid., 10–11

9. Ibid., 12. "Thus it took only one computer hacker in the Philippines to devise the 'I love you' virus and cause panic among hundreds of institutions and businesses (the virus was first encountered at the University of Oregon on May 4, 2000). It took only two individuals (perhaps with a few yet-unknown accomplices) to bomb the Murrah Federal Building in Oklahoma City (April 19, 1995) and terrorize an entire country."

10. Elaine Scarry, *The Body in Pain* (New York: Oxford University Press, 1985), 90.

11. Ibid., 128.

12. Ibid., 15.

13. Ibid., 18.

14. Girard, *Violence and the Sacred,* 31.

15. Chalmers Johnson, *Blowback: The Costs and Consequences of American Empire* (New York: Henry Holt, 2001), xi. Johnson published this work eighteen months before the 9/11 attacks, to a less than receptive American public (though it enjoyed a more enthusiastic response in areas outsides of the country and was quickly translated into German, Italian, and Japanese.) After the attacks, the book was reissued with a special introduction for the post-9/11 world. This edition was reprinted eight times in less than two months, and

quickly became a bestseller in the United States. See also John K. Cooley, *Unholy Wars: Afghanistan, America, and International Terrorism* (London and Sterling, Va.: Pluto Press, 2000).

16. Chalmers Johnson, *The Sorrows of Empire: Militarism, Secrecy, and the End of the Republic* (New York: Henry Holt, 2004), 9.

17. Johnson considers a number of instances that could be considered "blowback" — with examples of U.S. foreign policy in his 2000 work by that name, including Iran (1953), Guatemala (1954), Cuba (1959–present), Congo (1960), Brazil (1964), Indonesia (1965), Vietnam, Laos, Cambodia (1961–73), Greece (1967–74), Chile (1973), Afghanistan (1979 to the present), El Salvador, Guatemala, and Nicaragua (1980s), and Iraq (1991 to the present). In this study, he focuses primarily on U.S. involvement in South and North Korea, China, and Japan.

18. Noam Chomsky, interview by Michael Albert, in *9–11* (New York: Seven Stories Press, 2001), 67. Chomsky's quotes are from *Time*.

19. Christian Parenti lists three ways in which American involvement in the Afghan war later fed global *jihad:* first, the U.S. supplied the *Mujahideen* with Stinger anti-aircraft missiles, which hastened the end of the war; second, the United States (aided by British and Pakastani intelligence) encouraged expeditionary forces into the Central Asian Republics of the USSR, encountering there the Soviet's "soft Islamic underbelly"; and third, the CIA directly supported the ongoing recruitment of mercenaries and Islamist volunteers from around the world. "By 1988 this meant there were recruiting centers in numerous American cities including New York, Detroit, and San Francisco." Christian Parenti, "America's Jihad: A History of Origins" in Scraton, *Beyond September 11*, 12.

20. President Franklin Delano Roosevelt met with King Abd al-Aziz Ibn Saud, the founder of the modern Saudi regime, following the February 1945 conference in Yalta. According to Michael Klare, "it is widely believed that Roosevelt gave the king a promise of U.S. protection in return for privileged American access to Saudi oil — an arrangement that remains in full effect today and constitutes the essential core of the U.S.–Saudi relationship." Michael Klare, "The Geopolitics of War," in Burbach and Clarke, *September 11 and the U.S. War*, 32.

21. Ibid., 32–33.

22. From his essay "The Banality of Evil," quoted in John Pilger, "An Unconscionable Threat to Humanity," in Scraton, *Beyond September 11*, 29.

23. Richard T. Hughes, *Myths America Lives By*, 153.

24. See Robert N. Bellah, *The Broken Covenant: American Civil Religion in Time of Trial*, 2nd ed. (Chicago: University of Chicago Press, 1992).

25. Hughes, *Myths America Lives By*, 155.

26. "In 1987, the American Academy of Arts and Sciences sponsored a six-year research project that brought together academics from around the world to study the global

phenomenon of modern religious fundamentalism. After much discussion on the appropriateness of using what was essentially a western term to reflect the cultural and religious diversity of the movements under scrutiny, it was decided that there were sufficient 'family resemblances' among these groups to justify describing them in common as fundamentalist." These fundamentalist constants include: a concern over the erosion of religion's role in society, the goal to reshape society in accordance with group beliefs and ethics, the rejection of individualism and relativism, the highly selective use of particular aspects of the tradition and sacred texts along with an absolute confidence in the inerrancy of their own interpretation of divine revelation, a dualistic worldview that allows them to demonize anyone who challenges their positions. Oliver McTernan, *Violence in God's Name: Religion in an Age of Conflict* (London: Darton, Longman & Todd, 2003), 33. The aforementioned research project is presented in Martin E. Marty, "The Future of World Fundamentalisms," *Proceedings of the American Philosophical Society* 3 (September 1998).

27. Stuart Sim, *Fundamentalist World: The New Dark Age of Dogma* (Cambridge: Icon, 2004), 13. These fundamentals, or core principles of the Christian faith, are summarized by the historian George M. Marsden: the inerrancy of Scripture, the Virgin Birth of Christ, his substitutionary atonement, his bodily resurrection, and the authenticity of his miracles. Ibid.

28. Ibid., 21–22.

29. This is not to say that a specific personality "type" could not exist as a manifestation of this common disposition. See Adorno et al., *The Authoritarian Personality.* The problem, however, is that there is not just one type of personality that seems attracted to fundamentalism.

30. Sim, *Fundamentalist,* 22.

31. Brian Jenkins, "The Organization Men," in In Hoge and Rose, *How Did This Happen?* 5.

32. AbuKhalil, *Bin Laden,* 30.

33. Kelton Cobb, "Violent Faith," in Markham and Abu-Rabi, *September 11: Religious Perspectives on the Causes and Consequences,* 138.

34. Bruce Lincoln, *Holy Terrors: Thinking about Religion after September 11* (Chicago: University of Chicago Press, 2003), 10.

35. Ruthven, *A Fury for God,* 35.

36. Osama bin Laden, videotaped address, October 7, 2001, in Appendix C of Lincoln, *Holy Terrors,* 102.

37. George W. Bush, "Address to the Nation," October 7, 2001, in Appendix B, Lincoln, *Holy Terrors,* 100–101.

38. Ibid., 100.

39. Lincoln, *Holy Terrors,* 22–23.

40. Peter Singer, *The President of Good and Evil: Taking George W. Bush Seriously* (London: Granta, 2004), 208.

41. Ibid., 211.

42. Ruthven, *A Fury for God,* 272. The author also points out that, while many Israelis abhor this Christian fundamentalist premillenial scenario, "Israeli politicians opposed to any withdrawal from 'biblical' Israel have not always balked at the fundamentalists to bolster their cause inside the United States."

43. Sim cites the critique of Tariq Ali, who considers the geo-political and cultural dominance that America exerts to be not only a detriment to local cultural values throughout the world, but also the chief reason for the resurgence of Islamic fundamentalism in our time. Sensing a bit of the fundamentalist's typical paranoia over conspiracy, Sim critiques him decisively: "Ali's vision of imperialist fundamentalism is of a vast conspiracy which is systematically moving towards its goal of world domination, ruthlessly eliminating all competitors as it goes" (170).

44. Sardar and Davies, *Why Do People Hate America?* 195–96.

45. Ibid., 117. Sim invokes the Islamic scholar Akbar S. Ahmed, for the latter's critique of the ethic behind the International Monetary Fund (IMF) and the World Bank's policies toward the Third World. "Ahmed's argument is that such fundamentalism begets fundamentalism in return; the more zeal there is for the market on the part of the IMF and World Bank, the more zeal will be created in the cause of Islam as a defense mechanism. A beleagured society tends to close ranks and go back to basics; to favor *taqlid* (blind obedience) rather than *ijtihad* (independent reasoning)" (106–7).

46. Samuel P. Huntington, *The Clash of Civilizations and the Remaking of World Order* (New York: Simon & Schuster, 1996).

47. Ruthven, *A Fury of God,* 289.

48. Sim, *Fundamentalist,* 26–27.

49. In 1997, *Concilium* published a special issue on the topic: Wim Beuken and Karl-Josef Kuschel, eds., *Religion as a Source of Violence?* (1997/4). Among the contributors, François Houtart in his sociological analysis argues against the overly facile view that religions are essentially nonviolent and that it is its practitioners that often divert it toward violent ends; he determines that the roots of violence can be found within religion itself, and that explains why religions can also easily serve as vehicles for violent tendencies. Houtart acknowledges three such roots: the sacrificial element central to most religions, the struggle between good and evil, and the history of religious expansion. In addition, he describes three main mechanisms that seem to play a part in the association between religion and violence in the function of societies: the religious reading of social relationships, religion as a factor of identity, and the ethical legitimization or de-legitimization of a particular society's religion. François Houtart, "The Cult of Violence in the Name of Religion: A Panorama," trans. John Bowden, 1–8. Edward Schillebeeckx, on the other hand, explains that because religion is always mediated by culture and society it can associate itself with violent aspects in the given culture and can thereby become violent as religion. According to Schillebeeckx, religious violence has a twofold foundation of a nonreligious

kind: the claim to be the only true religion and the idea that religion is the first civic duty because one's relation to the Absolute has a direct connection with the preservation of an established order or to the call to revolution. The idea of divine covenant and election is potentially problematic unless we realize that election has to be subordinate to God's over-all creative intention, which is salvation for all (Edward Schillebeeckx, "Documentation: Religion and Violence," 129–42).

50. McTernan, *Violence in God's Name,* 22.

51. Ibid., 23.

52. George W. Bush, remarks at National Day of Prayer and Remembrance Service, Washington, D.C., September 14, 2001, in *Beauty for Ashes,* 177.

53. McTernan, *Violence in God's Name,* 22. McTernan examines those societal influences in the West that have contributed to the widespread failure to take seriously the place of religion in the world today. He holds that the "secularization thesis" is chiefly responsible: the view based on the premise that the decline in religion is an irreversible process, initiated by the Enlightenment's scientific paradigm, and further bolstered by the critiques of Marx, Freud, and Durkheim. See McTernan's critique in chapter 2, "Religion Matters." One factor of McTernan's critique is especially visible in his disagreement with author Salman Rushdie, who has claimed that in order for Muslim societies to become thoroughly modern, they must depoliticize and privatize religion: "he [Rushdie] fails to recognize that religious people, other than those who follow a distinctively Protestant individualistic concept of religion, do not understand faith to be a private affair. Political power is 'indispensable' to the establishment of Islamic society, and therefore political action in Islam has 'a religious goal'" (41).

54. Juergensmeyer, *Terror in the Mind of God.* Although this source was published before the 9/11/01 terrorist attacks, it examines terrorist activity throughout history while focusing on the chief terrorist events occurring at the turn of the last century, including the first terrorist attack on the World Trade Center in New York City, February 26, 1993.

55. Ibid., 123.

56. Ibid., 122.

57. Ibid., 124. The issue of performative acts can obviously be compounded when we consider the problem of the literal rendering of those religious texts that suggest that God is the one doing the acting. "As did the Jews and the later Christians, Muhammad saw reason for his victory in the hand of God or Allah. In the records of his sayings, the Qur'an, he told his followers after Badr: 'It was not you but Allah who slew them. It was not you who smote them. Allah smote them so that He might richly reward His faithful. He hears and knows all. He will surely destroy the designs of the unbelievers.'" Andrew Sinclair, *An Anatomy of Terror* (London: Macmillan, 2003), 14.

58. Juergensmeyer, *Terror in the Mind of God,* 124–25.

59. Ibid., 188.

60. Many if not most examples of terrorist conceptions and practices of Islamic *jihad* trace their influence to the Islamist founder of the Muslim Brotherhood, Sayyid Qutb (1906–65). See "Sayyid Qutb and the Fundamentalist Pattern of Activism," in Appleby, *The Ambivalence of the Sacred*, 91–95.

61. Juergensmeyer, *Terror in the Mind of God*, 146.

62. It is interesting to note that Juergensmeyer disagrees with Girard's understanding that sacrifice should be regarded as the context for viewing all other forms of religious violence. For Juergensmeyer, war is the context for sacrifice rather than the other way around (ibid., 169).

63. Ibid., 161–62.

64. Paul Gilbert, *New Terror, New Wars* (Edinburgh: Edinburgh University Press, 2003), 74–75.

65. *The New Oxford American Dictionary* (2001), s.v. "humiliate."

66. Quoted in Juergensmeyer, *Terror in the Mind of God*, 187.

67. Ibid., 186.

68. Paul Ricoeur, *Oneself as Another*, trans. Kathleen Blamey (Chicago: University of Chicago Press, 1992), 318. In this work Ricoeur explores his important distinction between identity as sameness (*idem*) and identity as selfhood (*ipse*), which becomes crucial with regard to the question of permanence in time. Identity in the sense of *ipse*, he explains, cannot imply some unchanging core of the personality. He asks the question: "Is there a form of permanence in time which can be connected to the question 'who?' inasmuch as it is irreducible to any question of 'what?'? Is there a form of permanence in time that is a reply to the question 'Who am I?'?" (118). He finds an answer in his observation that whenever we speak of ourselves we have available two models of permanence in time: character and faithfulness to oneself in keeping one's word. In brief, for Ricoeur, character expresses the overlapping of *idem* and *ipse* whereas keeping one's word expresses the gap between them. This polarity suggests "an intervention of narrative identity in the conceptual constitution of personal identity in the manner of a specific mediator between the pole of character, where *idem* and *ipse* tend to coincide, and the pole of self-maintenance, where selfhood frees itself from sameness" (118–19). "Because the major distinction between them [*ipse* and *idem*] is not recognized...the solutions offered to the problem of personal identity which do not consider the narrative dimension fail" (116).

69. Ibid., 320.

70. Ibid.

71. Ibid.

72. Volf, *Exclusion and Embrace*, 65.

73. Ibid., 66.

74. Ibid., 67.

75. Noam Chomsky, *Middle East Illusions* (Lanham, Md.: Rowman & Littlefield, 2003), 13.

76. Volf, *Exclusion and Embrace,* 67.

77. Edward W. Said, *Peace and Its Discontents: Essays on Palestine in the Middle East Peace Process* (New York: Vintage Books, 1996), 102–3.

78. Tanya Reinhart, *Israel/Palestine: How to End the War of 1948,* 2nd ed. (New York: Seven Stories Press, 2005), 117. Reinhart argues that the Oslo agreements deepened this dependence by giving Israel complete control over the Palestinian workforce and over other aspects of the economy, such as trade (118).

79. Mitchell Geoffrey Bard, *Myths and Facts: A Guide to the Arab-Israeli Conflict* (Chevy Chase, Md.: American-Israeli Cooperative Enterprise, 2001), 174.

80. Ibid. Bard notes that according to a 2002 report: "An Arabic translation of Adolf Hitler's *Mein Kampf* has been distributed in East Jerusalem and territories controlled by the Palestinian Authority (PA) and became a bestseller" (151). He further notes that "even Palestinian crossword puzzles are used to de-legitimize Israel and attack Jews, providing clues, for example, suggesting the Jewish trait is 'treachery' " (153).

81. And yet we can hardly claim that the majority of ordinary Palestinian "people" or the majority of the Israeli population are the ones instigating these various breakdowns of interconnectedness. In "Two Peoples in One Land," originally published in 1994, Said observed, "Ironically, most Palestinians and Israelis are now exhausted by the futility of conflict, and in various ways have expressed their willingness to live as neighbors in two independent states." Said, *Peace and Its Discontents,* 119.

82. Bard, *Myths and Facts,* 157–71.

83. Ibid., 165.

84. Psychologist B. J. Berkowitz describes six psychological types who might try to use weapons of mass destruction: paranoids, paranoid schizophrenics, borderline mental defectives, schizophrenic types, passive-aggressive personality types, and sociopath personalities. See B. J. Berkowitz et al., *Superviolence: The Civil Threat of Mass Destruction Weapons* (Santa Barbara, Calif.: ADCON Corporation, 1972) quoted in Rex Hudson, *Who Becomes a Terrorist and Why: The 1999 Government Report on Profiling Terrorists* (Guilford, Conn.: Lyons Press, 2002), 7–8.

85. According to Rex Hudson, there are various approaches to terrorism analysis, among them: the multicausal approach, see Paul Wilkinson, *Terrorism and the Liberal State* (New York: Macmillan, 1977); the political approach, see Chalmers Johnson, "Perspectives on Terrorism," reprinted in Walter Laqueur, ed., *The Terrorism Reader* (New York: New American Library, 1978); and the organizational approach, see Martha Crenshaw, "Questions to Be Answered, Research to Be Done, Knowledge to Be Applied," in *Origins of Terrorism: Psychologies, Ideologies, Theologies, States of Mind,* ed. Walter Reich (Cambridge: Cambridge University Press, 1990), 23–28. Hudson's own study can be characterized as a sociopsychological approach. "Attempts to explain terrorism in purely psychological terms

ignore the very real economic, political, and social factors that have always motivated radical activists, as well as the possibility that biological or physiological variables may play a role in bringing an individual to the point of perpetrating terrorism," 34.

86. Volf, *Exclusion and Embrace*, 66.

87. Robert A. Pape, *Dying to Win: The Strategic Logic of Suicide Terrorism* (New York: Random House, 2005), 11. Pape's typology includes demonstrative terrorism (political theater as much as it is violence), destructive terrorism (a more aggressive form that attempts to inflict real harm at the risk of losing sympathy for the cause), and suicide terrorism (10).

88. Ibid., 14. According to Pape, most instances of suicide terrorism occurring before 1980 should be understood as suicide missions rather than attacks, as exemplified by Japanese Kamikaze pilots of World War II. He cites the two earliest and best known examples: the Jewish Zealots from 4 B.C.E. to 70 C.E., and the eleventh- and twelfth-century Muslim Assassins. "The world's first suicide terrorists were probably two militant Jewish revolutionary groups, the Zealots and the *Sicarii*. Determined to liberate Judea from Roman occupation, these groups used violence to provoke popular uprising.... They attacked their victims in broad daylight in the heart of Jerusalem and other centers using small, sickle-like daggers (*sicae* in Latin) concealed under their cloaks. Many of these must have been suicide missions, since the killers were often immediately captured and put to death — typically tortured and then crucified or burned alive.... The Ismaili Assassins, a Shi'ite Muslim sect based in northwestern Iran in the eleventh and twelfth centuries, created an effective organization for the planned, systematic, and long-term use of political murder that relied on suicide missions for success. For two centuries, the Assassins' daggers terrorized and demoralized the mainly Sunni rulers of the region as well as leaders of Christian Crusader states, chalking up more than fifty dramatic murders and inspiring a new word: 'assassination....' The first successful Assassin, who killed the vizier to the Great sultan Malikshah of Persia in 1092, exclaimed before himself being killed: 'The killing of this devil is the beginning of bliss'" (11–12).

89. Pape, *Dying to Win*, 23. For a historical overview of American militaristic interference around the globe, see Gore Vidal, *Perpetual War for Perpetual Peace: How We Got to Be So Hated* (New York: Thunder's Mouth Press, 2002), 22–41.

90. Pape, *Dying to Win*, 86. "The wider the difference between the identities of the foreign occupier and of the local community — the fewer prominent attributes they share — the more the local community is likely to view the occupier as 'alien,' the more it will fear that the occupation will lead to radical and permanent transformation of its national characteristics, and the more it will seek to end the occupation at any price. The occupying power already is stronger than any military force in the occupied community — otherwise, the condition of occupation would not exist — and so has the power to damage its political, economic, social, and religious institutions with inevitable effects on other aspects of local culture as well. Even if the occupier does not directly use this power, it necessarily poses

an existential threat to the ability of the local community to determine and perpetuate its national identity" (87).

91. Ibid., 87–88.

92. Ibid., 218–26.

93. Adrian Karatnycky, "Under Our Very Noses, the Terrorist Next Door," *National Review,* November 5, 2001; available online.

94. Thomas Friedman, "The 2 Domes of Belgium," *New York Times,* January 27, 2002.

95. Quoted in ibid. As R. Scott Appleby explains: "Late modernity, in its technologically driven assault on the confines of time, space, and custom, erodes traditional orthodoxies and liberates people from social roles and behaviors considered obligatory." Appleby, *The Ambivalence of the Sacred,* 57.

96. Friedman concludes, "Belgium is a microcosm of the whole story. There are 300 mosques in Belgium today, with 300 domes. But there is another famous dome here: the huge radar dome of NATO headquarters in Mons. Somewhere in the cultural encounter between these two domes of Belgium — the dome of NATO and the dome of the mosques — lies the key to this September 11 and maybe the next."

Conclusion to Part 2

1. Mary Flannery O'Connor, "The Fiction Writer and His Country," 1957, in *Collected Works* (New York: Library of America, 1988), 805–6.

2. For an interesting study of apocalypse, see James Alison, *Living in the End Times: The Last Things Re-imagined* (London: SPCK, 1997). Here Alison develops the idea that the eschatological imagination is the subversion from within of the apocalyptic imagination and at the root of this subversion is found the criterion of the victim. It is an insertion of God's time in our own time, the beginning of eternity now.

Part 3. 9/12

1. Rowan Williams, *The Truce of God: Peacemaking in Troubled Times* (Grand Rapids: Eerdmans, 2005), 19–20. Williams here refers to the research of psychotherapist Nini E. Ettlinger, M.D.

2. Ibid., 18–19.

3. Daniel J. Louw, "Fides Quaerens Spem: A Pastoral and Theological Response to Suffering and Evil," *Interpretation* 57, no. 4 (October 2003): 384.

4. Ibid.

5. As such this first thesis already stands in rebuttal to the well-known dictum of Immanuel Kant: "Absolutely nothing worthwhile for the practical life can be made out of the doctrine of the Trinity, taken literally, when one believes that one has understood it adequately, but even less when one perceives that it exceeds all our concepts." Immanuel Kant, *Der Streit der Facultaten,* A 50, 57, quoted in Jürgen Moltmann, "The Trinitarian History of God," *Theology* 78 (1975): 633.

Chapter 9. Hope in an Age of Terror

1. Kevin L. Hughes, "The Crossing of Hope, or Apophatic Eschatology," in Volf and Katerberg, *The Future of Hope,* 103.

2. Ibid. *Apophasis,* literally the "flight from speech," is also called "negative theology." It is theology "that struggles to remain aware of what we do not and cannot know or say about God and the mysteries of faith. It is the disciplined speech of 'unknowing' and 'learned ignorance' before the mysterious presence of God." Ibid. As we shall see below, one category particularly promising in allowing us to look for traces of God as mystery in our midst is the category of the personal.

3. Hughes, "The Crossing of Hope," 103–4. Hughes here critiques Caputo reading Derrida. See John D. Caputo, *The Prayers and Tears of Jacques Derrida: Religion without Religion* (Bloomington: Indiana University Press, 1997).

4. Michael Albus, "Ground Zero: Wo war Gott am 11 September?" in Kässmann, *Glauben nach Ground Zero,* 39. Albus condemns the dead-end of "either/or" thinking characteristic of so much talk on religion and civilization: "The clearing of the Either-Or leaves only a wasteland behind it. All messengers of the pure teaching leave a bloody trace behind them in history and are therefore themselves accomplices of that Evil One that they want to destroy with all violence" (38–39).

5. *Faith and Doubt at Ground Zero.* Directed by Helen Whitney, Ron Rosenbaum, and Kathryn Walker. Helen Whitney Productions and PBS Home Video. New York: PBS Home Video, 2002. Available from *www.pbs.org/wgbh/pages/frontline/shows/faith/ect/script.html.*

6. Interview with Tim Lynston, in *Faith and Doubt at Ground Zero,* 10.

7. Interview with Rev. Joseph Griesedieck, in *Faith and Doubt at Ground Zero,* 11.

8. Interview with Rabbi Brad Hirschfield, in *Faith and Doubt at Ground Zero,* 11.

9. Interview with Josh Simon, in *Faith and Doubt at Ground Zero,* 11.

10. Interview with Joel Meyerowitz, in *Faith and Doubt at Ground Zero,* 26.

11. Eugene Kennedy, *9–11: Meditations at the Center of the World* (Maryknoll, N.Y.: Orbis Books, 2002), 22–23.

12. Interview with Rabbi Irwin Kula in *Faith and Doubt at Ground Zero,* 13.

13. Dietrich Bonhoeffer, *Letters and Papers from Prison,* enlarged ed., ed. Eberhard Bethge (New York: Macmillan, 1972), 286.

14. Ibid.

15. Ibid., 281.

16. Maria Hinojosa, "On September 11, Final Words of Love," CNN.com/U.S., America Remembers, *http://archives.cnn.com/2002/US/09/03/ar911.phone.calls/.* November 20, 2008. All subsequent portraits are taken from this same website or its internal links, unless otherwise indicated.

17. Jim Dwyer et al., "102 Minutes: Last Words at the Trade Center; Fighting to Live as the Towers Died," *New York Times,* November 30, 2008.

18. Ibid.

19. Ibid.

20. Ibid.

21. Jennifer Senior, "The Fireman's Friar," *New York Magazine,* November 30, 2008.

22. Sam Harris, *The End of Faith: Religion, Terror, and the Future of Reason* (New York: W. W. Norton, 2004). The book won the 2005 PEN/Martha Albrand Award for Nonfiction and has been endorsed by, among others, Harvard University professor of law Alan Dershowitz, Princeton professor of ethics Peter Singer, and Union Theological Seminary president Joseph C. Hough Jr.

23. Ibid., 15.

24. David Cunningham, *These Three Are One: The Practice of Trinitarian Theology* (Oxford: Blackwell, 1998), 53. "A specifically Trinitarian account of God, with all kinds of practical ramifications following in its wake, cannot be brought into the nation-state's embrace: it thus poses a genuine threat to the state's idolatrous demand that it receive our highest allegiance."

25. And there are many problems with Harris's argument that could be examined, such as the obvious problem of deciding *which* rationality will ground a spirituality based on *whose* evidence.

26. Juan Luis Segundo, for example, sees faith, in an anthropological sense, as that which structures life around specific meaning, and which prioritizes, and points out those values which are contributive to that meaning. Religious faith alters or radically specifies the scale of values making certain value structures worthwhile. He further distinguishes faith from *trust,* a more fundamental and less specified, less personal level, and *religion,* more the realm of instrumentality rather than value-structure and often accompanied by a sacral connotation. Anthropological faith points to the primacy of importance that *meaning* enjoys for all human beings, the reality toward which all human beings are compelled in order to redeem personal value. See Juan Luis Segundo, S.J., *Faith and Ideologies,* trans. John Drury (Maryknoll, N.Y.: Orbis Books, 1984), 8–14.

27. Harris, *The End of Faith,* 65. Kasper has explored the relationship between modern atheism and Christianity's failure to maintain the integrity of a truly Trinitarian faith. See *The God of Jesus Christ* (New York: Crossroad, 1984). See also Michael J. Buckley, S.J., *At the Origins of Modern Atheism* (New Haven: Yale University Press, 1987), and *Denying and Disclosing God: The Ambiguous Progress of Modern Atheism* (New Haven: Yale University Press, 2004).

28. Bonhoeffer, *Letters,* 380.

29. Ibid., 381.

30. Regardless of Bonhoeffer's own theological perspective on the concept at this time, the notion of participation is large and encompassing enough a term to include the (typically Barthian) accent on God's grace, i.e., a *being taken up into the Trinitarian reality,* as well as the more (typically Catholic) activist sense of the term, i.e., a *taking part in.*

31. Louw, "Fides Quaerens Spem," 386.

32. Ibid., 397.

33. Paul S. Fiddes, *Participating in God: A Pastoral Doctrine of the Trinity* (Louisville: Westminster John Knox, 2000), 8. See also Stephen Pattison and James Woodward, "An Introduction to Pastoral and Practical Theology," in *The Blackwell Reader in Pastoral and Practical Theology,* ed. Pattison and Woodward (Oxford: Blackwell, 2000), 7.

34. Dorothee Sölle admits: "Omnipotence is a fundamental concept of classical theology that I can't live with. I consider it a human illusion; one doesn't need to know a lot of Freud in order to understand this projection of human wishes onto God. It has been some thirty years since I have been able to say this clearly. It has become clear to me as the fundamental theme of German history: I think God was very small in Auschwitz and very small in the two Babylonian towers in New York." Sölle, "Von der Macht, Allmacht und Ohnmacht Gottes," in Kässmann, *Glauben Nach Ground Zero,* 54.

35. Tyron L. Inbody, *The Transforming God: An Interpretation of Suffering and Evil* (Louisville: Westminster John Knox, 1997), 178.

36. Louw, "Fides Quaerens Spem," 384.

37. Zabala, Introduction to Richard Rorty and Gianni Vattimo, *The Future of Religion,* ed. Santiago Zabala (New York: Columbia University Press, 2005), 16.

Chapter 10. Pursuing the Personal

1. Fiddes, *Participating in God,* 5. It is impossible and, for our aims, pointless to provide a comprehensive history of the development of Trinitarian thought and Trinitarian controversy throughout the ages. A great many thoughtful and systematic historical investigations have already been written. Two recent works of note are Anne Hunt, *Trinity: Nexus of the Mysteries of Christian Faith,* Theology in Global Perspective Series (Maryknoll, N.Y.: Orbis Books, 2005), and, for his helpful compendium of recent interest in Trinity organized in terms of "radicalizers" and "restricters" of "Rahner's Rule," or *Grundaxiom* (The economic Trinity is the immanent Trinity, and vice versa) Fred Sanders, *The Image of the Immanent Trinity: Rahner's Rule and the Theological Interpretation of Scripture,* Issues in Systematic Theology 12 (New York: Peter Lang, 2005).

2. Elaine Scarry, "The Difficulty of Imagining Other Persons," in *The Handbook of Interethnic Coexistence,* ed. Eugene Weiner (New York: Continuum, 1998), 43.

3. Ibid, 50–55. In light of our discussion of narrative in chapter 4, it is interesting to note Scarry's claim that the act of imagining oneself as another person is central to literature.

4. Among others, Catherine Mowry LaCugna concurs with Zizioulas. She holds that the primary reason for the "defeat" of the doctrine of the Trinity, that is, for its widespread irrelevance to Christian believers, is because Trinitarian discourse became dislodged from popular religiosity and worship, its biblical base, by speculative theology's esoteric and metaphysical pursuits. Catherine LaCugna, *God for Us: The Trinity and Christian Life* (San

Francisco: HarperSanFrancisco, 1991), 243. Patricia Fox aptly sums up the point: "While retaining 'persons' in the theological language of the dogma, de facto it was separated from the personal lives and experience of believers, from the 'economy' of their salvation. Revelation of the triune God did not impinge on them personally in any way and therefore faded from the existential imagination of Christian life." Patricia A. Fox, *God as Communion: John Zizioulas, Elizabeth Johnson, and the Retrieval of the Symbol of the Triune God* (Collegeville, Minn.: Liturgical Press, 2001), 31.

5. John D. Zizioulas, *Being as Communion: Studies in Personhood and the Church* (London: Darton, Longman & Todd, 2004), 16. This pivotal work was first published in 1985 in the United States by St. Vladimir's Seminary Press, New York.

6. Zizioulas stresses that neither the apologists, such as Justin Martyr, nor the Alexandrian catechetical theologians, such as Clement and Origen, could completely avoid the ontological monism of Greek thought: "they were above all 'doctors,' academic theologians interested principally in Christianity as 'revelation.' By contrast, the bishops of this period, pastoral theologians such as St. Ignatius of Antioch and above all St. Irenaeus and later St. Athanasius, approached the being of God through the experience of the ecclesial community, of *ecclesial being*." Ibid.

7. Because, of course, the primitive faith had already been handed down from generation to generation since the earliest years of the church in the practice of baptism in the name of the Father, Son, and Spirit. Ibid., 36. We shall further examine the concept of "ecclesial being" below.

8. Zizioulas, *Being as Communion*, 17. But Zizioulas explains, "this communion is not a relationship understood for its own sake, an existential structure that supplants 'nature' or 'substance' in its primordial ontological role. . . . Just like 'substance,' 'communion' does not exist by itself: it is the *Father* who is the cause of it." Ibid.

9. John Zizioulas, "The Doctrine of the Holy Trinity: The Significance of the Cappadocian Contribution," in *Trinitarian Theology Today: Essays on Divine Being and Act,* ed. Christoph Schwöbel (Edinburgh: T. & T. Clark, 1995), 53.

10. "True being in its genuine metaphysical state, which concerns philosophy *par excellence,* is to be found in God, whose uncreated existence does not involve the priority of the 'One' or of nature over the 'Many' or the persons. The way in which God exists involves simultaneously the 'One' and the 'Many', and this means that the person has to be given ontological primacy in philosophy." Ibid.

11. More accurately, Zizioulas locates the limitation not in Greek thought in particular but in philosophy in general. He argues that "person" as an ontological category cannot be extrapolated from experience. See Zizioulas, "On Being a Person: Towards an Ontology of Personhood," in Schwöbel and Gunton, *Persons, Divine and Human,* 37.

12. For such a concept to be developed, two basic presuppositions were necessary, the first of which could only be obtained from biblical thought, the second only from Greek: "(*a*) a radical change in cosmology which would free the world and man from ontological

necessity; and (*b*) an ontological view of man which would unite the person with the *being* of man, with his permanent and enduring existence, with his genuine and absolute identity." Zizioulas, *Being as Communion,* 35.

13. Ibid., 36.

14. Fox, *God as Communion,* 36.

15. John Zizioulas, "The Doctrine of the Holy Trinity," 54. Technically, the Cappadocians were able to achieve this by taking the term *hypostasis,* which had hitherto been identified with substance or *ousia,* and making it instead equivalent with *prosopon.* Zizioulas explains that this was done chiefly in order to make the expression "three persons" free from Sabellian (modalistic) interpretations. See Ibid., 47. Zizioulas also contends that it is precisely this identification of substance with hypostasis that culminated in all the difficulties and disputes concerning the Trinity in the fourth century: "The term 'person,' which had already been used in the West from the time of Tertullian for the doctrine of the Holy Trinity (*una substantia, tres personae*) did not meet with acceptance in the East *precisely because the term 'person' lacked an ontological content* and led toward Sabellianism (the manifestation of God in three 'roles')." Zizioulas, *Being as Communion,* 36–37. See Tertullian, *Against Praxeas* 11–12 (PL 2, 1670D). Moreover, the Eastern preference for the word *hypostases* (substance) in reference to the three also presented problems of its own (tritheism).

16. Zizioulas, *Being as Communion,* 18.

17. Ibid., 41. "For this communion is a product of freedom as a result not of the substance of God but of a person, the Father — observe why this doctrinal detail is so important — who is Trinity not because the divine *nature* is ecstatic but because the Father as a *person* freely wills this communion." Ibid., 44.

18. Ibid., 55–56.

19. Ibid., 56.

20. According to Zizioulas, individualism and death represent a distortion of eros and the body, created goods that are necessary for hypostasis. "The body, which is born as a biological hypostasis, behaves like the fortress of an ego...which hinders the hypostasis from becoming a person, that is, from affirming itself as love and freedom. The body tends towards the person but leads finally to the individual." Ibid., 51. Death, then, is the sealing of hypostasis as individuality.

21. Ibid., 46.

22. John D. Zizioulas, *Communion and Otherness: Further Studies in Personhood and the Church* (London: T. & T. Clark, 2006), 141. Colin Gunton looks at some of the main contributors to the typically Western individualistic tradition of thinking about God, including Boethius's definition of person as *naturae rationabilis individua substantia* (an individual substance of rational nature). Colin E. Gunton, *The Promise of Trinitarian Theology,* 2nd ed. (London: T. & T. Clark, 1997), 92. See Boethius, *Contra Eutychem,* III, 4f.

23. Zizioulas, *Communion and Otherness*, 141.

24. Ibid., 224. "The right notion of the person is of crucial importance for theology. The individualistic and psychological conceptions of personhood which have prevailed throughout the history of Western thought have led inevitably to a rejection of the understanding of God as person (e.g., Fichte, Feuerbach, Tillich, etc.). This is an additional reason why we should seek an understanding of personhood away from the ideas of individuality and consciousness." Ibid. See chapter 6, originally published as "Human Capacity and Human Incapacity: A Theological Exploration of Personhood," *Scottish Journal of Theology* 28 (1975).

25. Zizioulas, *Communion and Otherness*, 48. In fact, Zizioulas claims that Levinas approximates the patristic understanding of otherness better than other philosophers such as Husserl and Buber. "Levinas' attempt to liberate western philosophy from the primacy of consciousness, from the reduction of the particular to the general, from grasping, comprehending, controlling and using being by the human mind is most remarkable indeed. It brings us closer than any other philosophy to the Greek patristic view of otherness as irreducible to the universal, and of consciousness as belonging to the universal rather than to the particular, at least with regard to the Holy Trinity." Ibid., 49.

26. Ibid.

27. Levinas, *Otherwise Than Being*, 52.

28. Zizioulas, *Communion and Otherness*, 49.

29. Ibid., 50. Zizioulas here sharply contrasts Levinas with St. Maximus, for whom *eros*, or the movement of desire, finds its rest in the other.

30. Ibid., 51. See Dionysius Areopagite, *De div. nom.* 4.14 (*Patrologia Graecae* 3, 712AB), and Maximus *Amb.* 23 (*Patrologia Graecae* 91, 1260C).

31. Ibid., 55. Zizioulas is utilizing here Maximus's distinction between "logos" and "mode of being." See Maximus, *Amb.* 7 (*Patrologia Graecae* 91; 1088); *Amb.* 34 (*Patrologia Graecae* 91, 1288 B.C.E.). Here, also, Zizioulas makes an important clarification between the patristic "other," which preserves the particular and is the cause of and resting place of desire, and the postmodern other, which he claims passes over the particular in constant destabilization. See pp. 52–53.

32. There are, of course, theologians who would disagree with Zizioulas's reception of the Greek fathers. See, e.g., G. F. Wilks, "The Trinitarian Ontology of John Zizioulas," *Vox Evangelica* 25 (1995): 63–68.

33. Zizioulas, *Communion and Otherness*, 55. Thus, in his fear of totalizing reduction, Levinas must safeguard particularity ultimately in the realm of ethics for whom, we recall, it serves as first philosophy. But as we have seen, otherness, which is not erased by communion but is generated through it, is a more fundamental matter. Ethics is not enough. Otherness is an ontological reality, though via an ontology of personhood rather than substance.

34. Ibid.

35. Fiddes, *Participating in God*, 66.

36. Zizioulas, *Being as Communion,* 15.

37. Zizioulas, *Communion and Otherness,* 149. "Reconciliation with God is a necessary pre-condition for reconciliation with any 'other.'" Ibid., 2.

38. Baptism is "the application to humanity of the very filial relationship which exists between the Father and the Son." Zizioulas, "Human Capacity and Human Incapacity," 438. The concrete realization of this relationship is Eucharist, at once the gathering and movement toward its realization in the future. "As a liturgical act of eschatological orientation and progressive movement, the Eucharist proves that ecclesial existence is not of this world but 'from above.' It belongs to the eschatological transcendence of history and so the person has roots in the future." Edward Russell, "Reconsidering Relational Anthropology: A Critical Assessment of John Zizioulas's Theological Anthropology," *International Journal of Systematic Theology* 5, no. 2 (July 2003): 176.

39. Zizioulas, *Communion and Otherness,* 2.

40. Edward Russell, "Reconsidering Relational Anthropology," 178. Russell cites as examples Paul Ricoeur, *Oneself as Another,* trans. Kathleen Blamey (Chicago: University of Chicago Press, 1992), and Alistair I. McFadyen, *The Call to Personhood: A Christian Theory of the Individual in Social Relationships* (Cambridge: Cambridge University Press, 1990).

41. Ibid., 179. Russell sees a docetic tendency in Zizioulas's theology: "To put it bluntly, given the centrality of baptism to Zizioulas's anthropology, one wonders how significant the cross and resurrection really are for him."

42. Volf, *Exclusion and Embrace,* 127. We recall Metz's own criticism of the notion of a suffering God as itself an attempt at theodicizing.

43. Inbody, *The Transforming God,* 182.

44. Winton D. Persaud, "The Cross of Jesus Christ, the Unity of the Church, and Human Suffering," in Tesfai, *The Scandal of a Crucified World,* 115. Persaud is stressing that the church reflects Trinity, and not that the Trinity is derived from church.

45. Here Cunningham engages the thesis of Girard that Jesus, as victim who does not victimize in return, breaks the ancient cycle of revenge by accepting nonviolently the violence that is inflicted upon him. Cunningham, however, is right to identify the Trinitarian deficiency in Girard's view of the "wise man" Jesus who accomplishes this deed; as a result, Girard fails to give a convincing account of how the cycle is thus broken. "Jesus is not merely a wise man, but is the Wellspring who became flesh and dwelt among us; thus, the one who suffers (and absorbs, and does not return) the world's violence is *God....* And thus, despite the human fall to violence, and even in spite of the violent acts of God within the created order, we can still speak of God as 'the God of peace.'" Cunningham, *These Three Are One,* 251.

46. Ibid., 238.

47. Volf, *Exclusion and Embrace,* 24. See Jon Sobrino, *Jesus the Liberator: A Historical-Theological Reading of Jesus of Nazareth,* trans. Paul Burns and Francis McDonagh (Maryknoll, N.Y.: Orbis Books, 1993), 245ff.

48. It is difficult to trace a simple causal link between terrorists' deeds of self-donation and a view of personhood that fails to see, as Zizioulas claims was apparent to the Greek fathers, personhood as a mystery of relationship. Still, we cannot ignore the connection between nihilism and certain modern understandings of person in terms of radical individualism. "The modern dilemma of personhood is that by emphasizing self-existence in freedom as the true essence of personhood the question of suicide as the ultimate expression of freedom and therefore of self-actualization cannot be avoided or answered." Roger E. Olson and Christopher A. Hall, *The Trinity,* Guides to Theology Series, ed. Sally Bruynell, Alan G. Padgett, et al. (Grand Rapids: Eerdmans, 2002), 113.

49. Cunningham, *These Three Are One,* 165.

50. For an exploration of Christian ministry as participating in Christ's *kenotic* love see Kevin M. Cronin, O.F.M., *Kenosis: Emptying Self and the Path of Christian Service* (New York: Continuum, 1999).

51. Moltmann stresses the importance of a thoroughly Trinitarian understanding of kenosis, that is, one in which the divine being encompasses the human being and vice versa, and not one which implies a simple dialectical relation between divine and human being, leaving each unaffected. "It must understand the event of the cross in God's being in both Trinitarian and personal terms. In contrast to the traditional doctrine of the two natures in the person of Christ, it must begin from the totality of the person of Christ and understand the relationship of the death of the Son to the Father and the Spirit.... If the kenosis of the Son to the point of death upon the cross is the 'revelation of the entire Trinity', this event too can only be presented as a God-event in Trinitarian terms. What happens on the cross manifests the relationships of Jesus, the Son, to the Father, and vice versa. The cross and its liberating effect makes possible the movement of the Spirit from the Father to us. The cross stands at the heart of the Trinitarian being of God; it divides and conjoins the persons in their relationships to each other and portays them in a specific way." Moltmann, *The Crucified God,* 205–6.

52. Volf, *Exclusion and Embrace,* 128.

53. Fiddes, *Participating in God,* 71. According to Fiddes, the verb *choreo* was sometimes used to explain what was already accepted by fathers of both East and West at the end of the fourth century regarding the unity of *ousia* in God: the way that each person penetrated or was contained in the others. In the noun form, *perichoresis* was used in reference to the Trinitarian persons first by Pseudo-Cyril in the sixth century (*De Sacrosancta Trinitate* 24) and then by John of Damascus in the eighth (*De Fide Orthodoxa* I.14). Ibid.

54. Ibid., 71–72. See Aquinas, *Summa Theologica* Ia.42.5: trans. Fathers of the English Dominican Province (New York: Benzinger Bros., 1948), vol. 1, 218; Bonaventure, *Liber Sententiarum* I, Dist. 19, I.I.4, conl. [sic].

55. Volf and Welker, *God's Life in Trinity*, 6.

56. Fiddes, *Participating in God*, 72.

57. Aquinas, *Summa Theologica*, Ia.29.4, 159.

58. Fiddes, *Participating in God*, 35. See Aquinas, *Summa Theologica*, Ia.27.1; Ia.28.4. Fiddes, however, points out that the potential for developing here a truly dynamic ontology based on action and relationship was spoiled when Aquinas, influenced by Aristotle's view of the divine essence as simple and radically unified, went on to explain that the relationships subsist, or self-exist, because they are the same as the one divine substance, which itself has self-existence. The result is that the relations in God have the same reality as the one essence, which misses out on the Eastern theologians' understanding of the being of God as communion. As Aquinas puts it, "And this is to signify relation by way of substance, and such a relation is a hypostasis subsisting in the divine nature, although in truth that which subsists in the divine nature is the divine nature itself. Thus it is true to say that the name *person* signifies relation directly, and the essence indirectly; not, however, the relation as such, but as expressed by way of a hypostasis. So likewise it signifies directly the essence, and indirectly the relation, inasmuch as the essence is the same as the hypostasis: while in God the hypostasis is expressed as distinct by the relation: and thus relation, as such, enters into the notion of the person indirectly." Aquinas, *Summa Theologica*, Ia.29.4. Fiddes, *Participating in God*, 35–36.

59. Ibid., 36. Fiddes invokes Barth's understanding of event, with regard to the being of God, as final. Although we are not pursuing the present investigation from the perspective of interreligious dialogue, it is certainly worthwhile to consider that such a view of Trinity—understood as subsistent relationships, or movements in relation, rather than as three individual subjects at the end of such movements—might have positive implications for Christian-Muslim discussion on God. Fiddes writes: "Of course, it is not possible to visualize, paint, or etch in stone or glass three interweaving relationships, or three movements of being characterized by their relations, without subjects exercising them. But then this ought to be a positive advantage in thinking about God, who cannot be objectified like other objects in the world; the triune God must not, as I have been suggesting, be visualized as three individual subjects who *have* relationships" (36–37).

60. Ibid., 37.

61. Ibid.

62. Volf, *Exclusion and Embrace*, 100.

63. Ibid.

64. Ibid., 141.

65. Ibid.

66. Ibid., 144–45. In addition to these four steps of embrace, Volf discusses four notable features of a successful embrace: the fluidity of identities, the nonsymmetricity of the relationship, the underdetermination of the outcome, and the risk of embrace (145–47).

Chapter 11. An Anatomy of Forgiveness

1. Miroslav Volf, "Forgiveness, Reconciliation, and Justice: A Christian Contribution to a More Peaceful Social Environment," in *Forgiveness and Reconciliation: Religion, Public Policy, and Conflict Transformation,* ed. Raymond G. Helmick, S.J., and Rodney L. Petersen (Philadelphia: Templeton Foundation Press, 2001), 45.

2. Dietrich Bonhoeffer, *The Cost of Discipleship,* trans. R. H. Fuller (New York: Macmillan, 1931), 211. Donald Shriver examines those historical factors that contributed to the shift in perception with regard to forgiveness, from essentially a community-building practice and discipline in the New Testament to a more privatized option as Christianity became the established religion of Europe. He highlights Augustine's struggle with the Donatists in the fifth century and, in 1215, the Fourth Lateran Council's authoritative formulation of the discipline of penance characterized by the confidentiality of the priest-penitent relation, as well as later Reformation and Enlightenment influences. See his chapter 2, "Forgiveness in Politics in Christian Tradition," in Donald W. Shriver Jr., *An Ethic for Enemies: Forgiveness in Politics* (Oxford: Oxford University Press, 1995), 2–62.

3. Fiddes, *Participating in God,* 192.

4. Bonhoeffer, *The Cost of Discipleship,* 100.

5. Fiddes, *Participating in God,* 195.

6. Volf, "Forgiveness," 46.

7. Fiddes, *Participating in God,* 195.

8. Ibid.

9. Ibid., 197.

10. For an investigation of postwar relations between the United States and Germany and Japan, see Shriver, *An Ethic for Enemies,* 73–169. On the topic of the reconciliation process in South Africa, see Rodney L. Petersen, "A Theology of Forgiveness," in Helmick and Petersen, *Forgiveness and Reconciliation,* 3–26.

11. Fiddes, *Participating in God,* 199.

12. Ibid., 210. For a discussion on the psychotherapeutic benefits of forgiveness, see Richard Fitzgibbons, "Anger and the Healing Power of Forgiveness: A Psychiatrist's View," in Enright and North, *Exploring Forgiveness,* 63–74. However, for a critique of this trend, see L. Gregory Jones, *Embodying Forgiveness: A Theological Analysis* (Grand Rapids: Eerdmans, 1995), especially chapter 2: "Therapeutic Forgiveness: The Church's Psychological Captivity in Western Culture," 35–69.

13. Jones, *Embodying Forgiveness,* 26.

14. Ibid., 4. See Rom. 6:1–11.

15. Ibid.

16. Miroslav Volf, *The End of Memory: Remembering Rightly in a Violent World* (Grand Rapids: Eerdmans, 2006), 45.

17. Ibid., 50.

18. Ibid., 64–65.

19. Ibid., 68–69.

20. Ibid., 78.

21. Ibid., 77.

22. Ibid., 80. Stanley Hauerwas has made a similar point from a pacifist stance: "Christians are acutely aware that we seldom are faithful to the gifts God has given us, but we hope the confession of our sins is a sign of hope in a world without hope. This means that pacifists do have a response to September 11, 2001. Our response is to continue living in a manner that witnesses to our belief that the world was not changed on September 11, 2001. The world was changed during the celebration of a Passover in 33 A.D." Stanley Hauerwas, "September 11, 2001: A Pacifist Response," in *Performing the Faith: Bonhoeffer and the Practice of Nonviolence* (Grand Rapids: Blazos Press, 2004), 209. And, in "September 11, 2001: A Sermon a Year Later": "The story that makes the Jesus people a storied people is the story of God and God's unfailing love for us. How extraordinary. How wonderful. It is really not all about 'us.' It is about God. A God not rendered powerless by events like September 11, 2001, but the God who has made his church, the Jesus people, the alternative to those who would rule the world in the name of putting right the terror of September 11, 2001." In Ibid., 214.

23. Volf, *The End of Memory,* 84.

24. Volf, *Exclusion and Embrace,* 138.

25. Ibid., 139. Volf uses the term "backgrounding" or *Aufhebung* to signify this way of dealing with the memories of horrors within history: "they are the pre-eschatological anticipations of the eschatological nonremembering." Ibid. However, Volf does not appear to endorse the term in this more recent book we have been highlighting in this section, *The End of Memory* (2006). One wonders if the term "backgrounding" smacks of the connotation of repression, something that Volf obviously does not intend.

26. Volf, *Exclusion and Embrace,* 110.

27. Ibid., 156.

28. Ibid., 160, 163.

29. Ibid., 156–64.

30. Ibid., 165.

31. Volf, "Forgiveness, Reconciliation, and Justice," 35. Volf acknowledges that the term "cheap reconciliation" originated in the Kairos Document, a theological critique of the South African regime before the end of apartheid.

32. Ibid., 36.

33. Ibid., 40. The approach also fails to recognize the *gift* that is forgiveness. See Volf, *Free of Charge: Giving and Forgiving in a Culture Stripped of Grace: The Archbishop's Official 2006 Lent Book.* Grand Rapids: Zondervan, 2005.

34. Volf, *Exclusion and Embrace,* 125.

35. Ibid., 126

36. Ibid., 127.

37. Volf, "Forgiveness, Reconciliation, and Justice," 41.

38. Ibid., 43.

39. Ibid., 44–45.

40. Volf quotes Rowan Williams: "the inconceivable self-emptying of God in the events of Good Friday and Holy Saturday is no arbitrary expression of the nature of God: this is what the life of the Trinity is, translated into the world," in *Exclusion and Embrace*, 127.

41. Ibid., 128.

42. Ibid., 129.

43. Ibid.

44. Volf, "Forgiveness, Reconciliation and Justice," 33. Volf is contesting the thesis of Regina Schwartz in *The Curse of Cain: The Violent Legacy of Monotheism* (Chicago: University of Chicago Press, 1997). See also Miroslav Volf, "Jehovah on Trial," in *Christianity Today* (April 27, 1998): 32–35.

General Conclusion. Theology That Re-members

1. See *www.projectrebirth.org*.

2. Kirk Semple, "Bombers Said to Blow Up 2 Children Used as Decoys," *New York Times*, March 21, 2007.

3. The notion of "hierarchy of truths" was explored at the Second Vatican Council as is evidenced in the Decree on Ecumenism, *Unitatis Redintegratio*.

4. Dietrich Bonhoeffer, "Was heisst die Wahreit sagen?" *Werke*, 16:619–29, quoted in Robert E. Pollack, "The Religious Obligation to Ask Questions of Nature and the State," in *Union Seminary Quarterly Review* 60, nos. 1–2 (2006): 110.

5. Louw, "Fides Quaerens Spem," 395. According to Louw, it is this faithfulness that the Bible presents as the primary way of understanding God's power.

6. Ibid., 394. Louw concludes that practical theology must highlight the importance of recognizing God's presence in concrete acts of *diakonia*. In this sense, we can see that the very concrete depiction of the 9/11 attacks offered at the beginning of part 2, as a way of avoiding theodicy's tendency toward the abstraction of evil, is answered by the investigation of the very concrete acts of selfless giving and service taking place in the aftermath of the attacks: in the countless acts of courage and rescue and in the powerful scenes of embrace in the moment of death.

7. Alasdair MacIntyre, "Epistemological Crises, Dramatic Narrative and the Philosophy of Science," in *The Monist* 60, no. 4 (1977): 453–72.

8. Alasdair MacIntyre, *Whose Justice? Which Rationality?* (Notre Dame, Ind.: University of Notre Dame Press, 1988), 364.

9. Ibid., 362–63. According to MacIntyre, the resolution of an epistemological crisis depends on three requirements: first, it must solve the problem in question; second, it must

explain why the tradition failed to solve the problem; third, the answer it provides must stand in continuity with the "shared beliefs" of the tradition (362).

10. L. Gregory Jones, "Crafting Communities of Forgiveness," in *Interpretation: A Journal of Bible and Theology* 54, no. 2 (April 2000): 123.

11. Todorov, *Hope and Memory,* 195.

12. Ibid.

13. Oscar Romero, *The Violence of Love,* quoted in David Potorti, *September 11th Families for Peaceful Tomorrows: Turning Our Grief into Action for Peace* (New York: RDV Books, 2003), 11.

14. Jones, "Crafting Communities of Forgiveness," 131–32.

15. Stephen Nolt, "Perspectives: Amish Forgiveness," Televised interview by Bob Abernathy. *Religion and Ethics Newsweekly,* September 21, 2007.

16. Potorti, *September 11th Families for Peaceful Tomorrows,* 7.

17. Ibid., 8.

18. Ibid., 195.

19. Ibid., 137.

20. Augustine, *Confessions,* trans. R. S. Pine-Coffin (Harmondsworth, Middlesex, U.K.: Penguin, 1961), 218.

Afterword

1. Liam De Paor, *St. Patrick's World: The Christian Culture of Ireland's Apostolic Age* (Dublin: Four Courts, 1993), 96. According to the *Annals of Ulster,* Patrick lived from 373 to 493.

Bibliography

Abate, Frank R., and Elizabeth Jewell. *The New Oxford American Dictionary.* New York: Oxford University Press, 2001.

AbuKhalil, As'ad. *Bin Laden, Islam, and America's New "War on Terrorism."* Open Media Pamphlet Series. New York: Seven Stories Press, 2002.

Adorno, Theodor W., Else Frenkel-Brunswik, Daniel Levinson, and R. Nevitt Sanford, *The Authoritarian Personality.* Studies in Prejudice 3. New York: Harper, 1950.

Agamben, Giorgio. *Remnants of Auschwitz: The Witness and the Archive.* New York: Zone, 1999.

Albus, Michael. "Ground Zero: Wo War Gott Am 11 September?" In Kässmann, *Glauben Nach Ground Zero,* 37–51.

Alison, James. *The Joy of Being Wrong: Original Sin through Easter Eyes.* New York: Crossroad, 1998.

———. *Living in the End Times: The Last Things Re-Imagined.* London: SPCK, 1997.

American Jewish Committee. "Deny Intolerance." In Farina, *Beauty for Ashes,* 48.

Améry, Jean. "On the Necessity and Impossibility of Being a Jew." In Morgan, *A Holocaust Reader,* 27–42.

Ammerman, Nancy T. "Grieving Together: September 11 as a Measure of Social Capital in the U.S." In Markham, *September 11: Religious Perspectives on the Causes and Consequences,* 53–73.

Amnesty International. "The Backlash: Human Rights at Risk throughout the World." Available online.

Appleby, R. Scott, and Carnegie Commission on Preventing Deadly Conflict. *The Ambivalence of the Sacred: Religion, Violence, and Reconciliation.* Carnegie Commission on Preventing Deadly Conflict Series. Lanham, Md.: Rowman & Littlefield, 2000.

Arendt, Hannah. "The Concentration Camps." In Morgan, *A Holocaust Reader,* 47–63.

———. *Between Past and Future: Eight Exercises in Political Thought.* Enl. ed. New York: Viking Press, 1968.

———. *Eichmann in Jerusalem: A Report on the Banality of Evil.* Penguin Twentieth-Century Classics. Rev. and enl. ed. New York: Penguin Books, 1963.

———. *The Human Condition.* Garden City, N.Y.: Doubleday, 1959.

Ashley, James Matthew. "Johann Baptist Metz." In Scott and Cavanaugh, *The Blackwell Companion to Political Theology,* 250.

————. *Interruptions: Mysticism, Politics, and Theology in the Work of Johann Baptist Metz.* Studies in Spirituality and Theology 4. Notre Dame, Ind.: University of Notre Dame Press, 1998.

Auden, W. H., and Edward Mendelson. *Selected Poems.* New ed. New York: Vintage Books, 1979.

Augustine and R. S. Pine-Coffin. *Confessions.* Penguin Classics. Vol. L114. New York: Penguin Books, 1961.

Austin, William G., and Stephen Worchel, eds. *The Social Psychology of Intergroup Relations.* Monterey, Calif.: Brooks/Cole, 1979.

Banks, Robert. *Reconciliation and Hope: New Testament Essays on Atonement and Eschatology Presented to L. L. Morris on His 60th Birthday.* Grand Rapids: Eerdmans, 1974.

Barber, Benjamin R. *Jihad vs. McWorld.* New York: Ballantine Books, 1996.

Bard, Mitchell Geoffrey, and American-Israeli Cooperative Enterprise. *Myths and Facts: A Guide to the Arab-Israeli Conflict.* Chevy Chase, Md.: American-Israeli Cooperative Enterprise, 2001.

Barker, Jonathan. *The No-Nonsense Guide to Terrorism.* Oxford: New Internationalist in association with Verso, 2003.

Barron, Robert. *The Priority of Christ: Toward a Postliberal Catholicism.* Grand Rapids: Brazos Press, 2007.

Bartov, Omer. *Mirrors of Destruction: War, Genocide, and Modern Identity.* Oxford: Oxford University Press, 2000.

Baudrillard, Jean. *The Spirit of Terrorism and Requiem for the Twin Towers.* Trans. Chris Turner. London: Verso, 2002.

Bauer, Yehuda. *Remembering for the Future: Working Papers and Addenda.* New York: Pergamon Press, 1989.

Baum, Gregory. *The Twentieth Century: A Theological Overview.* Maryknoll, N.Y.: Orbis Books, 1999.

Bauman, Zygmunt. *Modernity and the Holocaust.* Cambridge: Polity Press, 1989.

Baur, Michael. "What Is Distinctive about Terrorism." In Shanahan, *Philosophy 9/11,* 3–22.

Becker, Ernest. *The Denial of Death.* New York: Free Press, 1973.

Beliefnet et al. *From the Ashes: A Spiritual Response to the Attack on America: Experience, Strength, and Hope from Spiritual Leaders and Extraordinary Citizens.* Emmaus, Pa.: Rodale, 2001.

Bellah, Robert Neelly. *The Broken Covenant: American Civil Religion in Time of Trial.* 2nd ed. Chicago: University of Chicago Press, 1992.

Bellinger, Charles K. *The Genealogy of Violence: Reflections on Creation, Freedom, and Evil.* Oxford: Oxford University Press, 2001.

Bemporad, Jack, John Pawlikowski, and Joseph Sievers. *Good and Evil after Auschwitz: Ethical Implications for Today.* Hoboken, N.J.: KTAV, 2000.

Bernstein, Richard J. "Evil and the Temptation of Theodicy." In Critchley and Bernasconi, *The Cambridge Companion to Levinas,* 252–67.

Berquist, Jon L., ed. *Strike Terror No More: Theology, Ethics, and the New War.* St. Louis: Chalice Press, 2002.

Beuken, Wim, and Karl-Josef Kuschel. *Religion as a Source of Violence.* Concilium. Vol. 1997/4. Maryknoll, N.Y.: Orbis Books, 1997.

Blanchot, Maurice. *The Writing of the Disaster.* Lincoln: University of Nebraska Press, 1986.

Blumenthal, David R. *Facing the Abusing God: A Theology of Protest.* Louisville: Westminster John Knox, 1993.

Boersma, Hans. *Violence, Hospitality, and the Cross: Reappropriating the Atonement Tradition.* Grand Rapids: Baker Academic, 2004.

Boeve, Lieven. "God Interrupts History: Apocalypticism as an Indispensable Theological Conceptual Strategy." *Louvain Studies* 26 (2001): 196–206.

Bonhoeffer, Dietrich. *Letters and Papers from Prison.* Enlarged ed. New York: Macmillan, 1972.

———. *The Cost of Discipleship.* Rev. and unabridged, containing material not previously translated. New York: Macmillan, 1963.

Booth, Ken, and Timothy Dunne, eds. *Worlds in Collision: Terror and the Future of Global Order.* New York: Palgrave Macmillan, 2002.

Boulnois, Olivier. "The Concept of God after Theodicy." *Communio* (Fall 2002): 444–68.

Bresheeth, Haim, Stuart Clink Hood, and Litza Jansz. *The Holocaust for Beginners.* 2nd ed. Cambridge: Icon, 2000.

Brewer, Marilynn B. "The Psychology of Prejudice: Ingroup Love or Outgroup Hate?" *Journal of Social Issues* 55 (1999): 429–44.

Buckley, Michael J. *Denying and Disclosing God: The Ambiguous Progress of Modern Atheism.* New Haven, Conn.: Yale University Press, 2004.

———. *At the Origins of Modern Atheism.* New Haven: Yale University Press, 1987.

Burbach, Roger, and Ben Clarke. *September 11 and the U.S. War: Beyond the Curtain of Smoke.* San Francisco: City Lights and Freedom Voices, 2002.

Burns, J. Patout. *Theological Anthropology.* Sources of Early Christian Thought. Philadelphia: Fortress, 1981.

Bush, George W. *President's Address at National Day of Prayer and Remembrance Service, September 14, 2001, National Cathedral, Washington, D.C.* 2001.

———. "Address to the Nation, Sept. 11, 2001." *www.whitehouse.gov/news/releases/2001/09/20010911-16.html.*

Caldecott, Stratford. "War without Boundaries." In Farina, *Beauty for Ashes,* 228–30.

Caputo, John D. *The Prayers and Tears of Jacques Derrida: Religion without Religion.* Indiana Series in the Philosophy of Religion. Bloomington: Indiana University Press, 1997.

Chomsky, Noam. *Middle East Illusions: Including Peace in the Middle East? Reflections on Justice and Nationhood.* Lanham, Md.: Rowman & Littlefield, 2003.

———. *9–11.* New York: Seven Stories Press, 2001.

Cobb, Kelton. "Violent Faith." In Markham, *September 11: Religious Perspectives on the Causes and Consequences,* 136–63.

Cohn-Sherbok, Dan. *Holocaust Theology: A Reader.* New York: New York University Press, 2002.

Colijn, G. Jan, and Marcia Sachs Littell. *Confronting the Holocaust: A Mandate for the 21st Century.* Studies in the Shoah 19. Lanham, Md.: University Press of America, 1997.

Colombani, Jean-Marie. "Nous sommes tous Américains." *Le Monde,* September 12, 2001, trans. Mary-Alice Farina, in Farina, *Beauty for Ashes,* 5–8.

Cooley, John K. *Unholy Wars: Afghanistan, America, and International Terrorism.* New ed. London and Sterling, Va.: Pluto Press, 2000.

Cousins, Ewert. "A Meditation at the Site of the Destruction of the World Trade Center: October 11, 2001." *Chicago Studies* 41, no. 1 (Spring, 2002): 7.

Crenshaw, Martha. "Questions to Be Answered, Research to Be Done, Knowledge to Be Applied." In *Origins of Terrorism: Psychologies, Ideologies, Theologies, States of Mind.* Ed. Walter Reich and Woodrow Wilson International Center for Scholars, Washington, D.C. New York: Woodrow Wilson International Center for Scholars, 1990.

Critchley, Simon, and Robert Bernasconi. *The Cambridge Companion to Levinas.* Cambridge and New York: Cambridge University Press, 2002.

Croner, Helga B., ed. *Stepping Stones to Further Jewish-Christian Relations.* Studies in Judaism and Christianity 1. London and New York: Stimulus Books, 1977.

Cronin, Kevin, O.F.M. *Kenosis: Emptying Self and the Path of Christian Service.* Rockport, Mass.: Element, 1992.

Cunningham, David S. *These Three Are One: The Practice of Trinitarian Theology.* Challenges in Contemporary Theology. Malden, Mass.: Blackwell, 1998.

Davies, Oliver. *A Theology of Compassion: Metaphysics of Difference and the Renewal of Tradition.* London: SCM Press, 2001.

de Beek, A. van. *Why? On Suffering, Sin, and God.* Trans. John Vriend. Grand Rapids: Eerdmans, 1990.

Deutsch, Eliot. *Culture and Modernity: East-West Philosophic Perspectives.* Honolulu: University of Hawaii Press, 1991.

Dwyer, Jim, Eric Lipton, Kevin Flynn, James Glanz, and Ford Dessenden. "102 Minutes: Last Words at the Trade Center; Fighting to Live as the Towers Died." *New York Times,* November 30, 2008.

Eimer, Colin. "Jewish and Christian Suffering." In Cohn-Sherbok, *Holocaust Theology: A Reader,* 135–37.

Ellwood, Wayne. *The No-Nonsense Guide to Globalization.* No-Nonsense Guides. Oxford: New Internationalist Publications, Verso, 2001.

Enright, Robert D., and Joanna North. *Exploring Forgiveness*. Madison: University of Wisconsin Press, 1998.

Fackenheim, Emil L. *God's Presence in History: Jewish Affirmations and Philosophical Reflections*. Deems Lectures 1968. New York: New York University Press, 1970.

Faith and Doubt at Ground Zero. Directed by Helen Whitney, Ron Rosenbaum, and Kathryn Walker. Helen Whitney Productions and PBS Home Video. New York: PBS Home Video, 2002. Available from *www.pbs.org/wgbh/pages/frontline/shows/faith/ect/script.html*.

Farina, John, ed. *Beauty for Ashes: Spiritual Reflections on the Attack on America*. Trans. Mary-Alice Farina. New York: Crossroad, 2001.

Fasching, Darrell J. *Narrative Theology after Auschwitz: From Alienation to Ethics*. South Florida Studies in the History of Judaism 212. Atlanta: Scholars Press, 1999.

Feenstra, Ronald Jay, and Cornelius Plantinga. *Trinity, Incarnation, and Atonement: Philosophical and Theological Essays*. Library of Religious Philosophy 1. Notre Dame, Ind.: University of Notre Dame Press, 1989.

Fiddes, Paul S. "The Holocaust and Divine Suffering." In Cohn-Sherbok, *Holocaust Theology: A Reader,* 127–29.

———. *Participating in God: A Pastoral Doctrine of the Trinity*. Louisville: Westminster John Knox, 2000.

———. *The Creative Suffering of God*. New York: Oxford University Press, 1988.

Fitzgibbons, Richard. "Anger and the Healing Power of Forgiveness: A Psychiatrist's View." In Enright and North, *Exploring Forgiveness,* 63–74.

Fox, Patricia. *God as Communion: John Zizioulas, Elizabeth Johnson, and the Retrieval of the Symbol of the Triune God*. Collegeville, Minn.: Liturgical Press, 2001.

Friedman, Thomas. "The 2 Domes of Belgium." *New York Times*, January 27, 2002, sec. A.

Frost, Robert. "God's Speech to Job." In Rodman, *100 Modern Poems,* 113–14.

Gilbert, Paul. *New Terror, New Wars*. Contemporary Ethical Debates. Edinburgh: Edinburgh University Press, 2003.

Girard, René. *I See Satan Fall like Lightning*. Maryknoll, N.Y.: Orbis Books, 2001.

———. *Things Hidden since the Foundation of the World*. Trans. Stephen Bann and Michael Metteer. Stanford, Calif.: Stanford University Press, 1987.

———. *The Scapegoat*. Baltimore: Johns Hopkins University Press, 1986.

———. *Violence and the Sacred*. Baltimore: Johns Hopkins University Press, 1977.

Girard, René. *Deceit, Desire, and the Novel: Self and Other in Literary Structure*. Trans. Yvonne Freccero. Baltimore: Johns Hopkins University Press, 1965.

Glover, Jonathan. *Humanity: A Moral History of the Twentieth Century*. Yale Nota Bene. New Haven, Conn.: Yale University Press, 2001.

Goldhagen, Daniel Jonah. *Hitler's Willing Executioners: Ordinary Germans and the Holocaust*. New York: Knopf, 1996.

Gollwitzer, Helmut, Käthe Kuhn, Reinhold Schneider, and Reinhard Clifford Kuhn. *Dying We Live: The Final Messages and Records of Some Germans Who Defied Hitler.* London: Fontana, 1958.

Govier, Trudy. *Forgiveness and Revenge.* London and New York: Routledge, 2002.

Griffin, David Ray. *Evil Revisited: Responses and Reconsiderations.* Albany: State University of New York Press, 1991.

———. *God, Power, and Evil: A Process Theodicy.* Lanham, Md.: University Press of America, 1990.

Gunton, Colin E. *The Promise of Trinitarian Theology.* 2nd ed. Edinburgh: T. & T. Clark, 1997.

Habermas, Jürgen, Jacques Derrida, and Giovanna Borradori. *Philosophy in a Time of Terror: Dialogues with Jürgen Habermas and Jacques Derrida.* Chicago: University of Chicago Press, 2003.

Haers, Jacques. "Defensor vinculi et conversationis: Connectedness and Conversation as a Challenge to Theology." In Haers and De Mey, *Theology and Conversation,* 1–40.

Haers, Jacques, and P. De Mey. *Theology and Conversation: Towards a Relational Theology.* Bibliotheca Ephemeridum Theologicarum Lovaniensium 172. Dudley, Mass.: Peeters, 2003.

Halliday, Fred. *Two Hours That Shook the World: September 11, 2001: Causes and Consequences.* London: Saqi Books, 2002.

Hancock, Ian. "Uniqueness, Gypsies and Jews." In Bauer, *Remembering for the Future,* 2017–25.

Harris, Sam. *The End of Faith: Religion, Terror, and the Future of Reason.* New York: W. W. Norton, 2004.

Harte, Liam. "A Taxonomy of Terrorism." In Shanahan, *Philosophy 9/11,* 23–50.

Harvey, John. "To War." *Commonweal,* September 13, 2002, 9.

Hauerwas, Stanley. *Performing the Faith: Bonhoeffer and the Practice of Nonviolence.* London: SPCK, 2004.

Hauerwas, Stanley, Richard Bondi, and David B. Burrell. *Truthfulness and Tragedy: Further Investigations in Christian Ethics.* Notre Dame, Ind.: University of Notre Dame Press, 1977.

Helmick, Raymond G., and Rodney Lawrence Petersen. *Forgiveness and Reconciliation: Religion, Public Policy, and Conflict Transformation.* Philadelphia: Templeton Foundation Press, 2001.

Hick, John. "Soul-Making Theodicy." In Rowe, *God and the Problem of Evil.*

———. *Philosophy of Religion.* Prentice-Hall Foundations of Philosophy Series. 4th ed. Englewood Cliffs, N.J.: Prentice-Hall, 1990.

———. *Evil and the God of Love.* New York: Harper & Row, 1966.

Hilberg, Raul. *The Destruction of the European Jews.* Rev. and definitive ed. 3 vols. New York: Holmes & Meier, 1985.

Hillesum, Etty. *An Interrupted Life: The Diaries of Etty Hillesum, 1941–1943.* Trans. Arnold J. Pomerans. New York: Pantheon Books, 1984.

Hinojosa, Maria. "On September 11, Final Words of Love," CNN.com/U.S., America Remembers. *http://archives.cnn.com/2002/US/09/03/ar911.phone.calls/.* November 20, 2008.

Hinton, Alexander Laban. *Annihilating Difference: The Anthropology of Genocide.* California Series in Public Anthropology 3. Berkeley: University of California Press, 2002.

Hirsch, David. "The Gray Zone, or the Banality of Evil." In Roth and Grob, *Ethics after the Holocaust,* 102.

Hitler, Adolf. *Hitler's Table Talk, 1941–1944.* New York: Oxford University Press, 1988.

Hoge, James F., and Gideon Rose, eds. *How Did This Happen? Terrorism and the New War.* New York: Public Affairs, 2001.

Horgan, John, and Frank Geer. *Where Was God on September 11?* San Francisco, Calif.: Brown Trout, 2002.

Houtart, François. "The Cult of Violence in the Name of Religion: A Panorama." In Beuken, *Religion as a Source of Violence,* 1–9.

Hubert, Henri, and Marcel Mauss. *Sacrifice: Its Nature and Function.* Chicago: University of Chicago Press, 1964.

Hudson, Rex A., and Library of Congress. Federal Research Division. *Who Becomes a Terrorist and Why: The 1999 Government Report on Profiling Terrorists.* Guilford, Conn.: Lyons Press, 2002.

Hughes, Kevin L. "The Crossing of Hope, or Apophatic Eschatology." In Volf, *The Future of Hope,* 101–24.

Hughes, Richard T. *Myths America Lives By.* Urbana: University of Illinois Press, 2003.

Hunt, Anne. *Trinity: Nexus of the Mysteries of Christian Faith.* Theology in Global Perspective Series. Maryknoll, N.Y.: Orbis Books, 2005.

Huntington, Samuel P. *The Clash of Civilizations and the Remaking of World Order.* New York: Simon & Schuster, 1996.

Inbody, Tyron. *The Transforming God: An Interpretation of Suffering and Evil.* Louisville: Westminster John Knox, 1997.

Jacobs, Steven L. *The Holocaust Now: Contemporary Christian and Jewish Thought.* East Rockaway, N.Y.: Cummings & Hathaway, 1996.

——. *Contemporary Christian Religious Responses to the Shoah.* Studies in the Shoah 6. Lanham, Md.: University Press of America, 1993.

——. *Contemporary Jewish Religious Responses to the Shoah.* Studies in the Shoah 5. Lanham, Md.: University Press of America, 1993.

Jenkins, Brian. "The Organization Men." In Hoge and Rose, *How Did This Happen?* 1–14.

Jhally, Sut, and Jeremy Earp, eds. *Hijacking Catastrophe: 9/11, Fear and the Selling of American Empire.* Northampton, Mass.: Olive Branch Press, 2004.

John Paul II. "General Audience, September 12, 2001." In Farina, *Beauty for Ashes,* 15–18.

———. "Pope's Address to New Ambassador to the Holy See." *America* (October 8, 2001): 6.

Johnson, Chalmers A. *The Sorrows of Empire: Militarism, Secrecy, and the End of the Republic.* New York: Henry Holt, 2004.

———. *Blowback: The Costs and Consequences of American Empire.* New York: Henry Holt, 2001.

———. "Perspectives on Terrorism." In Laqueur, *The Terrorism Reader.*

Johnson, William Stacy. "Probing the 'Meaning' of September 11, 2001." *Princeton Seminary Bulletin,* new series (2002): 42.

Jones, L. Gregory. *Embodying Forgiveness: A Theological Analysis.* Grand Rapids: Eerdmans, 1995.

Juergensmeyer, Mark. *Terror in the Mind of God: The Global Rise of Religious Violence.* Comparative Studies in Religion and Society 13. Updated edition. Berkeley: University of California Press, 2000.

Karatnycky, Adrian. "Under Our Very Noses, the Terrorist Next Door." *National Review,* November 5, 2001.

Kasper, Walter. *The God of Jesus Christ.* New York: Crossroad, 1984.

Kässmann, Margot, ed. *Glauben Nach Ground Zero: Von der Macht, Allmacht und Ohnmacht Gottes.* Stuttgart, Zurich: Kreuz Verlag, 2003.

Katz, Steven T. "The Uniqueness of the Holocaust." In Cohn-Sherbok, *Holocaust Theology: A Reader.*

Kennedy, Eugene C. *9–11: Meditations at the Center of the World.* Maryknoll, N.Y.: Orbis Books, 2002.

Kirk-Duggan, Cheryl A. "Civil War, Civil Rights, World Trade Center." In Berquist, *Strike Terror No More,* 36.

LaCugna, Catherine Mowry. *God for Us: The Trinity and Christian Life.* San Francisco, Calif.: HarperSanFrancisco, 1992.

Laqueur, Walter, ed. *The Terrorism Reader: A Historical Anthology.* New York: New American Library, 1978.

Laytner, Anson. *Arguing with God: A Jewish Tradition.* Northvale, N.J.: J. Aronson, 1990.

Leiser, Burton M. "The Catastrophe of September 11 and Its Aftermath." In Primoratz, *Terrorism: The Philosophical Issues,* 194.

Lerner, Michael. *Healing Israel/Palestine: A Path to Peace and Reconciliation.* Berkeley, Calif.: Tikkun Books/North Atlantic Books, 2003.

Levi, Primo. "Survival in Auschwitz." In Morgan, *A Holocaust Reader,* 19–27.

———. *The Drowned and the Saved.* Trans. Raymond Rosenthal. London: Abacus, 1988.

Lévinas, Emmanuel. *Entre Nous: On Thinking-of-the-Other.* European Perspectives. Trans. Michael B. Smith and Barbara Harshav. New York: Columbia University Press, 1998.

———. *Proper Names* London: Athlone Press, 1996.

———. *Totality and Infinity; an Essay on Exteriority.* Duquesne Studies. Philosophical Series 24. Trans. Alphonso Lingis. Pittsburgh: Duquesne University Press, 1969.

Lévinas, Emmanuel. *Collected Philosophical Papers.* Trans. Alphonso Lingis. The Hague: Martinus Nijhoff, 1987.

Lévinas, Emmanuel, and Philippe Nemo. *Ethics and Infinity: Conversations with Philippe Nemo.* Trans. Richard A. Cohen. Pittsburgh: Duquesne University Press, 1985.

Lévinas, Emmanuel, Adriaan Theodoor Peperzak, Simon Critchley, and Robert Bernasconi. *Emmanuel Lévinas: Basic Philosophical Writings.* Studies in Continental Thought. Bloomington: Indiana University Press, 1996.

Lincoln, Bruce. *Holy Terrors: Thinking about Religion after September 11.* Chicago: University of Chicago Press, 2003.

Littell, Franklin H., and Philadelphia Center on the Holocaust, Genocide, and Human Rights. *Hyping the Holocaust: Scholars Answer Goldhagen.* East Rockaway, N.Y.: Cummings & Hathaway, 1997.

Louw, Daniel J. "Fides Quaerens Spem: A Pastoral and Theological Response to Suffering and Evil." *Interpretation* 57, no. 4 (October 2003): 384–97.

Maduro, Otto. *Judaism, Christianity, and Liberation: An Agenda for Dialogue.* Maryknoll, N.Y.: Orbis Books, 1991.

Maguire, Ken. "Muslims Reflect on How Their Lives Have Changed." Associated Press. *www.boston.com/news/packages/sept11/anniversary/wire_stories/0905_muslims.htm.*

Markham, Ian S., and Ibrahim Abu-Rabi, eds. *September 11: Religious Perspectives on the Causes and Consequences.* Oxford: Oneworld, 2002.

Marty, Martin. "The Future of World Fundamentalisms." *Proceedings of the American Philosophical Society* no. 3 (September 1998).

May, Todd. *Reconsidering Difference: Nancy, Derrida, Levinas, and Deleuze.* University Park: Pennsylvania State University Press, 1997.

Maybaum, Ignaz. *The Face of God after Auschwitz.* Amsterdam: Polak & Van Gennep, 1965.

McFadyen, Alistair I. *The Call to Personhood: A Christian Theory of the Individual in Social Relationships.* Cambridge: Cambridge University Press, 1990.

McTernan, Oliver J. *Violence in God's Name: Religion in an Age of Conflict.* London: Darton, Longman & Todd, 2003.

Mead, Andrew C. "Sermon Preached on September 16, 2001." In Farina, *Beauty for Ashes,* 113–18.

Merkin, Daphne. "Terror-Filled." *New York Times Magazine,* August 15, 2004, 42.

Metz, Johann Baptist. "Toward a Christology after Auschwitz." *Theology Digest* 48 (Summer 2001): 103–7.

———. *A Passion for God: The Mystical-Political Dimension of Christianity.* Ed. and trans. James Matthew Ashley. New York: Paulist Press, 1998.

———. *Faith in History and Society: Toward a Practical Fundamental Theology.* Trans. David Smith. New York: Seabury Press, 1980.

Metz, Johannes Baptist, and Jürgen Moltmann. *Faith and the Future: Essays on Theology, Solidarity, and Modernity.* Concilium Series. Maryknoll, N.Y.: Orbis Books, 1995.

Middle East Council of Churches. "Caught Up in the Agony." In Farina, *Beauty for Ashes,* 34–36.

Mitchell, Peter R., and John Schoeffel. *Understanding Power: The Indispensable Chomsky.* New York: New Press, 2002.

Mitford, Jessica. *The American Way of Death.* New York: Simon and Schuster, 1963.

Moltmann, Jürgen. *The Experiment Hope.* Trans. M. Douglas Meeks. Reprint ed. Eugene, Ore.: Wipf & Stock, 2003.

———. "Im Ende — Der neue Anfang: Apocalyptischer Terror und christliche Hoffnung." In Kässmann, *Glauben nach Ground Zero,* 25–35.

———. "The Trinitarian History of God." *Theology* 78 (1975): 633.

———. *The Crucified God: The Cross of Christ as the Foundation and Criticism of Christian Theology.* Ed. R. A. Wilson. Trans. John Bowden. London: SCM, 1974.

Morgan, Michael L. *A Holocaust Reader: Responses to the Nazi Extermination.* New York: Oxford University Press, 2001.

National Commission on Terrorist Attacks upon the United States. *The 9/11 Commission Report: Final Report of the National Commission on Terrorist Attacks upon the United States.* New York: W. W. Norton, 2004.

National Council of Churches of Christ in the U.S.A. "Deny Them Their Victory: A Religious Response to Terrorism." *Midstream: The Ecumenical Movement Today* 41, no. 1 (January, 2002): 75.

Neiman, Susan. *Evil in Modern Thought: An Alternative History of Philosophy.* Princeton, N.J.: Princeton University Press, 2002.

New York Times. *Portraits 9/11/01: The Collected "Portraits of Grief" from the New York Times.* New York: Times Books/Henry Holt, 2002.

New York Times Editorial. "Harnessing the Spirit of September 11." *New York Times,* November 5, 2001, sec. A.

O'Connor, Flannery. *Collected Works.* Library of America 39. New York: Library of America, 1988.

O'Donnell, John J. *Trinity and Temporality: The Christian Doctrine of God in the Light of Process Theology and the Theology of Hope.* Oxford Theological Monographs. Oxford: Oxford University Press, 1983.

Olson, Roger E., and Christopher A. Hall. *The Trinity.* Guides to Theology Series, ed. Sally Bruynell, Alan G. Padgett, et al. Grand Rapids: Eerdmans, 2002.

Pape, Robert Anthony. *Dying to Win: The Strategic Logic of Suicide Terrorism.* New York: Random House, 2005.

Parenti, Christian. "America's Jihad: A History of Origins." In Scraton, *Beyond September 11th,* 10–19.

Parenti, Michael. *The Terrorism Trap: September 11 and Beyond.* San Francisco: City Lights, 2002.

Pawlikowski, John. "Uniqueness and Universality in the Holocaust: The Need for a New Language." In Colijn and Littell, *Confronting the Holocaust,* 51–62.

Pepper, Margot. "The Smell of Smoke." In Burbach and Clarke, *September 11 and the U.S. War,* 77–81.

Persaud, Winston D. "The Cross of Jesus Christ, the Unity of the Church, and Human Suffering." In Tesfai, *The Scandal of a Crucified World,* 111–29.

Petersen, Rodney Lawrence. "A Theology of Forgiveness." In Helmick and Petersen, *Forgiveness and Reconciliation,* 3–26.

Pilger, John. "An Unconscionable Threat to Humanity." In Scraton, *Beyond September 11th,* 19–30.

Pinnock, Sarah Katherine. *Beyond Theodicy: Jewish and Christian Continental Thinkers Respond to the Holocaust.* SUNY Series in Theology and Continental Thought. Albany: State University of New York Press, 2002.

Plant, Richard. *The Pink Triangle: The Nazi War against Homosexuals.* New York: Henry Holt, 1986.

Plantinga, Cornelius. *Not the Way It's Supposed to Be: A Breviary of Sin.* Grand Rapids; Leicester, U.K.: Eerdmans; Apollos, 1995.

———. "Social Trinity and Tritheism." In Feenstra and Plantinga, *Trinity, Incarnation, and Atonement,* 21–47.

Polkinghorne, J. C., and Michael Welker. *The End of the World and the Ends of God: Science and Theology on Eschatology.* Theology for the Twenty-First Century. Harrisburg, Pa.: Trinity Press International, 2000.

Pollack, Robert E. "The Religious Obligation to Ask Questions of Nature and the State." *Union Seminary Quarterly Review* 60, no. 1–2 (2006): 78–110.

Pollefeyt, Didier. "The Holocaust and Evil." In Cohn-Sherbok, *Holocaust Theology: A Reader,* 166–69.

———. "Auschwitz, or How Good People Can Do Evil." In Colijn and Littell, *Confronting the Holocaust,* 101.

Pollefeyt, Didier, and G. Jan Colijn. "Leaving Evil in Germany: The Questionable Success of Goldhagen in the Low Countries." In Littell, *Hyping the Holocaust,* 3–18.

Potorti, David, and September 11th Families for Peaceful Tomorrows. *September 11th Families for Peaceful Tomorrows: Turning our Grief into Action for Peace.* New York: RDV Books, 2003.

Primoratz, Igor. *Terrorism: The Philosophical Issues.* Houndmills, Baskingstoke, Hampshire and New York: Palgrave Macmillan, 2004.

Proctor, Robert. *Racial Hygiene: Medicine under the Nazis.* Cambridge, Mass.: Harvard University Press, 1988.

Raheb, Mitri, Rev. Dr. "Palestinian Christians Grieve over U.S. Tragedy." In Farina, *Beauty for Ashes,* 12–14.

Rahner, Karl, and Herbert Vorgrimler. *Concise Theological Dictionary.* Freiburg: Herder, 1965.

Redekop, Vern Neufeld. *From Violence to Blessing: How an Understanding of Deep-Rooted Conflict Can Open Paths to Reconciliation.* Ottawa: Novalis, 2002.

Reich, Walter, and Woodrow Wilson International Center for Scholars, eds. *Origins of Terrorism: Psychologies, Ideologies, Theologies, States of Mind.* Woodrow Wilson Center Series. Washington, D.C.; New York: Woodrow Wilson International Center for Scholars; Cambridge England; Cambridge University Press, 1990.

Reinhart, Tanya. *Israel/Palestine: How to End the War of 1948.* 2nd ed. New York: Seven Stories Press, 2005.

Ricoeur, Paul. *Oneself as Another.* Trans. Kathleen Blamey. Chicago: University of Chicago Press, 1992.

———. *The Symbolism of Evil.* Religious Perspectives 17. New York: Harper & Row, 1967.

Ringelheim, Joan. "The Strange and the Familiar." In Signer, *Humanity at the Limit.*

Roberts, Robert H. "A Shameful Distortion of Justice." In Farina, *Beauty for Ashes,* 37–38.

Robertson, Pat. "God Almighty Is Lifting His Protection." In Farina, *Beauty for Ashes,* 122–26.

Rodman, Selden. *100 Modern Poems.* New York: Pellegrini & Cudahy, 1949.

Rorty, Richard, Gianni Vattimo, and Santiago Zabala. *The Future of Religion.* New York: Columbia University Press, 2005.

Roth, John K., and Leonard Grob. *Ethics after the Holocaust: Perspectives, Critiques, and Responses.* St. Paul, Minn.: Paragon House, 1999.

Roumani, Rhonda. "I'm an American Muslim — and I'm Afraid." In Beliefnet et al., *From the Ashes,* 147–8.

Rowe, William L. *God and the Problem of Evil.* Blackwell Readings in Philosophy 1. Malden, Mass.: Blackwell, 2001.

Rubenstein, Richard L. "Apocalyptic Rationality and the Shoah." In Jacobs, *Contemporary Jewish Religious Responses to the Shoah,* 157–72, 207–10.

———. *After Auschwitz: Radical Theology and Contemporary Judaism.* Indianapolis: Bobbs-Merrill, 1966.

Rubenstein, Richard L., and John K. Roth. *Approaches to Auschwitz: The Legacy of the Holocaust.* London: SCM, 1987.

Ruether, Rosemary Radford. "The Holocaust: Theological and Ethical Reflections." In Baum, *The Twentieth Century,* 76.

Russakoff, Dale. *Memories Haunt WTC Survivors.* MSNBC broadcast, March 9, 2002. *http://www.msnbc.com/news/721921.asp.*

Russell, Edward. "Reconsidering Relational Anthropology: A Critical Assessment of John Zizioulas's Theological Anthropology." *International Journal of Systematic Theology* 5, no. 2 (July 2003): 168–86.

Rutherford, Donald. *Leibniz and the Rational Order of Nature.* New York: Cambridge University Press, 1995.

Ruthven, Malise. *A Fury for God: The Islamist Attack on America.* New York: Granta Books, 2002.

Sabbah, Michel. "Homily of the Mass for Peace and Remembrance of the Victims in the U.S.A." In Farina, *Beauty for Ashes,* 31–34.

Sacks, Jonathan. *The Dignity of Difference: How to Avoid the Clash of Civilizations.* Rev. ed. New York: Continuum, 2003.

Said, Edward W. *Peace and Its Discontents: Essays on Palestine in the Middle East Peace Process.* New York: Vintage Books, 1996.

Sakabe, Megumi. "Surrealistic Distortion of Landscape and the Reason of the Milieu." In *Culture and Modernity: East–West Philosophic Perspectives,* ed. Eliot Deutsch, 343–53. Honolulu: University of Hawaii Press, 1991.

Sanders, Fred. *The Image of the Immanent Trinity: Rahner's Rule and the Theological Interpretation of Scripture.* Issues in Systematic Theology 12. New York: Peter Lang, 2005.

Sardar, Ziauddin, and Merryl Wyn Davies. *Why Do People Hate America?* Cambridge: Icon, 2002.

Scarry, Elaine. "The Difficulty of Imagining Other Persons." In *The Handbook of Interethnic Coexistence,* ed. Eugene Weiner, 40–62. New York: Continuum, 1998.

———. *The Body in Pain: The Making and Unmaking of the World.* New York: Oxford University Press, 1985.

Schillebeeckx, Edward. "The Mystery of Injustice and the Mystery of Mercy: Questions Concerning Human Suffering." *Stauros Bulletin* 15 (1975): 3–31.

Schillebeeckx, Edward C., and John Bowden. "Documentation: Religion and Violence." In Beuken, *Religion as a Source of Violence,* 129–42.

Schuster, Ekkehard, and Reinhold Boschert-Kimmig. *Hope against Hope: Johann Baptist Metz and Elie Wiesel Speak Out on the Holocaust.* Studies in Judaism and Christianity. New York: Paulist Press, 1999.

Schwartz, Regina M. *The Curse of Cain: The Violent Legacy of Monotheism.* Chicago: University of Chicago Press, 1997.

Schwöbel, Christoph, and King's College. Research Institute in Systematic Theology. *Trinitarian Theology Today: Essays on Divine Being and Act.* Edinburgh: T. & T. Clark, 1995.

Scott, Peter, and William T. Cavanaugh, eds. *The Blackwell Companion to Political Theology.* Blackwell Companions to Religion. Oxford: Blackwell, 2004.

Scraton, Phil, ed. *Beyond September 11th: An Anthology of Dissent.* London: Pluto Press, 2002.

Segev, Tom. *Soldiers of Evil: The Commandants of the Nazi Concentration Camps.* New York: McGraw-Hill, 1987.

Segundo, Juan Luis. *The Liberation of Dogma: Faith, Revelation, and Dogmatic Teaching Authority.* Maryknoll, N.Y.: Orbis Books, 1992.

———. *Faith and Ideologies.* Jesus of Nazareth, Yesterday and Today. Vol. 1. Maryknoll, N.Y.: Orbis Books, 1984.

Senior, Jennifer. "The Fireman's Friar." *New York Magazine,* November 30, 2008.

Shanahan, Timothy. *Philosophy 9/11: Thinking about the War on Terrorism.* Chicago: Open Court, 2005.

Sherman, Franklin. "Speaking of God after Auschwitz." In Morgan, *A Holocaust Reader,* 196–208.

Shlaim, Avi. "The United States and the Israeli-Palestinian Conflict." In Booth and Dunne, *Worlds in Collision,* 172–83.

Shriver, Donald W., Jr. *An Ethic for Enemies: Forgiveness in Politics.* New York: Oxford University Press, 1995.

Signer, Michael Alan. *Humanity at the Limit: The Impact of the Holocaust Experience on Jews and Christians.* Bloomington: Indiana University Press, 2000.

Sim, Stuart. *Fundamentalist World: The New Dark Age of Dogma.* Cambridge: Icon Books, 2004.

Sinclair, Andrew. *An Anatomy of Terror: A History of Terrorism.* London: Macmillan, 2003.

Singer, Peter. *The President of Good and Evil: The Ethics of George W. Bush.* New York: Dutton, 2004.

Skillen, James. "Not without Criticism." In Farina, *Beauty for Ashes,* 127–29.

Slouka, Mark. "A Year Later: Notes on America's Intimations of Mortality." *Harper's Magazine* (September 2002): 36.

Sobrino, Jon. *Jesus the Liberator: A Historical-Theological Reading of Jesus of Nazareth.* Trans. Paul Burns and Francis McDonagh. Maryknoll, N.Y.: Orbis Books, 1993.

Sobrino, Jon, and Felix Wilfred. *Globalization and Its Victims.* Concilium. Vol. 2001/5. London: SCM Press, 2001.

———. "Introduction: The Reasons for Returning to this Theme." In Sobrino and Wilfred, *Globalization and Its Victims,* 11–15.

Sölle, Dorothee. "Von der Macht, Allmacht und Ohnmacht Gottes." In Kässmann, *Glauben Nach Ground Zero,* 53–58.

———. "God's Pain and Our Pain." In Maduro, *Judaism, Christianity, and Liberation.*

———. *Suffering.* Philadelphia: Fortress, 1975.

Stevens, Brin. "Six Critics Review Walter Wink's *The Human Being: Jesus and the Enigma of the Son of the Man.*" *Cross Currents* 53 (Summer 2003): 264–317.

Surin, Kenneth. *Theology and the Problem of Evil*. Signposts in Theology. Oxford: Black-well, 1986.

Tajfel, Henri, and John C. Turner. "An Integrative Theory of Intergroup Conflict." In Austin and Worchel, *The Social Psychology of Intergroup Relations*, 33–47.

Taylor, Christopher C. "The Rwandan Genocide of 1994." In Hinton, *Annihilating Difference*, 137–78.

Tesfai, Yacob, ed. *The Scandal of a Crucified World: Perspectives on the Cross and Suffering*. Maryknoll, N.Y.: Orbis Books, 1994.

Thomas Aquinas. *Summa Theologica*. Trans. Dominicans of the English Province. Westminster, Md.: Christian Classics, 1981.

Tilley, Terrence W. *The Evils of Theodicy*. Eugene, Ore.: Wipf & Stock, 2000.

Todorov, Tzvetan. *Hope and Memory: Reflections on the Twentieth Century*. Trans. David Bellos (London: Atlantic Books, 2003).

———. *Facing the Extreme: Moral Life in the Concentration Camps*. New York: Henry Holt, 1996.

———. *Story Theology*. Collegeville, Minn.: Liturgical Press, 1990.

Townshend, Charles. *Terrorism: A Very Short Introduction*. Very Short Introductions 78. Oxford: Oxford University Press, 2002.

Tyrnauer, Gabrielle. "Holocaust History and the Gypsies." *The Ecumenist* 12 (September–October 1988): 90–94.

U.K. Religious Leaders, Lambeth Palace. "Joint Statement, September 12, 2001." In Farina, *Beauty for Ashes*, 36–37.

United Nations General Assembly. "A Call for International Cooperation." In Farina, *Beauty for Ashes*, 14–15.

University of Oklahoma. Institute of Group Relations and Muzafer Sherif. *Intergroup Conflict and Cooperation: The Robbers Cave Experiment*. Norman: University Book Exchange, 1961.

USA Today editors. "Casualty Figures for 9/11." *USA Today*, October 29, 2003.

Vardy, Peter, and Julie Arliss. *The Thinker's Guide to Evil*. Alresford, U.K.: John Hunt Publishing, 2003.

Vidal, Gore. *Perpetual War for Perpetual Peace: How We Got to Be So Hated*. New York: Thunder's Mouth Press/Nation Books, 2002.

Volf, Miroslav. *The End of Memory: Remembering Rightly in a Violent World*. Grand Rapids: Eerdmans, 2006.

———. *Free of Charge: Giving and Forgiving in a Culture Stripped of Grace: The Archbishop's Official 2006 Lent Book*. Grand Rapids: Zondervan, 2005.

———. "Forgiveness, Reconciliation, and Justice: A Christian Contribution to a More Peaceful Social Environment." In Helmick and Petersen, *Forgiveness and Reconciliation*, 27–49.

———. *Exclusion and Embrace: A Theological Exploration of Identity, Otherness, and Reconciliation.* Nashville: Abingdon Press, 1996.

———. Concluding remarks at the U.N. annual International Prayer Breakfast, September 11, 2001. *www.calvin.edu/worship/stories/volf.php.*

Volf, Miroslav, and Dorothy C. Bass. *Practicing Theology: Beliefs and Practices in Christian Life.* Grand Rapids: Eerdmans, 2001.

Volf, Miroslav, and William H. Katerberg. *The Future of Hope: Christian Tradition amid Modernity and Postmodernity.* Grand Rapids: Eerdmans, 2004.

Volf, Miroslav, and Michael Welker. *God's Life in Trinity.* Minneapolis: Fortress, 2006.

Waller, James. *Becoming Evil: How Ordinary People Commit Genocide and Mass Killing.* Oxford: Oxford University Press, 2002.

Weinandy, Thomas G. *Does God Suffer?* Edinburgh: T. & T. Clark, 2000.

Whitlock, Craig. "Pope Prays at Auschwitz Death Camp." *Providence Journal,* May 28, 2006, 2006, sec. A.

Wiesel, Elie. *Night.* London: Macgibbon & Kee, 1960.

Wilkinson, Paul. *Terrorism and the Liberal State.* London: Macmillan, 1977.

Williams, Rowan. *The Truce of God: Peacemaking in Troubled Times.* Norwich: Canterbury Press, 2005.

———. *Writing in the Dust: Reflections on 11th September and Its Aftermath.* London: Hodder & Stoughton, 2002.

Wink, Walter. *The Powers That Be: Theology for a New Millennium.* New York and London: Doubleday, 1998.

———. *Naming the Powers: The Language of Power in the New Testament.* Vol. 1 of *The Powers.* Philadelphia: Fortress, 1984.

Woodward, Bob. "Interview with Condolezza Rice." *Washington Post,* October 24, 2001.

Woodward, James, and Stephen Pattison. "An Introduction to Pastoral and Practical Theology." In Woodward, Pattison, and Patton, *Blackwell Reader,* 7.

Woodward, James, Stephen Pattison, and John Patton. *The Blackwell Reader in Pastoral and Practical Theology.* Blackwell Readings in Modern Theology. Oxford: Blackwell, 2000.

Žižek, Slavoj. *Welcome to the Desert of the Real! Five Essays on September 11 and Related Dates.* New York: Verso, 2002.

Zizioulas, Jean. *Communion and Otherness.* New York: Continuum, 2006.

———. "The Doctrine of the Holy Trinity: The Significance of the Cappadocian Contribution," in Schwöbel, *Trinitarian Theology Today,* 53.

———. "On Being a Person: Towards an Ontology of Personhood," in Schwöbel and Gunton, *Persons, Divine and Human.* London: T & T Clark, 1991, 33–46.

———. *Being as Communion: Studies in Personhood and the Church.* Contemporary Greek Theologians 4. Crestwood, N.Y.: St. Vladimir's Seminary Press, 1985.

Index

Of Related Interest

Maureen O'Connell

Compassion

Loving Our Neighbor in an Age of Globalization

ISBN 978-1-57075-845-4

An exploration of the role Christian compassion can play in today's world.

"With insight, precision, and nuance, O'Connell builds on current debates about human nature, the emotions, the imagination, justice, virtue, and globalization, and brings theoretical questions alive by tying them to realities like 9/11, Katrina, and white privilege. *Compassion* will enlighten theologians, inspire students, and challenge all to re-think our responsibilities today."

—Lisa Sowle Cahill, Boston College

Roberto S. Goizueta

Christ Our Companion

Toward a Theological Aesthetics of Liberation

ISBN 978-1-57075-853-9

How do Christians resolve the dissonance between the truth of Christ's life, death, and resurrection as the universal key to human meaning, and our increased consciousness of the diverse, pluralistic world in which we live? In such a world, how can a Christian proclaim that message credibly and responsibly? How can one speak of Jesus Christ in the wake of 9/11?

Roberto Goizueta raises important questions about the ethical and theological defensibility of any religious position, particularly when the rationales for so much of the violence we see around us are grounded in religious principles.